ETHICS–POLITICS–SUBJECTIVITY

Radical Thinkers ▼

ETHICS–POLITICS–SUBJECTIVITY

Essays on Derrida, Levinas and
Contemporary French Thought

Simon Critchley

VERSO

London • New York

First published by Verso 1999
© Simon Critchley 1999
Reprinted 2009

3 5 7 9 10 8 6 4 2

Verso
UK: 6 Meard Street, London W1F 0EG
US: 20 Jay Street, Suite 1010, Brooklyn, NY 11201
www.versobooks.com

Verso is the imprint of New Left Books

ISBN-13: 978-1-84467-351-3

British Library Cataloguing in Publication Data
A catalogue record for this book is available from the British Library

Library of Congress Cataloging-in-Publication Data
A catalog record for this book is available from the Library of Congress

Typeset in the UK by The Running Head Ltd, London and Cambridge
Printed in the US

For Edward

Contents

Preface and Acknowledgements

What is ethical experience?

What can be said of the subject who has this experience?

What, if any, is the relation of ethical experience to politics?

This book brings together essays written on topics in contemporary French thought insofar as they have a common thematic concern with the questions of ethics, politics and subjectivity. The main focus for the elaboration of these questions is the work of Jacques Derrida and Emmanuel Levinas, and to that extent the work presented here is an anticipation (chapters 1 and 2), extension (chapters 3, 4, 5, 6) deepening (chapters 8, 9, 10, 11) and modification (chapters 7 and 12) of the argument of *The Ethics of Deconstruction: Derrida and Levinas*.[1] Happily enough, I am not in complete agreement with some of my earlier pronouncements in two regards. First, I am more doubtful about the persuasive force of Levinasian ethics in the way it was presented in *The Ethics of Deconstruction*, which leads me to give a critical reconstruction of Levinas's work with particular reference to the question of the subject (chapter 3) and to Freudian and Lacanian psychoanalysis (chapters 8 and 9). Second, based on a reading of Derrida's work since 1992, I am more positive about the political possibilities of deconstruction, specifically insofar as the latter is mediated through a reading of Marx and an account of friendship, democracy and the political decision (chapters 4, 7 and 12).

However, apart from the central foci of Derrida and Levinas, the reader will also find discussions of the work of other French thinkers, such as Jean Genet (chapter 2), Jacques Lacan (chapters 9 and 10), Jean-Luc Nancy (chapter 11) and Maurice Blanchot (chapter 12), as well as extended accounts of certain decidedly less French thinkers, like Hegel (chapter 1), Heidegger (chapters 1, 3, 10 and 11), Freud (chapters 8, 9 and 10), Richard Rorty (chapters 4 and 5) and Ernesto Laclau (chapters 5 and 7). In chapter 6, I take up the questions of race and imperialism, and try and consider whether the concept of hybridity, so pervasive as a category in recent cultural theory, can be productively extended into a reflection on philosophy and the philosophical tradition. In chapter 10, I develop a critique of what I see as the tragic-heroic paradigm in philosophy and psychoanalysis and, against the latter, propose a comic anti-heroic paradigm and an accompanying sketch of a theory of humour and laughter.

I would like to let the essays speak for themselves, rather than trying to freeze their various and overlapping strands of argumentation and exposition into a decontextualized summary. Although over half this book (chapters 1–7) was written sporadically over the past several years, the occasion to bring together these essays, as well as adding a number of new pieces (chapters 8–12), was provided by the generosity of the Alexander Von Humboldt Stiftung, through whose support I spent 1997–98 as a Research Fellow in Philosophy at the University of Frankfurt. The fact that I spent much of my year in Germany working on French philosophy in a Frankfurt context that has not exactly been noteworthy for its appreciation of certain French variants on the philosophical discourse of modernity, makes for a pleasing irony. But insofar as this book implicitly seeks to challenge and correct the way in which a good deal of contemporary French thought has been received in Germany, much of it is written out of my experience of that context.

I would like to thank Axel Honneth for his intellectual openness, friendship and practical support during my time in Frankfurt. I would also like to thank the following for intellectual – and much non-intellectual – stimulation during my stay: Rahel Jaeggi, Rainer Forst, Christine Pries, Mechthild Groß-Forst, Espen Hammer, Kristin Gjesdal, Felicia Herrschaft, Andreas Niederberger, Amy Morgenstern, Caitlin Dempsey, Devin Pendas, Eric Oberle, Carolin Emcke, Stephen White, Lena Inowlocki, Gerald Siegmund, Rainer Emig, Martin Bauer, Nancy Fraser and Eli Zaretsky.

Original publication details, where appropriate, can be found at the beginning of each essay. Many of the texts collected here have an occasional and oral origin, and I would like to thank the many friends, colleagues and institutions that have provided an audience for my work over the years. Much of the argument and exposition of chapters 8, 9 and 10 is indebted to Cecilia Sjöholm. Thanks especially to Ernesto Laclau and Chantal Mouffe for commissioning this book and then tactfully coaxing it out of me well after its deadline. I would particularly like to thank Ernesto for being such an excellent interlocutor over the years; traces of our many conversations will be found scattered over the pages of several of the chapters in this book.

Note

1. Oxford: Blackwell, 1992; expanded second edition, Edinburgh: Edinburgh University Press, 1999.

Derrida's Reading of Hegel in *Glas*[1]

Introduction

Glas is a tour de force of Hegel scholarship. Although primarily concerned with the *Philosophy of Right* and the *Phenomenology of Spirit*, Derrida also offers detailed discussions of *The Spirit of Christianity and its Fate*, the *First Philosophy of Spirit* of 1803–04, the 1803 essay 'Scientific Ways of Treating Natural Law', the *Lectures on Aesthetics* and the introduction to the *Lectures on the Philosophy of World History*. In addition – and this list is not exhaustive – there are discussions of and references to the *Logic*, the *Encyclopaedia*, the *Lectures on the Philosophy of Religion*, the *Differenzschrift*, *Faith and Knowledge* and abundant quotations from Hegel's correspondence.

It must be stressed at the outset that the Hegel column is for the most part a straightforward and closely argued commentary on Hegel, interrupted by a series of excurses on Marx, Feuerbach, Kant and Freud, and a number of significant allusions to Heidegger that I will come to below. Derrida's persistent mode of demonstration is through quotation rather than reconstruction or exposition. He quotes, often at extraordinary length; his assertions are nearly always textually verified with reference to Hegel's works. When Derrida is read with the care with which he reads Hegel, his reading practice appears largely irrefutable, employing an implicit conception of truth as *adaequatio* between text and commentary. When he wishes to offer a parenthetical remark or a quotation from a different source, he uses the formal device of the judas, a marginal window in the main text, which acts as a commentary upon his commentary and should not be judged to be of subordinate importance to the main text. It should be noted, however, that there are far fewer judases in the Hegel column than in the Genet column.

However, the apparent linearity of the Hegel commentary is disrupted as soon as one glances to the right (reading the Hegel column on the left-hand page), or to both left and right (reading the Hegel column on the right-hand page). These planned or aleatory intertextual effects, in the judases and opposing columns, and the oscillating movement between text and intertext, between commentary and what exceeds it, mark the rhythm of deconstructive reading. Yet, however true that may be, I shall try to fix an unblinking, Cyclopean eye on the Hegel column in order to try and understand the precise nature of the reading of Hegel being attempted in *Glas*.

Method: Systematic Reading and the Family

The only secondary text on Hegel that Derrida refers to at any length is Bernard Bourgeois's *Hegel à Francfort: Judaisme – Christianisme – Hegelianisme* (Gtr 83).[2] According to Derrida, Bourgeois reads the Hegelian system as if it were a book of life, where one would speak of an 'adolescent' Hegelianism, an 'early' Hegelianism, an 'incipient', 'mature', 'later' and 'accomplished' Hegelianism, with the truth of Hegel only being actualized at the end of a development. For Derrida, such an approach to Hegel represents 'the logical reading' (Gtr 84a) against which he opposes his own, refusing to distinguish the young from the old and objecting that the logical approach overlooks 'the systematic chains' (Gtr 84a) at work in the first texts. This passing remark is useful for it helps the reader to understand that Derrida gives very much a *systematic* reading of Hegel, a reading that is always focused on the concept of system and which treats individual texts, from whatever period, as morsels or constituent articulations of the greater system. To approach *Glas* as a systematic reading of Hegel illuminates a number of features of Derrida's commentary: firstly, it explains the privilege that Derrida gives to texts from the Frankfurt and Jena periods, like *The Spirit of Christianity* and *The First Philosophy of Spirit*. Secondly, and to choose an example, it explains why, when Derrida wants to give an account of *Sittlichkeit*, he begins with the *Differenzschrift, Faith and Knowledge* and the essay on natural law, in which Derrida claims to find 'the essential traits of *Sittlichkeit*' (G 137a/Gtr 97a). These traits are early traces of the 'great syllogism' (G 137a/Gtr 98a) of *Sittlichkeit* contained in the *Philosophy of Right*. Thirdly, it explains Derrida's choice of the 'thread' (G 5a/Gtr 4a) with which he draws out his reading: the concept of the family. But, one is entitled to ask, why the family?

The opening of the Hegel column is graphically complex and alludes to themes that become clearer as the reading develops. After a brief discussion of two seemingly peripheral passages from Hegel – the paragraph that mentions 'flower religion' (*Blumenreligion*) from the *Phenomenology* (PS 372/ PStr 420) and the short discussion of the phallic columns of India from the *Aesthetics* (A 641), which function as leitmotifs for both columns and are more fully discussed in the closing sections of *Glas* – Derrida raises the methodological problem of how one is introduced (*eingeführt*) or led into Hegel. Derrida remarks, 'the problem of the introduction to Hegel's philosophy is *all* of Hegel's philosophy [*c'est* toute *la philosophie de Hegel*]' (G 5a/Gtr 4a). This familiar issue implies that whatever point one chooses to enter the circle of speculative dialectics will presuppose all the other points on the circumference and thus the entirety of the Hegelian system. The point where *Glas* introduces itself into the system is with the theme of the family. Derrida's central text is the *Philosophy of Right*, where the family is the first moment in the syllogism of *Sittlichkeit*, the other two being Civil Society and the State. The family occurs therefore immediately after the transition from *Moralität* to *Sittlichkeit* (an important transition in *Glas*), that is to say, from the abstract diremption of the Good and subjectivity to their unification in the Concept. As well as being the first moment in the syllogism of *Sittlichkeit* and the beginning of the third moment in the syllogism of Abstract Right, *Moralität* and *Sittlichkeit*, the family also has its own syllogistic structure: marriage, family property and capital, and the education of children and the dissolution of the family (PR 152/PRtr 111). Thus, the immediate unification of the family in monogamous marriage and the family's external embodiment in capital are *aufgehoben* in the education of the children, which brings the latter to 'freedom of personality' and 'holding free property' (PR 163–4/PRtr 118) and leads to the family's dissolution. The truth of the family is its dissolution and transition to Civil Society, 'the stage of difference' (PR 168/PRtr 122).

Derrida draws on the thread of the family for a number of reasons: firstly, he admits that this choice, which is far from innocent, is made because, 'the concept family very rigorously inscribes itself in the system' (Gtr 5a); and again, 'the whole system repeats itself in the family' (Gtr 20a). The concept of the family, and this is true of every moment of the dialectic, exemplifies the system of which it is a part. Secondly, the family is a crucial transitional hinge in the Philosophy of Right and the system as a whole:

> Its interpretation directly engages the whole Hegelian determination of right on one side, of politics on the other. Its place in the system's structure and development, in the encyclopaedia, the logic, and the Hegelian ontotheology, is such that the displacements or the desimplifications of which it will be the object would not know how to have a simply local character. (Gtr 4–5a)

The transition from *Moralität* to *Sittlichkeit*, from abstract freedom to the actuality of freedom, from Kant to Hegel, hinges upon the passage through the family. However, this is no safe passage in the sense that Derrida's commentary upon the family would leave it and the system intact. Rather, Derrida analyses the family, 'in order to make a problematic within the whole field appear in the family' (Gtr 16a). Thus, the Derridian claim is that there is something in the concept of the family which both repeats the system and renders its entire field problematic. If Derrida can be said to read Hegel systematically, then this is not done in order to maintain the system, but rather to find a moment of '*rupture*' (G 5a – a key word in *Glas*) within the system's development. As Derrida writes later in the Hegel column, 'Development then, and rupture: response to the question of method' (Gtr 97a). Derrida's method of reading Hegel has a rhythm of development and rupture, of 'fits and starts, jolts, little successive jerks' (G 7a/Gtr 5a), that follows the course of the family and the speculative dialectic 'like a machine in the course of a difficult manoeuvre' (G 7a/Gtr 5a). In the closing pages of *Glas*, Derrida describes the dialectic as 'the three-stroke engine [*le moteur à trois temps*]' (G 350a/Gtr 252a), which seeks to run smoothly through the repeated triadic pattern of in-itself, for-itself and in-and-for-itself. The mechanism of reading in *Glas* attempts to throw a spanner in the works of this engine, transforming Hegel's text into a cumbersome and ineffective machine lumbering slowly across difficult terrain.

A deconstructive reading, then, which rigorously and minutely follows or 'will have to feign to follow' (Gtr 6a) the family circle of the dialectic whilst continually disrupting its circumference. In an allusion to Genet, Derrida calls his method of reading 'a bastard course [*démarche bâtarde*]' (G 8a/Gtr 6a), a reading of the family in terms of that which exceeds and resists it.

Christian Love and Hegel's Judaism

Derrida begins with the concept of love, which specifically characterizes the family for Hegel (PR 151/PRtr 110). After a brief exposition of the transition from *Moralität* to *Sittlichkeit* in the *Philosophy of Right*, Derrida comments on Hegel's introductory discussion of *Sittlichkeit* (PR 144–51/PRtr 105–10), out of which the concept of the family emerges. The family is defined as the immediate substantiality of Spirit, or, more precisely, 'ethical Spirit [*sittliche Geist*] (PR 151/PRtr 110). The unity of *Geist* in the family, that which unifies the three moments of its syllogism, is love. In a

Zusatz, Hegel defines love as 'the consciousness of my unity with another' (PR 152/PRtr 261), a unity where I only win my self-consciousness through the renunciation of my independence or 'selfish isolation'. Love has two moments for Hegel: (i) where I do not wish to be an independent person and where I experience my autarchy as a lack or defect; (ii) where I attain my independence and 'find myself in another person' (ibid.), the beloved. Hegel – and Derrida is following him to the letter here – identifies 'the most tremendous contradiction [*der ungeheuerste Widerspruch*]' within the concept of love. In a characteristic move, Derrida simply pauses with this contradiction, a contradiction found within Hegel's text and not imposed upon it. He is not interested in turning such a contradiction into a vicious circle, but rather, alluding to Heidegger's *Was heisst Denken?*, Derrida wishes to follow the hermeneutic circle that is the product of an apparent contradiction and which cannot be avoided in thinking (Gtr 20). Suspending his commentary on the family in the *Philosophy of Right* at this contradictory moment, Derrida moves on to a further account of the family given in 'a very late text' (Gtr 21a), the Introduction to the *Lectures on the Philosophy of World History*.

In the latter, Spirit is defined as the inseparability within self-consciousness of self-knowledge and objective knowledge (Gtr 21a). Derrida discusses the relation of Spirit to freedom (Gtr 22a), activity (Gtr 24a) and the notion of the *bei sich* (Gtr 22a), rendered by Derrida as '*être auprès de soi*' (G 30a). He shows how the Hegelian concept of Spirit is dependent upon a number of exclusions: firstly, the exclusion of matter, defined as exteriority, as that which is not *bei sich*. Secondly, the constitution of humanity is dependent upon the exclusion of nature, animality, and of everything that Hegel designates with the word *Trieb*. However, although humanity is spiritual and is constituted upon the exclusion of the natural, the material and the animal – 'a powerful and ample chain from Aristotle, at least, to our day, it binds ontotheological metaphysics to humanism' (Gtr 27a) – the human is only an example of finite Spirit. As the example of infinite Spirit, Hegel names God. However, the infinite is not without relation to the finite, for what distinguishes the Christian religion for Hegel – which raises it above its antecedent, Judaism – is that infinite Spirit can become finite in the person of Christ. In the incarnation, God becomes an object for himself, he knows and recognizes himself in his son. The relation that binds the father to the son, the infinite to the finite, is the Holy Spirit, the third person of the Trinity. Spirit, then, is filiation, a familial relation between father and son.

Derrida then asks, 'What is the function of this Christian model?' (Gtr 33a). This brings the reader to the next major transition in Derrida's reading where, 'within the system' and its 'very precise homology' (Gtr 33a), he steps back to Hegel's 1799 Frankfurt text, *The Spirit of Christianity and its Fate*. Note once again that the same systematic reading is at work, 'one enters the analysis of Christianity and of the Christian family elaborated by the young Hegel as the conceptual matrix [*la matrice conceptuelle* – the conceptual womb] of the whole systematic scene to come' (G 78a/Gtr 55a). Derrida's reading of this text extends for some sixty pages of the translation (Gtr 33a–93a). It is one of the most thorough sections of *Glas* and essential reading for anyone researching into Hegel's concept of Christianity and, in particular, his attitude to Judaism.[3] Derrida's general point here is that the transition from *Moralität* to *Sittlichkeit* described in the *Philosophy of Right*, whose first moment is the family unified by love, is replicated and reinforced in the transition from Judaism to Christianity. That is to say, there is no love before Christianity (Gtr 34a). It is the person of Christ who relieves (*relever* is Derrida's French translation of *aufheben*) the abstract rights of Judaism into ethical love. There is no true family before Christianity, for the concept of the family is only unified by love and therefore the Judaic family – Derrida discusses the example of Noah (Gtr 38–9a) – is based upon 'dutiful fidelity' (Gtr 34a). Thus, the advent of *Sittlichkeit* and the family is synonymous with the *Aufhebung* from a religion based upon duty and commandment to a religion based on love and freedom. To this extent, Derrida parenthetically and provocatively remarks, 'Kantianism is, in this respect, structurally a Judaism' (Gtr 34a).

For Hegel, the essence of the family is filiation; it is bound by the thread that binds the father to the son and where the mother is but 'a short detour' (Gtr 36a) into materiality and the daughter does not even figure. The essence of Christianity consists in the filiation of God the Father and God the Son through the material medium of the Virgin birth. The revelation of Christ consists in the loving recognition of his divine incarnation and the realization that human beings are the children of God (Gtr 78a). The incarnate human family is an echo of divine filiation.

It is precisely the doctrine of incarnation that Judaism (and Kantianism) cannot understand and which indeed surpasses the formal abstraction of the understanding. With his tongue lodged firmly in his cheek, Derrida asks 'What do the Jews make of Hegel?' (Gtr 84a). He responds, 'They cry out scandal. How can Jesus identify himself with God, regard himself equal to God, and believe that possible by naming God his father?' (Gtr 84a). The Jew, then, is 'enclosed in this double, non-dialectical onesidedness, he accedes neither to the divine nor to the spiritual sense of filiation. For the spirit has not yet spoken in him. He has not yet become an adult in himself' (Gtr 85a). Within the system, the Jew understands neither Christianity nor Hegelianism, he is a child who, moreover, does not even understand his childishness (Gtr 85a). The Jew does not love, he cannot love, he is the circumcised and dutiful subject of a 'dieu transcendant, jaloux, exclusif, avare, sans présent' (G 62a/Gtr 44a). The Jew attains neither self-presence nor presence to God, he or she is not *bei sich*, but is rather condemned to wander homelessly and nomadically like Abraham in the desert (Gtr 41a). The Jew is a materialist whose circumcision is based upon a materialistic misunderstanding, and who, like the Gorgon's head, turns everything to stone, petrifying and materializing Spirit (Gtr 45a).

Worst of all, the Jews 'have no sense of freedom' (Gtr 48a) and cannot become citizens of a *polis*. For Hegel, citizenship in the Greek sense is conditional upon the holding of property rights, where freedom is synonymous with the ownership of private property. On Hegel's reading, in virtue of the fact that Jews hold their possessions on loan and not as private property, they are denied both full citizenship and freedom (Gtr 53a). Consequently, a Jewish state could not possess political freedom and would inevitably be governed by violence (Gtr 52a). Derrida cites the following chilling passage from *The Spirit of Christianity*:

> All the subsequent circumstances of the Jewish people up to the mean, abject, wretched circumstances in which they still are today, have all of them been simply consequences and developments of their primordial destiny. By this destiny – an infinite power which they have set over against themselves and could never conquer – they have been maltreated and will be continually maltreated until they reconcile it by the spirit of beauty and so relieve (*aufheben*) it by reconciliation. (Gtr 55a, SC 199–200)

History has given such statements a terrifying irony. In order to indicate some paths of investigation that cannot be followed here, I would suggest that Hegel's attitude to Judaism is not simply or empirically anti-semitic, after all it could be argued, for reasons to be shown below, that Hegelianism is equally anti-Christian. Rather, Hegel's attitude is perhaps *philosophically* anti-semitic, that is to say, the conceptual matrix of family, love, community and property has no place for the Jew, if the latter is defined as the other to Greco-Christian philosophical conceptuality. Can philosophical dialectics approach the otherness of the other, that is to say, can it entertain an alterity that cannot be comprehended or reduced to an object of cognition or recognition? Does not the maintenance of the other within the horizon of cognition, self-recognition and the Concept, and the privilege of love over duty, reduce the alterity that ensures respect for the other person? Is not the very desire for love, family, community and cognition predicated upon a reduction of the other's otherness, hence upon a violence to the other person? And if this is the case, then might not anti-semitism be defined as a failure to respect that otherness?

Opening these questions out onto both columns of *Glas*, Sartre remarks in *Saint Genet* that 'Genet is anti-Semitic. Or rather he plays at being so' (SGtr 203/SG 192). What is one to make of the arguably pro-Nazi eroticism of Genet's third novel *Funeral Rites*, or, more recently, the anti-Zionism of his posthumously published *Prisoner of Love*, discussed in chapter 2? Is this a philosophical anti-semitism or is it not rather a prejudice of a more empirical kind? And what of Derrida's relation to this complex anti-semitism working in both columns of *Glas*? How would it relate to the poignant, seemingly autobiographical remarks on the double-columned Torah held aloft by colonists in an Algerian synagogue during Derrida's childhood (Gtr 240bi)? Is *Glas* a kind of anti-Torah, a memory or 'dream' of the sacred text that would 'organize all the pieces and scenes' (ibid.) of *Glas* whilst continually bringing the authority of the sacred text into question?

The *Aufhebung* of the Family and Sexuality

For Hegel, Christianity is the absolute religion which has the Absolute for its content. As such, Christianity is the *Aufhebung* of Judaism. However, although Christianity possesses the Absolute as content, it only represents this content in the form of *Vorstellung*, or picture-thinking. Therefore, Christianity must itself be *aufgehoben* in order for Absolute Knowledge to be achieved: religion is superseded by philosophy. As Derrida remarks, Hegel's reading of Christianity is double (Gtr 92a); or, more precisely, Christianity possesses this duplicity within itself, where it is both the truth of religion and that which only attains its truth in philosophy. Now, it is precisely this *Aufhebung* of religion by philosophy, the passage to Absolute Knowledge, that is Derrida's most general concern in *Glas* and which ultimately guides the subsequent transitions in his reading. He writes, 'The most general question would now have the following form: how is the relief of religion into philosophy produced?' (Gtr 93a). However, Derrida then immediately adds the following question, 'How, on the other hand, is the relief of the family structure into civil (bourgeois) society produced?' (Gtr 93a). How are these two questions analogous? Derrida's hint is that the family will have a determining function in the passage to Absolute Knowledge and will somehow disrupt that passage. Alluding to the closing paragraph of the 'Religion' chapter in the *Phenomenology*, Derrida notes how, in the transition from Absolute Religion to Absolute Knowledge – the *Aufhebung* of the form of Christianity – the family reappears in the guise of the Holy Family:

> Just as the *individual* divine Man has a father *in principle* and only an *actual* mother, so too the *universal* divine Man, the community, has for its father its own doing and knowing, but for its mother, eternal love which it only feels, but does not behold in its consciousness as an actual immediate *object*. Its reconciliation, therefore, is in its heart, but its consciousness is still divided against itself and its actual world is still disrupted. (PS 421/PStr 478, Gtr 94)

The Holy Family thus represents a moment of 'dehiscence' (Gtr 221a) or divorce between the 'father *in principle*' (God) and 'an *actual* [wirkliche] mother' (Mary) that produces 'the *individual* divine Man' (Christ) who does not fully reconcile Absolute Spirit and self-consciousness, and because of whom the 'actual world is still disrupted'. On the very threshold of Absolute Knowledge, both the Holy Family and the universal family of the community are dirempt and divorced and thus have to be *aufgehoben*. Thus, by choosing the guiding thread of the family, Derrida foregrounds a concept that is crucial to the passage to Absolute Knowledge or philosophy and with which the latter might be deconstructed.

Looking quickly ahead, Derrida's claim will be that 'The *Aufhebung*, the economic law of the absolute reappropriation of absolute loss, is a family concept' (Gtr 133a), and furthermore, that philosophy itself 'is properly familial' (Gtr 134a). By this, Derrida appears to be claiming that the movement of speculative dialectics always results in reappropriation, 'the guarding of the proper [*la garde du propre*]' (Gtr 134a), bringing back all phenomena within the circle of the proper, of property, of propriety, of one's own: love, home, family, community, cognition. It is precisely the circumference of this circle that Derrida seeks to deconstruct.

After a brief discussion of 'The Need for Philosophy' from the *Differenzschrift* (D 10–14), Derrida returns to the concept of *Sittlichkeit*, the context for the family, and traces its emergence in the 1803 essay on natural law, the *Philosophy of Nature* and the *First Philosophy of Spirit*. The place of the family in the *First Philosophy of Spirit* is the 'Third Level' of the 'Formal Concept of Consciousness' (FPS 231–5). The family forms part of a theory of consciousness, where it is characterized by love, marriage and procreation, and is *aufgehoben* in the transition to 'The People', or absolute *Sittlichkeit* (FPS 242). Derrida's claim here is that, despite some modifications, the treatment of the family in the *First Philosophy of Spirit* essentially predicts the fuller treatment given fifteen years later in the *Philosophy of Right*.

Consciousness, for Hegel, is the *Aufhebung* of nature by Spirit, and this prompts Derrida to make an excursus into the *Philosophy of Nature*, in order to give an account of the natural sex differences which are superseded by the spiritual sexual desire that founds the family (FPS 231). Derrida focuses on the short section of *Philosophy of Nature* that treats 'The Sex-Relationship' (PN vol. III 172–5). Beneath the apparently anatomical description in Hegel's text, Derrida detects the most traditional, Aristotelian interpretation of sexual difference, which repeats the hierarchical oppositions of male to female, form to matter, and activity to passivity, that characterize classical phallocentrism:

> The clitoris moreover is inactive feeling in general; in the male on the other hand, it has its counterpart in active sensibility, the swelling vital, the effusion of blood into the corpora cavernosa and the meshes of the spongy tissue of the urethra. (PN vol. III 175)

Derrida shows the wider complicity between phallocentrism and philosophy with a discussion of Kant's *Anthropology from a Pragmatic Point of View*. Kant's account of sex differences is even more repugnant than Hegel's. One reads:

> Whenever the refinement of luxury has reached a high point, the woman shows herself well-behaved (*sittsam*) only by compulsion, and makes no secret in wishing that she might rather be a man, so that she could give larger and freer playing room to her inclinations; no man, however, would want to be a woman. (ANT 221, Gtr 221a)

However, as well as being sexist and anti-feminist, classical phallocentrism is also *heterosexist*. A possible reading of Hegel that cannot be fully explored here would have to show how homosexuality is excluded from *Sittlichkeit*, where spiritualized sexual desire is at once familial, monogamous and heterosexual. With reference to Jean Genet, it should be asked whether speculative dialectics has a place for the homosexual other than in prison?

Antigone: The Quasi-Transcendental

Such themes of sexual difference are taken up and focused in the next major transition in *Glas*. After a discussion of the 'struggle for recognition' in the *First Philosophy of Spirit* (FPS 235–42), Derrida moves on to a detailed and fascinating discussion of Hegel's interpretation of the *Antigone* in the *Phenomenology of Spirit*. Note that one is once again within the context of *Sittlichkeit*, the first moment of its syllogism, which itself forms the first moment of the great syllogism of *Geist* in the *Phenomenology*. Derrida chooses two 'foci' (Gtr 142a) upon which to concentrate his reading: the sepulchre (*sépulture*) and the liaison between brother and sister (ibid.). Derrida begins by reiterating the cluster of oppositions that govern Hegel's reading: Antigone–Creon, divine law–human law, family–state, woman–man, law of singularity (*Gesetz der Einzelheit*)–law of universality (*Gesetz der Allgemeinheit*). With respect to the first focus, it is the function of the family, defined as the space of woman, the singular, the divine, to deal with the burial of the dead. The feminine work of mourning is rigorously distinguished from the masculine labour of the *polis*. Although, within this schema, the sepulchre is the proper or property (*le propre* – Gtr 144a) of man, it is the wife or the daughter who is entrusted with the funeral rites (*pompes funèbres*, Gtr 143a – which is also the title of Genet's third novel, an extended work of mourning for his dead lover, Jean Décarnin – J.D. –, an intertextual allusion that is far from incidental in this context). The building of the sepulchre is woman's work, as is the embalming, shrouding and interring of the corpse and the preparation and erection of the slab or stele. When the corpse is placed in the sepulchre, its singularity and materiality decompose, allowing it to ascend into the universality of Spirit.

Enter Antigone: for it is she who demands a sepulchre for her brother Polynices in the name of the divine law. This introduces the second focus of Derrida's reading, where he draws on two related phenomena: firstly, Antigone's declaration, 'I could have had another husband/And by him other sons, if one were lost;/But, father and mother lost, where would I get another brother' (AN lines 906–10). And secondly, Hegel's reading of this passage and his consequent privileging of the brother/sister relation over those of husband and wife or parents and children (PS 246–8/PStr 273–5). The relation of sister to brother is an 'unmixed' (PS 247/PStr 274) recognition of spiritual and ethical essence where the two parties neither desire one another, nor do they enter into a 'life and death struggle' or a 'struggle for recognition'. Although Antigone is 'Never a bride, never a mother' (AN line 911), Hegel recognizes that 'the feminine, in the form of the sister, has the highest *presentiment* of ethical essence [*Das Weibliche hat daher als Schwester die höchste* Ahnung *des sittlichen Wesens*]' (PS 247/PStr 274). Derrida's argument here is that Antigone and Polynices are:

the two sole consciousnesses that, in the Hegelian universe, relate to each other without entering into war. Given the generality of the struggle for recognition in the relationship between consciousnesses, one would be tempted to conclude from this that at bottom *there is no* brother/sister bond, there is no brother or sister. If such a relation is unique and reaches a kind of repose (*Ruhe*) and equilibrium (*Gleichgewicht*) that are refused to all others, that is because the brother and the sister do not receive their for-self from the other and neverthe-less constitute themselves as 'free individualities'. – The for-selves [*les pour-soi*] recognize, without depending on, each other; they no more desire one another than tear each other to pieces [*ne se désirent pas plus qu'ils ne se déchirent*]. (G 208a/Gtr 149a)

Thus far, Derrida has been pushing very hard at these paragraphs of the *Phenomenology*, but following them to the letter. However, he now raises a question with regard to this brother/sister relation, 'Is it impossible [the trans-lation has 'possible' here]? Is it in contradiction with the whole system?' (G 208a/Gtr 149a). Following Hegel's remark that the relation between the sister and the brother represents the limit at which the life of the family breaks up and goes beyond itself (PS 248/PStr 275), Derrida suggests that the sister's presentiment of the essence of *Sittlichkeit* cannot be contained within the limits of the system. Because Antigone and Polynices constitute themselves as free individualities that have not 'given to, or received from one another this independent being-for-self [*Fursichseyn*]' (PS 247/PStr 274), and because they do not engage in a 'struggle for recognition', their relation somehow exceeds the system of which it is a part. The figure of Antigone gazing with impassive rage at the unburied body of her brother cannot be dialectically appropriated and stands outside any attempt at assimilation. She exemplifies the femininity of the ethical relation with the other that is not based upon dialectical structures of recognition, reconciliation and reciprocity.

The effect of focusing on this 'impossible place' (Gtr 151a) within Hegel's reading of *Antigone*, and *a fortiori* within the family, within *Sittlichkeit* and within the system, is to propose a second question that will radicalize this impossibility:

What if the inassimilable, the absolutely indigestible, played a fundamental rôle within the system, abyssal rather, the abyss playing . . . [and here there is an interruption of eleven pages, where Derrida cites lengthy passages from Hegel's correspondence with his lover/friend Nanette Endel, his fiancé/wife Marie von Tucker and his friend Friedrich Niethammer, which offer insights into Hegel's opinions on love, friendship, marriage and teaching] a quasi transcendental role and letting be formed above it, like a sort of effluvium, a dream of appeasement? Is there not always an element excluded from the system which assures the space of the system's possibility? . . . And what if the sister, the brother/sister relation here represented the transcendental position or ex-position? (G 21–7a/Gtr 151–62a)

These questions, and note that they are still only questions, deconstructively turn the reading and suggest that what cannot be assimilated within the Hegelian system, the abyss, functions as a quasi-transcendental condition of possibility for the system. The peculiar character of Derrida's transcendental claim is that it not only establishes the condition for the possibility of the system, it also indicates the condition for the system's *impossibility*. The figure of Antigone is the quasi-transcendental condition for the possibility and impossibility of the Hegelian system, its *Grund* and *Abgrund*.

The above argumentation very much typifies Derrida's reading practice in *Glas* and elsewhere: he focuses on a seemingly minor point in a text, a point that one might easily overlook in a casual reading, and then shows how this point is the text's blind spot from which its entire conceptual edifice can be deconstructed. Derrida summarizes his reading in the following way:

Like Hegel, we have been fascinated by Antigone, by this unbelievable relation, this powerful liaison without desire, this immense impossible desire that could not live, capable only of reversing, paralysing or exceeding a system and a history, of interrupting the life of the Concept, of taking its breath away [*de lui couper le souffle*] or, indeed, which comes back to the same thing [*ce qui revient au même*], of supporting it from the outside or the beneath of a crypt. Crypt – one would have said, of the transcendental or of the repressed, of the unthought or the excluded – that organizes the ground to which it does not belong. (G 232a/Gtr 166a)

The twin foci of sepulchre and sister finally combine in the figure of the crypt, where Antigone is imprisoned and hangs herself. Ultimately, for Derrida, it is Antigone's death that sounds the knell or *glas* of the system and announces nothing less than the end of history, 'Nothing should be able to survive Antigone's death. Nothing more should follow, go out of her, after her. The announcement of her death should sound the absolute end of history [*la fin absolue de l'histoire*]' (ibid.). Antigone's death *should* bring the system, history and the movement of cognition to a halt, and yet speculative dialectics incorporates this crypt within itself, making of Antigone a moment to be *aufgehoben*. For Derrida, Antigone's death *should* exceed the

Hegelian system and make Spirit stumble on its path to Absolute Knowledge, and yet Spirit barely loses its footing for an instant and relentlessly
continues its ascent.

Once again, it should be noted how the choice of the family as the
example of the system is crucial here, because Antigone *exemplifies* the family, following its duties to the letter and showing the point at which the
family, *Sittlichkeit* and the system exceed the intentions of Hegel's text and
deconstruct themselves. Starting from Derrida's reading, I would want to
argue that by exemplifying the essence of ethical life, of *Sittlichkeit*, Antigone
marks a place ('an impossible place') within the Hegelian system where an
ethical moment irreducible to dialectics is glimpsed. Such an ethics would
not be based upon the recognition of the other, which is always self-
recognition, but would rather begin with the expropriation of the self in
the face of the other's approach. Ethics would begin with the recognition
that the other is not an object of cognition or comprehension, but precisely
that which exceeds my grasp and powers. The formal structure of such an
ethics might well be analogous to that of mourning in the Freudian sense:
Antigone's mourning for Polynices, Haemon's mourning for Antigone,
Genet's mourning for Jean Décarnin. In mourning, the self is consumed by
the pain of the other's death and is possessed by the alterity of that which
it cannot possess: the absence of the beloved.[4] Might not the death of the
beloved, of love itself, and the work of mourning be the basis for a non-
Christian and non-dialectical ethicality and friendship? Although such remarks give only hints and guesses, the claim that I will try and make good
in this book is that such an ethics is the perpetual horizon of Derrida's
deconstructive reading of Hegel, and of Derrida's work as a whole.

Derrida closes his reading of Hegel on *Antigone* by focusing on the final
paragraphs of 'Ethical Action. Human and Divine Knowledge. Guilt and
Destiny' (PStr 287–9), where the combat of Eteocles and Polynices provides the backdrop for the conflict between the spirit of community and
the rebellious principle of singularity, of the family (PS 257/PStr 286). In
refusing to administer the proper funeral rites to Polynices, the community
represses the singular; but in so doing, the community dishonours and
destroys the family pieties which underpin it. The community is avenged,
and Antigone revenged, by destructive war with other cities which results
in the ruin of *Sittlichkeit* (PS 260/PStr 289). In Hegel's much-cited words,
womankind, the feminine, the singular, is the community's 'internal enemy'
and 'everlasting irony' (PS 259/PStr 288).

At this point, one might attempt a rapprochement between Antigone
and Genet. Both are criminals, both are emprisoned or entombed, both are

orphans (Gtr 165–6a); and, more importantly, both are excluded by and reject the human law, what Hegel calls 'the manhood [*die Männlichkeit*] of the community' (PS 258/PStr 287). Whatever the community might do to repress the singular, there always remains the everlasting possibility of irony. Irony is the genre of ethical discourse. Emprisoned at Fresnes, Genet, the effeminate, the homosexual, the masturbator, the thief, silently ironizes the customs and legislature of the community in his writing. In *Funeral Rites*, Genet's irony of the Libération in France in 1944, he works through his mourning for Jean Décarnin. Like Antigone gazing at the corpse of Polynices, Genet contemplates Décarnin's face in his coffin, writing of the 'funereal flavor' that 'has often filled my mouth *after love*' (my emphasis – FR 25–7). As Cocteau remarked, Genet will one day have to be recognized as a moralist (SG 513/SGtr 558). Sartre extends this insight, arguing that although Genet's works 'are criminal assaults upon his readers, they are, at the same time, presented as systematically conducted ethical experiments' (SG 514/SGtr 559). However, rather than seeing the ethical content of Genet's work in terms of Sartre's totalizing narrative of liberation, the ethical status of a text like *Funeral Rites*, as well as Derrida's methodology of reading in *Glas*, lies precisely in its resistance to totalization, its everlasting ironization of totality.

Derrida's Post-Hegelian Kantianism

At this point in Derrida's reading, he interrupts his discussion of the *Phenomenology* in order to return to the *Philosophy of Right*, precisely at the point in the discussion of marriage when Hegel mentions Antigone and refers the reader back to the *Phenomenology* (PR 158/PRtr 114–15, Gtr 188–9). For Hegel, marriage is in essence monogamy and is characterized as 'ethico-legal love [*rechtlich sittliche Liebe*]' (PR 153/PRtr 262). It is our 'ethical duty' (PR 153/PRtr 111) to enter marriage, and therefore, as Derrida remarks, 'The ethical and the political are reached only on condition of being married' (Gtr 192) – which, of course, excludes both Antigone and Genet from Hegelian *Sittlichkeit*.

Derrida interests himself in two presuppositions of marriage: inhibition or repression (*Hemmung* – which Knox translates as 'restraint' PRtr 114), and the incest prohibition. Firstly, the ethical aspect of love consists in 'the higher inhibition and depreciation of purely natural pressure [*die höhere Hemmung und Zurücksetzung des bloßen Naturtriebs*]' (PR 156/PRtr 114). Thus, the entrance into marriage, the family and *Sittlichkeit* is founded upon the repression of the natural drive. Secondly, marriage is founded upon the incest prohibition, where the ethical transaction of marriage is denied to blood relatives like Antigone and Polynices (PR 159/PRtr 115).

This discussion occasions an excursus into the 'children' of Hegel's philosophy: Feuerbach, Marx and, very briefly, Kierkegaard (Gtr 200ai – see also Gtr 232ai–33ai). Derrida focuses on Feuerbach's *Principles of the Philosophy of the Future* and *The Essence of Christianity*, and on Marx's critique of Feuerbach in the 1844 *Economic and Philosophical Manuscripts* and the *Theses* of 1845. The purpose of this rare excursus into Marx in Derrida's work prior to *Spectres of Marx* would appear to demonstrate simply that Marx's and Feuerbach's critique of Hegel is largely a critique of religion. For Feuerbach, 'Speculative philosophy is the true, consistent, rational theology' (Gtr 201a).

The mention of religion slowly turns Derrida's reading back, somewhat circuitously, to the problem of the transition from Absolute Religion to Absolute Knowledge and to the guiding question, 'how is the relief of religion into philosophy produced?' After a discussion of fetishism in Hegel's account of African religion in the *Lectures on the Philosophy of World History* (Gtr 207–11a), Derrida takes up once again Hegel's critique of Kant's conception of religion. In the Introduction to the *Lectures on the Philosophy of Religion*, Hegel criticizes the Kantian claim according to which 'we can know nothing of God' (LPR 36–7, Gtr 211a). For Hegel, Christianity is the revealed religion, indeed it is the *only* revealed religion, and the essence of the revealed, *das Offenbare*, is that the content of religion, Absolute Spirit, is revealed to self-consciousness as an object of knowledge in the form of *Vorstellung*. The Hegelian conception of revealed religion is speculatively expressed in the closing pages of the *Encyclopaedia*, 'God is God only in so far as he knows himself: his self-knowledge is, further, a self-consciousness in man and man's knowledge of God, which proceeds to man's self-knowledge in God' (PM 298).

The Kantian claim that God is not an object of cognition fails to comprehend both the nature of revelation and the relation between the human and the divine. In these respects, Derrida claims, Kantianism is Judaic:

> To claim to found Christianity on reason and nonetheless to make non-manifes-tation, the being-hidden of God, the principle of this religion is to understand nothing about revelation. Kant is Jewish [*est juif*]: he believes in a jealous, envi-ous God . . . (G 297a/Gtr 213a)

In the *Encyclopaedia* (PM 298), Hegel repeats the exclusion of jealousy as a predicate of the divine that was established in Plato's *Phaedrus* and Aristotle's *Metaphysics*.[5] The enigmatic guardedness of jealousy is opposed to the phenomenal revelation of Spirit (PM 2898), and the former can have no place in either Absolute Religion or Absolute Knowledge:

> In *Sa* [i.e. *Savoir Absolu*], jealousy no longer has a place. Jealousy always comes from the night of the unconscious, the unknown, the other. Pure sight relieves all jealousy. Not seeing what one sees, seeing what one cannot see and who cannot present himself, such is the jealous operation. It always has to do with the trace, never with perception. Seen from *Sa*, the thought of the trace would thus be a jealous thought. (Gtr 215)

The structural analogies between Kantianism, Judaism, jealousy and the thought of the trace (i.e., the thought of that which will never have been revealed or incarnated and which exceeds the order of phenomenality and presence) are highly suggestive, recalling above discussions and provoking others that cannot be followed in this context. If Hegelianism is, as Derrida claims, a philosophy of presence, where philosophy is the truth of religion and where self-consciousness is presented with the Absolute as an object of cognition, then, one might ask, must not Kantianism bear a more complex relation to the philosophy of presence? Might not the deconstruction of *Sittlichkeit* and the thought of an ethics irreducible to dialectics signal a return to a form of *Moralität*? Is *Glas* implicitly postulating a post-Hegelian Kantianism?[6]

Such questions would, at the very least, have to pass through Hegel's critique of Kant in the *Phenomenology* and the *Philosophy of Right* and focus in particular on the status of the Postulates of Pure Practical Reason. It would be necessary to ask whether the postulation of an 'infinite progress' towards the complete fitness of the will to the Moral Law (immortality) and of morality to happiness (God), can be contained within the horizon of presence. Might not the infinite deferral of the presentation of the postulates to self-consciousness open out onto the thought of *différance*, where God and immortality would only be present as traces of that which will never have been present? In this regard, it is worth noting that when Derrida locates the thought of *différance* in Husserl's use of the 'Idea in the Kantian sense', he adds, 'La critique de Kant par Hegel vaudrait sans doute aussi contre Husserl.'[7] My claim is that this remark, read against the grain and in the knowledge of *Glas*, is a good deal more Kantian or Husserlian than might at first appear.

Luminous Essence: The Non-Metaphysical Gift of Holocaust

Derrida continues with the extraordinary *mise en scène* of a fictive dialogue between Kant and Hegel (Gtr 216–18a), with parenthetical remarks by Freud (Gtr 217ai), before summarizing the relation between religion and philosophy with Hegel's remark, 'Thus religion and philosophy come to be one . . . Philosophy is only explicating itself when it explicates religion, and when it explicates itself it is explicating religion' (LPR 20, Gtr 218a). Indeed it is the precise and paradoxical nature of the limit dividing and uniting religion and philosophy at the end of the *Encyclopaedia* and the *Phenomenology* that fascinates Derrida here. The paradox is that Absolute or Revealed Religion is not yet Absolute Knowing and yet it is already Absolute Knowing. Derrida expresses this structure more elegantly and untranslatably as 'l'absolu du déjà-là du pas-encore ou de l'encore du déjà plus' (G 306a/Gtr 219a). Although a digression would be necessary here upon the function of the 'we' and the concept of *Erinnerung* in the *Phenomenology*, as well as upon the circle metaphors that recur in Hegel's text (see PS 429/PStr 488, PR 17/PRtr 225, A 24–5), it can be justifiably claimed that Absolute Religion is only the *Vorstellung* of the unification between self-consciousness and Absolute Spirit, a unification only 'in principle [*an sich*]' (PS 425/PStr 483) and therefore neither actual nor fully present.

> The reconciliation has produced itself and yet it has *not yet* taken place, it is *not present*, only represented or present as remaining before, ahead of, to come, present as not-yet-there and not as presence of the present. But as this reconciliation of Being [*l'être*] and the same [*même*] (reconciliation itself [*même*]) is absolute presence, absolute parousia, we must say that in religion, in absolute revelation, presence is present as representation. (G 308a/Gtr 220a)

Parousia, as the presence to self-consciousness of the consciousness of the Absolute and the completion of Spirit's circular phenomenology, is minimally but decisively deferred in Absolute Religion. Absolute Knowledge is the unification of the content of religion, substance or being-in-itself (PS 421/PStr 478), with the form of Spirit (PS 362/PStr 409), subject or being-for-self, in the thinking of the Concept, what Hegel calls 'comprehensive knowing [*begreifendes Wissen*]' or Science (PS 427–8/PStr 485–6). It is only with Absolute Knowledge that the Concept attains its passage into consciousness and where the latter experiences the certainty of immediacy, thereby returning to the beginning of its phenomenological path in sense-certainty (PS 432/PStr 491). Thus begins the labour of recollection.

Derrida ascends with Hegel to the peak of Absolute Knowledge, but instead of remaining at the summit, he descends a little into the 'Religion' chapter of the *Phenomenology*. As I will show, such a move is neither contingent nor a product of vertigo. Derrida schematizes the three moments of religion: natural, aesthetic and revealed (Gtr 236a). The immediacy of natural religion (light, plants and animals, and the artificer) is superseded by the religion of art (the abstract, living and spiritual works of art), and these two forms are unified in revealed religion which is the true shape ('*wahren Gestalt*' PS 368/PStr 416) of Spirit. Now, although Christianity is the true shape of Spirit, this shape will itself have to be overcome in order to pass over into Absolute Knowledge. Derrida infers from this that 'le *Sa* n'a pas de figure' (G 330a/Gtr 237a) and that it is precisely shapeliness or figuration that must be superseded in Absolute Knowledge. From this inference, Derrida draws a circle around the syllogism of religion in order to link up the immediacy of natural religion with that of Absolute Knowledge (Gtr 237a). This would appear to be justified insofar as the first moment of natural religion, *das Lichtwesen* (translated by Miller as 'God as Light' PStr 418, and by Hyppolite as '*L'essence lumineuse*' PE vol. II 214 – Derrida follows the latter translation), shares the same shape, or rather 'shape of shapelessness [*Gestalt der Gestaltlosigkeit*]' (PS 371/PStr 419, and see LPR vol. II 78) as sense-certainty.

Crudely stated, the *Phenomenology* contains two movements, that from subject to substance in chapters I to VI ('Sense-Certainty' to 'Spirit'), and that from substance to subject described in chapter VII ('Religion'). All that remains in chapter VIII ('Absolute Knowing'), is for these two moments to be unified into the comprehensive thinking of the Concept. Thus, the return to sense-certainty that occurs at the end of the *Phenomenology*, as well as being a return to the beginning of chapter I, is also a return to the beginning of chapter VII; although, of course, religion presupposes that the moments of consciousness, self-consciousness, Reason and Spirit 'have run their full course' (PS 365/PStr 413). Thus, for Derrida, the discussion of natural religion is a way of obliquely analysing the claim to Absolute Knowledge and of answering the question that appears as the subtitle to the French paperback edition of *Glas*, 'Que reste-t-il du savoir absolu?'

I would argue that the pages of *Glas* that deal with natural religion (especially Gtr 236a–45a), together with the discussion of the *Antigone*, constitute the core of Derrida's reading and the clearest deployment of its thesis. Perhaps the enduring importance of these pages for Derrida can be judged by the fact that he quotes from them at great length in a 1987 publication, *Feu la cendre* (FC 26–32). What specifically interests Derrida here is the page-and-a-half of '*das Lichtwesen*' and the precise nature of the transition to 'Plant and Animal'. The 'shapeless shape' of the first moment of natural religion 'is the pure, all-embracing and all-pervading *essential light* of sunrise, which preserves itself in its formless substantiality [*das reine, alles enthaltende und erfüllende Lichtwesen des Aufgangs, das sich in seiner formlosen Substantialität erhält*]' (PS 371/PStr 419). As Derrida points out, this conception of religion, that of ancient Parsis or Persia, corresponds to the Zoroastrian cult of light discussed by Hegel in the *Lectures on the Philosophy of Religion* (LPR 77). In Zoroastrian religion, light is worshipped not as a symbol or sign of the Good, but as the Good itself, its pure manifestation (LPR 76 and 78).[8]

Essential light is, Derrida writes, 'Pure and without shape, this light burns all [*brûle tout*]. It burns itself in the all-burning [*brûle-tout*] that it is, leaves of itself, of itself or anything, no trace, no mark, no sign of passage' (G 332a/Gtr 238a). The 'torrents of light' or 'streams of fire' emanating from *das Lichtwesen* are 'destructive of all structured form' (PS 371/PStr 419). Hegel concludes that the content of essential light is 'pure Being [*das reine Seyn*]', 'an essenceless by-play [*ein wesenloses Beyherspielen*] in this substance which merely ascends, without descending into the depths to become a subject' (ibid.). Essenceless substance without subject, 'the many-named one' that 'lacks a self' (ibid.), is the thought that interests Derrida here. To express this differently, to think essenceless substance without subject is akin to thinking Being (*das Sein*) prior to its determination with regard to particular beings (*das Seiende*). Derrida asks, 'How can the self and the for-itself [*pour-soi*] appear?' (G 334a/Gtr 239a). That is to say, how can the transition from the in-itself to the for-itself that opens dialectics and history begin? How is the transition from this Oriental sunrise to Occidental sunset to be accomplished?

As always, it is a question of a transition from immediacy to mediation, or being-in-itself to being-for-self. Derrida, citing and retranslating what is perhaps the most important passage from Hegel for his reading, writes:

> But this reeling (tottering, tumultuous, *taumelnde*) life must (*muß*; why must it?) [*pourquoi doit-elle?*] determine itself as being for self and give its evanescent figures a stable subsistence . . . Pure light disseminates (*wirft . . . auseinander*) [Miller has 'disperses' and Hyppolite '*éparpille*'] its simplicity as an infinity of separated forms and gives itself as a holocaust to the for-itself [*se donne en holocauste au pour-soi*] (*gibt sich dem Fürsichseyn zum Opfer*) [Miller has 'sacrifice' for *Opfer*, Hyppolite also has '*holocauste*'], so that the singular [*das Einzelne*] may take its subsistence from its substance. (PS 371–2/PStr 420, PE vol. II 216, G 336/Gtr 241)

Thus, the total burning and consumation of essential light gives itself to being-for-self as a holocaust, that is, as a whole (*holos*) that is burnt (*caustos*). With the advent of this gift, the fire of light goes out and the sun begins to set; the dialectical, phenomenological and historical movement of occidentalization that will result in Absolute Knowledge has begun. Within the syllogism of natural religion, there occurs a transition from the religion of light to the pantheism of the religion of flowers, a move which mirrors the transition from sense-certainty to perception (PS 372/PStr 420) and which lets Derrida complete a circle that refers the reader back to the beginning of the Hegel column and the prefatory discussion of flower religion (Gtr 2a). Yet, one might ask, why is all this important? As Derrida writes, 'what is at stake in this column?' (G 337a/Gtr 241a). He responds:

> This perhaps: the gift, the sacrifice, the putting in play or to fire of all, the holocaust, are in the power of ontology [*en puissance d'ontologie*]. They bear and overflow it but cannot not give birth to it. Without the holocaust the dialectical movement and the history of Being could not open themselves, engage themselves in the annulus of their anniversary, could not annul themselves in producing the solar course from the Orient to the Occident. (G 337/Gtr 242a)

En puissance d'ontologie: ontology would here seem to be understood simply as discourse (*logos*) about beings (*onta*). As discourse about beings, ontology always thinks that which is – Being – with respect to its determination through beings. Heidegger defines metaphysics as onto-theo-logy, that is to say, the Aristotelian investigation of *to on e on*, Being *qua* Being, which asks after the totality of beings with respect to their most universal traits (ontology), but also with respect to the highest and therefore divine being (theology). Metaphysics or, more properly, first philosophy, conceives of beings in terms of a unifying *ousia* and ultimately a divine *ousia*. Heidegger therefore describes metaphysics as discourse which states what beings are as beings ('*Die Metaphysik sagt, was das Seiende als das Seiende ist*'). However, in its discourse upon beings, what does not get asked about is Being itself prior to its determination in terms of beings. Heidegger writes, 'Metaphysics, insofar as it always represents only beings as beings [*das Seiende als das Seiende vorstellt*], does not recall Being itself [*das Sein selbst*]'.[9]

Returning to Derrida, his claim would appear to be that although the gift of the Holocaust is in the power of ontology *qua* metaphysics, it simultaneously bears and overflows ontology and the dialectical or metaphysical determination of Being in terms of the subject, or being-for-self. Derrida is here attempting the thought of a sacrificial giving which is a moment within the Hegelian text which that text cannot master and which engages and exceeds ontology, dialectics and metaphysics. Recalling the above discussion of *Antigone*, the gift of holocaust is perhaps the condition for the possibility and impossibility of the Hegelian system. Derrida continues:

> before everything, before every determinable being [*étant*], there is [*il y a*], there was [*il y avait*], there will have been [*il y aura eu*] the irruptive event of the gift [*don*]. An event which no longer has any relation with what one currently designates under this word. One can no longer think the giving [*la donation*] starting from Being [*être*] . . . In *Zeit und Sein*, the gift of the *es gibt* gives itself to be thought before the *Sein* in the *es gibt* Sein and displaces all that is determined under the name of *Ereignis*, a word often translated by event [*événement*]. (G 337a/Gtr 242a)

With this allusion to Heidegger's 1962 lecture *Zeit und Sein*, the ultimate orientation of Derrida's reading of Hegel becomes apparent. There are scattered references to Heidegger in *Glas*, but the above allusion is the most important.[10] Derrida appears to be understanding Hegel in terms of the ontological difference between *Sein* (*être*) and *Seiende* (*étant*), and focuses in particular upon the thought of the gift contained in the phrase *es gibt Sein* ('it gives Being' or 'there "is" Being'; in French, *il y a être*), which returns the thinking of Being to that of a primordial giving.

In *Zeit und Sein*, Heidegger's continuation and radicalization of the thinking begun in *Sein und Zeit*, he seeks to raise the question of Being and time anew as a matter for thinking. To think Being in terms of beings, where the former is the ontological ground for the latter, is to think metaphysically (SD 4/TB 4). Heidegger replaces the customary expressions, namely that 'Being is' or 'time is' ('*Sein ist, Zeit ist*' SD 5/TB 5) with the formulations '*es gibt Sein*' and '*es gibt Zeit*' (ibid.). Thus, Heidegger displaces the problem of Being and time onto the horizon of an 'it' that 'gives' or provides the primordial donation of Being. This giving is ultimately thought as the appropriating event (*das Ereignis*, SD 20/TB 19) or, more precisely, as the appropriating of appropriation ('*das Ereignis ereignet*' SD 25/TB 24), which permits a thinking of the conjunction of Being and time without regard for beings, that is, without regard for metaphysics ('*Sein ohne das Seiende denken, heißt: Sein ohne Rücksicht auf die Metaphysik denken*' SD 25/TB 24).

What fascinates Derrida in the formulation *es gibt Sein* is the way in which Being is divorced from the language of metaphysics and shown to belong to a prior giving, the giving of an 'It' ('*Sein gehört als die Gabe dieses Es gibt in das Geben*' SD 6/TB 6). The gift of an 'It', in Derrida's text *Ça*,

and the homonym for *Sa*, Savoir Absolu, exceeds the metaphysical determination of Being. For Heidegger, Being is not ('*Sein ist Nicht*') but, rather,
gives 'It' as the unconcealing of presence ('*Sein gibt es als das Entbergen von
Anwesen*' SD 6/TB 6).

To think Being without beings, the essenceless, burning by-play of light,
is to think without metaphysics. The aim of Derrida's deconstructive reading of Hegel is the location of a non-metaphysical moment within dialectical metaphysics. Yet this non-metaphysical moment of *das Lichtwesen*
completely burns itself, becoming a holocaust that is then given to being-
for-self, *das Seiende*, and from which the metaphysical movement of the
dialectic begins. Hegelian dialectic thinks the meaning of Being with regard
to beings, as self-conscious subjectivity. Yet Derrida's claim appears to be
that, in its destination, as Absolute Knowledge, and in its beginning, as
sense-certainty and *das Lichtwesen*, Hegelian dialectic contains that which it
cannot contain: the primordial and non-metaphysical donation of the gift.
To formulate this more radically, one might say that Absolute Knowledge
(*Sa*) transforms itself into an It (*Ça*) that gives.

Derrida continues:

> the process of the gift (before exchange), process which is not a process but a
> holocaust, a holocaust of the holocaust, *engages* the history of Being but does not
> belong to it. The gift *is not*, the holocaust *is not*, if at least there is some [*il y en
> a*]. But as soon as it burns (the blaze is not a being) it must [*il doit*], burning itself,
> burn its operation of burning and begin to be. (G 338a/Gtr 242a)

The blaze of fire is not a being, yet in its burning it *must* (and the ethical
modality of this *doit* and its corresponding duty or *devoir* is of interest here)
become a being, begin to be and set the history of Being – understood as
Being's oblivion in the history of metaphysics – in motion. Derrida gener-
alizes his claim:

> The dialectic of religion, the history of philosophy (etc.), produces itself as the
> reflection–effect [*l'effet-reflet*] of a *coup de don* [a gift's blow] in holocaust. But if
> the blazing is not yet philosophy (and the remains) [*le reste*], it cannot not never-
> theless give rise [*donner lieu*] to philosophy, to dialectical speculation . . . (ibid.)

Philosophy, understood historically and dialectically as metaphysics, is the
effect of a *coup de don*, a primordial giving that is otherwise than philosophy.
Philosophy begins with a non-philosophical event which it both cannot
contain and cannot not give rise to philosophy. This claim has the status of
a necessity in *Glas*:

> There is there [*il y a là*] a fatum of the gift, and this *necessity* [my emphasis]
> was said in the 'must' (*muß*) we indicated above: the *Taumeln*, the vertigo, the
> delirium *must* determine itself as for-itself and take on subsistency. (G 338a/
> Gtr 242–3a)

It is necessary for the gift to be given, for the non-philosophical event that
gives rise to philosophy to be received as philosophy's beginning. At this
point in the text, inexplicably, Derrida slips into the language of personal
pronouns: 'I give you [*je te donne*] – a pure gift, without exchange, without
return – but whether I want this or not, the gift guards itself and from then
on you must, you owe [*tu dois*]' (G 338a/Gtr 243a). The necessity of giving
the gift without receiving anything in return, also implies the necessity of
receiving the gift. I am bound to give you the gift, and from that moment
you are duty-bound in a responsible relation where you must respond,
where you owe (*dois*) the gift to me. The discourse of philosophy has as its
unthought horizon an event of holocaust, of primordial giving that informs
and exceeds it, 'The gift [*don*], the giving of the gift [*la donation du don*], the
pure cadeau does not let itself be thought by the dialectics to which it,
however, gives rise [*donne lieu*]' (G 339a/Gtr 243a).

Yet, once again it is necessary to ask, what is at stake in this column?
Derrida's tireless labour of reading results in the location of the thought of
the gift and the Holocaust, notions which deny dialectical or even philosophical comprehension. Such a gift *must* (*doit*), however, give rise to philosophy. It is the nature and fatality of this *must* and its association with a
notion of ethical *duty* (*devoir*) that is of interest here. Connecting this discussion with the reading of the *Antigone* and the hypothesis of an ethics
irreducible to dialectics, might one not ask whether *Glas* is also delineating
an ethics of holocaust, of a primordial gift or sacrifice that is the unthought
limit of philosophical conceptuality? Can philosophy think holocaust, its
ashes, its remains? Can ontology, even fundamental ontology or the question of the truth of Being, responsibly break its silence on the Holocaust?
What is at stake here?[11]

This perhaps: the gift or holocaust that I must give to the other and
which the other owes to me, is to regard the other as he or she for whom
I would sacrifice myself. Prior to my concern with myself, with my death
and with all that is proper to me, arises the primacy of the other's death over
my own and the consequent possibility of regarding myself as a sacrifice or
holocaust for the other. An ethics of holocaust would describe a radical
expropriation, a movement of charity, where I give to the other without
hope of remuneration and yet, from that moment, you are also obliged.[12]

At the Origin of Literature

However, *Glas* does not end with the discussion of the gift. Indeed, the text does not have an end, in the sense of an organized telos, like Absolute Knowledge, towards which the reading tends. The final pages (Gtr 245a–62a) continue the reading of Hegel, working through the remaining sections of 'Natural Religion' and discussing the first two moments of 'Religion in the Form of Art' (PS 376–88/PStr 424–39). Derrida begins by examining flower religion and digresses onto Hegel's remarks on plants from the *Philosophy of Nature* (PN 67–91). Bringing together themes from both the Genet column and the discussion of the *Antigone*, Derrida writes: 'the plant is a sort of sister' (Gtr 245a); that is, it is innocent, without desire, and its subjectivity is 'not yet for-itself' (Gtr 245a). The plant or flower, Antigone or Genet, becomes a figure for the singular entity that receives the gift of the light, the life-giving sustenance of the sun, and in so doing, recognizes its debt, its *devoir*. From the innocence of the flower religion and 'the guilt of *animal* religions' (PS 372/PStr 420), Derrida passes onto the third moment of 'Natural Religion', 'The Artificer' ('*Der Werkmeister*'). By focusing on the way in which the artificer employs 'plant life' as 'mere ornament' (PS 374/PStr 422), Derrida joins a further textual circle and returns to the passage from the *Aesthetics* which was the second of the figures with which he began his commentary. The phallic stone columns of India themselves derive from plant forms (A 657–8) and become objects of religious adoration.

The final pages of the Hegel column discuss the moments of abstract and living works of art, analysing the notions of hymn, oracle and cult (PS 378–85/PStr 427–35), before returning once again to what was called above the *Taumel*, the scene of 'Bacchic enthusiasm' (PS 388/PStr 439, Gtr 261a). Derrida follows Hegel's discussion of Dionysian religion, where 'the mystery of bread and wine is not yet the mystery of flesh and blood' (PS 387/PStr 438), and where Dionysus must pass over into the figure who represents revealed religion, the person of Christ. This explains the closing lines of *Glas*, where Derrida writes of 'A time to perfect the resemblance between Dionysus and Christ. Between the two (already) is elaborated in sum the origin of literature' (Gtr 262a). In Dionysian enthusiasm, the self is in rapture and 'beside itself [*ausser sich*]' (PS 388/PStr 439); it has become a god. Yet, Hegel argues, the self in rapture is unbalanced and the only element in which a balance between the self and the Absolute, or the interior and the exterior, can be achieved is through language. However, language here understood is no longer that of the hymn, oracle or Dionysian 'stammer' (ibid.), but rather literature: epic (Homer), tragedy (Sophocles and

Aeschylus) and comedy (Aristophanes). *Glas* ends at the origin of literature and the overcoming of Dionysian religion in a development that recalls the analyses of Nietzsche's *The Birth of Tragedy*.

The Hegel column finishes with the following incomplete sentence, 'But it runs to its ruin [*elle court à sa perte* – it is heading for disaster], for having counted without [*sans*]' (G 365a/Gtr 262a). The pronoun 'elle' seems to refer back to 'littérature' in the previous sentence, and indeed Hegel's analysis of literature ends with the dissolution of both divine transcendence and, significantly, Greek *Sittlichkeit*, in the irony and mockery of Aristophanean comedy. But what does literature count without? Does it count without Genet, the thief who single-handedly destroys and reinvents literature (SG 407/SGtr 439)? Is the reader encouraged to progress from the reading of Hegel to the beginning of the Genet column? Perhaps – although joining the two columns together in this manner risks missing the graphic complexity of *Glas*. For this is a book that seeks to escape linearity and circularity, the metaphorics of speculative dialectics. By concluding without climax or apocalypse – without even a full stop – *Glas* nevertheless makes its point. During his discussion of Genet, Derrida notes that 'The object of the present work, and its style too, is the morsel [*morceau*]' (G 166b/ Gtr 118b). By repeating the Hegelian system, largely in the manner of a commentary, and by letting Hegel speak for – and against – himself, the system somehow begins to decompose, morsels fall off and remain outside the grasp of the dialectic. The rhythm of reading Hegel with Derrida is not governed by the smooth three-stroke engine of the dialectic, but rather by a jerking rhythm of interruption and recommencement – the music of Genet's masturbation.

Notes

1. First published in a special issue of the *Bulletin of the Hegel Society of Great Britain*, on the topic 'Hegel and Deconstruction', no. 18, 1988, pp. 4–32. It was reprinted with modifications in S. Barnett, ed., *Hegel After Derrida*, London: Routledge, 1998. Chapters 1 and 2 form part of an abandoned commentary on Derrida's massive 1974 book, *Glas*, and deal with Hegel and Genet respectively. These two texts were to be accompanied by a third piece, speculatively entitled 'Sartre's France', which focused in detail on the context and methodology of *Glas*, where I approached Derrida's reading of Genet in relation to what is undoubtedly a significant precursor text for *Glas*, namely Sartre's *Saint Genet*. Derrida describes Sartre in *Glas* in the most critical terms as 'the ontophenomenologist of the liberation' and condemns his interpretation of Genet as 'a pre-Heideggerian misontologism and a vague Mallarméism'. My ambition in the comparison of Sartre and Derrida

was to read *Glas* as a cultural pathology and critique of post-war France, a context marked by both a certain Kojèvian-Hegelianism and an existential heroism, strands which come together in Sartre's exhaustive and exhausting existential-dialectical interpretation of Genet.

2. Paris: Vrin, 1970.

3. Derrida's relation to Jewish philosophy, theology and tradition is discussed, albeit with a rather limited and non-philosophical understanding of Derrida's work, by Susan Handelman in 'Reb Derrida's Scripture', in *The Slayers of Moses. The Emergence of Rabbinic Interpretation in Modern Literary Theory*, Albany: State University of New York Press, 1982, pp. 163–78. An expanded version of the same argument appears in Mark Krupnick, ed., *Displacement. Derrida and After*, Bloomington: Indiana University Press, 1983, pp. 98–129. It is the latter article that is discussed by Habermas in a long footnote of the *Philosophical Discourse of Modernity*, Cambridge: Polity Press, 1987, pp. 406–7, and in which Habermas finds support for his interpretation of Derrida. Habermas's thesis is that

> even Derrida does not extricate himself from the constraints of the paradigm of the philosophy of the subject . . . Derrida passes beyond Heidegger's inverted foundationalism, but remains in its path. As a result, the temporalised *Ursprungsphilosophie* takes on clearer contours. The remembrance of the messianism of Jewish mysticism and of the abandoned but well circumscribed place once assumed by the God of the Old Testament preserves Derrida, so to speak, from the political-moral insensitivity and the aesthetic tastelessness of a New Paganism spiced up with Hölderlin. (pp. 166–7)

Habermas's claim is that the deconstruction of the (Christian) metaphysics of presence is ultimately the attempt to renew a specifically Judaic relation to God. Regardless of the truth of Habermas's argument, which might be truer than he imagines, and whose crude reductionism is sadly only fuelled by Handelman's analysis, my question is: why should the accusation of Judaism be an accusation? What is the possible force of Habermas's argumentation? If traces of religious or mystical thinking are 'discovered' by Habermas in Derrida's work, then why should this have the force of a refutation?

4. See Freud, 'Mourning and Melancholia', in *On Metapsychology. The Theory of Psychoanalysis*, Harmondsworth: Penguin Books, 1984, pp. 251–68.

5. *Phaedrus*, 247a; *Metaphysics*, 983a.

6. I discuss the link between deconstruction and Kantian ethics in 'Deconstruction and the Thought of an Unconditional Ethical Imperative', in *The Ethics of Deconstruction*, Oxford: Blackwell, 1992, pp. 31–44.

7. *La voix et la phénomène*, Paris: PUF, 1967, p. 114.

8. Mention of Zoroaster is suggestive here and alerts the reader to the two references to Nietzsche's *Also Sprach Zarathustra* (Leipzig: Alfred Kroner Verlag, 1930; *Thus Spake Zarathustra*, transl. R. J. Hollingdale, Harmondsworth: Penguin Books, 1961) that occur during the discussion of Genet (Gtr 102bi and 262b). At the close of the Genet column, Derrida cites six lines from 'Before Sunrise' (G 180–1/Gtr 184–5), where Zarathustra speaks to the sky: 'You abyss of light! [*Du Lichtabgrund*]' and of the god that came to him before the sun. Zarathustra speaks of the friendship between himself and the god of light, in which they have both 'the sun in common' and 'the vast and boundless Yes [*das ungeheure unbegrenzte Ja*–]'. The parallels between, on the one hand, Zarathustra and the God of Light

and, on the other, Derrida and Genet are clear, even if their precise implications are not. Pulling a remark out of context, one might suggest that in *Glas*, 'you have here at your disposal, as if in contraband, everything necessary for an almost complete, literally literal [*littéralement littérale*] reading of Zarathustra. You can verify' (G I43bi/ Gtr I 02bi).

9. See Heidegger, 'Der Rückgang in den Grund der Metaphysik', in *Was ist Metaphysik?* Frankfurt: Vittorio Klostermann, 1969, pp. 19–20; 'The Way Back into the Ground of Metaphysics', transl. Walter Kaufmann, in *Existentialism from Dostoevsky to Sartre*, New York: Meridian, 1975, pp. 275–6.

10. See Gtr I 1–12ai, 20a, 22–3ai, 57a; and references to onto-theo-logy (33a), the history of Being (94a), and an earlier important reference to *Zeit und Sein* (167a), which occurs, significantly enough, during the discussion of *Antigone*.

11. But what holocaust is Derrida discussing here? Is it the Greco-Christian ecclesiastical notion of *to holocauston*, a burnt offering, or the *Shoah*, or indeed both at once? If Derrida is referring to the *Shoah* with the word *holocaust*, then – and here one need only allude to debates current within Holocaust studies – would this not unwittingly constitute a Hellenization or Christianization of the *Shoah*, its assimilation into the language of Greek metaphysics? The deliberateness of Derrida's translation of *Opfer* by *holocauste* leads one to conclude that he is discussing the *Shoah* in terms of the gift and the sacrifice. But is this a felicitous language in which to discuss the *Shoah*? And, perversely, what of Heidegger's intervention in this context? What of Heidegger's much-discussed silence or near silence on the Holocaust? And what of Derrida's use of the Heideggerian notion of *es gibt Sein* to open up the non-metaphysical thought of the gift or holocaust in Hegel?

12. On the issue of an ethics of sacrifice with reference to the 'Heidegger affair', see Emmanuel Levinas's 'Mourir Pour', in *Heidegger. Questions ouvertes*, Paris: Éditions Osiris, 1988, pp. 254–64.

Abbreviations

A – Georg Wilhelm Friedrich Hegel, *Aesthetics: Lectures on Fine Art*, transl. T. M. Knox, 2 vols, Oxford: Clarendon, 1975.

AN – Sophocles, *Antigone* (in *The Theban Plays*), transl. E. F. Watling, Harmondsworth: Penguin Books, 1947.

ANT – Immanuel Kant, *Anthropology from a Pragmatic Point of View*, transl. Victor Lyle Dowdell, revised and ed. Hans H. Rudnick, Carbondale: Southern Illinois University Press, 1978.

D – Georg Wilhelm Friedrich Hegel, *The Difference Between the Fichtean and Schellingian Systems of Philosophy*, transl. Jere Paul Surber, Atascadero: Ridgeview Publishing, 1978.

FC – Jacques Derrida, *Feu la cendre*, Paris: Éditions des femmes, 1987.

FPS – Georg Wilhelm Friedrich Hegel, *System of Ethical Life and First Philosophy of Spirit*, ed. and transl. H. S. Harris and T. M. Knox, Albany: State University of New York Press, 1979.

FR – Jean Genet, *Funeral Rites*, transl. Bernard Frechtman, London: Anthony Blond, 1969.

G – Jacques Derrida, *Glas*, 2 vols, Paris: Denoël/Gonthier, 1981.

GL – John P. Leavey Jr., *Glassary*, Lincoln and London: Nebraska University Press, 1986.

GS – Jean Hyppolite, *Genesis and Structure of Hegel's Phenomenology of Spirit*, transl. Samuel Cherniak and John Heckman, Evanston: Northwestern University Press, 1974.

Gtr – Jacques Derrida, *Glas*, transl. John P. Leavey and Richard Rand, Lincoln and London: Nebraska University Press, 1986.

LPR – Georg Wilhelm Friedrich Hegel, *Lectures on the Philosophy of Religion*, transl. Rev. E. B. Speirs and Burdon Sanderson, 3 vols, London: RKP, 1895.

PE – Georg Wilhelm Friedrich Hegel, *Phénoménologie de l'Esprit*, transl. Jean Hyppolite, 2 vols, Paris: Montaigne, 1941.

PM – Georg Wilhelm Friedrich Hegel, *Hegel's Philosophy of Mind: Part Three of the 'Encyclopaedia of the Philosophical Sciences'*, transl. A. V. Miller, Oxford: Clarendon Press, 1971.

PN – Georg Wilhelm Friedrich Hegel, *Hegel's Philosophy of Nature*, ed. and transl. M. J. Petry, 3 vols, London: George Allen and Unwin, 1970.

PR – Georg Wilhelm Friedrich Hegel, *Grundlinien der Philosophie des Rechts*, ed. Helmut Reichelt, Frankfurt am Main: Ullstein, 1972.

PRtr – Georg Wilhelm Friedrich Hegel, *Philosophy of Right*, transl. T. M. Knox, Oxford: Oxford University Press, 1952.

PS – Georg Wilhelm Friedrich Hegel, *Phänomenologie des Geistes*, Gesammelte Werke Band 9, ed. Wolfgang Bonsiepen and Reinhard Heede, Hamburg: Felix Meiner, 1980.

PStr – Georg Wilhelm Friedrich Hegel, *Phenomenology of Spirit*, transl. A. V. Miller, Oxford: Oxford University Press, 1977.

SC – Georg Wilhelm Friedrich Hegel, *The Spirit of Christianity and its Fate*, transl. T. M. Knox, in *Early Theological Writings*, Philadelphia: University of Pennsylvania Press, 1948, pp. 182–301.

SD – Martin Heidegger, *Zur Sache des Denkens*, Tübingen: Max Niemeyer, 1969.

SG – Jean-Paul Sartre, *Saint Genet: comédien et martyr*, Paris: Gallimard, 1952.

SGtr – Jean-Paul Sartre, *Saint Genet: Actor and Martyr*, transl. Bernard Frechtman, London: Heinemann, 1988 [1963].

TB – Martin Heidegger, *On Time and Being*, transl. Joan Stambaugh, New York: Harper and Row, 1972.

2

Writing the Revolution: The Politics of Truth in Genet's *Prisoner of Love*[1]

Saintliness cannot be placed in question.

Emmanuel Levinas

Introduction

The last thing Jean Genet's work needs is another philosopher's commentary. After Sartre's monumental *Saint Genet* and Derrida's equally monumental – although anti-Sartrean – *Glas*, it might seem prudent, indeed respectful, to refrain from any further philosophical discussion of Genet. However, in this chapter I would like to discuss a work of Genet's that neither Sartre nor Derrida were able to deal with in their commentaries: the posthumously published *Prisoner of Love* (*Un captif amoureux*). I shall discuss this work in terms of the problem of truth – philosophy's problem – and more particularly in terms of how one tells the truth about a political event, in this case, the Palestinian revolution. How is the revolution to be written? Can the revolution be truthfully described? I shall proceed by placing *Prisoner of Love* in both its historical context and in the context of Genet's earlier prose work, paying particular attention to *The Thief's Journal*. After surveying the differences between Genet's earlier and later prose work, I shall then try to show how the problem of writing the revolution is raised and finally resolved in *Prisoner of Love*. In this moment of resolution or, as I will claim, redemption, our understanding of Genet will hopefully undergo an inversion.

Breaking the Silence? The Biographical and Historical Context

The very appearance of *Prisoner of Love* five weeks after Genet's death in April 1986 was both surprising and significant, for it represented the only published piece of extended prose by Genet in the period following the publication of *The Thief's Journal* in 1949. Why did he break this silence? And was there indeed a silence to be broken?[2] At least, why should Genet resume writing for publication after such an extended break? Towards the end of *The Thief's Journal*, and at the beginning of the short sequence of pages that form the *philosophical* climax of that book and, indeed, of Genet's early prose *œuvre*, he writes:

> Unless there should occur an event of such gravity that my literary art, in the face of it, would be imbecilic and I should need a new language to master this new misfortune, this is my last book . . . For five years I have been writing books: I can say that I have done so with pleasure, but I have finished. (JV 217/ TJ 170)

Genet's promise appeared to be confirmed by the fact that in the intervening years he only produced three plays – albeit of major importance: *The Balcony* (1956), *The Blacks* (1958) and *The Screens* (1961) and a trickle of occasional prose pieces on the theory of art, literature and theatre, most notably 'Ce qui est resté d'un Rembrandt déchiré en petits carrés bien reguliers, et foutu aux chiottes' (1967). After 1968, much of Genet's energy was given over to political writing, whether for the student movement in France, the Black Panthers, the Red Army Faction or the Palestinian resistance. Yet these occasional writings by no means constitute a large body of work; as Derrida notes in *Glas* (1974), 'he almost never writes anymore, he has interred literature like no one' (G 50/Gtr 36).

An explanation often offered for Genet's relative silence after *The Thief's Journal* is that Sartre's *Saint Genet* had entombed Genet's *œuvre*, burying his corpus alive and imprisoning him within a totalizing narrative of liberty to which he was condemned and from which it was impossible to escape through writing. Indeed, if one accepts Sartre's thesis that Genet's prose work is akin to an extended psychoanalytic cure, where writing becomes the means for self-liberation from trauma, then it is necessary to read *The Thief's Journal* 'as a literary testament or at least as a conclusion' (SG 502/SGtr 545). Soon after the publication of *Saint Genet* in 1952, Genet remarked in a letter to Jean Cocteau, 'You and Sartre have turned me into a monument. I am somebody else, and this somebody else must find something to say.'

In response, Cocteau notes in his journal, 'Jean has changed since the publication of Sartre's book. He looks as if he were at once trying to follow
it and to escape it.'[3] Whether interring literature in *Glas* or being himself
interred within the pages of *Saint Genet*, the question remains: what could
have provoked Genet to write a 504-page book after a break of nearly
thirty years?

Genet writes *Prisoner of Love* in order to tell the truth about the Palestinian revolution:[4] 'Before I started to write it I'd sworn to myself to tell the
truth in this book' (CA 503/PL 374–5). It is a book which has truth as
its goal, insofar as Genet wants to achieve a correspondence or *adaequatio*
between his writing and a set of empirical events. Very broadly, *Prisoner of
Love* is a collection of *souvenirs* of the time Genet spent amongst the Palestinian revolutionaries – the *fedayeen* – between 1970 and 1972. Although
originally only intending to stay for a week (CA 331/PL 244), Genet ended
up spending two years with the Palestinians in their camps on the East Bank
of the Jordan. Genet arrived at the moment when the Palestinians, frus-
trated by the dismal performance of the Arab League – Egypt, Jordan and
Syria – against Israel in the Six Day War in 1967, had begun to use their
bases in Jordan as a springboard for guerrilla attacks on Israeli targets, which
included some extraordinary acts of air piracy.[5] Genet was forcibly evicted
from Jordan at the end of 1972, but between that time and 1983, when he
began writing *Prisoner of Love*, he returned to the area on numerous occasions. Genet's book narrates, through a powerful and non-linear photo-
montage of notes and anecdotes, the fate of the Palestinian people, from
their dream-like optimism of the late 1960s and early 1970s to their betrayal
and humiliation at the hands of the Jordanians, the Israelis and even their
own leadership. Although the book was very loosely commissioned by
Yasser Arafat – an anecdote wryly related by Genet as an inconsequential
act of 'politeness' ('Why don't you write a book?' asks Arafat. '*Bien sûr*'
replies Genet – CA 126/PL 90) – *Prisoner of Love* is persistently critical of
the Palestinian leadership; Genet writes, 'I found the manners of almost all
the ordinary Palestinians, men and women, delightful. But their leaders
were a pain in the neck [*emmerdants*]' (CA 328/PL 243). The real heroes of
Prisoner of Love are the ordinary Palestinian people, the men and women of
the resistance, and one man and woman in particular; but I shall return to
this below.

Genet's initial reflection upon Arafat's suggestion was, 'I didn't believe
in the idea of that or any other book; I meant to concentrate on what I saw
and heard' (CA 126/PL 91). Genet's transition from literature to action, from
langage to *l'engagement*, appears irreversible; and yet, he adds, 'without my

quite realizing it, everything that happened and every word that was spoken set itself down in my memory' (ibid.). It is this storehouse of memories that Genet struggles to write down in *Prisoner of Love*. A more direct spur to the writing of this book was the massacre of the Palestinians in the Lebanese camps at Sabra and Chatila in 1982. Finally, after numerous requests for his memoirs from Palestinian acquaintances, Genet started writing in either August or October 1983 (unsurprisingly perhaps, he contradicts himself: see CA 331/PL 245 and CA 456/PL 338). He paid his final and, for the book, most significant visit to the area in June 1984, spending a few months in Irbid and Chatila. The writing of the book was completed in 1986 and, after suffering from throat cancer for some years, he died on the night of 14–15 April 1986, whilst correcting proofs of *Prisoner of Love*.

Genet's death is not accidental to *Prisoner of Love*, rather it is the horizon against which the book is written and behind which the author eventually vanishes (CA 161/PL 117). Genet's death is the book's genesis. In a concluding remark, he writes:

> Perhaps the massacres at Chatila in September 1982 were not a turning point. They happened. I was affected by them. I talked about them. But while the act of writing came later, after a period of incubation, nevertheless in a moment like that or those when a single cell departs from its usual metabolism and the original link is created of a future, unsuspected cancer, or a piece of lace, so I decided to write this book. (CA 502/PL 373)

The fabrication of a book is like the growth of a cancer, where a cell departs from its usual metabolism, connecting with and infecting other cells, interconnecting to form the sentences on a page. Death is the event that prompts the book, watches over its growth, disrupts its progress and prevents its completion – Genet died before completing his corrections to the proofs. In order to remain as lucid as possible during the writing of *Prisoner of Love*, Genet refused pain-killing drugs (PL xxi); and indeed, every page presents the reader with the agony of the book's creation, a struggle which results in a fractured and quasi-cinematic narrative technique, leaping back and forth in time, moving randomly between spaces and cutting quickly from image to reportage, to reminiscence. Genet's frustration at not being able to relate facts as they happened, his lapses of memory, his repetitions and strange leaps of thought, make it an agonizing book to read and agony to have written: 'One thing a book tries to do is show, beneath the disguise of words and causes and clothes and even grief, the skeleton and the skeleton dust to come. The author too, like those he speaks of, is dead' (CA 414/PL 307). And yet, if mortality is the horizon of the book's production, a horizon which repeatedly returns to haunt its narrative style, *Prisoner of Love* perhaps also represents Genet's intimation of immortality, not the literary immortality of *les grands écrivains*, but rather the immortality or eternity of what Genet calls 'the joy of being [*le bonheur d'être*]':

> A little while ago I wrote that though I shall die, nothing else will. And I must make my meaning clear. Wonder at the sight of a cornfield, at a rock, at the touch of a rough hand – all the millions of emotions of which I'm made – they won't disappear even though I shall. Other men will experience them, and they'll still be there because of them. More and more I believe I exist in order to be the terrain and proof which show other men that life consists in the uninterrupted emotions flowing through all creation. The happiness my hand knows in a boy's hair will be known by another hand, is already known. And although I shall die, that happiness will live on. 'I' may die, but what made that 'I' possible, what made possible the joy of being, will make the joy of being live on without me. (CA 423–4/PL 314)

Prisoner of Love presages and prefaces its author's death, presupposing it as both the condition for the book's possibility and also for the possibility of the transcendence of that death through the continuity of humanity and the eternity of creation – 'the happiness my hand knows in a boy's hair will be known by another hand'.

From Saintliness to Solidarity: *The Thief's Journal* and *Prisoner of Love*

We already seem far from the truth of the Palestinian revolution. However, proceeding negatively, it is important to stress what sort of book *Prisoner of Love* is not. Firstly, it is not a straightforward reportage of historical events in the Near East; one learns little history from the book, and at the end the reader is left rather with a bundle of disorderly facts. The book needs to be read *with* a history of the period rather than *as* such a history. Secondly, *Prisoner of Love* is not a piece of political propaganda for the PLO. The book shows the Palestinian leadership to be vain and corrupt, and Genet ex presses little hope for the future of the movement. What could be said to be the book's political motto is spoken by a young *fedayee* in the form of a question: 'Having been slaves, shall we be terrible masters when the time

comes?' (CA 133/PL 96). The belief that political life is a continual nego-
tiation with evil, relieved only by scintillating moments of revolution, is a
recurrent theme in *Prisoner of Love*.

However, a third and more substantial point needs to be made, namely,
that *Prisoner of Love* is not simply the second volume of Genet's autobio-
graphy and a sequel to *The Thief's Journal*. The two books differ substantially
both at the level of form and content. At the level of form, *Prisoner of Love*
lacks the poise, lyrical self-assurance and thematic coherence of *The Thief's
Journal*. In *Prisoner of Love*, Genet's style is simple, direct and without pretension, whilst his images and recollections are almost photographic, offering snapshots which yet manage to express great poignancy and depth. For
example:

> Though I was lying still in my blankets as I looked up into the sky, following the
> light, I felt myself swept into a maelstrom, swirled around and yet smoothed by
> strong but gentle arms. A little way off, through the darkness, I could hear the
> Jordan flowing. I was freezing cold. (CA 19/PL 9)

Or again, Genet will suddenly expand the focus of an image in order to
move from the particular to the general, letting the reader survey a wider
historical or political horizon. For example:

> As I squatted down, resting, I was drinking tea – noisily, for it was hot and in
> those parts it's the custom to proclaim the pleasures of tongue and palate. I was
> also eating olives and unleavened bread. The fedayeen were chatting in Arabic
> and laughing, unaware of the fact that not far away was the spot where John the
> Baptist baptized Jesus. (CA 55/PL 37)

The reader of *Prisoner of Love* is presented with a long series of these images:
luminous, highly coloured and randomly sequenced. Of course, such a non-
linear accretion of images, anecdotes, snatches of dialogue, maxims and
reflections is characteristic of Genet's earlier prose, but *Prisoner of Love* takes
this technique a stage further, mixing genres and almost entirely abandoning the linear logic of story-telling. The book is bitty and flows awkwardly,
employing or rather being employed by a language that at times appears to
be out of control. Genet remarks that this 'probably shows what a relief it is
to open the floodgates and release pent-up memories' (CA 255/PL 186). Yet
at the same time the narrative maintains a sinuous continuity which holds
the book together by the slenderest skein. Genet writes: 'I've only to hear
the phrase "Palestinian revolution" even now and I'm plunged into a great

darkness in which luminous, highly coloured images succeed and seem to
pursue one another' (CA 407–8/PL 302). And again, 'I feel now like a little
black box projecting slides without captions' (CA 408/PL 303).

The logic and argument of *Prisoner of Love* is advanced through bursts of
images involuntarily dredged up from Genet's memory. And yet, *Prisoner
of Love* is not *À la recherche du temps perdu*; Genet always remained a kind of
anti-Proust. In *The Thief's Journal*, Genet argues that any attempt to recom-
pose the past through the activity of involuntary memory is impossible. For
Genet, a book 'is not the quest of time gone by [*une recherche du temps passé*],
but a work of art whose pretext-subject is my former life' (JV 75/TJ 58).
This experience of the impossibility of recomposing the past into a present
act of writing is radicalized in *Prisoner of Love*, for although the book is, for
the most part, a work of involuntary memory, the book itself does not and
cannot claim *à retrouver* that past and bring it to life. The reader is continually faced with the failure of recollection in the form of writing. Genet asks
the reader, 'do you remember?' (CA 261/PL 190) and remarks to himself,
're-reading what I've written' (CA 167, 325/PL 121, 240) as if to underline
the inadequacies of writing as a means for the presentation of remembrance. *Prisoner of Love* is a book of *flawed* memory, a flaw that is caused
by the failure of writing itself. If this is indeed the case, then the question
that must be asked and to which I shall return is: how does Genet's narrative technique in *Prisoner of Love* recall the truth about the Palestinian
revolution?

At the level of content, *Prisoner of Love* at the very least complicates the
triad of betrayal, theft and homosexuality that combine to form the counter-
morality of *The Thief's Journal* (JV 181/TJ 141). Theft is not discussed, and
although the book's central theme is perhaps the eroticism of the revolutionary act, a sensuousness expressed in Genet's descriptions of the *fedayeen*,
homo-eroticism is not used as a means of linguistic, moral and political subversion and does not have the shocking intensity of Genet's earlier work,
particularly *Our Lady of the Flowers*. Rather, a different eroticism pervades
Prisoner of Love, what might be called revolutionary love, where Genet,
when presented with the beauty of the *fedayeen* – 'decked with guns, in
leopard-spotted uniforms and red berets tilted over their eyes, each not
merely a transfiguration but also a materialization of my fantasies. And
apparently at my disposal' (CA 244/PL 178) – is surprised at himself 'for
not feeling any desire for them' (ibid.). This overcoming of desire in the
act of revolutionary love recalls the themes of 'Ce qui est resté d'un Rembrandt . . .', where, in a third-class railway compartment travelling between
Salon and Saint-Rambert-d'Albon, Genet exchanges a brief *regard* with a

rather ugly traveller sitting opposite. This *regard* has the force of a revelation for Genet, a revelation of the 'identité universelle à tous les hommes' (CQ 22), where Genet feels himself flowing away from himself into the other ('Je m'écoulais . . . Je m'ec', CQ 22–3 and see G 21/Gtr 16 et passim). Genet's problem here, as Jean-Bernard Moraly expresses it, is 'If every man is worth the same as another, how can one desire?' (VE 112). Beneath the sexual eroticism that seeks to reduce the other to the self and whose desire is premised upon the uniqueness of the other person, Genet locates a fragile *regard* which produces the revelation, '*que tout homme est tout autre homme et moi comme tous les autres* [that each man is every other man and myself like all the others]' (CQ 30–1). This conception of love as the recognition of alterity and revolutionary solidarity – truly an ethical metamorphosis, to use Sartre's terminology – signals a break with the egoistic, masturbatory desire that informs Genet's earlier work. It is this revolutionary love for the Palestinians which holds Genet captive and to which he alludes in the book's title.

The concept of betrayal undergoes a similar and complex shift between Genet's earlier and later work. In *The Thief's Journal*, betrayal – low or abject betrayal (*la trahison abjecte*) (JV 257/TJ 202) – becomes the unique mode of access to a state of moral and aesthetic perfection which enables Genet 'to break the bonds of love uniting him with mankind' (JV 258/TJ 202) and to found a morality opposed to that of the social order – *la sainteté*. For Genet, saintliness is '*le plus beau mot du langage humain* [the most beautiful word in the human language]' (JV 226/TJ 178) and is the central ethico-religious concept of Genet's earlier prose. Saintliness is a form of 'ascesis' (JV 227/TJ 178) achieved through an experience of abjection that demands the recognition of evil, pain and degradation. Yet it is precisely this recognition of degradation, of actions that run counter to accepted notions of human self-interest, that opens the possibility of total altruism and goodness. It is in saintliness that we learn to value the other human being more than ourselves. With a paradoxical logic reminiscent of the narrative voice of Dostoevsky's *Notes from Underground*, Genet's early homo-erotic prose should be read as a course of spiritual instruction or purification into saintliness, a form of ethical life in revolt against the Social Darwinism of European society. Returning to betrayal, the use of this concept is complicated in *Prisoner of Love*. In a couple of passages, Genet employs formulations strongly reminiscent of *The Thief's Journal*, 'Anyone who hasn't experienced the ecstasy of betrayal knows nothing about ecstasy at all' (CA 85/PL 59); and later on, 'Anyone who's never experienced the pleasure of betrayal doesn't know what pleasure is' (CA 367/PL 271). But in other contexts, Genet condemns the betrayal committed by the Israelis (CA 155–7/PL 112–13), the Circassians (CA 233/PL 169) and there is a debate throughout the book about the betrayal of the *fedayeen* by elements within their leadership. Indeed, what distinguishes the *fedayeen* for Genet is precisely their resistance to the temptation of betraying the revolution: '[the *fedayeen*] were beset by the temptation to betray, though I think it was *almost* always resisted' (CA 368/PL 273). Furthermore, if Genet writes *Prisoner of Love* in order to tell the truth about the Palestinian revolution, then it is precisely this truth that he does not want to betray.

The Triumph of Truth over Art: Genet's Inverted Nietzscheanism

In *The Thief's Journal*, Genet quips: 'to speak of my work as a writer would be a pleonasm' (JV 115/TJ 90). He claims that he wrote in prison in order to take refuge in his past life, and that later, when free, 'I wrote again in order to earn money' (ibid.). The motivation for *Prisoner of Love*, as I will show, is quite different: Genet is not writing to make money, he is not even writing in order to produce a work of art, but rather he writes in order to tell the truth. This contrasts strongly with Genet's proclamations on the truth content of his writing in, for example, *Our Lady of the Flowers*: 'What's going to follow is false, and no one has to accept it as gospel truth. Truth is not my strong point' (OLF 169). It also announces an aesthetics totally at odds with the views of 'Ce qui est resté d'un Rembrandt . . .', where Genet writes:

> It is only these sorts of truths, those which are not demonstrable and which are even '*false*', those that cannot be led without absurdity to their extreme point without leading to their and our own negation, it is these sorts of truths that must be exalted by the work of art. (CQ 21)

For these reasons, *Prisoner of Love* does not sit at all easily with the rest of Genet's prose *œuvre*; it rather undermines it, causing a *collapse* within its values and vocabulary:

> In other days I think I'd have avoided words like heroes, martyrs, struggle, revolution, liberation, resistance, courage and suchlike. I probably *have* avoided the words homeland and fraternity, which still repel me. But there's no doubt that the Palestinians caused a kind of collapse in my vocabulary. (CA 367/PL 272)

And again, when Genet refers to himself in the third person as an old man with the dream of a house on the coast with a view of Cyprus, he writes:

> An old man travelling from country to country, as much ejected by the one he was in as attracted by the others he was going to . . . rejecting the repose that comes from even modest property, was amazed by the collapse that took place in him. (CA 430/PL 318–19)

The massive scale of this collapse is recorded on the pages of *Prisoner of Love*: Genet was *at home* in Palestine (CA 463/PL 344), *bei sich* in a country that didn't exist. *Prisoner of Love* proclaims the *triumph of truth over art*. It is a work of *reverted Platonism*, or *Inverted Nietzscheanism*, which elevates the true – the identity of thought and its object – over the aesthetic – the metaphorical and non-identical relation of thought and its object. My hypothesis here is that *Prisoner of Love* is a book about the conditions of possibility for truthful narration, and, more precisely, about what sort of narrative technique is required in order to tell the truth about a revolution. The question then becomes, and it is this problem that Genet struggles with on the pages of *Prisoner of Love*: can writing tell the truth? Or must writing always exist within an economy of betrayal?

I want to explore these questions by looking in detail at some extended passages from *Prisoner of Love*. The book begins with the following words:

> The page that was blank to begin with is now crossed from top to bottom with tiny black characters – letters, words, commas, exclamation marks and it's because of them that the page is said to be legible. But a kind of unease, a feeling close to nausea, an irresolution that stays my hand – these make me wonder: do these black marks add up to reality? [*la realité est-elle cette totalité des signes noirs?*] The white of the paper is an artifice that's replaced the translucency of parchment and the ochre surface of clay tablets; but the ochre and the translucency and the whiteness may all possess more reality than the signs that mar them.
>
> Was the Palestinian revolution really written on the void, an artifice superimposed on nothingness, and is the white page, and every little blank space between the words, more real than the black characters themselves? Reading between the lines is a level art; reading between the words a precipitous one. If the reality of the time spent among – not with – the Palestinians resided anywhere, it would survive between all the words that claim to give an account of it. They claim to give an account of it, but in fact it buries itself, slots itself exactly into the spaces, recorded there rather than in the words that serve only to blot it out. Another way of putting it: the space between the words contains

more reality than does the time it takes to read them. Perhaps it's the same as the time, dense and real, enclosed between the characters in Hebrew . . .

So did I fail to understand the Palestinian revolution? Yes, completely. I think I realized that when Leila advised me to go to the West Bank. I refused, because the occupied territories were only a play acted out second by second by occupied and occupier. The reality lay in involvement, fertile in love and hate; in people's daily lives; in silence, like translucency, punctuated by words and phrases. (CA 11–12/PL 3)

This passage raises the question that haunts the entirety of *Prisoner of Love* and to which Genet will repeatedly return, namely: 'do these black marks add up to reality?' Do the legible written signs of a book correspond to the reality they are said to describe? Genet replies emphatically in the negative. The reality of the Palestinian revolution does not reside in the written signs that attempt to describe it; rather, reality buries and conceals itself in the space between the written signs. The white space between the words contains more reality than the words themselves; a point that Genet perversely illustrates by analogy with the Hebrew language. The corollary of this is that Genet cannot claim to understand the reality of the Palestinian revolution within writing; rather, its reality lies elsewhere, in the everyday life of the Palestinians, in involvement, in a silence that exceeds the written sign.

Thus, on the first page of *Prisoner of Love*, the reader is faced with the veridical inadequacy of the book he or she is about to read. There will be no adequation between language and reality, and no narrative technique will ever be able to tell what the revolution was really like (CA 302/PL 222). *True narration is impossible. Writing is betrayal.* Genet makes the point even more emphatically later in the book:

By transforming a fact into words and characters you create other facts that can never create the original one. I state this basic truth to put myself on guard. If it's only a question of ordinary morality [*commune morale*], I don't care if someone's lying or telling the truth. But I must stress that it's *my eyes* that *saw* what I thought I was describing, and *my ears* that heard it [*ce sont mes yeux, mon regard, qui ont vu ce que j'ai cru décrire, mes oreilles entendu*]. The form I adopted from the beginning for this account was never designed to tell the reader what the Palestinian revolution was really like.

The construction, organization and layout of the book [*récit*], without deliberately intending to *betray* [*trahir*] the facts, manage the narrative in such a way that I probably seem to be a privileged witness or even a manipulator . . . Sometimes I wonder whether I didn't live my life especially so that I might arrange its episodes in the same seeming disorder as the images in a dream.

All these words to say, *this is my Palestinian revolution*, told in my chosen order. As well as mine there is the other, probably many others. Trying to think the revolution is like waking up and trying to see the logic in a dream. (CA 416/ PL 308–9)

The transformation of a fact into words does not represent this fact truthfully, but rather creates a new and different verbal fact that does not correspond with the one that was to be described. However, this Nietzschean claim, which Genet's earlier prose both presupposes and promotes, causes a verbal collapse within *Prisoner of Love*, for, as Genet repeatedly and almost obsessively insists (CA 45, 405, 447, 482/PL 28, 300, 331, 358–9), the events that writing cannot understand and narrate *really happened*: 'Ce sont *mes yeux, mon regard*, qui ont *vu* ce que j'ai cru décrire, *mes oreilles* entendu.' Thus, if writing cannot truthfully describe factual events and yet those events occurred and are the ones to be described, then writing necessarily exists within an economy of betrayal. The betrayal of the truth which writing attempts to convey entails that the version of events eventually committed to writing will have a content imposed arbitrarily by the individual writer: 'ceci est ma révolution palestinienne'. As Genet notes in another passage, the order of the writing, the selection of events and the words chosen to describe those events will not 'be set down truthfully, as some transcendental eye [*l'oeil transcendant*] might see them, but as I myself select, interpret and classify them' (CA 280/PL 205). There is no transcendental key that will provide an understanding of the events of the Palestinian revolution, nor can the description of those events lay claim to universal or intersubjective validity. Yet Genet refuses to let this state of affairs collapse his writing into a vicious subjectivism freed from demands for communication and truth-telling. He is committed to telling the truth even when he knows that the truth cannot be told.

However, this problematic has to be nuanced with respect to the particular events that are being described. Genet is obliged to tell the truth about the Palestinian revolution. The question is then not simply, 'how is reality to be written?', but rather, 'how is the revolution to be written?' Genet repeatedly describes revolutionaries as dreamers and the revolution as a dream, a sublime and mysterious event that defies the linearity of conventional realist description and undermines any adequation between language and reality. Attempting to write the truth of the revolution is like trying to see the logic in a dream, and this imposes a form of writing that is neither realistic, historical nor doctoral, but rather fragmentary and imagistic. Thus, and here the form and the content of *Prisoner of Love* converge, the necessary failure to *understand* the truth of the revolution imposes a narrative technique that *evokes* the sublimity of the revolutionary event – its mystery, its infinity, its naïvety, its joyful optimism. *Prisoner of Love* is both a writing of revolution and a revolutionary writing; it is what Genet calls 'la celebration du mystère', or 'la fête' (CA 494/PL 367). Form and content combine in the following extraordinary passage, where an arbitrary enchainment of images becomes consequential within a revolutionary logic:

It may irritate me when a veteran tells me for the umpteenth time about the battle of the Argonne, or when Victor Hugo, in *Quatre-Vingt-Treize*, goes on about the forests in Brittany, but it won't stop me writing again and again that the days and the nights spent in the forests of Aljoun, between Salt and Irbid, on the banks of the Jordan, were a celebration, a fête. A celebration that can be defined as the fire that warmed our cheeks at being together despite the laws that hoped we'd have deserted one another. Or as the escape from the community into a place where people were ready to fight with us against that community. That exaltation may be felt when a thousand, a hundred, fifty, twenty or only two flames last as long as it takes the match that lighted them to burn out. And the only sound or song is that of the charred stick writhing until it's consumed.

This last image reminds me that a wake is a kind of fête. In fact, every fête is at once jubilation and despair. Think of the death of a Jew in France under the German occupation: he's buried in a country graveyard, and seven of the worst Jewish musicians come from seven different directions carrying seven black boxes. Badly but superbly the clandestine septet plays an air by Offenbach beside the grave, then each goes off on his own without a word being said. For the God of Isaiah, who is only a breath of wind on a blade of grass, that night was a fête.

The slight or subtle unease of the Mukabarats as I looked at the mother's white hair and face was necessary for the celebration of the mystery, and made it possible for that strange encounter to become a fête.

Of course it's understood that the words nights, forests, septet, jubilation, desertion and despair are the same words that I have to use to describe the goings-on at dawn in the Bois de Boulogne in Paris when the drag queens depart after celebrating their mystery, doing their accounts and smoothing banknotes out in the dew.

But every more or less well-meaning organization is bound to be gloomy not funereal. So they put loudspeakers in factories for the music to cheer up the assembly-line workers and increase their output. The owners of battery farms say music makes hens lay more eggs. Any celebration of a mystery is dangerous, forbidden. But when it takes place it's a fête. (CA 494–5/PL 367–8)

Prisoner of Love employs a form of writing that celebrates the mystery of the revolutionary event, an event which, like the sublimity of the moral law in

Kant, demands our respect. By limiting the claim of the understanding, that which resists understanding is better understood – that is to say, better evoked, celebrated or fêted. However, Genet focuses his revolutionary writing upon a single image that haunts the entire book. This, and the other themes that have been discussed so far, are brought together in the closing passage of *Prisoner of Love*:

> After giving his name and age, a witness is supposed to say something like, 'I swear to tell the whole truth . . .' Before I started to write it I'd sworn to tell the whole truth in this book, not in any ceremony but every time a Palestinian asked me to read the beginning or other passages from it or wanted me to publish parts of it in some magazine. Legally speaking, a witness neither opposes nor serves the judges. Under French law he has sworn to *tell the truth*, not to *tell it to the judges*. He takes an oath to the public – to the court and the spectators. The witness is on his own. He speaks. The judges listen and say nothing. The witness doesn't merely answer the implicit question *how?* – in order to show the *why?* He throws light on the *how?*, a light sometimes called artistic. The judges have never been to the places where the acts they have to judge were performed, so the witness is indispensable. But he knows a realistic description [*le vérisme d'une description*] won't mean anything to anyone, including the judges, unless he adds some light and shade which only he perceived. The judges may well describe a witness as valuable. He is.
>
> What's the point of that medieval, almost Carolingian, sounding oath in the courtroom? Perhaps it's to surround the witness with a solitude that confers on him a lightness *from which* he can speak the truth. For there may be three or four people present who are capable of hearing a witness.
>
> Any reality is bound to be outside me, existing in and for itself. The Palestinian revolution lives and will live only of itself. A Palestinian family, made up essentially of mother and son, were among the first people I met in Irbid. But it was somewhere else that I really found them.
>
> Perhaps inside myself. The pair made up by mother and son is to be found in France and everywhere else. Was it a light of my own that I threw on them, so that instead of being strangers whom I was observing they became a couple of my own creation? An image of my own making that my penchant for daydreaming had projected on to two Palestinians, mother and son, adrift in the midst of a battle in Jordan?
>
> All I've said and written happened. But why is it that this couple is the only really *profound* memory I have of the Palestinian revolution?
>
> I did the best I could to understand how different this revolution was from others, and in a way I did understand it. But what will remain with me is the little house in Irbid where I slept for one night, and fourteen years during which I tried to find out if that night ever happened. This last page of my book is transparent. (CA 503–4/PL 374–5)

Prisoner of Love ends with the image of a tribunal, where Genet is cast in the role of a witness, upon whom it is incumbent to tell the truth. The reader assumes the role of the judge, who is to listen quietly to the evidence and come to a decision. The value of the witness consists in describing acts that the judge did not witness, acts which are not simply to be described realistically, but are to be given 'some light and shade'. It is out of the transparent and memorial silence of past events that the witness, in his or her solitude, tells and betrays the truth. The only image that for Genet can evoke the truth of the revolution, that can bear the entirety of what Genet calls its 'enigma' (CA 242/PL 176), is the couple of mother and son that he met in Irbid. The revelation of this image is the truth of *Prisoner of Love*. But what is this image?

The Scene of Redemption: Genet Becomes God

In 1970, Genet spent a half-day and a whole night in the company of Hamza, a young *fedayee*, and his mother. After striking up a rapport, Hamza took Genet back to his house to meet his mother, who was also sympathetic to the revolution. After a simple meal of sardines, omelette and salad, Genet helped Hamza prepare his arms for that evening's action against the Jordanian *Bedouin*. That night, whilst Hamza was out fighting, Genet took his place and slept in his bed, where, in the middle of the night, Hamza's mother brought Genet some coffee and a glass of water.

Such are the bare facts of the story, which appear unremarkable in themselves. However, it is this event that *haunts* Genet for the next fourteen years, returning repeatedly like a spectre as the book develops and which ultimately prompts Genet's final visit to the area in 1984, when he meets Hamza's mother once again (CA 460–86/PL 341–61). Now, why does this image bear the entire mystery of the revolution? How is the sublime truth of the revolution redeemed in this image? What follows is the crucial moment in Genet's narrative:

> The fact that the Virgin Mary is called the Mother of God makes you wonder, since the chronological order is the same for parenthood human and divine, by what prodigy or by what mathematics the mother came after the Son but preceded her own Father. The order becomes less mysterious when you think of Hamza . . .
>
> I lay fully dressed on Hamza's bed, listening to the noise of battle. It grew less regular but remained just as deafening and apparently close. Then in the midst

of this aural chaos two little reports from nearby seemed to hurl the din of destruction back. I suddenly realized they were two peaceful taps at the door of my room. While iron and steel exploded in the distance, a knuckle was banging on wood a few feet away. I didn't answer, partly because I didn't know how to say 'Come in' in Arabic yet. But mainly because, as I said, I'd only just realized what had happened.

The door opened, light from the starry sky came into the room, and behind it I could see a tall shadow. I half-closed my eyes, pretending I was asleep, but through my lashes I could see everything. The mother had just come in. Was she taken in by my pretence? Had she come out of the now earsplitting darkness, or out of the icy night I carry about with me everywhere? She was carrying a tray, which she put down on the little blue table with yellow and black flowers, already mentioned. She moved the table near the head of the bed, where I could reach it. Her movements were as precise as a blind man's in daylight. Without making a sound she went out and shut the door. The starry sky was gone, I could open my eyes. On the tray were a cup of Turkish coffee and a glass of water. I drank them, shut my eyes and waited, hoping I hadn't made a noise.

Another two little taps at the door, just like the first two. In the light of the stars and the waning moon the same long shadow appeared, as familiar now as if it had come into my room at the same time every night of my life before I went to sleep. Or rather so familiar that it was inside rather than outside me, coming into me with a cup of Turkish coffee every night since I was born. Through my lashes I saw her move the little table silently back to its place and, still with the assurance of someone born blind, pick up the tray and go out, closing the door.

It all happened so smoothly that I realized the mother came every night with a cup of coffee and a glass of water for Hamza. Without a sound, except for four little taps at the door, and in the distance, as in a picture by Detaille, gunfire against a background of stars.

Because he was fighting that night, I'd taken the son's place and perhaps played his part in his room and his bed. For one night and for the duration of one simple but oft-repeated act, a man older than she was herself became the mother's son. For 'before she was made, I was' ['*j'etais avant qu'elle ne fût*']. Though younger than I, during that familiar act she was my mother as well as Hamza's. It was my own personal and portable darkness that the door of my room opened and closed. I fell asleep. (CA 229–31/PL 166–7)

This passage describes Genet's initiation into what he calls the 'mystères de la résistance' (CA 228/PL 166). The entire purpose of *Prisoner of Love* is the recovery in memory and writing of this event, of the simplicity of this routine act of a mother's giving a drink of coffee and water to her 'son'. It is the event of this gift that ultimately prompted Genet's visit to Irbid in 1984, where he felt compelled to meet Hamza's mother in order 'to establish that I knew something' (CA 476/PL 353). This event, the free and routine giving of coffee and water to a stranger mistaken to be a son, constitutes the book's *redemptive moment*; the point of transcendence that Genet attempts to recover in writing. Genet explains this event through the theological paradox of the Immaculate Conception (the very concept that resounds on both columns of *Glas*; Derrida asks, 'And what if the *Aufhebung* were a Christian mother' – G 280/Gtr 201), namely, that Mary is the mother of the God who inseminates her, precedes her and is ultimately the cause for her existence. The child is therefore older than the parent. The significance of this for Genet is that, for one night and for the duration of one oft-repeated everyday action, he becomes the son of a mother who is younger than he. This paradoxical event begins to haunt Genet and he comes to associate the couple of himself/Hamza and Hamza's mother with representations of *pietà*, of the Virgin Mary mourning the dead Christ, an image for which, incidentally, there is no Biblical source, but which is intended to illustrate both the Virgin's motherly love for her son – and *via* him for humanity – and the Christ's suffering for our salvation. What fascinates Genet is that in some representations of the *pietà*, Mary appears to be younger than the dead Christ (CA 240/PL 175). The paradox of both the *pietà* and the Immaculate Conception lends an essential ambiguity to the image of Hamza and his mother. If a son can be older than his mother, then Genet can identify himself both as the son of a mother who is younger than he and, more particularly, as Hamza himself. This image allows a number of themes to be reconciled:

1. Genet becomes Hamza, the brave *fedayee*, and thereby becomes an initiate of the mysterious truth of the revolution.

2. Genet becomes reconciled with a mother who, paradoxically, could be his own mother and is thereby reconciled symbolically with his absent mother, Gabrielle (JV 46/TJ 34).

3. Genet *qua* Hamza discovers a home, somewhere outside of France and Europe, where he can find proper repose.

4. *Genet becomes God*; he is not merely Saint Genet, but the dead Christ lying in his mother's arms. The truth of Genet's art is an act of auto-deification.

Although the various strands of meaning carried by the image of Hamza and his mother are knotted together in Genet's text and knot together the meaning of that text, the image is clearly contradictory. Why should the emblem of the Palestinian revolution be the Christian image of *pietà*? I think one has to believe Genet's sincerity when he says that he does not know why he chose this image; it remains for him a perplexity:

Perhaps it's not very important, but it's very strange, that for me the seal, the emblem of the Palestinian Revolution was never a Palestinian hero or a victory like Karameh, but that almost incongruous apparition: Hamza and his mother . . . But why had this oft-repeated, profoundly Christian couple, symbolizing the inconsolable grief of a mother whose son was God, appeared to me like a bolt from the blue as a symbol of the Palestinian resistance? And not only that. That was understandable enough. But why did it also strike me that the revolution took place in order that this couple should haunt me? (CA 242–3/PL 177)

It is now perhaps a little clearer why the image of Hamza and his mother should be Genet's 'only really profound memory' of the Palestinian revolution. With this image Genet achieves redemption and reconciliation, redeeming himself and the truth of the revolution in the reconciliation of his desire for a mother, a family, a home, love, property, community and God. The final page of *Prisoner of Love* is left transparent because at that moment Genet achieves the breakthrough into the reality of 'involvement, fertile in love and hate; in people's daily lives; in silence, like translucency, punctuated by words and phrases' (CA 12/PL 3). The economy of betrayal within which the writing of *Prisoner of Love* circulates, is broken by a redemptive moment of transcendence that cannot be comprehended in writing and, precisely because of this, is able to comprehend the truth of the Palestinian revolution. Writing the truth of the revolution is a writing of the truth of what lies outside of writing: redemption, reconciliation.

Palestinian *Sittlichkeit*: Genet becomes Hegel

But what is the meaning of this scene of reconciliation? Genet's redemption into the truth – what I called above his inverted Nietzscheanism – privileges love, family, home, property, community and divinity. Reconciliation is the dream of a community of presence, of co-presence; a community of self-recognition in otherness, where the other becomes an object of my amorous cognition; a Christian community bound by the bond of Holy Spirit and rooted in the Holy Family, of which each empirical family is an echo; an existing ethical community rooted in substantial customs and practices and through which the individual finds actual (Hegelian) and not merely abstract (Kantian) freedom. In short, the political truth that transcends Genet's writing is the dream of a *polis* of Palestinian *Sittlichkeit*, that is to say, a free ethical life rooted in the substantial *Sitten* of the community: family, marriage, love, heterosexuality, fecundity, property and divinity (see PRtr 105–10).

The curious paradox here is that it is precisely this concept of Hegelian *Sittlichkeit* that Derrida attempts to displace in *Glas*. The focus of Derrida's reading of Hegel is the concept of the family, which constitutes the first moment of *Sittlichkeit* in the *Philosophy of Right* (PRtr 110–22). Derrida's 'critical displacement' (G 6/Gtr 5) of the Hegelian system begins from a reading of the family, and his claim is that any displacement of the family will have deep implications for both the concept of *Sittlichkeit* and the Hegelian system as a whole (G 5–6/Gtr 4–5). Now, Derrida juxtaposes a commentary on Hegel with a text on Genet in order to aid this critical displacement and, alluding to Genet, he calls his methodological procedure in *Glas* 'a bastard course' (G 8/Gtr 6). A commentary on Genet – the bastard, the thief, the homosexual, the imprisoned ironist of communal morality – intertextually displaces the values inherent within Hegelian *Sittlichkeit*. The question is: has Genet, the enemy of European *Sittlichkeit*, become Hegelian in *Prisoner of Love*? In one of the strangely autobiographical moments in *Glas* from which a fragment was quoted above, Derrida writes:

> Not to stop the path of a Genet. For the first time I am afraid, while writing, as they say, 'on' someone, of being read by him. Not to stop him, not to draw him back, not to bridle him. Yesterday he let me know that he was in Beirut, amongst the Palestinians at war, the encircled outcasts. I know that what interests me always takes [its] place over there, but how do I show it? He almost never writes anymore, he has interred literature like no one, he leaps wherever it [*ça*] leaps in the world, wherever the Absolute Knowing of Europe takes a blow, and these stories of *glas*, *seing*, flower and horse must really piss him off [*doivent le faire chier*]. (G 50–1/Gtr 36–7, translation modified)

Would *Glas* really piss Genet off? And how can Derrida show that what really interests him takes place over there, in the concrete actuality of revolution or political resistance? How can Derrida show this interest through the writing of *Glas*? How can he too write the revolution? Of course, Genet's path was not stopped by *Glas* – indeed, epistolary evidence suggests that Genet was very appreciative of Derrida's work (VE 304) – and he writes the revolution in *Prisoner of Love* as a testament or souvenir of his blows against the Absolute Knowledge of Europe. Yet, paradoxically, the book's truth is the postulation of Palestinian *Sittlichkeit*, a form of political life which, whilst challenging the Absolute Knowledge of Europe, implicitly replicates its ethico-religious hierarchy: God, property, community, home, family, love, heterosexuality. *Prisoner of Love* is a replacement of that which was to be displaced by *Glas*. As such, *Prisoner of Love* enacts a profound inversion of the ethically privileged terms of Genet's earlier writing: homo-sexuality, betrayal, theft, solitude, alterity, abjection, and, most importantly, saintliness. To recall Jean Cocteau's remark, 'Sooner or later it will have to be recognized that he [Genet] is a moralist' (SG 584/SGtr 558). This was and remains true. But what takes place in *Prisoner of Love* is a collapse in Genet's ethical vocabulary which produces an inversion of values, from an ethic of saintliness which respects the other's alterity through an experience of aesthetized abjection, to an ethic of family and community, where the other is my mother or brother and is recognized as an object of loving cognition to which I am captive. With characteristic irony, it appears that Genet had the last laugh against both Derrida and Sartre.[6]

Notes

1. First published in *Radical Philosophy*, no. 56, 1990, pp. 25–34.

2. Jean-Bernard Moraly's *Jean Genet. La vie écrite* powerfully contests the legend of Jean Genet, namely that he was simply an untutored homosexual thief who suddenly became a writer, out of boredom, and just as suddenly gave up writing when he had achieved his desires for liberty and wealth. This legend is most deceptively apparent in *The Thief's Journal*, where Genet writes: 'through writing I have attained what I was seeking . . . To achieve my legend. I know what I want. I know where I'm going' (JV 217–18/TJ 170). It is this legend that Derrida writes of at the beginning of his discussion of Hegel in *Glas* (G 2/Gtr 1). In his conclusion Moraly writes:

> What has the legend shown us? A rebel who, by chance, wrote five books in prison and, through boredom, inadvertently wrote five plays. The theatre? He hates it. The desire to construct *une œuvre*? He despises literature and himself has never read and never written, or nearly. As hazardous as it may have been, our voyage in the realm of suppositions has the advantage of having shown Genet at work: ceaselessly reading and writing. (VE 339)

Moraly produces a great deal of persuasive evidence for unpublished or destroyed manuscripts by Genet, 'une œuvre-iceberg' (VE 340) of which only the tip was published (see VE 144). Contradicting the legend of Genet, Moraly constructs Genet's biography in terms of the problematic of writing, showing Genet's exten-sive acquaintance with literature – especially Proust, Gide, Dostoevsky, Rimbaud – and his obsession with the act of writing, finally asserting that 'Genet n'est qu'écriture' (VE 340). Moraly's thesis is supported by some challenging hypotheses and abundant empirical evidence, upon which I have drawn for biographical information about Genet. In this article, however, I shall remain within the param-eters of the legend of Jean Genet.

As a final remark on Moraly, it is interesting to note that although the tone of Moraly's book is fashionably anti-Sartrean throughout (see VE 95–110), he unwit-tingly employs Sartre's central concept of *metamorphosis*, a notion employed in existential psychoanalysis to explain the development of Genet's life and work.

According to Sartre, Genet undergoes three metamorphoses – thief, aesthete, writer – on his ascent to liberty. For Moraly, it is writing that determines Genet's life, and the metamorphoses of that life are explained in terms of writing: Genet is firstly the prose pornographer who is secondly metamorphosed into a playwright and finally becomes a political writer (see VE 127–8). The unity of these three metamorphoses establishes, in a thoroughly Sartrean manner, the unity of Genet's œuvre (VE 149).

3. Cited in Annie Cohen-Solal's *Sartre. A Life*, London: Heinemann, 1987, pp. 316–17. See also in this respect Genet's remarks in an interview with *Playboy* magazine, cited in Moraly's biography (VE 96).

4. I follow Genet here in describing the Palestinian insurgence as a revolution rather than a resistance. Of course, it is at the very least questionable whether the Palestinian struggle is assimilable to the Western concept of revolution.

5. See David McDowell, *Palestine and Israel. The Uprising and Beyond*, London: I. B. Tauris and Co., 1989, pp. 31–3. For a more comprehensive account of the Palestinian question, see Edward Said's *The Question of Palestine*, London and Henley: RKP, 1980.

6. For a fascinating discussion of Genet's *Prisoner of Love*, that parallels many of the points made above, see Félix Guattari, 'Genet retrouvé', in *Revue d'études palestiniennes*, special issue on 'Jean Genet et la Palestine', Washington DC: Institute for Palestinian Studies, 1997, pp. 49–64.

Abbreviations

CA – Jean Genet, *Un captif amoureux*, Paris: Gallimard, 1986.

CQ – Jean Genet, 'Ce qui est resté d'un Rembrandt déchiré en petits carrés bien reguliers, et foutu aux chiottes', in *Œuvres Complètes*, vol. 4, Paris: Gallimard, 1968, pp. 19–31.

G – Jacques Derrida, *Glas*, 2 vols, Paris: Denoël-Gonthier, 1981.

Gtr – Jacques Derrida, *Glas*, transl. John P. Leavey and Richard Rand, Lincoln and London: Nebraska University Press, 1986.

JV – Jean Genet, *Journal du voleur*, Paris: Gallimard, 1949.

OLF – Jean Genet, *Our Lady of the Flowers*, transl. Bernard Frechtman, London: Paladin, 1988.

PL – Jean Genet, *Prisoner of Love*, transl. Barbara Bray, London: Pan Books, 1989.

PRtr – Georg Wilhelm Friedrich Hegel, *Philosophy of Right*, transl. T. M. Knox. Oxford: Oxford University Press, 1952.

SG – Jean-Paul Sartre, *Saint Genet. Comédien et martyr*, Paris: Gallimard, 1952.

SGtr – Jean-Paul Sartre, *Saint Genet. Actor and Martyr*, transl. Bernard Frechtman, London: Heinemann, 1988.

TJ – Jean Genet, *The Thief's Journal*, transl. Bernard Frechtman, Harmondsworth: Penguin, 1967.

VE – Jean-Bernard Moraly, *Jean Genet. La vie écrite*, Paris: Éditions de la Différence, 1988.

3

Post-Deconstructive Subjectivity?[1]

The Subject as the Subject of Metaphysics (Heidegger)

What, or rather who, is the subject? 'Subject' derives from the Latin *subjectum*, literally, 'that which is thrown under'. Thus, the subject is that which is thrown under as a prior support or more fundamental stratum upon which other qualities, such as predicates, accidents and attributes may be based. *Subjectum* translates the Greek *hupokeimenon*, 'that which lies under', 'the substratum'; a term which refers in Aristotle's *Physics* and *Metaphysics* to that of which all other entities are predicated but which is itself not predicated of anything else.[2] In a classical context, then, the subject is the subject of predication; the *hupokeimenon* is that which persists through change, the substratum, and which has a function analogous to matter (*hule*). It is matter that persists through the changes that form (*morphe*) imposes upon it. In remembrance of this sense of the subject, one still speaks of a subject matter (*e hupokeime hule, subjecta materia*) as that with which thought deals, the matter of a discussion or the subject of a book or a painting. Indeed, one immediately here notes the oddity that the word *subject* can also designate an object. As Heidegger points out, during the Middle Ages the meaning of the words *subjectum* and *objectum* was precisely the reverse of their modern signification.[3] In the context of the English language, lexicographic evidence suggests that from the Middle Ages until the eighteenth century the word *subject* was used to name independently existing entities: the subject was that which was acted or operated upon, the 'object' upon which one exercised one's craft. For example, the dead body dissected for medical experimentation was, and still is, called a 'subject'. The modern philosophical use of the word *subject* as the conscious or thinking subject, as self or ego, as that to which representations are attributed or predicated (the subject as the subject of representation) first appears in the English language as late as 1796.[4]

Returning to Aristotle, we can see that *hupokeimenon* has the meaning of a foundation, as that upon which all other entities are based, the grounding principle upon which all entities become intelligible. Early in *Sein und Zeit*, Heidegger states that every idea of a subject, regardless of the protestations against the substantialization of the subject (i.e. the subject as a soul-substance or *res cogitans*), in Kant for example, always posits an *ultimum subjectum*, an absolute foundation (SuZ 46). Thus, from its context in Aristotle's *Metaphysics*, the subject is metaphysical: it is the very element of metaphysical thinking. To determine the subject as *hupokeimenon* is to make a claim to the meaning of Being, meaning being defined with Heidegger as the foundation or that upon which (*das Woraufhin* – SuZ 151) entities can be grasped as such. Metaphysics is here defined with Heidegger in fidelity to Aristotle as *philosophia prote*, as that science (*episteme*) that asks the question *ti to on*, What is an entity? (in German, *Was ist das Seiende?*); or again, what is an entity in its Being (*Was ist das Seiende in seinem Sein*)? Metaphysics does not ask after the Being of any particular region of entities; it is not a regional ontology like biology (the investigation of the Being of living things) or physics (the investigation of the Being of physical things, i.e. matter). Rather, metaphysics asks after what it means for any entity to be as such, and this question constitutes the guiding question of philosophy. Thus, for Heidegger, the question of Being (*die Seinsfrage*) is the guiding question of philosophy; and the history of philosophy, from Plato to Nietzsche, consists of a series of determinations or theses on the meaning of the Being of entities, what Heidegger also calls 'words for Being'.[5] Heidegger's fundamental insight into the history of philosophy is that, in this series of theses on Being that constitutes the history of metaphysics, the *question* of Being itself is forgotten or passed over. This is how Heidegger can claim that the history of metaphysics is a forgottenness or oblivion of Being (*Seinsvergessenheit*).

Modestly stated, the aim of Heidegger's thinking is simply to renew the experience of the question of Being as a question, as a source of perplexity about what it means for entities to be. This is the purpose of the quotation from Plato's *Sophist* on the untitled first page of *Sein und Zeit*, 'For manifestly you have been long aware of what you mean when you use the expression "being" [*seiend*]. We, however, who used to think we understood it have now become perplexed' (SuZ 1). Philosophy begins with a movement into perplexity (*aporia*) or questioning about the meaning of the Being of beings, and Heidegger's thinking begins with a certain repetition (*Wiederholung*) of this Greek beginning (PGZ 184, 187–8/HCT 135, 138). However, in order for philosophy to begin, for human beings to be attuned

to the philosophical mood of perplexity or wonder, the previous ontological tradition must be submitted to a de(con)struction (*Destruktion*), or what
the later Heidegger calls a dismantling (*Abbau*).

Keeping in mind this broad sense of the subject – and I am slightly
distorting Heidegger's account of metaphysics – metaphysics is always a
metaphysics of the subject, insofar as philosophy has always sought to name
the *subjectum*, the ultimate foundation or beginning point for an understanding of entities, or to offer a thesis on the Being of beings. In this broad
sense, the master words of premodern metaphysics – *eidos, ousia, causa sui* –
are all subjects. *The subject is the subject of metaphysics*, and philosophy deals
with the determination of the subject as the ultimate foundation upon
which entities become intelligible. The possibility of the subject is the very
possibility of philosophy.

Following the Heideggerian account of the history of philosophy more
faithfully (a narrative which remains illuminating even if one should continually want to question the scope of its applicability, what Gadamer calls its
unilateralism, or what Derrida sees as the univocity of its sending of Being),[6]
what is particular to modern metaphysics, and this means philosophy after
Descartes, is that this metaphysical foundation is no longer claimed to reside
in a form, substance, or deity outside of the human intellect but is, rather,
found in the human being understood as subject; Heidegger writes, 'Man
has become the *subjectum* [*Der Mensch ist das* subiectum *geworden*].'[7] The
human subject – as self, ego, or conscious, thinking thing – becomes the
ultimate foundation upon which entities are rendered intelligible, that in
virtue of which entities are understandable in their Being. As Hegel allegedly
shouted to his students during his lectures on the history of philosophy,
with the conception of the human being as *res cognitans* in Descartes we
have reached the *terra firma* of modern philosophy[8] – although, and this is
a massive caveat, one would be hard pressed to find the word *subject* used in
its modern sense in Descartes's *Meditations*.

The initial task, as I see it, is not to decide *sub specie aeternitatis* whether
human beings are subjects or not but to examine historically what happens
when the human being is conceived of as a subject, what metaphysical
presuppositions are implicit in the application of the philosophical concept
of the subject to the human being, and whether we should continue to
conceive of human beings as subjects.

In Kantian terms, the turn towards the subject is the Copernican turn,
where cognition no longer follows the object, but rather where the object
comes to depend upon the subject's constitution of objectivity. Although,
for Kant, the ground of the subject, which is the ground of thought itself,

cannot be known – for that one would need an intellectual intuition – the principle of apperception, where I can only grasp the manifold of representations insofar as they are mine, as the 'I think' accompanies all my representations, is, Kant writes, 'the highest principle in the whole sphere of human knowledge'.[9] It is the transcendental unity of apperception, a subjectivity that is, I would claim, logically rather than ontologically entailed as a place-holder in the argument of the Transcendental Deduction, that provides the principle of 'connexion' that Hume claimed was necessary to the constitution of personal identity, but which he found was wanting from his own 'deconstruction' of the Cartesian subject.[10]

Turning to Husserl's account of the subject in the *Cartesian Meditations*, he claims that philosophy begins with the turn toward the transcendental subject, that the *ego cogito* is the ultimate and apodictically certain foundation for my world.[11] Phenomenology, at least after the publication of *Ideas I* in 1913, begins with the subjective turn, the reduction or *epoche* of the naïve objectivism of the natural attitude, and the development of transcendental subjectivism: *phenomenology is an egology*. Returning to Heidegger, it is my suspicion that much of Heidegger's critique of the Cartesian subject is largely and parricidally directed against Husserl's Cartesianism. From the appearance of *Ideas* onwards, the phenomenological field is delimited as the field of pure consciousness: consciousness is pure and absolute Being.[12] For Heidegger – and this argument inspired both Levinas's critique of Husserl's theoreticism in his 1930 doctoral thesis and Sartre's 1937 *The Transcendence of the Ego*[13] – Husserl's Cartesian turn in *Ideas* is a failure to see through the radicality of the discovery of intentionality in the *Logical Investigations*. Husserl's metaphysical dogmatism consisted in rooting intentionality in consciousness and consequently failing to ask the question of the Being of intentional consciousness and ultimately the question of Being itself. With the publication of *Ideas*, Husserlian phenomenology 'moved into the tradition of modern philosophy', that is, sacrificed radicality for traditionality, falling prey to the tradition's temptation toward decadence and falling (*das Verfallen* – PGZ 178–80/HCT 128–30).

As Merleau-Ponty has elegantly shown,[14] this Heideggerian narrative of Husserl's increasing Cartesianism is, to say the least, somewhat complicated by the analyses of the body, perception and intersubjectivity given in *Ideas II*. Although the latter only appeared in 1952, Heidegger had a copy of the manuscript on his desk in 1925. In the lecture course of the same year, *History of the Concept of Time*, Heidegger rather precipitously remarks that even given the account of personalistic psychology given in *Ideas II*, which anticipates so much of the *Dasein*-analytic, 'everything remains ontologically the same' (PGZ 170/HCT 123) The originality of *Ideas II* is that Husserl engages in an empirical – not transcendental as in the *Cartesian Meditations* – analysis of the human being as a psychophysical unity that is constituted intersubjectively through an act of empathy (*Einfühlung*). Betraying Dilthey's influence, Husserl shows how the naturalistic attitude of the natural sciences is founded upon the personalistic attitude of life. For Merleau-Ponty, *Ideas II* is the shadowy preparation for an ontology of brute or savage Being (*l'être brut, l'être sauvage*), an ontology that would seem to have much in common with Heidegger's ontological critique of phenomenology. The point at issue here is that Heidegger's critique of the Cartesian Husserl is necessarily based upon a partial reading of the Husserlian text and premised upon an oversimplification of the extremely rich and complex history of subjectivity between Descartes and Husserl. In a moment of welcome humility, Heidegger seems to recognize this when he says: 'even today I still regard myself as a learner in relation to Husserl' (PGZ 168/HCT 121).

On a Heideggerian account, any determination of the subject, whether in terms of the *res cogitans*, the I think, the ego (Fichte), Spirit (Hegel), transcendental ego, Man (Dilthey), or person (Scheler), always remains within the closure of metaphysics, that is to say, within the limits of a traditional ontology characterized by the forgottenness or oblivion of Being. For Heidegger, symptomatic of this oblivion (an oblivion, incidentally, continued in much contemporary philosophy of mind) is the failure to ask the question of the Being of being human and the dogmatic and precipitous determination of the human being as subject or consciousness. Heidegger asks: what does it really mean for a human being to be determined as a subject or a consciousness? As Deleuze reminds us, the subject is a philosophical concept, and the question of the subject is a metaphysical question, *the* question of modern metaphysics; namely, that in order to understand what it means for entities to be, we have to begin with the subject as the principle or ground of philosophy.[15] The subject is, in Descartes's words, 'the sticking point' at which the sceptical, hyperbolic movement of doubt ends and philosophy begins: *ego sum, ego existo*. But, Heidegger would ask, what is the Being of the *sum*?

The determinations of the subject that have been discussed above – in Descartes, Kant and Husserl – would all seem to equate the subject with consciousness, self-consciousness, or reflection. They assume that I am the being who is conscious of having these doubting thoughts, and insofar as I have them it cannot be doubted that I exist at that moment as a thinking thing; or that I am the being who synthesizes these representations and who is self-conscious as the being to whom these representations belong; 'for otherwise,' writes Kant, 'I should have as many-coloured and diverse a self as I have representations of which I am conscious to myself'.[16] However, it should be noted that all attempts to break the bond linking the subject to consciousness, or reflection, for example Lacan's subject of the unconscious, remain profiled upon the same metaphysical horizon.[17] Without minimizing the importance of Lacan's decentring of the subject – what he calls Freud's 'Copernican turn' – an unconscious subject, a subject defined in terms of lack at the heart of its Being, a many-coloured and diverse self – it is still a subject and *ergo* a metaphysical fundament, even if it is an unknowable, ungraspable fundament. To determine the subject in terms of a lack of Being (*un manque-à-être*) is still to offer a determination of subjectivity (perhaps this is unavoidable for reasons I shall give below). The same Heideggerian argument could also be proposed with respect to all accounts of pre-reflective, pre-conscious or non-identical subjectivity, achieved through restitutions of Schelling, Schleiermacher, Sartre (for whom the subject or the *pour-soi* is also a lack of Being), or Levinas.[18]

In passing, I would like to turn this Heideggerian analysis onto Heidegger and ask: is *Dasein* – that is, the conception of the human being that is explicitly opposed to the subject – itself free from the traces of metaphysical subjectivity? Heidegger himself clearly thought this was the case, and *Dasein* is rigorously distinguished from metaphysical conceptions of the subject. Heidegger sought to demonstrate phenomenologically how the subject–object distinction basic to Kantian (or rather Heidegger's real target of neo-Kantianism; he is particularly critical of Heinrich Rickert, his former doctoral supervisor) epistemology is founded upon the ontological structures of *Dasein* understood as Being-in-the-world. For Heidegger, to posit the Being of being human in terms of the conscious subject is to reify the human being and to oppose the latter to a world which is understood as an objective realm posited over against the subject. Furthermore, the question of the subject's access to the objective realm, the sole concern of a philosophy that understands itself as a theory of knowledge, is presupposed as a theoretical or contemplative access through, in Husserlian terms, certain objectifying acts. For Heidegger, the subject–object dualism constitutive of epistemology understands both the subject and the world as entities that are *vorhanden*, 'present-at-hand', or objectively present to a theoretical regard. The modern philosophical positing of the conscious subject silently and constantly presupposes the massive privileging of *Vorhandenheit* over *Zuhandenheit* and of theory over practice. In his final seminar held at Zähringen in 1973, Heidegger reiterates how consciousness (*Bewußtsein*) is rooted in *Dasein* and how both presuppose a certain givenness or openness to *das Sein selbst*.[19]

The path of Heidegger's thinking moves from *Bewußtsein*, through *Dasein*, to *Sein*.

In *Sein und Zeit*, Heidegger displaces the Cartesian starting point for philosophy in the *res cogitans* by defining *Dasein* as *Mitsein* (Being-with). As he writes in the important 1924 lecture, *Der Begriff der Zeit*,

> *Dasein* is that entity which is characterized as *Being-in-the-world*. Human life is not some subject that has to perform some trick in order to enter the world . . . As this Being-in-the-world *Dasein* is, together with this, *Being-with-one-another* [Mit-einander-sein], being with others: Having the same world there [*da*] with others, encountering one another, being with one another in the manner of *Being-for-one-another* [Für-einander-sein].[20]

In its inauthentic everyday existence, *Dasein* is with and for others before it is with and for itself. Who is *Dasein*? *Dasein* is the entity *who comes before the subject*, who exists prior to the division or separation of entities into subjects and objects. As an aside, might it not be argued that what is truly novel with regard to the question of the subject in *Sein und Zeit* is the irreducibility of *inauthentic* modes of selfhood; Heidegger writes: 'Everyone is the Other and no one is himself' (SuZ 128). Or again, in *Der Begriff der Zeit*, *Dasein* is defined as *Niemand*, 'nobody'.[21] It should not be forgotten that the inauthenticity of *das Man*, 'the they' or 'the one', has the status of an *existential* for Heidegger and that authenticity arises as an *existentiell* modification of *das Man* (SuZ 130).

However, there are various modes of authentic selfhood in *Sein und Zeit*. The basic-attunement or *Grund-stimmung* of anxiety, where entities withdraw and *Dasein* becomes uncanny, individualizes *Dasein* and discloses it as a quasi-Cartesian *solus ipse*, a solipsistic self alone (SuZ 188). *Dasein* is also individualized in Being-towards-death, in the call of conscience that addresses the particular *Dasein* as guilty or indebted (*schuldig*), and the final account of selfhood in paragraph 64 – which emerges through a complex double reading of the Kantian 'I think' – in terms of the constancy of the self, leaves an individualized *Dasein* who is decidedly open or resolute (*ent-schlossen*) in the face of death. The question here is whether these authentic modes of selfhood remain free from the metaphysics of subjectivity. Another way of asking the same question: does the subject or self remain after it has been ecstatically temporalized in division 2 of *Sein und Zeit*? Jean-Luc Marion has convincingly demonstrated how *Dasein*'s authentic selfhood repeats the autarchy and auto-affection of the self-constituting ego and thus represents the last heir to the tradition of metaphysical subjectivity.[22] For example, it is *Dasein* who calls to itself in the phenomenon of conscience (SuZ 275), and the voice of the friend that calls *Dasein* to its most authentic ability to be (*eigenstes Seinkönnen*) is a voice that *Dasein* carries within it (*bei sich trägt* – SuZ 163).

Nevertheless, to do justice to the question of subjectivity in Heidegger, one would also have to consider patiently the later Heidegger's account of the essence of the human (*der Mensch*) in, for example, the 'Letter on Humanism', where the human is the entity that ek-sists ecstatically in nearness to the truth of Being. The Being of being human is defined in terms of an openness to the claim or call of Being (*Der Anspruch des Seins*), a claim that does not originate within *Dasein* but relates the human to the event of an alterity or exteriority that is irreducible to the self.[23] As Heidegger notes in the Zähringen seminar, 'The Da-sein is essentially ec-static [*ek-statisch*].'[24] For the later Heidegger, the human is no longer a subjective master of entities but, rather, the shepherd of Being ('*Der Mensch ist nicht der Herr des Seienden. Der Mensch ist der Hirt des Seins*'),[25] and it exceeds metaphysics in its ecstatic openness to the temporal donation of the truth of Being, the appropriative event of *das Ereignis. Das Ereignis* is the conjunction in the title *Sein und Zeit*, the 'and' that shows the belonging together of both Being and time and Being and the human.[26]

All of the above discussion is leading up to the question: is there a subject outside metaphysics? On the basis of the Heideggerian argument, the answer would have to be negative. If the question of the subject is a metaphysical question, if it is *the* question of modern metaphysics (it is what makes modern metaphysics modern), then the subject is the subject of metaphysics. However, can one not ask after a non-metaphysical determination of the subject? Or again, as philosophy is metaphysics for Heidegger, can one not ask after a non-philosophical account of what it means to be a human being? Now, is this possible? Is this even desirable? To pursue a non-metaphysical determination of the human being would entail, as Jean-Luc Nancy points out, that the question with which he frames a collection of papers on subjectivity, 'Who comes after the subject?', also be read as an affirmation: Yes, indeed, after the subject who comes? The 'who' that comes after the subject would thus be assumed somehow to stand outside the metaphysical tradition – a gesture which is, to say the very least, problematic. How is it that the 'who' should be somehow subtracted from the deconstruction of the metaphysical subject? (AS 96/WC 101). Who is 'who' such that it should stand outside of metaphysics? Is it *Dasein*, the being who, in *Sein und Zeit*, maintains a privileged relation to its 'who'? Is it the human being conceived ecstatically as an openness to the event of appropriation?

Or, following Nietzsche, might one speak of this 'who' as the *Übermensch*, as that being who, at the end of *Zarathustra*, leaves behind the superior or highest man, introducing a life free from the metaphysical determination of subjectivity.[27]

Which Subject? What Metaphysics?

It is time to raise some critical questions with regard to the above Heideggerian analysis. The question/affirmation, 'Who comes after the subject?/ Yes, after the subject who comes?', presupposes that there is an 'after' to come after the subject, as if an epochal break in the continuum of history had been achieved and that one could leave behind the epoch of subjectivity. For reasons that one might call 'classically' Derridian, all ideas of exceeding the metaphysical closure should make us highly suspicious, and the seductive illusions of 'overcoming', 'exceeding', 'transgressing', 'breaking through', and 'stepping beyond' are a series of tropes that demand careful and persistent deconstruction.

The above question/affirmation also implies the problematic presupposition that there was such a thing as the metaphysics of subjectivity that began in Descartes. In a discussion of Descartes's *Meditations*, Michel Henry has persuasively shown that the Heideggerian (and not just Heideggerian, although Heidegger does have a particular blindness to Descartes) caricature of the *res cogitans* as the subject of representation is based upon an extremely partial reading of Descartes (AS 141–52/WC 157–6). Etienne Balibar claims, with some justification, that the category of the Cartesian transcendental subject is something only retrospectively projected onto Descartes's *Meditations* from the *Critique of Pure Reason* (AS 26–7/WC 36). However, and *a fortiori*, it should not be doubted that the same nuancing of the history of the subject could certainly be given in a reading of Kant (Heidegger comes pretty close to this in paragraph 64 of *Sein und Zeit*) or Husserl (one need only think of Merleau-Ponty's 'The Philosopher and his Shadow' or the penultimate chapter of Derrida's *Speech and Phenomena*).

All of which leads one to ask sceptically: has there ever existed a unified conscious subject, a watertight Cartesian ego? Or is the subject some phantasy or abstraction that is retrospectively attributed to a past that one wants either to exceed, betray or ignore? That is to say, is not the subject a fiction that Kant finds in Descartes without it being in Descartes, that Heidegger finds in Kant without it being in Kant, or that Derrida finds in Husserl without it being in Husserl? However, if my critical suspicions are sustainable – and the very least I am arguing for is a more nuanced account of the history of subjectivity – then with what assurance can one speak of *an* epoch of subjectivity? To what extent can one periodize a 'modernity' in terms of a philosophy of the subject, a modernity that must be either supplemented by an intersubjective turn to communicative reason and mutual agreement, a turn (according to Habermas) not taken by the various discourses of modernity, or exceeded by a 'postmodernity' in which the subject would be somehow dispersed or fragmented?[28] Does not the periodization of modernity in terms of the philosophy of the subject – whether this prepares the way for an extension of modernity or a postmodern turn – presuppose a radically reduced and violent reading of the modern philosophical tradition? In the light of such sceptical questions, all we seem to be left with is a series of caricatures or cartoon versions of the history of metaphysics, a series of narratives based upon a greater or lesser misreading of the philosophical tradition. Such narratives may well be necessary and unavoidable fictions, but they are fictions nonetheless.

However, does metaphysics matter? If, following the Heideggerian account, there is no subject outside of metaphysics, then should this deter us from thinking the subject? Or might one argue, as Vincent Descombes has done, that the entire debate on the subject is simply *une querelle d'école*, based upon the fiction of a metaphysical subject that is simply not required in order to provide a philosophical explanation of our sense of individual agency (AS 115–29/WC 120–34)? Is not the debate on the subject, and here one rehearses Hume's critique of Descartes, based upon the grandiloquent and unintelligible presupposition of a founding conscious subject that is simply not shared by the English-speaking philosophical tradition, where one might more readily expect debates to focus on concepts of personhood or agency? To my mind, such a questioning would have to begin by thinking through the influence of the Wittgensteinian demolition of the metaphysical subject and those celebrated remarks on solipsism in the *Tractatus*: the subject is nothing in the world or part of that world, just as the eye is not in the perceptual field that it surveys; 'The subject does not belong to the world: rather it is a limit of the world.' For Wittgenstein, solipsism, rigorously followed through, coincides with realism: 'the I of solipsism shrinks to an extensionless point and there remains the reality coordinated with it'.[29]

Seeing the tradition through Heideggerian spectacles, one is inclined to see metaphysics as the site of a lack. The history of metaphysics is a history of the progressive covering over of the original sending of Being by the Greeks (Parmenides, Heraclitus) in a series of determinations or theses on

Being. The history (*Geschichte*) of metaphysics begins with a sending of Being (*Schickung des Seins*) that sends itself as a destiny (*das Seins-Geschick*) and where the sending holds itself back and undergoes a progressively more profound withdrawal. Heidegger calls this withholding of the sending of Being an *epoche*, and the history of metaphysics is a series of epochal trans-formations, where the original sending of Being undergoes deepening obfuscation. Metaphysics – that is, philosophy from Plato to Nietzsche – is an exhausted series of possibilities that has attained its completion or fulfilment (*Vollendung*) in the thoughtless technological domination of post-Nietzschean modernity, where the will-to-power has become the sheer power of the will-to-will (*der Wille zum Willen*), which is no longer under human control.[30]

On this Heideggerian picture, the question of the subject is entirely complicit with the metaphysical forgetfulness of the *Seinsfrage*, and indeed the history of modern metaphysics is the history of the progressive subject-ivization of Being (reading Heidegger, one sometimes feels that Descartes was simply a catastrophic error). Thus, for Heidegger, there is no subject outside metaphysics, and any conception of the subject is metaphysical. My suggestion here is that the *Heideggerian statement of the problem of metaphysics and subjectivity demands a Heideggerian solution*; that is to say, conceiving of the human being non-subjectively as an ecstatic openness to that which metaphysics is unable to think: the truth of Being, *das Ereignis*, the bivalence of *aletheia*. My sceptical question is: in virtue of what must one give exclus-ive priority to this Heideggerian approach to the question of metaphysics and subjectivity? What is the force of its claim? (Is it phenomenological? Is it historical? Is it more of a social-critical *Zeitdiagnose*?) Is it not too *reactive* and totalizing a solution to the question of the subject which presents one with an either/or alternative: *either* a metaphysically compromised concep-tion of the subject *or* an ecstatic *Dasein* open to the truth of Being? If a defence of subjectivity, say that given by Levinas in *Totality and Infinity* (TeI xiv/TI 26), coincides with a restitution of metaphysics (albeit a strange metaphysics of exteriority, which, as Derrida writes, is something 'new, quite new, a metaphysics of radical separation and exteriority'[31]), then how and why exactly is this problematic? Are we henceforth prohibited from thinking metaphysically about what it means to be a human being for fear of falling into nihilism? Or should we, paraphrasing Adorno, be suspicious at this point, claiming that all acts of overcoming are always worse than what they overcome?[32] Might not the entire problematic of the overcoming of metaphysics lead paradoxically to a deepening of nihilism? *Contra* Heidegger, do we not need more complex and nuanced accounts of metaphysics and subjectivity and of the relation between subjective experience and meta-physical experience, of the kind that Adorno finds in aesthetic experience and that Levinas finds in the ethical relation to the Other?

My view, broadly stated, is that the ambiguity of thinking the subject after Heidegger must be governed by the double bind of a double affirma-tion: firstly, by the need – ethically, politically, metaphysically – to leave the climate of Heidegger's thinking; and secondly, by the conviction that we cannot leave it for a philosophy that would be pre-Heideggerian.[33] That is, there is no going back behind Heidegger and no going forward without him; the break or paradigm shift occasioned by *Sein und Zeit* is, in my view, philosophically decisive. However, in what follows, I would like to employ the leverage of Levinas's critique of Heidegger to argue for a conception of the subject that will hopefully acknowledge our sense of self, the fact that I am someone (thereby retrieving the *haecceity* of the subject, its thisness, its uniqueness), a sense of self that might begin to meet the claims of respons-ibility, ethical and otherwise. I shall propose a determination of the subject in terms of responsibility or, better, responsivity,[34] a minimal, non-identical and pre-conscious subject defined in terms of sensibility, a subject that is ethical to the extent that it is sensibly responsive to the other's address. Levinas, I believe, presents us with the possibility for beginning to think a post-Heideggerian conception of the subject that will hopefully not be metaphysically or naïvely pre-Heideggerian, a conception that I shall even-tually describe as 'post-deconstructive'.

Levinas: the Subject is Subject

Levinas presents his work as a defence of subjectivity, but what is this Levinasian conception of subjectivity? Subjectivity is a central and constant theme in Levinas's work, and in his first post-war writings, *De l'existence à l'existent* and *Le temps et l'autre* (both published in 1947), Levinas describes the advent of the subject out of the impersonal neutrality of the *il y a*.[35] However, I shall sketch the notion of the subject as it is presented in Levinas's second major – and, I believe, greatest – work, *Otherwise than Being or Beyond Essence* (1974). I shall privilege the latter work because, in many ways, it is written from out of the context of the post-structuralist and anti-humanist critique of subjectivity. It is, in part, a response to the constellation of what Ferry and Renaut approximately refer to as *La pensée 68*, which Levinas also discusses in two essays: 'Humanism and Anarchy' (1968) (HAH 73–91/CPP 127–39) and the extraordinary 'Without Iden-tity' (1970) (HAH 95–113/CPP 141–51).[36]

In *Otherwise than Being* Levinas begins his exposition by describing the movement from Husserlian intentional consciousness to a level of pre-conscious sensing or sentience, a movement enacted in the title of the second chapter ('De l'intentionalité au sentir'). From the time he wrote his 1930 doctoral thesis on Husserl, Levinas had been critical of the primacy of intentional consciousness, claiming that consciousness *qua* intentionality maintains (despite the breakthrough of Husserl's *Logical Investigations*) the primacy of theoretical consciousness, where the subject maintains an objectifying relation to the world mediated through representation: the worldly object is the *noema* of a *noesis*. Such is Husserl's intellectualism. Now, in a gesture that remains constantly faithful to Heidegger's ontological undermining of the theoretical comportment toward the world (*Vorhandenheit*) and the subject–object distinction that supports epistemology, the movement from intentionality or sensing, or, in the terms of *Totality and Infinity*, from representation to enjoyment, shows how intentional consciousness is, to put it simply, conditioned by *life*, by the material conditions of my existence. Life is sentience, enjoyment and nourishment, it is *jouissance* and *joie de vivre*. It is a life that lives from (*vivre de*) the elements: 'we live from good soup, air, light, spectacles, work, sleep, etc. . . . These are not objects of representations' (TeI 82/TI 110). Life, for Levinas, is love of life and love of what life lives from: the sensible, material world. Levinas's work offers a *material phenomenology of subjective life*, where the conscious I of representation is reduced to the sentient I of enjoyment. The self-conscious, autonomous subject of intentionality is reduced to a living subject that is subject to the conditions of its existence. Now, for Levinas, it is precisely this I of enjoyment that is capable of being claimed or called into question ethically by the other person. Ethics, for Levinas, is simply and entirely this calling into question of myself – of my spontaneity, of my *jouissance*, of my freedom – by the other (TeI 13/TI 43). The ethical relation takes place at the level of sensibility, not at the level of consciousness; the ethical subject is a sensible subject, not a conscious subject.

For Levinas, *the subject is subject*, and the form that this subjection assumes is that of sensibility or sentience. Sensibility is the way of my subjection, vulnerability, or passivity towards the other, a sensibility that takes place 'on the surface of the skin, at the edge of the nerves' (AE 18/OB 15). The entire phenomenological thrust of *Otherwise than Being* is to found ethical subjectivity in sensibility and to describe sensibility as a proximity to the other, a proximity whose basis is found in what Levinas calls substitution (AE 23/OB 19). The ethical subject is an embodied being of flesh and blood, a being capable of hunger, who eats and enjoys eating. As Levinas writes, 'only a being that eats can be for the other' (AE 93/OB 74); that is, only such a being can know what it means to give its bread to the other from out of its own mouth. In what must be the shortest refutation of Heidegger, Levinas complains that *Dasein* is never hungry (TeI 108/TI 134), and the same might be said of all the various heirs to the *res cogitans*.

Ethics is not an obligation toward the other mediated through the formal and procedural universalization of maxims or some appeal to good conscience; rather – and this is what is truly provocative about Levinas – ethics is *lived* in the sensibility of a corporeal obligation to the other. It is because the self is sensible, that is to say, vulnerable, passive, open to wounding, outrage and pain, but also open to the movement of the erotic, that it is capable or worthy of ethics. As Levinas remarks in the autobiographical 'Signature', 'moral consciousness is not an experience of values but an access to the exterior being, and the exterior being par excellence is the other.'[37] Levinas's phenomenological claim – and by phenomenology Levinas means a methodological adherence to the spirit rather than the letter of Husserlian intentional analysis – is that the deep structure of subjective experience, what Levinas calls the 'psyche', is structured in a relation of responsibility or responsivity to the other. The psyche is the other in the same, the other within me in spite of me, calling me to respond.

Merleau-Ponty makes similar claims about the intersubjective constitution of subjectivity taking place at the level of sensibility on the basis of his reading of *Ideas II*.[38] He argues that the philosopher must learn to bear the shadow of the sensible world, the pre-theoretical core of brute or wild Being (*l'être brut, l'être sauvage*). It is at this pre-theoretical level that a phenomenological ontology must show the constitution of the self and the other prior to the formation of the subject: 'The idea of the subject, and that of the object as well, transforms into a cognitive adequation the relationship with the world and with ourselves that we have in the perceptual faith.'[39] The question here is whether the Levinasian account of sensibility and the intersubjective constitution of subjectivity can in any way be assimilated to Merleau-Ponty's account of Husserl. Although there is much room for proximity between Levinas and Merleau-Ponty on their privileging of sensibility, a certain distance would have to be recognized with regard to their conceptions of intersubjectivity. Merleau-Ponty embraces the Husserlian account of intersubjectivity described in *Ideas II*, where, at the empirical level, my psychophysical unity is not attained at the level of a solipsistic self-experience but is given only through a recognition of unity in the other person, a unity which is then transferred analogically to myself.[40] In Merleau-Ponty's words, the self and the other are intimately related like two hands touching, a handshake, the intertwining of a chiasmus. It is with this experience of the toucher-touched that Merleau-Ponty formulates a relation to the visible world irreducible to the consciousness–object distinction which still plagues the analyses of *The Phenomenology of Perception*.[41] For Merleau-Ponty, the intersubjective relation, conceived on analogy with the chiasmic relation to the visible, is one where the self and the other 'are like organs of one single intercorporeality.'[42]

For Levinas, on the other hand, ethics is not chiasmic. The relation between the self and the other is not analogous to two hands touching – ethics is not akin to a handshake. Levinas asks: 'Is the meaning of intersubjectivity at the level of sociality attained while being conceived by analogy with the image of the joining of a person's hands?'[43] For Levinas, the ethical relation to the other cannot be based on the fact that I need the other in order to achieve psychophysical integrity. Ethics is a movement of *desire* that tends towards the other and that cannot be reduced to a *need* that returns to self. Ethical intersubjectivity must be founded on the datum of an irreducible difference between the self and the other. The entire exposition of *Totality and Infinity* is intended to show that in the ethical relation the *relata* remain absolute – an absolute relation offensive to the principle of non-contradiction, what Levinas describes as 'formal logic'. Thus, although Merleau-Ponty's account of intersubjectivity is based on a necessary retrieval of sensibility, it remains an ontological – or what Levinas calls 'gnoseological' – relation that reduces the alterity of the other.

In 'Without Identity', Levinas concurs with Heidegger's determination of *Dasein* as an openness to the world, but the openness of the ethical subject is the openness of vulnerability, of sensibility. The subjectivity of the subject is a passivity that cannot be grasped or comprehended, that is beyond essence, otherwise than Being. In a manner similar to that of Lacan, the deep structure or truth of the subject is achieved when the ego opens itself to the Other (capital O), that is, to the structure of intersubjective communication that takes place at the level of the unconscious. *The identity of the subject is denied to consciousness, or to reflection, and is structured intersubjectively.* For Levinas, like Lacan, the subject cannot be grasped essentially, in its Being, and any metaphysical statement (*énoncé*) of the form, 'the Being of the subject is *x*' fails, by definition, to capture the subject of the *énonciation*. The subjectivity of the subject is *without identity*, because of the divergence or cut (*coupure*) between, in Lacan's terms, ego and subject, or *énoncé* and *énonciation*. The responsible or responsive structure of the psyche cannot be identified by consciousness and the subject is always missing from or lacking itself.[44]

Who is the subject? It is *me* and nobody else. As Dostoevsky's underground man complains, I am not an instance of some general concept or genus of the human being: an ego, self-consciousness, or thinking thing.[45] Levinas phenomenologically reduces the abstract and universal I to me, to myself as the one who undergoes the demand or call of the other. As Levinas puts it, 'La subjectivité n'est pas le Moi, mais moi' (HAH 111/CPP 150). That is, my first word is not *ego sum, ego existo*; it is, rather, *me voici!* (see me here!), the prophetic word that identifies the prophet as interlocuted by the alterity of God. The subject arises in and as a response to the other's call; this is what Levinas calls 'the religiosity of the self' (AE 150/OB 117). To put it another way, ethics is entirely my affair, not the affair of some hypothetical, impersonal or universal I running through a sequence of possible imperatives. Ethics is not a spectator sport; rather, it is my experience of a claim or demand that I both cannot fully meet and cannot avoid. The ethical subject is, in the true sense of the word, *an idiot*. No one can substitute themselves for me, and yet I am prepared to substitute myself for the other, and even die in their place. For Levinas, I cannot even demand that the other respond responsibly to my response, 'that is his affair', as Levinas remarks in an interview.[46] Subjectivity is hostage, both in the sense of being a hospitable host and also in the sense of being held captive by the other. The other is like a parasite that gets under my skin. It is *me* who is hostage to the other, who cannot slip away or escape this responsibility. This is the meaning of the concept of election for Levinas: I am elected or chosen to bear responsibility prior to my freedom. My subjectivity is a subjection to the other.

Anti-humanism and Post-structuralism: Clearing a Place for the Subject

Given the above, what consequences does the Heideggerian anti-humanist or post-structuralist critique of the subject have upon this Levinasian conception of subjectivity? Does the former in any way invalidate the latter? In order to illuminate this question, I want to focus on two passages from *Otherwise than Being* and a sentence from Levinas's short article on Derrida, 'Wholly Otherwise'. Towards the end of the central 'Substitution' chapter of *Otherwise than Being*, amnesically alluding to Heidegger, Levinas writes:

> Modern anti-humanism, which denies the primacy that the human person, free and for itself, would have for the signification of Being, is true over and beyond

the reasons it gives itself. It clears the place [*il fait place nette*] for subjectivity positing itself in abnegation, in sacrifice, in a substitution which precedes the will. Its inspired intuition is to have abandoned the idea of person, goal and origin of itself, in which the ego is still a thing because it is still a being. Strictly speaking, the other is the 'end'; I am a hostage, a responsibility and a substitution supporting the world in the passivity of assignation, even in an accusing persecution, which is undeclinable. Humanism has to be denounced only because it is not sufficiently human. (AE 64/OB 127–8)[47]

Thus, the anti-humanist critique of subjectivity clears a place for the subject conceived in terms of subjection, substitution and hostage. Rather than seeing anti-humanism as a threat to ethical subjectivity, Levinas claims that the former entails the latter by abandoning the philosophical primacy of the free, autonomous subject. The truth of anti-humanism consists in its claim that the subject can no longer support itself autarchically; it is, rather, overflowed or dependent upon prior structures (linguistic, ontological, socio-economic, unconscious, or whatever) outside of its conscious control. Levinas's point is that the humanity of the human signifies precisely through this inability to be autarchic, where the subject is overwhelmed by an alterity that it is unable to master. The subject is no longer the self-positing origin of the world; it is a hostage to the other. Humanism should not begin from the datum of the human being as an end-in-itself and the foundation for all knowledge, certainty, and value; rather, the humanity of the human is defined by its service to the other. Levinasian ethics is a humanism, but it is a humanism of the other human being.

Indeed, one finds a similar logic at work in Levinas's short article on Derrida, 'Wholly Otherwise', where Levinas suggests that the Derridian deconstruction of the subject prepares the way for an understanding of the human being in terms of the *creature*:

It will probably be less willingly acknowledged – and Derrida will probably deny it – that this critique of Being in its eternal presence of ideality allows, for the first time in the history of the West, the thought of the *Being of the creature* [l'être de la créature], without recourse to an ontic account of divine operation, without from the start treating the 'being' ['*être*'] of the creature like a being [*un étant*] . . .[48]

Thus, according to Levinas, Derrida would probably deny the most radical aspect of deconstruction, its insight into subjectivity as 'creaturality' (*la créaturalité*).[49] However, what does deconstruction have in common with creation, and what is the relation of the latter to ethical subjectivity? In a nutshell, the deconstruction of the autarchic humanist subject, and the claim that subjectivity is an effect of structures outside the conscious control of the subject, is assimilated by Levinas to the concept of creatureliness, which defines the human as that being who is overwhelmed by responsibility. Levinas writes in a note to *Otherwise than Being*: 'This freedom enveloped in a responsibility which it does not succeed in shouldering is the way of the creature, the unlimited passivity of a self, the unconditionality of a self' (AE 140/OB 195). Thus, creatureliness describes the responsibility that defines ethical subjectivity. The creature is that being who is always already in a relation of dependence to and distinction from the alterity of a creator, and it thus introduces a passivity into the heart of subjectivity.

Traditionally understood, creation is the production of entities from nothingness. In the Judaeo–Christian tradition, *creatio ex nihilo* is the summoning of the universe into existence, the emergence of a created temporal order from an eternal and uncreated God. Such a theological conception of creation has two important consequences: (1) the absolute distinction of God from his creation, thereby entailing the separation of the creator and the creature and the transcendence of the former over the latter; and (2) the absolute dependence of the creature and the created realm upon the creator for their continued existence. Now, Levinas criticizes this theological understanding of creation because, he claims, it treats the relation between the creator and the creature ontologically; that is, it conceives of eternal being and temporal being as a totality of being (TeI 269/TI 293). Consequently, this onto–theo–logical account of creation fails to account for the infinity and alterity of the creator and the dependence and passivity of the creature.

One might say that Levinas 'de-theologizes' the concept of 'creation' and employs it as a way of thinking the structure of ethical subjectivity. Creation should not be thematized ontologically in terms of totality but approached ethically in terms of alterity; that is, the absolute separation of the creator and the creature implies a complete dependence of the latter on the former. The relation of the creature to the creator, of the temporal to the eternal, is a relation between separated terms which cannot be closed over into a totality. Levinas employs this de-theologized concept of creation as a model for thinking a relation between beings who cannot be totalized and who together form a plurality. Indeed, this account of creation, given through Levinas's radicalization of Derrida, brings to mind Schleiermacher's concept of creation in *The Christian Faith*, where creation is the relation of absolute dependence of the creature on the creator, an absolute dependence that is the core of religious self-consciousness, or what was called above 'the religiosity of the self'.[50]

I would now like to turn to a second passage from *Otherwise than Being*, one that appears towards the end of the second chapter and deals more directly and polemically with structuralism and the human sciences. Levinas begins by setting out the context for the structuralist critique of the subject:

> In our days truth is taken to result from the effacing of the living man behind the mathematical structures that *think themselves out* in him, rather than he thinking them. For it is said in our day that nothing is more *conditioned* than the allegedly originary consciousness or the ego. (AE 74/OB 58)

After going on to argue that a conception of ethical subjectivity can be maintained despite the insights of structuralism, Levinas continues:

> One can, to be sure, invoke, against the signifyingness of the extreme situations to which the concepts formed on the basis of human reality lead, the conditioned nature of the human. The suspicions engendered by psychoanalysis, sociology and politics weigh on human identity such that we never know to whom we are speaking and what we are dealing with when we build our ideas on the basis of human facts. But we do not need this knowledge in the relationship in which the other is a neighbor, and in which before being an individuation of the genus *man*, a *rational animal*, a *free will*, or any essence whatever, he is the persecuted one for whom I am responsible to the point of being a hostage for him . . . One can ask if anything in the world is less conditioned than man, in whom the ultimate security a foundation would offer is absent. Is there anything less unjustified than the contestation of the human condition? Does anything in the world deliver more immediately, beneath its alienation, its non-alienation – its *holiness* [*sa* sainteté] – which may define the anthropological over and beyond its genus? . . . The influences, complexes and dissimulations that cover over the human do not alter this holiness, but sanction the struggle for exploited man. Thus it is not as a freedom – impossible in a will that is inflated and altered, sold or mad – that subjectivity is imposed as an absolute. It is sacred in its alterity with respect to which, in an unexceptionable responsibility, I posit myself deposed of my sovereignty. Paradoxically, it is qua *alienus* – foreigner and other – that man is not alienated. (AE 75–6/OB 58–9)

Once again, it must first of all be noted that Levinas does not deny the validity of the structuralist or post-structuralist insights into the conditioned nature of the human being. The claim here is that although it may be true to say that the human being is conditioned in the manner argued by psychoanalysis, sociology and political theory, *we do not need this knowledge when we enter into relation with the other*. Although the human being is undoubtedly and massively determined by the contexts – sociohistorical, psychobiographical, linguistic, biological – into which he or she is inserted, this in no way negates the unconditional priority of the ethical moment which rends those contexts. Thus, the insights of anti-humanism and post-structuralism might well be necessary conditions for the determination of subjectivity, but they are not sufficient to explain the extraordinary event of my responsibility for another, what Levinas calls, in a key word of his later work, the holiness or saintliness (*la sainteté*) of the human being. For Levinas, to recall the epigraph to the previous chapter and my discussion of Genet, it is precisely this saintliness, defined as the priority of the other over me, that cannot be placed in question.[51]

The Levinasian conception of the self does not react conservatively to the deconstruction of the subject by nostalgically trying to restore the primacy of the free autonomous ego, autarchic and for-itself. On the contrary, it is precisely because the discourse of anti-humanism or post-structuralism has deposed the subject from its position of sovereignty that the saintliness of the human being can be delineated. It is *qua* alien that the human being comes into its own, and what is proper to the subject is its expropriation by the other. Thus, anti-humanism and post-structuralism may be true in their analyses of the ontological, linguistic, psychological, or sociohistorical constitution of subjectivity, but this should not lead one – tragically, prophetically or cynically – to declare or celebrate the death of the subject. I must never be indifferent to the demand that the other places upon me, a demand which presupposes that I must be me and no one else. The deconstruction of the subject facilitates a novel account of the ethical subject *qua* me, without identity, an idiot, a creature, a hostage to the other.

Post-Deconstructive Subjectivity

During his conversation on the subject with Jean-Luc Nancy, Derrida makes the following intriguing remark:

> To be brief, I would say that it is in the relation to the 'yes' or to the *Zusage* presupposed in every question that one must seek a new (post-deconstructive) determination of the responsibility of the 'subject'. (AS 100/WC 105)

An adequate explication of this allusion to the *Zusage* (grant or pledge) would demand a commentary on Derrida's 1987 text on Heidegger, *De l'esprit*.[52] However, by way of summary, *De l'esprit* attempts to show that the primary datum of language for Heidegger is not the experience of questioning – the questioning that opens *Dasein* to the question of Being and which is characterized by the later Heidegger as 'the piety of thinking' – but rather *das Hören der Zusage*, listening to the grant or pledge of language. Prior to the putting of questions to language, Heidegger claims that language has already been granted or addressed to human beings. The significance of the *Zusage* for Derrida is that it shows that all forms of questioning are always already pledged to respond to a prior grant of language. The question and the questioning stance of philosophy is always already a response to and a responsibility for that which is prior and over which the question has no priority. One might say that the 'origin' of language is responsibility. As Derrida makes clear in his text on Michel de Certeau, the *Zusage is* understood as a moment of affirmation in Heidegger, 'in short, a yes'.[53]

Let us return to the above quotation. Derrida, despite his discomfort with the word *subject*, – he immediately goes on to say, 'it always seems to me to be more worthwhile, once this path has been laid down, to forget the word to some extent' (AS 100/WC 105) – claims that it is in relation to the dimension of responsibility prior to questioning opened by the affirmation of the *Zusage* that a new determination of the 'subject' is to be sought. My claim here is that the Levinasian account of subjectivity as responsibility to the other provides the framework for the kind of new determination of the 'subject' sought by Derrida.[54]

However, what intrigues me in Derrida's remark is the parenthesized adjective 'post-deconstructive' (and why parentheses? Does the word risk saying too much or too little outside of its brackets? Indeed, how does one mark parentheses in a conversation?). To my knowledge, this word is a novelty in Derrida's vocabulary. As to what 'post-deconstructive' might mean, this is illuminated by a later remark from the same conversation:

> In order to recast, if not rigorously refound a discourse on the 'subject' . . . one has to go through the experience of a deconstruction. This deconstruction (we should once again remind those who do not want to read), is neither negative nor nihilistic; it is not even a pious nihilism, as I have heard said. A concept (that is to say also an experience) of responsibility comes at this price. We have not finished paying for it. I am talking about a responsibility that is not deaf to the injunctions of thinking. As you [i.e. Nancy] said one day, there is duty in deconstruction. There has to be, if there is such a thing as duty. The subject, if subject there must be, is to come *after* this. (AS 102–3/WC 107–8)

The new determination of the 'subject' in terms of responsibility, of an affirmative openness to the other prior to questioning, is something that can only be attained after having gone through the experience of a deconstruction of subjectivity, that is, the kind of Heideggerian deconstruction outlined in the first part of this chapter. Post-deconstructive subjectivity would be a determination of the subject *after* deconstruction, a determination that succeeds the duty of deconstruction without lapsing back into the pre-deconstructive or classical conceptions of the subject that we sketched in Descartes, Kant and Husserl.

Nevertheless, a number of thorny problems arise with this notion of post-deconstructive subjectivity, not the least of which is the presupposition that there is a unity to deconstruction, that deconstruction is a singular and not a plural event. In speaking of the 'post-deconstructive', is there not also the implicit assumption of a 'before' and 'after' to deconstruction that can be specified or periodized in some kind of temporal succession – an epoch of deconstruction that is either preceded or succeeded by other epochs, or some kind of deconstructive *epoche* or withholding from determination or positivity that can be set aside in a return to pre- or post-deconstructive naïvety. Be that as it may, and it would have to be accepted that any post-deconstructive determination of the subject would itself have to be a candidate for renewed and persistent deconstruction, what is remarkable in the above quotations is Derrida's willingness to accept the need for new discourses on subjectivity, for new names and new determinations of the 'subject' that will supplement (in the full sense of the word) or succeed deconstruction. In brief, what is glimpsed here is the possible renewal of the 'subject' after its deconstruction.

Yet, how might such a post-deconstructive determination of the 'subject' be characterized? In a suggestive hint that is sadly not pursued (but upon which the entirety of my chapter might be seen as a commentary), Derrida says:

Some might say, quite rightly: but what we call 'subject' is not the absolute origin, pure will, identity to self, or presence to self of consciousness but precisely this non-coincidence with self. This is a riposte to which we'll have to return. By what right do we call this 'subject'? By what right, conversely, can we be forbidden from calling this 'subject'? I am thinking of those today who would try to reconstruct a discourse on the subject that *would not be pre-deconstructive* [my emphasis], around a subject that would no longer include the figure of mastery of self, of adequation to self, center and origin of the world, etc. . . . but which would define the subject rather as the finite experience of non-identity to self, as the underivable interpellation inasmuch as it comes from the other, from the trace of the other . . . [*l'expérience finie de la non-identité à soi de l'interpellation indérivable en tant qu'elle vient de l'autre, de la trace de l'autre* . . .] (AS 98/WC 103)

Look closely at Derrida's formulations in this passage: 'Non-coincidence with self', 'finite experience of non-identity to self', 'the underivable inter-pellation inasmuch as it comes from the other'. Although it would be un-necessarily reductive to read these remarks solely as allusions to Levinas's account of the subject, it is not difficult to see how the Levinasian con-ception of subjectivity described in this chapter, as hostage to the other, or as non-identical sensible responsivity, could be said to be consonant with the drift of Derrida's remarks. Levinas offers a determination of the sub-ject that is not pre-deconstructive but which takes place precisely in the space cleared by the anti-humanist and post-structuralist deconstruction of subjectivity.

However, and by way of conclusion, I would like to turn full circle back to the train of thought with which I began this chapter and ask: does not this tentatively post-deconstructive account of the subject itself fall prey to the Heideggerian deconstruction outlined above? Is not the Levinasian conception of the subject itself metaphysical? It was claimed above that, on a Heideggerian account, there is no subject outside of metaphysics and that, consequently, any determination of the subject, including any post-deconstructive determination, would remain within the closure of meta-physics. Remaining within the parameters of the Heideggerian problematic, there are two ways, it seems to me, of avoiding such a lapse back into the metaphysics of subjectivity: (1) to maintain a persistent and permanent deconstruction, without attempting to offer any positive theses; a kind of infinite vigilance or modesty that would renounce the attempt at a new determination of the subject or any other classical philosopheme;[55] and (2) to embrace the position of the later Heidegger and conceive of the human being non-metaphysically as an ecstatic openness to the truth of Being.

With regard to these two options, I have argued in this chapter that the task of thinking the subject after Heidegger must be governed by the double bind of a double affirmation; that is, both by the profound need to leave the climate of Heidegger's thinking and by the conviction that one cannot leave it for a philosophy that would be pre-Heideggerian. This en-tails, in John Llewelyn's formulation, the task of avoiding 'the metaphysics of subjectivity . . . without falling into the metaphysical denial of metaphy-sics by positing a power that has at most a contingent need of human or other being'.[56] Thus, against the above two options, I would argue that (1) the former merely sidesteps philosophy and perhaps risks conspiring with the very nihilism it seeks to deconstruct (recall that Heidegger condemns such a position as a false substitute for philosophy: 'the mere interpretation of the traditional texts of philosophy, the elaboration and slaving away at metaphysics [*das Ausarbeiten und Abarbeiten der Metaphysik*]'),[57] and (2) the latter offers an account of the subject that is too dehumanized and 'react-ive'. I would follow Janicaud here in refusing the strictness of Heidegger's opposition between the classical metaphysical subject and the human being conceived as ecstatic openness: 'The question is rather: what becomes of subjectivity when it loses its substantiality, its imperial sovereignty, its cer-tainties and perhaps even its will?'[58]

Nonetheless, the claim that the Levinasian subject is metaphysical would indeed seem to be in perfect accord with many of Levinas's own remarks on metaphysics. *Totality and Infinity* begins with a positive definition of meta-physics in terms of desire for the infinitely other: metaphysics is trans-cendence and the very movement of alterity (TeI 3–5/TI 33–5). A few pages further on, in 'Metaphysics precedes ontology', Levinas polemically rehearses the anti-Heideggerian arguments first formulated in the 1951 essay, 'Is Ontology Fundamental?' (TeI 12–18/TI 42–8).[59] For Levinas, the primacy of fundamental ontology in the early Heidegger decides the essence of philosophy: 'it is to subordinate the relation with *someone*, who is an existent (*un étant*) (the ethical relation) to a relation with the *being of existents* (*l'être de l'étant*)' (TeI 16/TI 45). To maintain this subordination of the human being to the being of beings is to privilege ontology over ethics, the Same over the Other, power over peace, and freedom over justice. For Levinas, the relation between ethics and ontology must be inverted ('*il faut intervertir les termes*' TeI 17/TI 47); that is, it must be shown that ontology presupposes metaphysics, not vice versa, and that the ethical relation with the Other is not grafted on to an antecedent *Seinsverständnis* but is rather a foundation or infrastructure. Ethics is first philosophy. In a letter appended to the 1962 paper, 'Transcendence and Height', Levinas writes, with an oblique but characteristic reference to Heidegger's political myopia:

> The poetry of the peaceful path that runs through fields does not simply reflect the splendour of Being beyond beings. That splendour brings with it more sombre and pitiless images. The declaration of the end of metaphysics is prema-ture. The end is not at all certain. Besides, metaphysics – the relation with the being (*étant*) which is accomplished in ethics – precedes the understanding of Being and survives ontology.[60]

Levinas opposes metaphysics to ontology and claims that *Dasein*'s *Seinsver-ständnis* presupposes a non-ontological relation with the other human being (*autrui*), the being to whom I speak and am obligated before being compre-hended. Fundamental ontology is fundamentally ethical metaphysics.

Thus, it would seem that Levinas's strategy with respect to Heidegger is one of reversal, an inversion of the priority of being over beings and a restitution of metaphysics against ontology. From a Heideggerian perspective, one might object that Levinas simply returns to a classical metaphysics of beingness (*Seiendheit*); that is, a determination of Being in terms of beings and a humanistic privilege of one particular entity, the human being. While still employing the ontological language he seeks to undermine, Levinas defines being as *exteriority* ('*l'être est extériorité*' TeI 266/TI 290); that is, what it means to be a human being is to be open to the radically non-comprehensible alterity of the Other. In addition to the performative self-contradiction entailed by employing the language of ontology to undermine ontology, Levinas's determination of being would appear to be metaphysical to the same extent as all previous determinations of being, from Plato to Nietzsche. What distinguishes Levinas would seem to be the fact that he is a retarded metaphysician, still producing theses on Being at the moment when philosophy has ended and we have entered the completion of metaphysics. By failing to see the radicality of the question of Being as a question, Levinas is logically, if not chronologically, pre-Heideggerian.

However, should one accept this 'Heideggerian' reading of Levinas? Is Levinas simply engaging in an inverted Heideggerianism? Although this view has its temptations, it does not, I believe, give the whole picture. Levinas is not only engaging in a reversal of Heidegger, which leads him to repeat the language of metaphysics, but also *enacting* a displacement of metaphysical language. This displacement can be seen in Levinas's use of palaeonyms like *ethics*, *metaphysics* and *subjectivity*, ancient words which undergo what Derrida has described as a 'semantic transformation' in Levinas's hands.[61] Levinas's language forms *a series of palaeonymic displacements*, where the ancient words of the tradition are repeated and in the iterability of that repetition semantically transformed: ethics signifies a sensible responsibility to the singular other, metaphysics is the movement of positive desire tending towards infinite alterity, subjectivity is pre-conscious, non-identical sentient subjection to the other, and so forth. The Levinasian text is swept across by a double movement or logic of ambiguity, between a metaphysical (in Heidegger's sense) or ontological (in Levinas's sense) language of being *and* the thought (if it is a thought, if it is not rather the break-up of thought before its matter) of the otherwise than Being that interrupts metaphysics or ontology. Levinas's writing, particularly after *Totality and Infinity*, is hinged or articulated around an ambiguous or double movement, between a palaeonymic repetition of the language of metaphysics and a displacement of that language, or between what Levinas calls, with deceptive simplicity, 'the Said and the Saying' (*le Dit et le Dire*).

On the question of the subject, my claim is that Levinas does not simply engage in an inversion of Heidegger that returns him to a pre-Heideggerian, pre-deconstructive determination of the metaphysical subject. As we saw above, Levinas accepts the Heideggerian deconstruction of the subject insofar as the latter maintains the privilege of theoretical, contemplative, objectifying consciousness. Indeed, if one reads Levinas's 1930 doctoral thesis alongside Heidegger's 1925 lectures on Husserl in the *History of the Concept of Time* (a reading unavailable to Levinas at that time, as the lectures were only published in 1979), then it is clear to what extent Levinas's critique of Husserl's intellectualist and theoreticist concept of 'intuition' is derived from Heidegger. Levinas's early reading of Husserl is 'inspired' by 'the intense philosophical life that runs through Heidegger's philosophy'.[62] For Levinas, 'knowledge of Heidegger's starting point may allow us to understand better Husserl's end point'; that is to say, there is a necessity to follow the movement from transcendental phenomenology to fundamental ontology and to focus on the existential problems of life, freedom, time and history.[63] As is clear from the 1932 essay 'Martin Heidegger et l'ontologie', the move from Husserl to Heidegger entails the deconstruction of the subject and the turn to *Dasein*.[64]

The persistence of Heidegger's critique of the theoreticism of Husserlian intentional consciousness in Levinas's work can be seen, to pick just one example, in the 1984 paper 'Ethics as First Philosophy'.[65] After defining metaphysics as that science or knowledge of the being of beings that is obtained through theoretical contemplation, Levinas uses the example of Husserl to show how the theoreticism of intentional consciousness that characterizes phenomenology as *philosophia prote* in fact presupposes a pre-theoretical, pre-intentional consciousness, the 'infinite subjection of subjectivity'.[66] For Levinas, the determination of the subject in terms of 'the passivity of the non-intentional' precedes 'any metaphysical ideas on the subject'.

However, although Levinas initially follows the ontological turn in Heidegger's deconstruction of the classical metaphysical subject, particularly with respect to Husserl, he then goes on to reformulate subjectivity in a way that undermines the fundamentality of *Dasein* and the claim of fundamental ontology to be first philosophy. If *Dasein* is defined as that being who is open to the question of being, *das Befragte*, then Levinas understands the ethical subject as the site of responsibility prior to questioning and ontology:

> The ego is the very crisis of the Being of beings [*de l'être de l'étant*] in the human domain. A crisis of Being, not because the sense of this verb might still need to

be understood in its semantic secret and might call on the powers of ontology, but because I begin to ask myself if my Being is justified, if the *Da* of my *Dasein* is not already the usurpation of somebody else's place.[67]

If *Dasein* is that being whose 'essence' lies in *Existenz*, then by what right does *Dasein* exist? If *Dasein* is disclosed through its *Da*, the 'there' of the world that Heidegger defines in *Sein und Zeit* as 'the clearing [*die Lichtung*]' (SuZ 133), then is this not 'my place in the sun', and thus – following Levinas following Pascal – 'the beginning and image of the usurpation of the entire earth'?[68] Prior to the *Jemeinigkeit* that is the condition of possibility for my authenticity (*Eigentlichkeit*), and an antecedent to the essential propriety that binds the human being to the event of appropriation (*das Ereignis*), it must be asked, *by what right do I exist?* What justification is there for me before the other? The basic question of philosophy is not Heidegger's Leibnizian question, 'why are there beings at all and why not rather nothing?'; it is, rather, 'how does being justify itself?'

Notes

1. An extended version of this text was first published in S. Critchley and P. Dews, eds, *Deconstructive Subjectivities*, Albany: State University of New York Press, 1995, pp. 13–45.

2. See, for example, *Metaphysics*, 1028b33–9.

3. '*Obiectum* signified that which was thrown before, held against our perceiving, imagination, judging, wishing and intuiting. *Subiectum*, on the other hand, signified the *hupokeimenon*, that which lies present before us from out of itself (and not brought before us by representation), whatever is present, e.g., things' (Martin Heidegger, *Wegmarken*, 2nd edn, Frankfurt am Main: Klostermann, 1978, p. 72). See similar remarks by Heidegger in 'Die Zeit des Weltbildes', in *Holzwege*, 6th edn, Frankfurt am Main: Klostermann, 1980, pp. 86, 103–4.

4. See the *Shorter Oxford English Dictionary*, s.v.v. subject, subjected, subjective, subjectivity, subject-matter.

5. For a list of these words for Being, see the 1962 lecture 'Zeit und Sein', in *Zur Sache des Denkens*, 3rd edn, Tübingen: Niemeyer, 1988, pp. 7, 9; *On Time and Being*, transl. J. Stambaugh, New York: Harper and Row, 1972, pp. 7, 9.

6. See Gadamer's remarks in a 1981 interview with *Le Monde*, republished in *Entretiens avec 'Le Monde', vol. 1, Philosophies*, Paris: 1984, p. 238; Derrida's 'Envoi', in *Psyché: Inventions de l'autre*, Paris: 1987, pp. 109–13.

7. Heidegger, 'Die Zeit des Weltbildes', p. 108.

8. Ibid., p. 124.

9. Kant, *Critique of Pure Reason*, B. 135.

10. Hume, *A Treatise of Human Nature*, ed. P. H. Nidditch, Oxford: Oxford University Press, 1978, pp. 251–63 and appendix, pp. 633–6.

11. Edmund Husserl, *Cartesian Meditations*, transl. Dorian Cairns, Dordrecht: Kluwer, 1960, pp. 1–26.

12. Edmund Husserl, *Ideas*, transl. W. R. Boyce Gibson, New York: Humanities Press, 1976, paras. 4–50, pp. 143–55.

13. Emmanuel Levinas, *The Theory of Intuition in Husserl's Phenomenology*, transl. A. Orianne, Evanston: Northwestern University Press, 1973; Jean Paul Sartre, *The Transcendence of the Ego*, transl. F. Williams and R. Kirkpatrick, New York: Harper and Row, 1972.

14. Merleau-Ponty, 'The Philosopher and his Shadow', in *Signs*, transl. R. McCleary, Evanston: Northwestern University Press, 1964, pp. 159–81.

15. Deleuze and Guattari emphasize that the subject is a philosophical concept, and that the task of philosophy as a discipline is that of 'creating concepts' (*Qu'est-ce que la philosophie?* Paris: Minuit, 1991). Consequently, the return to the subject in contemporary philosophy might simply show the incapacity of current thinking to live up to the demands of its history, that is, the demand to create new concepts. In lieu of the word *subject*, Deleuze proposes the concepts of 'pre-individual singularities and non-personal individuations' (AS 90/WC 95). In his conversation with Jean-Luc Nancy, Derrida makes a similar point about the need for new names for the 'subject', such as *subjectile* that occurs in Derrida's discussion of Artaud (AS 100/WC 104).

16. *Critique of Pure Reason*, B. 134.

17. For examples of such an argument, see Mikkel Borch-Jacobsen, 'The Freudian Subject: From Politics to Ethics' (AS 53–72/WC 61–78); Philippe Van Haute, 'Psychanalyse et existentialisme: À propos de la théorie lacanienne de la subjectivité', *Man and World*, vol. 23, 1990, pp. 453–72.

18. On the concept of the subject in Schelling, see Andrew Bowie's 'Re-thinking the History of Subjectivity: Jacobi, Schelling, and Heidegger', in S. Critchley and P. Dews, eds, *Deconstructive Subjectivities*, Albany: SUNY Press, 1995, pp. 105–26. On Schleiermacher, see Maciej Potepa, 'Die Frage nach dem Subjekt in der Hermeneutik Schleiermachers', in Manfred Frank, Gérard Raulet and Willem van Reijen, eds, *Die Frage nach dem Subjekt*, Frankfurt am Main: Suhrkamp, 1988, pp. 128–43. See also Manfred Frank's remarks on Schleiermacher and Sartre in *What is Neostructuralism?* transl. Sabine Wilke and Richard Gray, Minneapolis: University of Minnesota Press, 1989.

19. Heidegger, 'Seminar in Zähringen 1973', in *Seminare*, Frankfurt am Main: Klostermann, 1986, pp. 379–80.

20. Martin Heidegger, *Der Begriff der Zeit*, Tübingen: Niemeyer, 1989, p. 12; *The Concept of Time*, transl. William McNeill, Oxford: Blackwell, 1992, pp. 7–8.

21. Heidegger, *Der Begriff der Zeit*, p. 13; *The Concept of Time*, pp. 8–9. And see Philippe Lacoue-Labarthe's exploration of the theme of nobody (*personne*) in relation to Heidegger in 'The Response of Ulysses' (AS 153–60/WC 198–205).

22. See Jean-Luc Marion, 'The Final Appeal of the Subject' and Dominique Janicaud, 'The Question of Subjectivity in Heidegger's *Being and Time*', in *Deconstructive Subjectivities*.

23. 'Letter on Humanism', in Heidegger, *Wegmarken*, pp. 346–7; transl. F. Capuzzi and J. Glenn Gray, in *Martin Heidegger: Basic Writings*, ed., D. F. Krell, New York: Harper and Row, 1977, pp. 228–9.

24. Heidegger, *Seminare*, p. 383.

25. Heidegger, *Wegmarken*, p. 383; *Martin Heidegger: Basic Writings*, p. 221.

26. Heidegger, 'Zeit und Sein', pp. 20, 45; *On Time and Being*, pp. 19, 42.

27. Friedrich Nietzsche, *Also Sprach Zarathustra*, Leipzig: Kroner, 1930, pp. 359–63; *Thus Spoke Zarathustra*, transl. R. J. Hollingdale, Harmondsworth: Penguin, 1961, pp. 333–6.

28. Jürgen Habermas, *The Philosophical Discourse of Modernity*, transl. F. Lawrence, Cambridge: Polity, 1987, see esp. pp. 294–326.

29. Ludwig Wittgenstein, *Tractatus Logico-Philosophicus*, transl. C. K. Ogden, London and Henley: Routledge and Kegan Paul, 1922, proposition 5.6 ff.

30. Heidegger, 'Überwinding der Metaphysik', in *Vorträge und Aufsätze*, 6th edn, Pfullingen: Neske, 1990, pp. 67–95.

31. Derrida, *L'écriture et la différence*, Paris: Minuit, 1967, p. 132; *Writing and Difference*, transl. A. Bass, London: Routledge, 1978, p. 88.

32. Adorno, *Negative Dialectics*, transl. E. B. Ashton, New York: Continuum, 1973, p. 380.

33. Levinas, *De l'existence à l'existent*, 2nd edn, Paris: Vrin, 1986, p. 19; *Existence and Existents*, transl. A. Lingis, The Hague: Nijhoff, 1978, p. 19.

34. For this distinction, see Bernhard Waldenfels, 'Jenseits des Subjektprinzips', in *Der Stachel des Fremden*, Frankfurt am Main: Suhrkamp, 1990, pp. 72–9.

35. Levinas, *De l'existence à l'existent*; *Le temps et l'autre*, 2nd edn, Paris: PUF, 1979, transl. R. Cohen, Pittsburgh: Duquesne University Press, 1987.

36. See Ferry and Renaut, *La pensée 68: essai sur l'antihumanisme contemporain*, Paris: Seuil, 1985.

37. 'Signature', in *Difficile Liberté*, Paris: Livre de Poche 1976, p. 499.

38. Merleau-Ponty, 'The Philosopher and his Shadow', pp. 166–7.

39. Merleau-Ponty, *The Visible and the Invisible*, Evanston: Northwestern University Press, 1968, p. 23.

40. See 'The Constitution of Psychic Reality in Empathy', in *Ideas*, bk. 2, *Studies in the Phenomenology of Constitution*, transl. R. Rojcewicz and A. Schuwer, Dordrecht: Kluwer, 1989, p. 175.

41. See Merleau-Ponty's remarks in the working notes to *The Visible and the Invisible*, pp. 175–6, 183, 200.

42. Merleau-Ponty, 'The Philosopher and his Shadow', p. 168.

43. On Levinas's critique of Merleau-Ponty, see the two short essays (which are essentially two different drafts of the same text), 'Merleau-Ponty: Notes on Intersubjectivity' and 'Sensibility', in G. Johnson and M. Smith, eds, *Ontology and Alterity in Merleau-Ponty*, Evanston: Northwestern University Press, 1990, pp. 54–6.

44. I am here following Peter Dews's interpretation of Lacan in 'The Truth of the Subject: Language, Validity, and Transcendence in Lacan and Habermas', in *Deconstructive Subjectivities*, pp. 149–68. The comparison between Levinas and Lacan is continued below in chapter 9.

45. Dostoevsky, *Notes from Underground*, Harmondsworth: Penguin, 1972, p. 123.

46. Levinas, *Ethique et infini*, Paris: Livre de Poche, 1982, p. 92.

47. Strangely, Levinas's words here seem to echo those of Heidegger in his 'Brief über den "Humanismus" ', *Wegmarken*, p. 327: 'Humanism is opposed because it does not set the *humanitas* of man high enough.'

48. Levinas, 'Tout autrement', in *Noms propres*, Montpellier: Fata Morgana, 1976, p. 87; 'Wholly Otherwise', transl. S. Critchley, in R. Bernasconi and S. Critchley, eds, *Re-Reading Levinas*, Bloomington: Indiana University Press, 1991, p. 6.

49. 'Tout autrement', p. 98; 'Wholly Otherwise', p. 7.

50. Friedrich Schleiermacher, *The Christian Faith*, transl. H. R. Mackintosh and J. S. Stewart, Edinburgh: Edinburgh University Press, 1989.

51. Levinas, *Autrement que savoir*, Paris: Osiris, 1988, p. 72.

52. For a discussion of this text, see the essays collected in D. Wood, ed., *Of Derrida, Heidegger and Spirit*, Evanston: Northwestern University Press, 1993.

53. Derrida, 'Nombre de oui', in *Psyche. Inventions de l'autre*, Paris: Galilée, 1987, p. 646.

54. The problem that is left hanging here, and which would disrupt this happy homoiosis between Derrida and Levinas – although it is the only explicit criticism that Derrida makes of the Levinasian conception of the subject – concerns the limits of responsibility in Levinas. To whom am I responsible on a Levinasian view? Who is my neighbour? Derrida claims that, for all its novelty and force, the Levinasian conception of the subject conceives of responsibility as an obligation only to other human beings and not to animals and living things in general (AS 107–8/WC 112–13). Therefore, although Levinas engages in a critique of traditional humanism, his thinking (like that of Heidegger) remains humanistic insofar as ethical obligation is limited to other humans (AS 100/WC 105). To employ Derrida's neologism, Levinas would remain within the sphere of 'carnophallogocentrism', where carnivorous sacrifice is essential to the constitution of subjectivity. John Llewelyn has devoted an extended study to this question of whether an ecological ethics is derivable from Levinas (*The Middle Voice of Ecological Conscience*, London and Basingstoke: Macmillan, 1991). I would argue that it is indeed true that language is the condition of possibility for ethical obligation in Levinas and that one therefore has obligations only towards linguistic beings. However, what or who counts as a linguistic being? Are human beings alone capable of language and ethics? I think it can be shown that what Levinas means by language can be extended to include non-verbal as well as verbal communication, and therefore it could be claimed that insofar as animals and living things in general are capable of non-verbal language – i.e. that the language employed by living things does not necessarily have to conform to human intelligibility – a Levinasian ethics would still have obligations towards non-human sentient beings. The criterion for obligation would be sentience. However, in making this argument, I realize that I am perhaps taking Levinas where he would not want to be taken. (For a discussion of Levinas and humanism, see my *The Ethics of Deconstruction*, Oxford: Blackwell, 1992, pp. 176–82.)

55. A position outlined in the opening pages of Lacoue-Labarthe's *La fiction du politique: Heidegger, l'art et la politique*, Paris: Christian Bourgois, 1987, pp. 1–20; *Heidegger, Art and Politics*, transl. C. Turner, Oxford: Blackwell, 1990, pp. 1–7.

56. Llewelyn, *The Middle Voice of Ecological Conscience*, p. ix.

57. Heidegger, 'Zeit und Sein', p. 28; *On Time and Being*, p. 26.

58. Janicaud, 'The Question of Subjectivity in Heidegger's *Being and Time*', in *Deconstructive Subjectivities*, p. 57.

59. Levinas, 'L'ontologie est-elle fondamentale?' *Revue de Métaphysique et de Morale*, 56, no. 1, 1951, pp. 89–98; 'Is Ontology Fundamental?', transl. P. Atterton

and S. Critchley, in *Emmanuel Levinas: Basic Philosophical Writings*, A. Peperzak, S. Critchley and R. Bernasconi, eds, Bloomington: Indiana University Press, 1996, pp. 1–10.

60. Levinas, 'Transcendence et hauteur', *Cahiers de l'Herne*, M. Abensour and C. Chalier, eds, Paris: Éditions de l'Herne, 1991, p. 112; transl. T. Chanter, S. Critchley and N. Walker in *Emmanuel Levinas: Basic Philosophical Writings*, pp. 11–31. Interestingly, one finds a similar evaluation of the end of philosophy in Deleuze and Guattari: 'we have never had any problem concerning the death of metaphysics or the overcoming of philosophy: this is useless and tiresome drivel . . . Philosophy would willingly yield its place to any other discipline that could better fulfil the function of creating concepts, but as long as that function subsists, it will still be called philosophy, always philosophy' (Deleuze and Guattari, *Qu'est-ce que la philosophie*, Paris: Minuit, 1991, p. 14).

61. Jacques Derrida and Pierre-Jean Labarrière, *Altérités*, Paris: Osiris, 1986, p. 71.

62. Levinas, *The Theory of Intuition in Husserl's Phenomenology*, pp. 155, xxxiii.

63. Ibid., pp. 155–8.

64. Levinas, *En découvrant l'existence avec Husserl et Heidegger*, 3rd edn, Paris: Vrin, 1974, pp. 53–76.

65. Levinas, 'Ethics as First Philosophy', transl. S. Hand and M. Temple, in S. Hand, ed., *The Levinas Reader*, Oxford: Blackwell, 1989, pp. 75–87.

66. Ibid., p. 84.

67. Ibid., p. 85.

68. See the penultimate epigraph to AE/OB.

Abbreviations

AE – Emmanuel Levinas, *Autrement qu'être ou au-delà de l'essence*, The Hague: Nijhoff, 1974.

AS – Jean-Luc Nancy (ed.), *Après le sujet qui vient*, Paris: Cahiers Confrontation 20, 1989.

CPP – Emmanuel Levinas, *Collected Philosophical Papers*, transl. A. Lingis, Dordrecht: Kluwer, 1987.

HAH – Emmanuel Levinas, *Humanisme de l'autre homme*, Livre de Poche edn, Montpellier: Fata Morgana, 1972.

HCT – Martin Heidegger, *History of the Concept of Time*, transl. T. Kisiel, Bloomington: Indiana University Press, 1985.

OB – Emmanuel Levinas, *Otherwise than Being or Beyond Essence*, transl. A. Lingis, The Hague: Nijhoff, 1981.

PGZ – Martin Heidegger, *Prolegomena zur Geschichte des Zeitbegriffs*, Gesamtausgabe vol. 20, 2nd edn, Frankfurt am Main: Klostermann, 1988.

SuZ – Martin Heidegger, *Sein und Zeit*, 15th edn, Tübingen: Niemeyer, 1984. All references give the German pagination, included in the margins of the English translation. See *Being and Time*, transl. J. Macquarrie and E. Robinson, Oxford: Blackwell, 1962.

TeI – Emmanuel Levinas, *Totalité et infini*, The Hague: Nijhoff, 1961.

TI – Emmanuel Levinas, *Totality and Infinity*, transl. A. Lingis, Pittsburgh: Duquesne University Press, 1969.

WC – Eduardo Cadava, Peter Connor and Jean-Luc Nancy (eds), *Who Comes after the Subject?* London and New York: Routledge, 1991.

4

Deconstruction and Pragmatism: Is Derrida a Private Ironist or a Public Liberal?[1]

Introduction

Is pragmatism deconstructive? Is deconstruction pragmatist? At a superficial level, the response to the first question is clearly affirmative, insofar as pragmatism deconstructs all forms of foundationalism (Platonism, Metaphysical Realism, Analytic Neo-Kantianism, Pre-Heideggerian Phenomenology), and argues for the contingency of language, self and community. The pragmatist deconstructs the epistemological picture of truth as a glassy correspondence or clear and distinct representation between the mind and external reality, and replaces it with the claim that truth is what it is good to believe (James) or whatever one is warranted in asserting (Dewey). With regard to the second question, it can perhaps be said that deconstruction is pragmatist in two senses: firstly, that the deconstruction of texts from the history of philosophy (e.g. Plato, Rousseau or Husserl) in terms of the detection of what Derrida calls 'the metaphysics of presence' can be assimilated to an anti-foundationalist critique of philosophy; secondly, that the deconstructive claim that the ideality of meaning is an effect of the differential constitution of language – what Derrida calls the general text or, more helpfully, context – can be assimilated to a pragmatist conception of meaning as a function of context, i.e. the Wittgensteinian reduction of meaning to use (EHO 125).

So, at this superficial level, it would indeed seem that pragmatism is deconstructive and deconstruction is pragmatist. Yet, is this the whole story? In this chapter, I would like to disrupt this identification of deconstruction with pragmatism from the perspective of Derrida's work, and raise some critical questions about Rorty's understanding of deconstruction, particularly as this impinges on questions of ethics and politics. Thus, if I admit at the outset that deconstruction is allied to pragmatism, then the question is whether *deconstruction is pragmatist all the way down?* That is to say, is deconstruction consistently anti-foundationalist? Or is there a foundationalist claim in deconstruction which cannot be pragmatized: justice, for example, or responsibility for another's suffering? As we will see presently, this is the same question as to whether Derrida is *only* a private ironist, calling us to recognize the utter contingency of the philosophical tradition, a tradition that we are now in a position to circumvent (a favourite verb of Rorty's in his discussions of Derrida), and where Derrida's work functions as an exemplar of the forms of autonomy and individual perfection that might be available to anyone in a Utopian liberal society.

In texts like the 'Envois' to *La carte postale*, which is Rorty's prime example of what interests him in deconstruction, Derrida is clearly an ironist, in particular he ironizes about the validity or univocity of Heidegger's account of the history of Being.[2] But, is Derrida *only* an ironist? That is to say, in Rorty's vocabulary, is it not also possible for Derrida to be a liberal? For Rorty, Derrida can only be understood as a private thinker whose work has no public utility and therefore no interesting ethical or political consequences. Concealed in this claim is, I believe, a normative belief to the effect that Derrida *should* not be considered as a public thinker. The reason for this is that Rorty believes that if Derrida's work were extended into the public realm, then this would produce either useless, pernicious or possibly even *dangerous* ethical and political consequences. When Rorty discusses the question of the public significance of deconstruction, Derrida tends to get tarred with the same brush as Heidegger: namely, that Heidegger, for Rorty, is the most sublime theoretical imagination of his time (CIS 118), just as Derrida is the most ingenious and imaginative of contemporary philosophers (HDF 307), and just what one needs if one has felt the power of Heidegger's language but one does not want to describe oneself in terms of that language. However, Heidegger's work – and *a fortiori* Derrida's work – has no public utility; that is, it has no role in the political life of liberal society. Therefore, Derrida is a private ironist. Against this conclusion, I will try to show how, in Rorty's terms, it is possible both for Derrida to be a public liberal and for deconstruction to have overriding ethical and political consequences.

Rorty's Later Work: Presentation and Critique

To approach this issue, we need to define some terms and establish the general framework for Rorty's pragmatism. As a proviso, let me say that I will be restricting my discussion of Rorty to *Contingency, Irony, Solidarity*, to the reading of Derrida given therein and in some papers contemporary with and prior to that book.[3]

For Rorty, the liberal (and Rorty always personifies the positions he describes – 'the liberal ironist', 'the pragmatist' – which adds a helpful dramatic quality to the writing, but sometimes has the negative effect of reducing these positions to caricatures) is someone who believes that cruelty is the worst thing there is. Liberal society, therefore, must encourage the value of tolerance as a way of minimizing suffering. The ironist is someone who faces up to the contingency of their most central beliefs and desires – beliefs about the nature of language, the self and community and desires for autonomy and perfection. The heroine (Rorty always uses the feminine gender to describe the position he is advocating, whereas the liberal metaphysician – let's call him Habermas or the early Rawls – is always gendered male) of *Contingency, Irony, Solidarity* is the figure of the liberal ironist, someone who is committed to social justice and appalled by cruelty, but who recognizes that there is no metaphysical foundation to her concern for justice.

However, the core of Rorty's analysis – which has been the object of much hostile critical attention – is the distinction between the public and the private. It is important to point out that this distinction is not the Hellenistic or Arendtian demarcation of *oikos* and *polis*, between the domestic hearth and the public forum. The private is defined by Rorty as being concerned 'with idiosyncratic projects of self-overcoming', with self-creation and the pursuit of autonomy. The public is defined as being concerned with those activities 'having to do with the suffering of other human beings', with the attempt to minimize cruelty and work for social justice (HDF 307–8). Rorty's central claim in *Contingency, Irony, Solidarity* – a claim, moreover, that would be devastating to much work in philosophy if taken seriously – is that it is theoretically impossible to unite or reconcile the public and private domains. Such a desire for reconciliation lies at the basis of Platonism, Christianity, Kantianism and Marxism (other examples could be given), insofar as each of these has attempted to fuse the claims of self-interest, self-realization, personal salvation or individual autonomy with the *eidos* of justice, charity and love of one's fellow humans, the universality of the categorical imperative or the proletariat as the universal class and agent of history. The dominant legacy of the Platonist tradition is the attempt to reconcile private, individual autonomy with the public good of the community by erecting both upon a common philosophical foundation.

Rorty cuts the Gordian knot in which philosophy has long been entangled, between moral optimists like Kant, who claim that self-realization coincides with a commitment to human solidarity (the tie that binds individual autonomy, the moral law and the kingdom of ends), and moral sceptics like Nietzsche and Freud who would claim that the desire for human solidarity dissimulates either the will-to-power or libidinal drives. After Hegel – that is to say, for Rorty, after the historical turn in philosophy which coincides with a recognition of contingency, the idea that truth is something created rather than discovered – this contest between moral optimists and moral sceptics becomes a conflict between two forms of historicism. On the one hand, there are historicists for whom the desire for self-creation and autonomy dominates (for Rorty: Foucault and Heidegger), and on the other hand there are historicists for whom the desire for community dominates and who see the emphasis on self-creation as 'aestheticism' or 'irrationalism' (for Rorty: Dewey and Habermas). Rorty insists that there is no way of reconciling theoretically these two forms of historicism: 'there is no way to bring self-creation together with justice at the level of theory' (CIS xiv). We must reconcile ourselves to the fact that we have two irreconcilable final vocabularies, which function well in two different language games: the public and the private. To confuse the field of application for each of these two vocabularies would be to engage in a form of category mistake: on the one hand, to judge the public by the standards of the private gives rise to the kind of dangerous errors of which Heidegger was guilty in 1933; on the other hand, to judge the private by the standards of the public produces the kind of myopic readings of Heidegger and Derrida to be found in Habermas's *Philosophical Discourse of Modernity*.

For Rorty, the best that can be hoped for is a person – she, the liberal ironist – who would be able to discriminate public questions from private concerns, questions about cruelty and social justice from concerns about the significance of human life and the quest for autonomy. The liberal ironist would be the sort of person who would be able to distinguish properly the public from the private. Does such a person or community of persons exist? This question allows us to introduce the *Utopian* or *critical* element in Rorty's account. Most of the citizens of 'the rich North Atlantic democracies', for reasons of either religious belief or a vague, residual attachment to the humanistic values of the Enlightenment, are liberal metaphysicians. Such people are genuinely concerned with social justice, and they believe that there is one, final moral vocabulary – Christian love, classical liberalism, liberties underwritten by tradition – for deciding political questions, a vocabulary in touch with our essential humanity, our nature. On the other hand, although clearly outnumbered by the metaphysicians, there are non-liberal ironists who are concerned with their self-realization, and perhaps the realization of a small group, but who have no concern for traditional liberal questions of social justice. The critical, Utopian function of *Contingency, Irony, Solidarity* is to persuade liberal metaphysicians to become ironists (or at least commonsensical nominalists and historicists – CIS 87) and non-liberal ironists to become liberals. It is important to point out that Rorty believes that such persuasion will take place not through argument (as in philosophy) but through the *redescriptions* of metaphysics as irony, and of irony as consistent with liberalism. *Contingency, Irony, Solidarity* does not therefore belong to the genre of philosophy, but rather to literary criticism, which, for Rorty, is the only form of discourse that could be of moral relevance in our post-philosophical culture (CP 82) – liberal democracy needs literature not philosophy.

Rorty's Utopia is the vision of a society of liberal ironists, and progress towards such a Utopia will be achieved by the *universalization* (CIS xv) of liberal society. The obvious (if banal) question to be raised here is how such a commitment to universality can be consistent with Rorty's anti-foundational 'relativism' (between quotation marks, for I take it that relativism would be the name of a pseudo-problem for Rorty). To respond to this, it has to be understood that progress towards this liberal ironic Utopia itself depends upon Wilfrid Sellars's analysis of moral obligation, where the universality of a moral vocabulary – that of the liberal in this case – is dependent upon it being shared by a certain community with a similar set of moral intentions: 'we-intentions' (CIS 194–8). Thus, our moral vocabulary – that of 'we liberals' – is valid for us, for a community that sees the world the way that we do, as 'we Americans' or 'we citizens of the rich North Atlantic democracies'. Thus, progress towards Rorty's Utopia will be achieved by the progressive expansion of the frontiers of liberal democracies, a globalization of Western liberalism.

Of course, it would perhaps be too easy, but nonetheless still justified, to point towards the evidence of imperialism, racism and colonialism that has always accompanied – or perhaps has always been the reality behind the cynical veneer of a legitimating discourse – the expansionism of Western liberal democracy. Rorty's definition of liberalism is ethico-political and pays no attention to the *economic* liberalism – freedom defined in terms of free markets – which is indeed in the process of rapidly and violently globalizing itself, mostly without an accompanying commitment to tolerance and the abhorrence of cruelty (for example, China has successfully established itself as an economically liberal and politically non-liberal state).

Following C. B. Macpherson's classic analysis, it is evident that the historical basis for the development of liberal democracy was a liberal state
committed to both a competitive party political system and a competitive
market economy, onto which was eventually grafted, after much struggle
and bloodshed, a universal democratic franchise.[4] The important point to
grasp here is that liberalism denotes an economic as well as a political form
of society, and there is nothing *necessarily* democratic about the economically liberal state.

But, perhaps we are all liberals now. Perhaps the best we can hope for
politically speaking is a gradualist, reformist approach to politics that will
bring about a beautiful liberal society; all sublime dreams of revolutionary
transformation seem either hopelessly inadequate or merely quaint. Perhaps
Rorty is right to insist that the only response to objective political stagnation
is the privatization of the sublimity that radicals had come to expect from
politics between 1789 and 1968. Perhaps Rorty is also right to call for a
banalization of leftist political language and a subordination of the claims of
radical social theory to the facticity of democratic politics, which would
entail less *Ideologie-Kritik* and more social criticism of the kind that Rorty
finds in Orwell and which can be seen in the best investigative journalism.
Perhaps philosophy should be only an underlabourer to democracy, criticizing any drift towards reactionary political movements, intolerance
and cruelty and attempting to hegemonize the radical potentialities within
liberalism. Nonetheless, I am much less happy about the *tone* of Rorty's
statement that 'the rich democracies of the present day already contain the
sorts of institutions necessary to their reform' (HDF 326). Such remarks
risk political complacency and can be read as a (re)descriptive apologetics
for the inequality, intolerance, exploitation and disenfranchisement within
actually existing liberal democracies. As Hilary Putnam has recently pointed
out in a spirited defence of Dewey's radical democratic politics, 'the democracy that we have is not something to be spurned, but also not something
to be satisfied with'.[5] The problem that is caught sight of here, as pointed
out by Mark Warren,[6] is that Rorty's purportedly post-philosophical reconstruction of liberalism risks repeating the exhausted abstractions of classical
liberalism, against which the left–Hegelian and socialist critiques of liberalism are still largely valid.

I would like to conclude this section with four critical questions connected to the above remarks. First, the question of irony and the public
realm. As William Connolly points out,[7] by restricting irony and ironists to
the private sphere, Rorty might be said to refuse the possibility of a critique
of liberal society that would use the strategy of public irony to uncover the

violence that liberalism does so much to try and dissimulate. An example of this would be some of the neo-Nietzschean readings of the Gulf War, in terms of exposing liberalism's Janus face: one side turned towards legitimacy and universality, i.e. the mechanisms of the United Nations, and the other side turned towards the particularity of violence and war motivated by economic self-interest.[8] Rorty refuses the rich critical potential of seeing thinkers like Nietzsche and Foucault as public ironists, as critical both of the liberal democratic social and political formations that privatize autonomy, and of the slippery slope that allows the affirmation of the self's contingency to slide into a behaviouristic – and potentially barbaric (as in the case of psychiatry) – disciplining of the subject.

Second, although Rorty's liberalism does not presuppose the conception of the person *qua* possessive individual that one finds in classical liberalism, and although the liberal ironist has a Nietzschean awareness of themselves as a tissue of contingencies, the Rortian ironical self is just as private as the possessive individual and its conception of liberty is just as negative. Thus, although Rorty weakens the liberal conception of personhood, it does the same work as the possessive individual in underpinning liberalism, where freedom is defined negatively, that is to say, one is free insofar as one can distance oneself from social institutions.[9] Political freedom, for Rorty, is simply 'being left alone' (HDF 322); or, more polemically, he writes, 'My private purposes . . . are none of your business' (CIS 91). Against this negative conception of freedom, it is important to emphasize a positive conception of freedom, where liberty would not be found in the absence of normative constraint, but rather – the more Hegelian thought – that freedom would be precisely a product of such normative constraints (i.e. social practices); that is to say, freedom would be social and public and not a-social and private.[10]

Third, with regard to the public–private distinction; it seems strange that the fact that we become ironists in the private realm seems to have few implications for our relation to the public realm. It would appear that the public realm continues for 'we Rortians' in the same way as it did before we were transformed from metaphysicians into ironists. My question is a psychological one: namely, how can one be a Nietzschean ironist in the private sphere, which would mean understanding liberal principles of tolerance and abhorrence of cruelty as symptoms of *ressentiment*, and a liberal in the public sphere where one would respect and act on those principles? Does not the public–private distinction of the self into ironist and liberal yield an impossible psychological *bi-cameralism*, which would be a recipe for political cynicism (Nietzsche lurking behind a Millian mask)? To cite one of Rorty's own discussions, if one believes, with Freud, in the narcissistic origin of compassion, or that conscience is an ego-ideal for those unwilling to forgo the perfection of childhood (CIS 31), then doesn't this alter one's practical, public relation to acts of compassion and the fact of conscience? The question of the psychological impossibility of being both a liberal and an ironist is compellingly raised in *Contingency, Irony, Solidarity* (CIS 85), but is not convincingly dealt with in the ensuing discussion; Rorty raises the question extremely sharply and then proceeds to evade the issue. After having given no compelling reasons as to why a liberal should also be an ironist, Rorty goes on to claim, 'There is no reason the ironist cannot be a liberal.' This is true, but as it stands it still begs the psychological question of what it would feel like and what sort of psychological conflict would be produced by being a liberal ironist. Rorty just adds the caveat that an ironist 'Cannot be a "progressive" and "dynamic" liberal' (CIS 91) and cannot display the same degree of social hope as the liberal metaphysician. But isn't this just to suggest that the liberal ironist is regressive, sedentary and hopeless – and what good is *that* sort of liberal?

Fourth, there is a large issue about Rorty's definition of the liberal: if a liberal is a person for whom cruelty is the worst thing that there is, then what is the status of the implied appeal to minimize cruelty? Is this a universal principle or foundation for moral obligation? If it is, then how would this be consistent with Rorty's anti-foundationalism, and if it is not then what sort of binding power is it meant to have on members of liberal societies? Rorty goes on to qualify the abhorrence of cruelty by claiming that the recognition of a susceptibility to humiliation is the *only* social bond that is needed, and furthermore that this susceptibility to pain is pre-linguistic; suffering takes place outside of language (CIS 91, 94). To my mind, this would seem to ground Rorty's definition of the liberal in a universal fact about human nature. Thus, is not Rorty's definition of liberalism an attempt to ground the moral legitimacy of the political order in a claim about the pre-political state of nature, in a way that is strategically similar to Rousseau's appeal to *pitié* in the Second Discourse, which is defined as a pre-social, pre-rational, sentient disposition that provokes compassion in the face of the other's suffering?[11] Are we not here being offered a redescription of a criterion for moral obligation grounded not in reason but in the response to suffering, a criterion which can also be found in Bentham's argument for the extension of moral obligations towards animals: 'The question is not, Can they Reason? nor Can they *talk*? but *Can they suffer*?'[12] Let me say that I do not disagree with either Rousseau or Bentham (or Rorty, if this is what he is claiming). I will argue below for a criterion of ethical obligation located in the sensible or sentient disposition of the self towards the other's suffering, which is to be found in the work of Emmanuel Levinas. It will be claimed that such a criterion for ethical obligation yields a concept of justice that is taken up by Derrida and which establishes the public significance of deconstruction. Of course, this will mean reading Levinas as more of a secular pragmatist (what Derrida would call an empiricist[13]) and less of a religious metaphysician. But – and this is the present point – is not this recognition of cruelty or suffering as the ethical basis for Rorty's liberalism an appeal to an essentialist, foundationalist fact about human nature; and does this not sit rather uneasily with the general drift of Rorty's intentions? Despite Rorty's claims to irony and the ubiquity of contingency, is he not in fact attempting to base moral obligation and political practice upon a foundational claim about human susceptibility to humiliation, upon a recognition of the other's suffering? And even if one were to relativize this claim and argue that only 'we liberals' recognize the avoidance of cruelty as the basis for morals and politics and that such recognition is a product of a particular – and therefore contingent – social and political history, does it not nevertheless remain true that the claim has the status of a non-relativizable universal for 'we liberals', with our set of 'we-intentions'? Is cruelty something about which liberals can be ironic?

Rorty's Reading of Derrida

Having sketched the general picture of Rorty's position in *Contingency, Irony, Solidarity*, it is possible to see how the pragmatist critique of philosophy so powerfully articulated in *Philosophy and the Mirror of Nature* extends into moral and political concerns to produce a purportedly anti-foundationalist reformulation of liberalism. In the remainder of this chapter I want to address two questions: how does Derrida's work fit into this picture, and is Rorty's picture of Derrida justified?

Rorty's concern with Derrida goes back to the late 1970s and in particular to an influential essay, 'Philosophy as a Kind of Writing' (CP 90–109). In this essay, Rorty sees Derrida as an ally in his more general critique of neo-Kantian analytic philosophy and representationalism. It is claimed that Derrida's work is best understood as the latest development in a non-Kantian tradition of dialectical thinking that begins with Hegel's *Phenomenology of Spirit*, where narrative is substituted for veridicality and worlddisclosure for argument. Derrida recalls philosophy to its written status by the use of multi-lingual puns, allusions, typographical gimmicks, jokes and sexual innuendoes. In this way, Derrida shows that philosophy (with a lowercase 'p', rather than Philosophy) is best described as a kind of writing or as a sector of culture devoted to the discussion of a particular tradition and not as the master discourse by which all other disciplines are to be judged. Deconstruction lets us imagine the way things might look if we did not have the Kantian representationalist model of Philosophy built into our culture. This theme is continued in the 1984 essay 'Deconstruction and Circumvention' (EHO 85–106), where Rorty agrees with Habermas *avant la lettre* (and for quite un-Habermasian reasons), that deconstruction allows us to blur the distinction between philosophy and literature and to promote the idea of a 'seamless, undifferentiated general text' (EHO 85). In a nutshell, deconstruction does not engage us in an indeterminate task of deconstructing the tradition with the permanent risk of falling back within its limit, but rather allows us to *circumvent* the tradition, to go around it. Rorty claims that the Heidegger-inspired problematic of overcoming the tradition, or metaphysics, is a pseudo-problem that ought to be replaced by lots of little pragmatic questions.

Yet, from the very beginning of his encounter with deconstruction, Rorty inserts a note of caution with respect to both Derrida and, more particularly, Derrida's interpreters in the English-speaking world. For Rorty, Derrida's less interesting, less pragmatist side is revealed in his early work through his invocation of certain master-words like 'trace' and '*différance*'; words with a seemingly transcendental function in Derrida's discourse, which would risk deconstruction slipping back into the onto-theo-logical tradition it sought to undermine. Although Derrida, Rorty insists, always ultimately pulls back from this temptation to transcendentalize, unconditionalize or divinize words like 'trace', and where Derrida is careful to point out that *différance* is not a metaphysical name,[14] the same caution is not shown by many of Derrida's interpreters.

Is Derrida a transcendental philosopher? Rorty raises this question in a 1989 essay which responds directly to the publication of Rodolphe Gasché's *The Tain of the Mirror* (EHO 119–28). The appearance of Gasché's book allows Rorty to focus many of the objections he had to previous interpretations of Derrida, notably those of Jonathan Culler and Christopher Norris, each of which attempted to block Rorty's identification of deconstruction with pragmatism by claiming that Derrida's work was full of rigorous arguments and had to be judged by traditional philosophical standards. Rorty's main problem with these interpreters is that they tend to treat Derrida as a quasi-metaphysician and not as an ironist; they want 'to make

Derrida into a man with a great big theory about a great big subject' (HDF 8) and they show the kind of reverence for philosophy that Rorty believes is ridiculed in a text like *La carte postale*.

Everything turns here on the question of whether Derrida has arguments or not, that is to say, whether he can be admitted as a public thinker (and argumentation would be the criterion for admission) whose work has serious moral and political consequences. Gasché attempts to claim Derrida's work for serious philosophical consideration by showing that it forms what he calls 'a system beyond Being', that is to say, a series of infrastructures (*trace, différance, supplement, iterability, remark*) that are rigorously deduced from particular texts and which have a (quasi)-transcendental status, insofar as they make a claim to the conditions of possibility and impossibility for the particular text, or conceptual structure or institution under consideration.[15] Thus, Gasché's defence of Derrida as a rigorous philosopher turns on whether one can locate something akin to transcendental arguments in his work. If Derrida is a transcendental philosopher then, it is claimed, this will prevent deconstruction being caricatured as a mere private fantasy (although, for Rorty, to call Derrida a private fantasist is to pay him a much higher compliment than calling him a transcendental philosopher – EHO 121).

What, then, is an argument for Rorty? He follows Ernst Tugendhat (and, incidentally, the vast majority of philosophers in the European tradition) in claiming that argumentation has to be propositional, that is, argument can only be about the truth or meaning of propositions, and therefore philosophical discourse must be propositional if it is properly to be called argumentative (EHO 124–5).[16] There are only two directions one can follow on the basis of such a definition: either the language of argumentation (deductive or inductive) is antecedently given and stable, like the language of logic or what Rorty calls 'normal' science; or it is a disposable ladder-language of the kind employed by Wittgenstein in the *Tractatus*, a language that is to be left behind when *aufgehoben*. For Rorty, Derrida – like Wittgenstein and Hegel – is a master of *Aufhebung*. Thus, the claim that is central to Gasché's depiction of transcendental argumentation in Derrida – namely, that one can move from the propositional to some pre-propositional level (i.e. *différance*) which would provide the conditions of possibility and impossibility for the propositional and, moreover, that one can claim some sort of cognitive status for such a procedure – is a *misunderstanding* of the nature of argumentation. For Rorty, argumentation requires that the same language be employed in one's premises and conclusions. Such a definition of argumentation would not disqualify traditional, Kantian forms of transcendental argument (which were concerned with resolving sceptical doubts about the existence of the self and the external world), but it does disqualify Derridian forms of (quasi)-transcendental argumentation which would attempt to locate the conditions of possibility and impossibility for propositional language in some pre-propositional 'word' or 'concept'. Thus, Gasché's attempt to claim Derrida for serious philosophical attention by arguing that he employs (quasi)-transcendental arguments is based on a misunderstanding of the nature of argumentation. Hence, Rorty concludes, Gasché's project collapses.[17]

For Rorty, deconstruction is not (quasi)-transcendental philosophy, but must be understood as part of a tradition of philosophy as world-disclosure, a tradition that includes Plato, Hegel and Heidegger, where our old vocabularies of self- and world-description are challenged, redescribed and replaced by new vocabularies. Thus, the crucial distinction to draw is that between an argumentative form of language which addresses the problems of social justice – what we called 'the public' – and a non-argumentative, often oracular, form of language that is world-disclosive and concerned with the quest for individual autonomy – what we called 'the private'. Failure to draw the distinction between the public and the private will lead, on the one hand, to the sort of reading that Carnap gives of Heidegger, and Habermas gives of Derrida, and, on the other hand, to the reading that Gasché gives of Derrida and – perhaps – that Derrida gives of Austin.

Rorty concludes 'Is Derrida a Transcendental Philosopher?' with the rhetorical question: should one read Derrida with Gasché as a transcendental latter-day Hegel, or with Rorty as a kind of French Wittgenstein? (EHO 128). Rorty adds that the response to this question is not straightforward because 'Derrida makes noises of both sorts' (CIS 128). However, in order to persuade the reader to choose Rorty's interpretation over Gasché's, he offers what one might call a *developmental thesis* based on a distinction between Derrida's earlier and later work. Rorty divides Derrida's work into an earlier, professorial and scholarly period and a later eccentric, personal, original period. Derrida's early work, especially *De la grammatologie* is, for Rorty (and I think he is right) continuous with Heidegger's problematic of the overcoming of metaphysics, and attempts to locate the conditions of possibility and impossibility for logocentrism in certain infrastructures, like 'trace' and '*différance*'. Thus, in his early work, Derrida is indeed deploying forms of (quasi)-transcendental argumentation and therefore Gasché's reading is valid for Derrida's early work (which also entails that Derrida himself was subject to the misunderstanding about the meaning of argumentation that Rorty raised against Gasché above). However, if Derrida's early work is engaged in a form of what Rorty calls 'ironist theorizing', then the crucial moment in Derrida's development occurs, for Rorty, in the move from grandiose theory to more minimal and private forms of writing.

This developmental thesis is intimated in the title of Rorty's discussion of Derrida in *Contingency, Irony, Solidarity*: '*From* Ironist Theorizing *to* Private Allusions' (Rorty points out that he had originally wanted to entitle the discussion 'From Ironist Theorizing to Private *Jokes*' – EHO 120). For Rorty, the texts that best show this move from theory to privacy are *Glas* and, especially, *La carte postale*; neither of which are discussed by Gasché in *The Tain of the Mirror*. Thus, for Rorty, Derrida's early theoretical work is a 'false start' in the same way, he claims, that *Sein und Zeit* is a false start in the development of Heidegger's work and the *Tractatus* was a false start for Wittgenstein. Rorty argues for 'the superiority of later to earlier Derrida' (EHO 124), and claims that this superiority lies in the move away from quasi-transcendental forms of theorizing and towards new forms of writing, that give expression to privacy, fantasy and humour. The later Derrida privatizes his philosophical thinking, drops theory and gives free rein to fantasy. In an intriguing formulation, Rorty writes that Derrida 'privatizes the sublime, having learnt from the fate of his predecessors [i.e. Heidegger] that the public can never be more than beautiful' (CIS 125). Thus, on this view, in a text like *La carte postale*, Derrida does not resemble Heidegger so much as Proust, insofar as he is concerned less with the sublime ineffability of the word and more with the proliferation of beauty and the rearrangement of his memories. For Rorty, Derrida, 'has done for the history of philosophy what Proust did for his life story': he has achieved autonomy through art. The consequence of this developmental thesis is that Derrida's work has no ethical, political or public significance insofar as it has given up on the attempt to reconcile theoretically the public and the private. It is this claim that I want to challenge.

Is Rorty's Reading of Derrida Justified?

I want to direct two questions to Rorty's reading of Derrida: first, as to the validity of the developmental thesis, and second, as to whether deconstruction can be said to have no public utility. Let me say, however, that I think Rorty's reading of Derrida, especially his interpretation of *La carte postale* in *Contingency, Irony, Solidarity*, is an extremely strong reading that brings an honesty, humour and lightness of touch that are all-too infrequent in discussions of Derrida, and which also offers a plausible approach to Derrida's

more 'autobiographical' texts, like *Circonfession*.[18] Also, and this is where I
would part company with Gasché, I do not want to be drawn into a
transcendental defence of Derrida against Rorty's pragmatized deconstruction. I think this strategy is too 'reactive' (in Nietzsche's sense), where a
transcendental-philosophical defence of Derrida is itself a reaction to either
a 'literary' assimilation of deconstruction (in the work of Geoffrey Hartman,
Paul de Man and the Yale School) or to a Critical Theory-inspired critique
of Derrida (in the work of Habermas or Manfred Frank). Also, it sets up an
unhelpful opposition between the transcendental and the pragmatic, where
philosophy becomes identified solely with the former against the latter.

As we saw above, much of the force of Rorty's understanding of deconstruction turns on his developmental account of Derrida's work. The
question here is whether Derrida's early work is a false start and to what
extent Rorty is justified in periodizing Derrida's work into early and late,
particularly when the difference between early and late is only the matter of
a few years or so and when Derrida is, to say the least, still going strong.[19]
Can one really, with any plausibility, speak of a 'Derrida I' and a 'Derrida
II', in the same way as William Richardson interpreted Heidegger (a distinction that Heidegger himself sought to complicate)?[20] On the contrary,
I would claim that the difference between a text like *La voix et le phénomène*
and a text like *Glas* does not consist in any move from the public to the
private, but, rather, suggests a change in the mode of presentation of
Derrida's work, from a constative form of theorizing to a *performative* mode
of writing, or, in other terms, from meta-language to language.[21] Unlike
some (but by no means all) of Derrida's work from the 1960s, for example
the opening chapters of *De la grammatologie*, much of his work in the 1970s
is concerned less with formulating a theoretico-historico-interpretative
grid (a 'science' of grammatology) and more with deconstruction(s) as a
form of textual *enactment*, an event or series of events. Thus, the development of Derrida's work, if there is one, and this would have to be plotted
in some detail – and in my experience of reading Derrida, the closer one
looks the harder it is to find any substantial difference between earlier and
later work; I am always astonished by the extraordinary thematic continuity of Derrida's work and the persistence of his central concerns – would
not be found in any move from the public to the private, but from meta-
language to language, from constative to performative utterance, allowing
the performative constantly to overflow the constative.

And yet, writing now, nearly twenty-five years after the publication of
Glas, there is also a large issue as to how one is to understand Derrida's
more recent work, where the performative experiments of the 1970s have

not been continued at such length and where Derrida's work has, in my view, become dominated by the overwhelmingly *public* issue of *responsibility*, whether ethical, political, sexual, textual, legal or institutional. In order to address these issues, I would suggest – contentiously – that Derrida's style has become neither theoretical nor performative, but *quasi-phenomenological*. By this I mean that much of Derrida's recent work – his analyses of mourning, of the promise and the secret, of eating and sacrifice, of friendship and confession, of the gift and testimony – is concerned with the careful description and analysis of particular phenomena, in order to elucidate their deeply aporetic or undecidable structures. My contention here is that Derrida's work is moving towards a practice of deconstruction as a series of quasi-phenomenological micrologies that are concerned with the particular *qua* particular, that is to say, with the grain and enigmatic detail of everyday life.

This leads me to my second and more far-reaching question to Rorty's reading of Derrida, which arises as a consequence of his developmental thesis: namely, is it justified to claim that deconstruction has (or should have) no public significance, and can therefore have no ethical or political utility? In *The Ethics of Deconstruction*, I argued that Derridian deconstruction can and indeed should be understood as an ethical demand, provided one understands ethics in the particular and novel sense given to that word in the work of Emmanuel Levinas. Crudely stated, ethics for Levinas is defined as the calling into question of my freedom and spontaneity, that is to say, my subjectivity, by the other person (*autrui*). Ethics is here conceived, in the wake of Buber's I–thou relation (although Levinas is ultimately critical of Buber), in terms of an ethical *relation* between persons. What distinguishes an ethical relation from other relations (to oneself or to objects) is, Levinas claims, that it is a relation with that which cannot be comprehended or subsumed under the categories of the understanding. In Stanley Cavell's terms, it is the very unknowability of the other, the irrefutability of scepticism, that initiates a relation to the other based on acknowledgement and respect.[22] The other person stands in a relation to me that exceeds my cognitive powers, placing me in question and calling me to justify myself. Levinas's philosophical ambition is to subordinate claims to knowledge to claims to justice, or, in Kantian terms, to establish the primacy of practical reason (although, for Levinas, the ethical is the pre-rational foundation of the rational rather than the exemplification of reason). As Levinas is often given to write, *ethics is first philosophy*.

Although severely critical of Heidegger's philosophy after *Sein und Zeit* and his political myopia, Levinas shares his early critique of the theoreticism or intellectualism of Husserlian intentionality, where, it is claimed, the subject maintains an objectifying relation to the world mediated through representation: the worldly object is the *noema* of a *noesis*. As I argued in chapter 3, Levinas follows Heidegger's ontological undermining of the theoretical comportment towards the world (*Vorhandenheit*) and of the subject–object distinction that supports epistemology, by tracing intentionality back to a more fundamental stratum, namely, sentience or sensibility. Simply stated, Levinas shows how intentional consciousness is conditioned by *life*, by the material conditions of existence. His work offers *a material phenomenology of subjective life*, where the conscious subject of representation and intentionality is reduced to the sentient subject of sensibility. Levinas's phenomenological claim – and by 'phenomenology' Levinas means a methodological adherence to the spirit rather than the letter of Husserlian intentional analysis, that is to say, the description of the constitutive structures of naïve conscious life – is that the deep structure of subjective experience is always already engaged in a relation of responsibility or, better, responsivity to the other. The ethical relation takes place at the level of sensibility, not at the level of consciousness, and thus, in a way that recalls both Bentham's and Rousseau's criteria for ethical obligation mentioned above, it is in my pre-reflective sentient disposition towards the other's suffering that a basis for ethics and responsibility can be found.

What is the relation of this Levinasian account of ethics to the debate between Derrida and Rorty? First, with regard to Rorty, although he would doubtless criticize Levinas's claim that ethics is first philosophy as a neo-Kantian philosophical foundationalism, and although Levinas's qualified endorsement of Husserlian phenomenological method would sit rather uneasily with Rorty's pragmatism, there is room to ask how far apart Rorty and Levinas really are from each other. Are not Rorty's definition of liberalism and Levinas's definition of ethics essentially doing the same work, namely attempting to locate a source for moral and political obligation in a sentient disposition towards the other's suffering? Do they both not agree that cruelty is the worst thing that there is, and that, furthermore, this is the only social bond that we need?

Second, with regard to Derrida, I would like to make good a *rapprochement* between Levinas and Derrida by looking at one recent example from Derrida's work. My argument here can be more formally stated along the following lines: first, let us recall that Rorty defines the private as being concerned with 'idiosyncratic projects of self-overcoming', whereas the public is defined as 'having to do with the suffering of other human beings'. If I can make good the claim that deconstruction is ethical in the peculiarly

Levinasian sense identified above, then deconstruction would be concerned with the suffering of other human beings and would therefore qualify as public by Rorty's own criteria. Deconstruction could then have significant ethical and political consequences. If Rorty is a liberal, then, I would claim that Levinas and Derrida are also liberals – which perhaps begs the question as to the adequacy of Rorty's definition of liberalism.

The example I have in mind is the first half of Derrida's remarkable text on the question of justice, 'Force of Law: The "Mystical Foundation of Authority"'.[23] Derrida makes some remarkably provocative statements in this text; he writes: 'Justice in itself, if such a thing exists, outside or beyond law, is not deconstructible. No more than deconstruction itself, if such a thing exists. Deconstruction is justice' (pp. 14–15). Derrida's discussion proceeds from the distinction between law, which is deconstructible (and which, it is claimed, *must* be deconstructible if political progress is to be possible), and justice, which is not deconstructible, but is that in virtue of which deconstruction takes place. In a quasi-transcendental register, Derrida claims that justice is the undeconstructible condition of possibility for deconstruction, that 'nothing is more just than what I today call deconstruction' (p. 21). On the basis of references to Montaigne and Pascal (and even a rare allusion to Wittgenstein – p. 14), Derrida paradoxically defines justice as an experience of that which we are not able to experience, which is qualified as 'the mystical', 'the impossible' or 'aporia'. In Derrida's more habitual vocabulary, justice is an 'experience' of the undecidable. However, and this is crucial, such an undecidable experience of justice does not arise in some intellectual intuition or theoretical deduction, rather it always arises in relation to a particular entity, to the singularity of the other (p. 20). It is at this point (or, to be precise, at two points: p. 22 and p. 27) in the discussion that Derrida cites Levinas and employs the latter's conception of justice to illuminate his own account. In *Totality and Infinity*, justice defines and is defined by the ethical relation to the Other, 'la relation avec autrui – c'est à dire la justice' (p. 22); that is to say, justice arises in the particular and non-subsumptive relation to the Other, as a response to suffering that demands an infinite responsibility. Thus it can be seen that when Derrida is provoked into offering an illustration of the public significance of deconstruction by showing how it presupposes a conception of justice, he draws heavily from Levinas.

This allusion to Levinas seems unproblematic until one realizes that there are *two* conceptions of justice in Levinas. As Levinas points out in the 1987 Preface to the German translation of *Totalité et infini*, justice functions as a synonym for the ethical in the latter work, in just the way discussed by

Derrida.[24] However, in Levinas's later work, particularly *Autrement qu'être ou au-delà de l'essence*, justice is distinguished from the ethical relation, where Levinas argues that the question of justice arises when a third party arrives on the scene, obliging one to choose between competing ethical claims and reminding one that the ethical relation is always already situated in a specific socio-political context.[25] The fact that Derrida adopts an *ethical* and not a *political* concept of justice from Levinas does not mean, however, that the deconstructive account of justice is a-political. Derrida claims that it is linked to what he calls '*politicisation*' (p. 28), and as examples of this process he cites the Declarations of the Rights of Man and the abolition of slavery, that is to say, the emancipatory gains of classical liberalism. In a staggeringly blunt statement, Derrida writes: 'Nothing seems to me less outdated than the classical emancipatory ideal' (although we might want to ask: is Derrida's commitment to this emancipatory ideal necessarily a commitment to liber-alism, or might it not entail a more radical version of this ideal, one that one can be found, for example, in the socialist tradition?). Thus, the ethical conception of justice that drives the deconstructive enterprise and which is defined in terms of responsibility to the other would (Derrida, characteris-tically, adds 'perhaps' – p. 27) seem to be essentially connected to the pos-sibility of political reformation, transformation and progress, opening up a future of political possibilities.

To summarize, Derrida's claim here is that deconstruction is justice and justice is an 'experience' of the undecidable; that is to say, according to my interpretation, to be just is to recognize one's infinite responsibility before the singular other as something over which one cannot ultimately decide, as something that exceeds my cognitive powers. It is this 'experience' of justice that propels one forward into politics, that is to say, from undecidabil-ity to the decision, to what Derrida calls, following Kierkegaard, the mad-ness of the decision (p. 26).[26] Politics is the realm of the decision, of the organization and administration of the public realm, of the institution of law and policy. As I see it, the central aporia of deconstruction – an aporia that must not be avoided if any responsible political activity is to be undertaken – concerns the nature of this passage from undecidability to the decision, from the ethical 'experience' of justice to political action, to what we might call the moment of judgement. But how does this deconstruct-ive, ethical conception of justice translate into political judgement? Derrida insists that judgements have to be made and decisions have to be taken, provided it is understood that to be responsible they must pass through an experience of the undecidable. But my *critical* question to Derrida would be: *what* decisions are taken, *which* judgements are made?[27]

For Derrida, no political form can or should attempt to embody justice; the undecidability of justice must always lie outside the public realm, guiding, criticizing and deconstructing that realm, but never being instantiated within it. From a deconstructive perspective, the greatest danger in politics is the threat of totalitarianism, or what Jean-Luc Nancy calls 'immanentism',[28] in all of its most recent and terrifying disguises: neo-fascism, nationalism, ethnocentrism, theocracy. Totalitarianism is premised upon the identification of the political and the social and would claim that a particular political form and hence a particular state, community or territory embodies justice, that justice is immanent to the body politic. A deconstructive approach to politics, based upon the radical separation of justice from law, and the non-instantiability of the former within the latter, leads to what one might call the dis-embodiment of justice, where no state, community or territory could be said to embody justice. One might say that the 'experience' of justice is that of an absolute alterity or transcendence that guides politics without being fully present in the public realm. If we look back to Derrida's first published work on Husserl, we might say that justice is an 'Idea in the Kantian sense', an infinitely deferred ethico-teleological postulate that continually escapes the horizon of presence and the very idea of a horizon.[29]

If it is now asked what political form best maintains this dis-embodiment of justice, then I take it that Derrida's response would be *democracy*: not a democracy that claims to instantiate justice here and now, not an apologetics for actually existing liberal democracy (but neither a dismissal of the latter), but a democracy guided by the *futural* or *projective* transcendence of justice – what Derrida calls *une démocratie à venir*. To my mind, this would seem to commit Derrida to a Utopian and critical politics that does not differ substantially from the Deweyan tradition that seeks to link pragmatism to radical democracy – the very political tradition in whose lineage Rorty claims to stand. However, if my argument is not entirely aberrant, if Rorty and Derrida share similar public and political aspirations (even though they are quite differently articulated), then why is Rorty unable to see in Derrida a powerful political ally?

Conclusion

I hope to have shown that Derrida both conceives of himself as a public thinker, whose work has serious ethical commitments and political consequences, and that he can only be so understood on the basis of Rorty's own criteria for distinguishing the public from the private and liberalism from irony. The undeconstructible condition of possibility for deconstruction is a commitment to justice, defined in terms of an ethical relation to the other, a response to suffering that provokes an infinite responsibility and the attempt to minimize cruelty. Such an ethical conception of justice can never be fully instantiated in the public realm, nor can it be divorced from the latter; rather, justice regulates public space, making politics critical, Utopian and radically democratic.

In terms of the theme of this chapter, deconstruction and pragmatism, I hope it has been established that Rorty's picture of Derrida as only a private ironist falls rather short of the truth. Although, as I admitted at the outset, it might be valid to interpret concepts like '*différance*' in terms of a pragmatist notion of context, thereby showing the contingency of language, self and world, it is by now hopefully clear that what motivates the practice of deconstruction is an ethical conception of justice, that is, by Rorty's criteria, public and liberal. Thus, deconstruction is pragmatist, *but it is not pragmatist all the way down*. At the basis of deconstruction is a non-pragmatist (or at least non-Rortian) foundational commitment to justice as something that cannot be relativized, or at least cannot be relativized for 'we liberals'. Of course the consequence of my conclusion is that Derrida is still seeking to fulfil the classical philosophical project of reconciling the public and the private, believed by Rorty to be redundant. If deconstruction is justice, then this commitment to justice *goes all the way down*: in private self-creation as well as public responsibility.

However, the intriguing counter-balancing question that this chapter has thrown up is whether Rorty's pragmatism is in fact pragmatist *all the way down*; or whether its commitment to liberalism – in terms of a non-relativizable claim about the susceptibility of human beings to suffering and the need to minimize cruelty – transgresses the limits of Rorty's pragmatism. Can pragmatism maintain a genuine and non-cynical commitment to liberalism and still remain pragmatist *all the way down*?

Notes

1. First published in *European Journal of Philosophy*, vol. 2, no. 1, 1994, pp. 1–21. Reprinted with a response from Richard Rorty, in Chantal Mouffe, ed., *Deconstruction and Pragmatism*, London and New York: Routledge, 1996, pp. 19–40.

2. Might not Derrida also ironize about Rorty's conception of the history of philosophy, what Rorty calls 'the Plato–Kant succession': a vision of the history of philosophy that is just as totalizing, unilateral and univocal as Heidegger's, and which reads irony out of the pre-Kantian tradition (but what about Socrates? And

can we always take Descartes at his word?). From what vantage point does Rorty view history? If history is a series of successive metaphors and displaced final vocabularies, a history whose metaphoricity is now grasped fully for the first time, then it must be asked, from where and from what final vocabulary do we view that history? Is Rorty's not a God's-eye view on the impossibility of any God's-eye view?

3. With regard to Rorty's earlier work, particularly *Philosophy and the Mirror of Nature*, let me venture a couple of professions of mixed faith: firstly, I agree with Rorty's critique of the mind as the mirror of nature and hence with his critique of representationalism, epistemology and hence philosophy itself, if the latter is conceived in narrowly epistemological terms. My only caveat here is that I would arrive at the same conclusion as Rorty through Heidegger's critique of epistemology and Neo-Kantianism in *Sein und Zeit*. In my view, however, this would still leave open the possibility of a form of philosophizing, exemplified in the phenomenology of the early Heidegger, the later Merleau-Ponty and Levinas, that would be critical of the slide in Rorty's work from the critique of epistemology into naturalism (on this point, see Jay Bernstein, 'De-Divinization and the Vindication of Everyday Life: Reply to Rorty', *Tijdschrift voor Filosofie*, vol. 54, no. 4, 1992, pp. 668–92). Secondly, I am very sympathetic to Rorty's attempted de-divinization of the world, where a Davidsonian account of language, a Nietzschean/Freudian account of the self and culture, and a Darwinian account of nature all conspire to produce a relation to the world conceived as a web or tissue of contingencies. Yet, it seems to me that the outcome of the recognition of contingency might not be a move towards naturalism, but rather towards *romanticism*, namely the romantic victory of poetry over philosophy announced in *Contingency, Irony, Solidarity* (CIS 40), where the triumph of metaphor and self-creation over literalness and discovery leads to a romantic demand for a poeticization of the world, a re-enchantment of the world as a web of contingencies.

4. See C. B. Macpherson, *The Real World of Democracy*, New York: Oxford University Press, 1966, see esp. pp. 1–11.

5. See H. Putnam, *Renewing Philosophy*, Cambridge Mass.: Harvard University Press, 1992, p. 199.

6. See Warren's contribution to the 'Review Symposium on Richard Rorty', *History of the Human Sciences*, vol. 3, no. 1, pp. 101–22; see esp. pp. 118–20.

7. Ibid., pp. 104–8.

8. In this regard, see Paul Virilio, *L'écran du désert*, Paris: Galilée, 1991; and Michael Shapiro, 'That Obscure Object of Violence: Logistics and Desire in the Gulf War', in D. Campbell and M. Dillon, eds, *The Political Subject of Violence*, Manchester: Manchester University Press, 1993.

9. For a related line of criticism, with reference to Rorty's conception of autonomy, see J. Caputo, 'On not Circumventing the Quasi-Transcendental: The Case of Rorty and Derrida', in G. Madison, ed., *Working Through Derrida*, Evanston: Northwestern University Press, 1993, see esp. pp. 165–6.

10. This view is powerfully argued for by Robert Brandom, 'Freedom and Constraint by Norms', *American Philosophical Quarterly*, vol. 16, no. 3, 1979, pp. 187–96. In this connection, see Rorty's discussion of Brandom in 'Representation, Social Practice and Truth' in Rorty, ORT 151–61.

11. Rousseau, *Discours sur l'origine de l'inegalite parmi les hommes*, Paris: Garnier, 1962, p. 37.

12. Bentham, *An Introduction to the Principles of Morals and Legislation*, J. H. Burns and H. L. A. Hart, eds, London: Athlone, 1970, p. 283.

13. See Derrida, 'Violence et métaphysique', in *L'écriture et la différence*, Paris: Seuil, 1967, p. 224.

14. Rorty repeatedly cites sentences from the closing paragraphs of Derrida's 1968 paper 'La différance', in *Marges de la philosophie*, Paris: Minuit 1972, pp. 28–9, where Derrida claims that there is no unique name or name for Being, and that this must be thought without Heideggerian nostalgia or hope (see Rorty, CP 103, CIS 122 and EHO 95).

15. See Rodolphe Gasché, *The Tain of the Mirror. Derrida and the Philosophy of Reflection*, Cambridge Mass.: Harvard University Press, 1986.

16. See Tugendhat, *Selbstbewusstsein und Selbstbestimmung*, Frankfurt am Main: Suhrkamp, 1979. For example, Tugendhat writes, 'alles intentionale Bewusstsein überhaupt ist propositional' (p. 20).

17. For Gasché's critique of Tugendhat's position, where he argues that to restrict oneself to propositional truth is to deprive oneself of the possibility of thinking the foundations of the propositional, see Gasché, *The Tain of the Mirror*, pp. 76–7.

18. See G. Bennington and J. Derrida, *Jacques Derrida*, Paris: Seuil, 1991.

19. It would not be difficult, on the basis of textual evidence, to make the distinction between earlier and later Derrida begin to look absurd. For example, I take it that most of the essays from *Marges de la philosophie* (1972) would be judged by Rorty to belong to the style of the early Derrida, whilst portions of *Dissemination* (also 1972) and *Glas* (only two years later in 1974) would be classified as later Derrida.

20. See Heidegger's *Vorwort* to Richardson's *Through Phenomenology to Thought*, The Hague: Nijhoff, 1963, pp. xxii–xxiii.

21. I owe this thought to conversations with Gasché.

22. See 'Skepticism and the Problem of Others', in Cavell, *The Claim of Reason*, Oxford and New York: Oxford University Press, 1979, pp. 327–496.

23. See Derrida, 'The Force of Law: The "Mystical Foundation of Authority"', in D. Cornell, M. Rosenfeld and D. G. Carlson, eds, *Deconstruction and the Possibility of Justice*, London and New York: Routledge, 1992, pp. 3–67. All subsequent page references have been inserted into the text.

24. Levinas, *Totalité et infini*, Paris: Livre de Poche, 1990, p. 11.

25. Levinas, *Autrement qu'être ou au-delà de l'essence*, The Hague: Nijhoff, 1974, pp. 199–207.

26. A quote which also provided the epigraph to Derrida's celebrated essay on Foucault, see *L'écriture et la différence*, p. 51.

27. Such a question opens the large and difficult issue of specifying the precise relation between undecidability and the decision, justice and judgement, and ethics and politics in Derrida's work; which is, to say the least, a problem of which he is acutely aware, and which might be said to dominate much of his recent work. I take up this issue in more detail in chapters 7 and 12.

28. See J.-L. Nancy, *La communauté désœuvrée*, Paris: Christian Bourgois, 1990.

29. Derrida, *Introduction à L'origine de la géométrie*, Paris: Presses Universitaires de France, 1962.

Abbreviations

PMN – Richard Rorty, *Philosophy and the Mirror of Nature*, Princeton: Princeton University Press, 1980.

CP – Richard Rorty, *The Consequences of Pragmatism*, Minneapolis: University of Minnesota Press, 1982.

CIS – Richard Rorty, *Contingency, Irony, Solidarity*, Cambridge: Cambridge University Press, 1989.

ORT – Richard Rorty, *Objectivism, Relativism and Truth. Philosophical Papers Volume 1*, Cambridge: Cambridge University Press, 1991.

EHO – Richard Rorty, *Essays on Heidegger and Others. Philosophical Papers Volume 2*, Cambridge: Cambridge University Press, 1991.

HDF – Richard Rorty, 'Habermas, Derrida and the Functions of Philosophy', in *Truth and Progress. Philosophical Papers Volume 3*, Cambridge: Cambridge University Press, 1998.

5

Metaphysics in the Dark:
A Response to Richard Rorty and
Ernesto Laclau[1]

> A metaphysician in the dark, twanging
> An instrument, twanging a wiry string that gives
> Sounds passing through sudden rightnesses, wholly
> Containing the mind, below which it cannot descend,
> Beyond which it has no will to rise.
>
> Wallace Stevens, 'Of Modern Poetry'[2]

In a text published in 1996, 'Response to Simon Critchley', Richard Rorty took issue with my interpretation of his work and in particular with what I said about his understanding of Derrida's work. It is clear that the stakes of this debate are not simply philological, but touch on much larger issues of ethics, politics and the possibility of philosophy itself.[3] Before turning to the specifics of our disagreement, permit me to restate the basic claim I was seeking to advance. With regard to the interpretation of Derrida's work, I sought to show how, on the basis of Rorty's own definitional criteria, Derrida is a public thinker whose work has serious and, I believe, profound ethical commitments and political consequences. On my reading, the undeconstructible condition of possibility for deconstruction is *justice*, which I seek to interpret in Levinasian terms as a relation to the other, a response to suffering or an attempt to limit cruelty and humiliation; a relation that might be described with the adjective *ethical*. On my view, then, Rorty's picture of Derrida as a private ironist falls somewhat short of the truth.

This line of interpretation can be supported, I believe, with reference to Derrida's remarks in *Deconstruction and Pragmatism*, by three main points:

1. Derrida's refusal of the public–private distinction, where literature would cut across this distinction by being both *le droit à tout dire* and

intimately bound up with the secret; that is, as being both irreducibly public and that which refuses publicity, what we might think of as the depolit-
icizing condition for politicization. For Derrida, there is a historical and
systematic connection between literature and democracy. Literature is the
public articulation of a sphere of private and intimate experience, on the
basis of which 'the realm of the political can be and remain open'.[4]

2. Derrida's comments on the messianic as an apriori structure that, as
he puts it, 'belongs to all language', as that promisory, performative or illocutionary dimension to our speech acts, which, as he describes it in an interview, is 'the universal dimension of experience'.[5] Derrida writes:

> There is no language without the performative dimension of the promise, the
> minute I open my mouth I am in the promise. Even if I say that 'I don't believe
> in truth' or whatever, the minute I open my mouth there is a 'believe me' in
> play. And this 'I promise you that I am speaking the truth' is a messianic apriori,
> a promise which, even if it is not kept, even if one knows that it cannot be kept,
> takes place and *qua* promise is messianic.[6]

It is difficult to see how such a claim could be contained within the
limits of Rorty's neo-pragmatist nominalism. Indeed, Derrida's linking of
the messianic apriori as a structure of experience to what he calls 'the
discourse of emancipation', both gets him off the hook of any claim to
Utopianism and suggests the possibility of an unexpected rapprochement
with Habermas's understanding of the structure of communicative action.
The whole Derridian discussion of the promise as that illocutionary dimension of speech acts whose denial would lead one into a performative contradiction has obvious Habermasian echoes. And despite Habermas's moral
cognitivism and his insistence upon the symmetrical nature of intersubjectivity, it is clear at the very least that there is work to be done here and that
possibly Habermas and Derrida share more with each other than they both
share with Rorty, especially when it comes to political matters.

3. Most importantly, my line of interpretation can be supported by
Derrida's remarks on the need for infinite responsibility. I quote at length:

> I believe that we cannot give up on the concept of infinite responsibility, as
> Rorty seemed to do in his remarks, when he spoke of Levinas as a blind spot
> in my work. I would say, for Levinas and for myself, that if you give up the
> infinitude of responsibility, there is no responsibility. It is because we act and we
> live in infinitude that the responsibility with regard to the other is irreducible.
> If responsibility was not infinite, if every time that I have to take an ethical or
> political decision with regard to the other, this was not infinite, then I would

not be able to engage myself in an infinite debt with regard to each singularity. I owe myself infinitely to each and every singularity. If responsibility was not infinite, you could not have moral and political problems. There are only moral and political problems, and everything that follows from this, from the moment when responsibility is not limitable.[7]

To summarize rapidly, to my mind the above passage describes the ethical (or quasi- or proto-ethical, if you like) moment in deconstruction. It is an experience of infinite responsibility, which can be qualified as undeconstructible, unconditional, apriori and universal. But infinite responsibility only arises within the context of a singular experience; that is, within the empirical event of a concrete speech act, the performative dimension of the promise. However, and here we begin to see the limits to any rapprochement with Habermas, what takes place in the concrete linguistic event of the promise is a relation to an other, what Derrida calls a singularity, which is an experience of *infinite indebtedness*. Thus, the messianic apriori describes the structure of intersubjectivity in terms of an *asymmetrical* obligation that I could never meet, to which I would never be equal. It has been argued by Axel Honneth, and I am inclined to agree with him, that the symmetrical structure of intersubjectivity within Habermasian discourse ethics requires an additional moment of asymmetry, something that, for him, can be achieved through Winnicottian object-relations psychoanalysis or a naturalistic reconstruction of Levinasian ethics.[8]

For Derrida, it is on the basis of this infinite responsibility that one is propelled into moral and political problems, into the realm of the decision. It is important to point out here that this notion of the undeconstructible – justice, the messianic apriori or whatever – does not function like the Moral Law in Kant, namely as the basis for a decision procedure in ethics, a categorical imperative mechanism in the light of which one might propose and test specific maxims. On the contrary, *it is because responsibility is infinite that the decision is always undecidable*. It is because the field opened by deconstruction is limitless that no decision or choice made within this field can ever be thought of as wholly 'good', 'right' or 'adequate'. In politics, it is always a question of the least bad. Each choice I might make in favour of *x* might work against *y* and *z*, not to mention *a*, *b*, and *c*. For Derrida, it is because responsibility is infinite that the field of undecidability is not a moment to be overcome or left behind. It is because of infinite responsibility that there is what Derrida calls *politicisation*; that is, an occurrence of the decision which is ungrounded, incalculable and – to a greater or lesser extent – unjust. There could never be a wholly just decision, and this is why all decisions are political. Thus, the infinite responsibility or messianic apriori that opens in and as the singular experience of the other – whether human, animal, vegetable or mineral – does not close down or limit the field of aporia and undecidability, rather, it expands that field because the other always exceeds the context within which the encounter takes place. The ethical moment is not the dilution of aporia, but rather its exacerbation. Thus, although according to me there is a moment of formal universality in Derrida's work, which constitutes something like an ethical criterion – what I see in chapter 12 as not so much a *Faktum der Vernunft* as a *Faktum des Anderen* – political decisions must always be singular and context-sensitive acts of invention.

Now, it is precisely this notion of infinite responsibility, this Levinasian moment in deconstruction, that both Richard Rorty and Ernesto Laclau have difficulties with, for quite different reasons. Rorty's recently published *Achieving our Country. Leftist Thought in Twentieth-Century America* – despite its admirable ambition to reinvigorate a reformist, hopeful Left that would be an agent within and not a mere spectator upon American society – sadly wastes much of its energy tilting irritatingly at the windmills of the so-called 'Foucauldian Left', and Rorty's demand for American national pride is only a cigarette paper away from a rather unpalatable chauvinism of American exceptionalism. In it he remarks:

> The notion of 'infinite responsibility', formulated by Emmanuel Levinas and sometimes deployed by Derrida . . . may be useful to some of us in our individual quests for private perfection. When we take up our public responsibilities, however, the infinite and the unrepresentable are merely nuisances.[9]

I am happy to be a nuisance to Rorty and will continue to be so presently, but permit me a couple of words on Laclau. In chapter 7, I attempt to link the work of Derrida and Laclau and their respective logics of deconstruction and hegemony because I find this the most productive way of broaching the question of the relation between deconstruction and politics, namely the relation between undecidability and the decision. It is this question that is the *Brennpunkt* of Laclau's rigorous and interesting intervention in *Deconstruction and Pragmatism*.[10] His argument can be summarized in the following three steps:

1. Deconstruction has widened the field of structural undecidability in terms of which basic social and political categories – like toleration, power and representation, but equally race, nation and gender – can be understood. A deconstructive discourse analysis can show how the legitimating discourse of a particular regime – Apartheid say – is based on a set of presuppositions

whose status is ultimately undecidable. In this sense, deconstruction can be employed to show how the terrain of the social does not attain closure, the sort of closure or achievement imagined by Rorty's allusion to James Baldwin's notion of 'achieving our country',[11] but is an ever incomplete, undecidable structure. In this sense, Laclauian discourse analysis is powerfully analogous to what we might call a deconstructive genealogy, where the apparent stabilization of a society – what appears to be the natural order of things – is shown to be the consequence of the operation of hegemonic articulations, traces of power which are always political.

2. On the basis of this understanding of the hegemonic institution of the social, Laclau argues that the field is cleared for a theory of the decision taken on an undecidable terrain. In more common parlance, one might say that once the political origin of the social has been grasped through a genealogical deconstruction, then one is in a position to reactivate a fully *political* theory without the illusory comfort of social sedimentation, a sedimentation implicit within all appeals to a concept of *Lebenswelt*, Habermasian or otherwise.

3. However, by virtue of the fact that for Laclau all structures, including social structures, are undecidable at the level of their categorial articulation and are therefore incapable of closure, political decisions cannot ultimately be grounded on anything external to themselves. For Laclau, we cannot base political decisions on the basis of a prior programme, for example the Marxism of the Second International, or in the light of the universality of a rule or some sort of regulative idea, for example any metaphysical or post-metaphysical reworking of the Kantian moral law. To do so, and this is where Laclau follows Carl Schmitt, would be to engage in a form of depoliticization. Therefore, the instant of the political decision is madness.

The point at issue, then, is that of the mediation between undecidability and the decision, an issue which Laclau interestingly pursues through what he calls 'the absent fullness of the subject' as the space of a contingent, provisional and ever-revisable decision.[12] Laclau then suggests that one possible line of mediation between undecidability and the decision is with reference to a 'primordial ethical experience, in the Levinasian sense'.[13] This is the position that Laclau ascribes to my work, a position which, for him, leaves the question of deconstruction and politics in an impasse because he cannot see in what sense an ethical injunction can work here other than as a universal rule that precedes and governs any decision. Permit me a couple of words of clarification and self-defence:

1. As indicated in my opening remarks above, the injunction that governs deconstruction, whether one qualifies it as ethical, quasi-ethical or

whatever, is an unconditional, apriori, universal dimension of experience – the messianic – which is *undeconstructible*. Thus, and this is the point I want to emphasize, the place of the ethical moment in deconstruction is *not* that which mediates the passage from undecidability to the decision, but rather is that which *governs* the whole field of undecidability opened by deconstruction. I agree that the question of the passage from undecidability to the decision is political rather than ethical – every decision is political. But, the ethical moment in deconstruction is the undeconstructibility of justice that precedes the passage from the ethical to the political (it is interesting to note that Laclau does not deal with the issue of the undeconstructible, and I ask myself what place he could find for this notion).

2. This messianic experience of justice as the undeconstructible arises, as I also indicated above, in an experience of singularity, namely the infinite responsibility that arises in the relation to the other, however the latter is understood. Thus, the experience of singularity as that illocutionary, promisory dimension to our linguistic activity produces a structure that belongs to, or accompanies, all language, and is therefore universal. As such, the messianic apriori cannot be reduced to context, and it refuses the pragmatist reduction of ethicality to context, which is a point on which Laclau seems happy to follow Rorty, despite his criticism of the latter's parochialism. Now, the insistence on the ultimate non-determinability or non-saturatability of context has been an explcit theme of Derrida's work since the 1971 paper 'Signature, Event, Context'. What is perhaps clearer now, and what Derrida's 1988 'Afterword to *Limited Inc.*' eloquently shows, is that although there exists nothing outside context, although it is limitless, context is motivated by an unconditional appeal or affirmation – a Nietzschean 'yes, yes' or, better, 'a "yes" to emancipation'[14] – that Derrida, somewhat reluctantly, describes in terms that recall Kant's categorical imperative.[15]

3. These clarifications of the messianic apriori or infinite responsibility as the ethical moment in deconstruction, an ethical moment that is not itself a norm but which provokes the subject into the context-specific *invention* of political norms, allows a question of more general import to be raised. To put it crudely, what is the difference between hegemony and *democratic* hegemony for Laclau? At the level of genealogical deconstruction, the theory of hegemony shows the irreducibly political institution of the social: social sedimentation is simply the masking of the operations of power, contingency and antagonism. That is to say, the fixing of the meaning of social relations is the consequence of a decision, and every decision is political. However, Laclau's and Mouffe's work famously and rightly also invokes notions of 'the democratic revolution' and 'radical democracy' as

the consequence of the genealogical critique of Marxism. That is, the recognition of contingency, antagonism and power does not lead to political
pessimism or the collapse of the public–private distinction, but is, rather,
as Laclau puts it, the condition for a 'new militancy and new optimism'.[16]
But if all decisions are political, then in virtue of what is there a difference
between democratizing and non-democratizing forms of decisions? It seems
to me that there are two ways of answering this question, one normative
and the other factual, but both of which leave Laclau sitting uncomfortably
on the horns of a dilemma. On the one hand, one might say that democratic decisions are more participatory, egalitarian, pluralistic or directed
towards promoting the other's freedom. But if one grants any such version
of this thesis then one has admitted some normative claim – and hence
depoliticization – into the theory of hegemony. On the other hand, if one
simply says that the theory of hegemony and radical democracy is the
description of a fact, i.e. that democratization is simply taking place, or
that freedom is a consequence of existing social dislocations, then one risks
collapsing any *critical* difference between the theory of hegemony and that
which this theory purports to describe. If the theory of hegemony is simply
the description of a positively existing state of affairs, then one risks empty-
ing the theory of any critical function, that is, of leaving open any space
between things as they are and things as they might otherwise be. If the
theory of hegemony is the description of a factual state of affairs, then it
risks identification and complicity with the logic of contemporary capitalist
societies. My view is that there is the risk of a kind of 'normative deficit' in
the theory of hegemony, a deficit that can be made good on the basis of
another understanding of the logic of deconstruction. That is, if Laclau is
justified in his claim that what deconstruction lacks in its thinking of the
political is a theory of hegemony, then this needs to be balanced by the
second claim that what the theory of hegemony can learn from deconstruction is the kind of messianic, ethical injunction to infinite responsibility.

Let me now turn in more detail to Rorty's response to my paper. On
a first listening or reading, Rorty's remarks on deconstruction and pragmatism and his responses to Laclau and myself seem to restate implacably
the interpretation of Derrida's work given in *Contingency, Irony, Solidarity*.
However, on closer inspection, I think important modifications in Rorty's
position can be noted, modifications that can also be tracked in Rorty's
paper on Bennington's commentary on Derrida.[17]

As I stated above, my main claim was to show the inadequacy of Rorty's
belief that Derrida should be understood as a private ironist, whose work
had no public, ethical or political significance. However, I argued that this

claim was premised upon a certain picture of Derrida's work, what I called in my paper the 'developmental thesis', where the reason for choosing Rorty's view of Derrida over that of Gasché, say, is found in the fact that, in works like *Glas* and *La carte postale*, Derrida appears to abandon the theoretical ambitions of his early work, the 'quasi-professional noises' of 'a young philosophy professor', in favour of private irony devoted to the business of self-creation. So, to no small extent, the hermeneutic plausibility of Rorty's interpretation of Derrida depends on the tenability of the developmental thesis. However, from the first lines of his response to me, it is clear that he is prepared to abandon this thesis: 'I agree with Simon Critchley that I have, in the past, made too much of the difference between earlier and later Derrida . . . The more one reads either Heidegger or Derrida, the more continuities between the earlier and later writings appear.'[18] Now, if the developmental thesis is abandoned, then how exactly does the claim for Derrida as a private ironist still stand? And yet, this claim would also seem to have been subtly modified in Rorty's interventions. But before looking at this question, let me take a step back.

Rorty writes: 'I have trouble with the specifically Levinasian strains in his [i.e. Derrida's] thought. In particular, I am unable to connect Levinas's pathos of the infinite with ethics and politics.'[19] As my response should already have shown, Derrida cannot give up on the notion of infinite responsibility because it is in virtue of this that there are, for him, moral and political problems. On a Derridian view, if you give up the infinitude of responsibility, then the moral and political realm risks contracting into an untroubled, uncritical complacency. I think this is what Laclau means by the danger of parochialism within pragmatism, a parochialism that becomes worryingly explicit in Rorty's belief in the need for American national pride in 'achieving our country'. For my part, I think this explains why Rorty feels able to express the very American sentiment, 'Neither my child nor my country is very much like a Levinasian other.'[20] Indeed, and this is precisely the problem! In Pascalian terms, when I say, 'this is my country, my child, my place in the sun', the usurpation of the whole world begins. When the infinitude of ethics contracts into the finite space of an *ethos* – a site, a plot, a space for the sacred, 'the country of Whitman's and Dewey's dreams'[21] – then the very worst becomes possible. I admit that ethics without *ethos* or, better, without a relation to a plurality of *ethoi*, is empty, and this is a weakness of Levinas's work, a weakness that runs like an open wound through his exaggerated polemics against Heidegger and his inability to criticize Israel as a nation-state. However, Rorty's identification of *ethos* with the territory of the nation misses one of the crucial lessons of

Derrida's work, namely its persistent deconstruction of the concept of the frontier, the nation and territory. If there is a deconstructive politics, then it is *de-territorialized*, which is something that Derrida tries to capture with his notion of The New International.

For Rorty, ethics is what we need when 'we face a choice between two irreconcilable actions'. Of course, this is not what Levinas means by ethics, where, as I have claimed, he provides a material phenomenology of inter-subjective experience whose ultimate structures can be (but they *need* not be) described with the adjective 'ethical'.[22] For Levinas, as for Derrida and Laclau, the sphere of choice and decision is political rather than ethical, it is the realm of political justice. If, however, for the sake of argument, we accept Rorty's account of ethics then it would appear, interestingly, that he no longer believes that Derrida's work has no ethical, political or public significance. Rorty writes that reading Derrida, like reading Proust or Dewey, can make a significant difference to our descriptions of ourselves and our projects, but he qualifies this by adding that one should not assign too much political significance to Derrida's work.[23] These remarks can be extended with reference to Rorty's comments on humanism, where he interprets Derrida's remarks about *la démocratie à venir* as sharing Dewey's and Mill's 'utopian social hope'. For Rorty, then, Derrida is a thinker who belongs to what he would probably call the *sentimental* side of Western democracy. Although, for reasons I hope to have shown, I find this an inadequate understanding of Derrida, my immediate point here is to show that Rorty's response to me represents a subtle but important shift in his assessment of Derrida insofar as he is willing to see his work as having valid ethical significance, although its political utility is limited. As a separate argument, I would want to question the utility of Rorty's notion of utility, which risks reducing politics to the business of state administration and social engineering.

In the conclusion to his response, I think that Rorty is right to suggest that the big difference between him and myself is 'straightforwardly polit-ical rather than philosophical'.[24] At its crudest, Rorty thinks that we do not require a critique of liberal society and I think that we do. Furthermore, I would argue that the measure of any society that calls itself liberal is its capacity for critique, for encouraging citizens, through the education pro-cess and the to and fro of cultural and public life, to take up the standpoint of reflective critique towards their social and political practices, a reflective critique indexed to emancipation. On my view, deconstruction offers an exemplary version of such a reflective, emancipatory critique. Without this capacity for critique, neo-pragmatism risks collapsing into what I called in my paper 'a (re)descriptive apologetics for the inequality, intolerance, exploitation and disenfranchisement within actually existing liberal society'.[25] We do not, as Rorty suggests we do, simply require 'more liberal societies', pleasant as that might be for some of us, for the simple reason that such a view would exempt liberal societies from critique, as if liberalism were indeed the end of history. Rather, what is required is that democracy be driven by a concern for justice, an infinite responsibility, a formal universality, that arises in a singular experience or in the experience of indebtedness towards a specific singularity, and which is the condition (but not a recipe) for politicization. In my view, political decisions have to be invented in relation to a conception of justice that is never integrable or presentable within the institutions and practices of a given society.[26] There is no just society, no just decision and justice can never be done; which does not mean that the demand for justice should be given up, but precisely the reverse. This is what I meant in my paper by the disembodiment of justice, where no state, nation or territory could be said to embody justice, and where all claims to 'achieving our country' have to be abandoned in the name of justice. As I see it, the difference between Rorty and myself is essentially the difference between a pragmatized and parochial liberalism and a critical and emancipatory politics driven by a non-territorial conception of justice, what I call below 'deterritorialized democratization' (see chapter 12). Such a view still requires, *contra* Rorty, both '*Ideologiekritik* and . . . the romantic notion of the philosopher'.[27]

In my paper, I raised a critical worry about the cogency of an antifoundationalist liberalism. I suggested that Rorty's pragmatism might not be pragmatic *all the way down* and that its commitment to liberalism transgresses the limits that he sets for his pragmatism. My critical question here is simple: if Rorty defines liberalism in terms of a claim about the need to minimize cruelty, reduce humiliation, or be responsive to suffering, then what is the status of this claim? More particularly, can this claim be relativized? And more sharply, is cruelty something about which liberals can be ironic? I think not. But the consequence of such questions is that the recognition of cruelty or suffering as the ethical basis for Rorty's liberalism seems to involve an appeal to an essential, foundational fact about human beings, namely that we are the sort of beings who respond to the other's suffering, in a way that recalls Rousseau's notion of compassion as a pre-social, pre-rational, sentient disposition that is common to all human beings. But if this claim is plausible, then doesn't it sit rather uneasily with the general drift of Rorty's intentions? Despite Rorty's claims to irony and the ubiquity of contingency, is he not in fact attempting to base moral obligation and political practice upon a foundational claim about human susceptibility to humiliation, upon a recognition of the other's suffering? And even if one were to relativize this claim and argue that only 'we liberals' recognize the avoidance of cruelty as the basis for morals and politics, and that such recognition is a product of a particular – and therefore contingent – social and political history, does it not nevertheless remain true that the claim has the status of a non-relativizable universal for 'we liberals', with our set of 'we-intentions'?

Unsurprisingly, Rorty quickly rebuts this argument, claiming that

> I do not see the point of delving down to the roots of the difference between people who care about others' suffering and those who don't . . . Maybe it's acculturation in some people and genes in others. I don't see why this should matter.[28]

However, this misses my point. Of course it is clear that Rorty is not *trying* to locate a source for moral obligation in an abhorrence to cruelty, understood as a universal feature of human behaviour. My worry is rather about the coherence of his position, namely that if cruelty is something about which liberals cannot be ironic, then the attempt to diminish suffering must have the status of a non-relativizable universal, if only for 'we liberals'. This is why a pragmatist liberalism cannot be pragmatic *all the way down*. However, a wider point can be made here, for surely research into the sources of our moral intuitions *does* matter and Rorty's remark is simply flippant. If one thinks of the work of moral psychologists like Nietzsche, Freud or Adorno, or for example of the Oliners' study into the nature of altruism with specific reference to the behaviour of rescuers of Jews in the Second World War, then to my mind it does matter what sort of account we can give of our moral intuitions, especially when those intuitions lead to hatred, cruelty, suffering and murder. In short, what Rorty is disregarding is the whole field of *social pathologies* and the possibility of empirical research into certain deformations of subjectivity that have occurred in history, and which continue to reoccur with depressing regularity. It is not clear to me that the implementation of liberal political structures, combined with what Rorty blithely calls 'affluence and security'[29] will be sufficent – they were hardly sufficent in the case of the Oklahoma bombings.[30]

However, I cannot finish this response without discussing Rorty's 'ultimate weapon' against me, namely that my philosophical attitudes strike him as *metaphysical*. For Rorty, the metaphysician is the person who believes that there is a 'Right Context' (Rorty's capitalization) and that consequently the search for 'ultimate sources of this, and indefeasible presuppositions of that' is valid.[31] Rorty goes on to suggest that I believe that moral seriousness requires us to conduct such a metaphysical search. Well, am I a metaphysician? In a word, as Laurence Sterne would say, 'Yes and No'. I take it that one of the most important lessons of Derrida's early thinking – and here he follows Heidegger – is that our relationship to the metaphysical tradition is caught in a double bind. That is, any attempt either to enclose oneself within the metaphysical tradition by postulating some new thesis on Being, or to leave metaphysics behind in some move to post-metaphysical thinking, is equally doomed to failure and is a candidate for deconstruction. I take it that this is the situation that Derrida describes as 'the closure of metaphysics', a crucial notion because it permits one to undermine any formalist understanding of deconstruction by situating it in relation to a specific historical or epochal conjuncture, namely the post-Heideggerian understanding of the philosophical tradition.[32]

I see the closure of metaphysics as the double recognition that the metaphysical tradition is theoretically exhausted with Heidegger's reflections on the history of philosophy as the oblivion of Being, but that any belief that we can step across into an overcoming of metaphysics or any notion of the post-metaphysical always risks collapsing back into a pre-Heideggerian naïvety or non-dialectical positivity. Deconstruction takes place at the limit between metaphysics and its other(s), as the rigorous disruption of that limit. From a deconstructive perspective, the relation to metaphysics should be governed by the figure of aporia, which denies both the security of an inside or an outside to metaphysics. I take it that is why Derrida can consistently deconstruct *both* Plato, Rousseau or Husserl for attempting to buttress a metaphysics of presence *and* Bataille, Foucault or Artaud for attempting to step outside of metaphysics.

As I see it, our relation to metaphysical questioning is analogous to that of transcendental questioning, where, as Derrida notes in his 'Remarks on Deconstruction and Pragmatism', 'this new form of transcendental questioning only mimics the phantom of classical transcendental seriousness without renouncing that which, within this phantom, constitutes an essential heritage'.[33] Although it has received too little attention from his readers, and although it is a word that has to be wrested from too close an identification with Heidegger's notion of *Erbe* as the authentic historicity of *Dasein*,[34] *heritage* is a key item in Derrida's vocabulary for it describes a historically self-conscious or reflexively reactivated relation to any sedimented notion of tradition. In this sense, metaphysics, like transcendental philosophy, constitutes part of an essential heritage. Now, this heritage might well be exhausted and incapable of innovation – we cannot expect any new theses in the realm of *prima philosophia* – but such a recognition does not automatically entail that one can simply abandon metaphysical questioning, or cogently speak from outside of metaphysics. I think this is what Derrida means when he speaks of *mimicry* in relation to a tradition that has become *spectral* or when he uses terms such as the 'quasi-transcendental', a word incidentally also employed by Habermas. But the point here is that although metaphysics has become spectral, it is a phantom that continues to haunt our philosophical present.

As a consequence, the neo-pragmatist attempt to step outside metaphysics, by leaving it to itself, forgetting about it, or subjecting its claims to banalization, simply understates how shot through our language and history are with metaphysical categories and the ghosts of the metaphysical tradition. A similar point could be made with reference to Habermas, when one thinks of how brusquely he dismisses metaphysics and makes a move to the post-metaphysical in the opening three paragraphs of the Introduction to *The Theory of Communicative Action*.[35] Returning to Rorty's main point, however, I think that moral seriousness, for reasons of historical, social and linguistic embeddedness, might in some cases (but not all) entail the use of metaphysical categories and the resources of the metaphysical tradition. The attempt to exclude certain forms of inquiry as being 'too metaphysical' might be said, strangely perhaps, to be *too philosophical*, that is, as requiring too much in the way of apriori assurance, i.e. everything must be either empirical or normative, which is simply a new version of Occam's razor. It is in terms of such claims to heritage and mimicry that I make sense of someone like Levinas's palaeonymic talk of 'ethics as first philosophy', although I always read him through a deconstructive looking glass, that is to say, through Derrida's decisive dismantling of his pretension to ethical metaphysics. Part of the problem with neo-pragmatism is that it refuses to recognize our linguistic, social, historical and philosophical entanglement with the metaphysical tradition as an element in its programme of the banalization of philosophical vocabularies. As a consequence this banalization risks a double alienation: both from a philosophical audience infuriated by its deflationary redescriptions and the non-philosophical audience of the 'folks at home' who, in its rather patronizing way, neo-pragmatism imagines as its touchstone of authenticity.

Happily enough, Rorty finally seems to have got this point about the closure of metaphysics in his 1995 paper, 'Derrida and the Philosophical Tradition'. Under the pressure of Bennington's powerful presentation of Derrida's work, Rorty is finally forced to admit defeat or at least a strategic retreat. He begrudgingly concedes,

Maybe what Bennington calls 'the impossibility in principle of cutting oneself cleanly from the metaphysical logos' is, as we nominalists like to think, at most a local, transitory and empirical impossibility – one that prevails only over half the planet's surface and will last, even there, only another few centuries. But those words – Plato's and Kant's words – certainly helped make *some* of us . . . what we are.[36]

So who are we then? To return to my epigraph from Wallace Stevens, *some* of us are 'metaphysicians in the dark', and if that is the case 'only for another few centuries', then this is some comfort. Of course, such metaphysics in the dark can no longer claim insight into some ultimate reality or the Right Context. For us, this is as Stevens points out earlier in the poem, 'a souvenir', the reminder of an essential heritage. But such realization does not entail a wholesale abandonment of the metaphysical tradition. Rather, the metaphysical task is one of 'twanging a wiry instrument that gives/ Sounds passing through sudden rightnesses . . .'. The metaphysician in the dark, like Stevens's man with the blue guitar, plays 'a tune beyond us, yet ourselves',[37] who achieves through these sudden rightnesses what Stevens calls 'the finding of a satisfaction'. Stevens describes the condition to which such a thinking should be equal in the following terms, which seem to me to have a rightness that I cannot improve upon:

It has to be living, to learn the speech of the place.
It has to face the men of the time and to meet
The women of the time. It has to think about war
And it has to find what will suffice. It has
To construct a new stage.

Notes

1. First published in *Political Theory*, vol. 26, no. 5, 1998, pp. 803–17.

2. *Collected Poems*, London: Faber, 1955, p. 240. I owe this allusion to Tracy Strong.

3. Rorty's response and my original paper (reprinted above as chapter 4) can be found, in Chantal Mouffe, ed., *Deconstruction and Pragmatism*, London and New York: Routledge, 1996, pp. 41–6 and 19–40. In the time since my original paper was written in 1993, Derrida's work has, characteristically, evolved. In particular, it seems to me that a consideration of *Spectres of Marx*, London and New York: Routledge, 1994 and *Politics of Friendship*, London: Verso, 1997, would lead me to modify significantly elements of my interpretation of Derrida. I attempt to do this below in chapters 7 and 12.

4. Derrida, 'Remarks on Deconstruction and Pragmatism', *Deconstruction and Pragmatism*, p. 80.

5. See Derrida, 'The Deconstruction of Actuality', *Radical Philosophy*, no. 68, Autumn 1994, p. 36.

6. Derrida, 'Remarks on Deconstruction and Pragmatism', p. 82.

7. Derrida, 'Remarks on Deconstruction and Pragmatism', p. 86.

8. I take up these questions in greater detail in a debate with Axel Honneth, 'Habermas und Derrida werden verheiratet: Antwort auf Axel Honneth', *Deutsche Zeitschrift für Philosophie*, vol. 42, no. 6, 1994, pp. 981–92.

9. Rorty, *Achieving our Country. Leftist Thought in Twentieth-Century America*, Cambridge Mass.: Harvard University Press, 1998.

10. 'Deconstruction, Pragmatism, Hegemony', in *Deconstruction and Pragmatism*, pp. 47–67.

11. Rorty, *Achieving our Country*, p. 13.

12. See 'Deconstruction, Pragmatism, Hegemony', pp. 54–60. Incidentally, as I argue in chapter 3, I completely agree with Laclau that one cannot do away with the category of the subject, understood as the subject of a lack, a failed structural identity, because it is, as Laclau admits, 'part of the structure of experience' ('Deconstruction, Pragmatism, Hegemony', p. 56). But if one accepts this, might one not also ask: if, for Laclau, the subject is a freedom that is condemned because it is defined in terms of failure and lack, then *who* is the subject condemned to be in relation towards? More simply, if the subject is part of the structure of experience, then is not the other also part of that structure? One thinks here of Sartre's celebrated remark 'Hell is other people', but also of the transformation of the Hegelian dialectic of intersubjectivity in Lacan's thinking of the subject in relationship to the big Other. What is the relation between Laclau's theorization of the subject and the problematic of intersubjectivity and is not the latter ultimately constitutive of the former?

13. 'Deconstruction, Pragmatism, Hegemony', p. 53.

14. 'Remarks on Deconstruction and Pragmatism', p. 82.

15. I am compressing a much longer argument that can be found in 'From Text to Context: Deconstruction and the Thought of an Unconditional Ethical Imperative', from *The Ethics of Deconstruction*, Oxford: Blackwell, 1992, pp. 31–42.

16. Laclau, *New Reflections on the Revolution of our Time*, London: Verso, 1990, p. 82.

17. See G. Bennington and J. Derrida, *Jacques Derrida*, Chicago: University of Chicago Press, 1993. Rorty's essay, 'Derrida and the Philosophical Tradition' appears in *Truth and Progress. Philosophical Papers Volume 3*, Cambridge: Cambridge University Press, 1998, pp. 327–50. In his conclusion, Rorty writes:

> Bennington has convinced me that I cannot get away with my stance of tough-minded, hypostatization-bashing empiricism without falling a bit too much under the sway of the metaphysical *logos* . . . I still cannot help becoming impatient with the bloodless ballet that Bennington very skillfully choreographs, but I think I now understand better why he thinks it has to be done – why he thinks we can't just let deconstruction go hang if we still want to hang on to Derrida. (p. 349)

18. *Deconstruction and Pragmatism*, p. 41.

19. Ibid., p. 17.

20. Ibid., p. 41.

21. *Achieving our Country*, p. 107.

22. See *Deconstruction and Pragmatism*, p. 33.

23. Ibid., p. 44.

24. Ibid., p. 45.

25. Ibid., p. 24.

26. Chantal Mouffe makes the same argument using Cavell's critique of Rawls in 'Deconstruction, Pragmatism and the Politics of Democracy', *Deconstruction and Pragmatism*, pp. 9–11.

27. *Deconstruction and Pragmatism*, p. 45.

28. Ibid., p. 42.

29. Ibid., p. 42.

30. For the sake of completeness, I would like to point out two further infelicities in Rorty's response: (1) I did not write 'justice is an experience of the unexperienceable' (*Deconstruction and Pragmatism*, p. 41) which is a perhaps fructive contradiction in terms, but 'an "experience" of the undecidable', which is something quite different. I take it that Rorty's subsequent remarks about my 'pointless hype' would have to be moderated by the fact that they do not refer to my paper. (2) As far as I am aware, I do not speak of a 'supreme ethical principle' (ibid., p. 42).

31. Ibid., p. 43.

32. I discuss this in detail in 'The Problem of Closure in Derrida', in *The Ethics of Deconstruction*, Oxford: Blackwell, 1992, pp. 59–106.

33. *Deconstruction and Pragmatism*, p. 82.

34. Heidegger, *Being and Time*, transl. J. Macquarrie and E. Robinson, Oxford: Blackwell, 1962, pp. 383–6.

35. *The Theory of Communicative Action, Volume 1: Reason and the Rationalization of Society*, transl. T. McCarthy, Cambridge: Polity, 1984, pp. 1–3.

36. 'Derrida and the Philosophical Tradition', *Philosophical Papers Volume 3*, p. 350.

37. 'The Man with the Blue Guitar', *Collected Poems*, p. 165.

6

Black Socrates?
Questioning the Philosophical
Tradition[1]

Inconsiderateness in the face of tradition is reverence for the past.

Martin Heidegger, *Sophistes*

Funk not only moves, it can remove.
George Clinton, *P. Funk (Wants to Get Funked Up)*

Philosophy tells itself stories. One might go further and claim that the life of philosophy, the memory that ensures its identity and its continued existence as something to be inherited, lived and passed on, consists in the novel repetition of certain basic narratives. And there is one story in particular that philosophy likes to tell, which allows philosophers to reanimate, theatrically and sometimes in front of their students, the passion that founds their profession and which, it seems, must be retold in order for philosophy to be capable of inheritance. It concerns, of course, Greece – or rather, as General de Gaulle might have said, a certain idea of Greece – and the passion of a dying Socrates.

Philosophy as De-traditionalization

Socrates, the philosopher, dies. The significance of this story is that, with it, we can see how philosophy constitutes itself as a tradition, affects itself with narrative, memory and the chance of a future, by repeating a scene of radical *de-traditionalization*. For Hegel and Nietzsche,[2] to choose two examples of philosophers who affect themselves with a tradition – although from seemingly opposed perspectives – the historical emergence of philosophy, the emergence of philosophy into history, that is to say, the decisive break with mythic, religious or aesthetic world-views, occurs with Socrates' death.

Who is Socrates? So the story goes, he is an individual who claims that the source of moral legitimacy cannot be said to reside in the traditional customs, practices and forms of life of the community, what Hegel calls *Sittlichkeit*; nor – as for Nietzsche – in the aesthetico-religious practices that legitimate the pre-philosophical Greek *polis*, that is to say, Attic tragedy. Rather, Socrates is an individual who demands that the source of moral legitimacy must lie in the appeal to universality; it must have a universal form: what is justice? The philosopher does not ask, 'What is justice for the Athenians?' or 'What is justice for the Spartans?'; rather, the philosopher focuses on justice in general, seeking its *eidos*. Socrates announces the vocation of the philosopher and establishes the lines of transmission that lead from individuality to universality, from the intellect to the forms – a route which by-passes the particular, the communal, the traditional, as well as conventional views of ethical and political life.

The vocation of the philosopher is *critique*, that is, an individual interrogation and questioning of the evidence of tradition through an appeal to a universal form. For Hegel and Nietzsche, Socrates' life announces the death of tragedy, and the death of the allegedly *sittlich* community legitimated through pre-philosophical aesthetico-religious practices. In Hegel's words, Socrates' death marks the moment when tragedy comes off the stage and enters real life, becoming the tragedy of Greece.[3] Socrates' tragic death announces both the beginning of philosophy and the beginning of the irreversible Greek decline that will, for Hegel and Nietzsche, take us all the way from the legalism of the Roman Republic to the eviscerated *Moralität* of post-Kantian Germany. Of course, one's evaluation of Socrates' death will vary, depending on whether one is Hegel or Nietzsche. For the former (not without some elegaic regret for the lost Sophoclean *polis*) it is the first intimation of the principle of subjectivity; for the latter, Socrates' death ignites the motor that drives (Platonic-Christian) nihilism. But, despite these differences of evaluation, the narrative structure is common to Hegel and Nietzsche; the story remains the same even if the moral is different: Socrates' death marks the end of tragic Greece and the tragic end of Greece.

It is a beautiful story, and as I recount it I am once again seduced by its founding passion: the historical emergence of philosophy out of the dying Socrates is the condition of possibility for de-traditionalization. It announces the imperative that continues to drive philosophy, *critique*, which consists in the refusal to recognize the legitimacy of tradition without that tradition having first submitted itself to critical interrogation, to dialogue *viva voce*.

Philosophy as Tradition

However, if in my view philosophy is de-traditionalization, that which calls into question the evidence of tradition, then what is philosophy's relation to its own tradition? What is the relation of philosophy to the stories it tells about itself?

With the admittedly limited examples given above, one might say that the philosophical tradition is a tradition of de-traditionalization, of stories where the authority of tradition is refused. As Descartes famously writes, 'I will devote myself sincerely and without reservations to the general demolition of my opinions.'[4] As we will see presently with reference to Husserl and Heidegger, the philosopher's appeal to tradition is not traditional; it is, in Derrida's words, 'an appeal to tradition which is in no way traditional'.[5] It is a call for a novel repetition or retrieval of the past for the purposes of a critique of the present, often – for example in Husserl – with a view to the construction of an alternative ethical teleology. But, slightly getting ahead of myself, should we believe the stories that philosophy tells to itself? Should these stories themselves be exempt from philosophical critique? More particularly, what about the story of the dying Socrates? What more can I say about this story apart from feeling its beauty and pathos despite (or perhaps because of) its being so often recounted?

To ventriloquize a little: *one might point out that the story of Socrates' death is a Greek story, a narrative that recounts and reinforces the Greek beginning of philosophy. Indeed, it is a story that can be employed to assert the exclusivity of the Greek beginning of philosophy. Philosophy speaks Greek and only Greek, which is to say that philosophy does not speak Egyptian or Babylonian, Indian or Chinese and therefore is not Asian or African. Philosophy can only have one beginning and that beginning has to be the Greek beginning. Why? Because we are who we are. We are Europeans and Europe has a beginning, a birthplace, that is both geographical and spiritual, and the name of that birthplace is Greece. What takes place in Greece, the event that gives birth to our theoretical-scientific culture, is philosophy. By listening to the story that philosophy tells to itself, we can retrieve our beginning, our Greek beginning, the Greek beginning of the European Spiritual adventure. Furthermore, by appropriating this beginning as our own we will be able to come into our own as authentic Europeans, to confront the crisis of Europe, its spiritual sickness, a malaise which consists in the fact that we have forgotten who we are, we have*

*forgotten our origins and immersed ourselves unquestioningly in tradition. We must
de-traditionalize the tradition that ails us and allows us to forget the crisis – be it
the crisis of objectivism (Husserl), rationalization (Weber), commodification (Marx),
nihilism (Nietzsche) or forgetfulness of Being (Heidegger). We must project another
tradition that is truly our own. The only therapy is to face the crisis as a crisis, which
means that we must tell ourselves the story of philosophy's Greek beginning, of
philosophy's exclusively Greek beginning – again and again. If philosophy is not
exclusively Greek, we risk losing ourselves as Europeans, since to philosophize is to
learn how to live in the memory of Socrates' death.*

This troubling ventriloquy is very loosely based on Husserl's 1935
Vienna lecture, 'Philosophy and the Crisis of European Humanity', which
in many ways perfectly exemplifies the concerns of this chapter and the
position I am seeking to question.[6] We could also quote examples from
Hegel, Nietzsche, Heidegger, Merleau-Ponty, Arendt, Gadamer, Levinas,
and an entire German and English romantic tradition. What such remarks
testify to, I believe, is the importation of a certain model of ancient history, centred on the exclusivity of Greece, into philosophy as the foundation stone of its legitimating discourse. I would briefly like to explore and
question the historical basis for this belief.

Philosophy as Invented Tradition

One of the most challenging consequences of reading Martin Bernal's *Black
Athena*[7] – regardless of its many alleged scholarly infelicities, which I am
simply not in a position to judge – is the way in which he traces the
genealogy of the invented historical paradigm upon which Husserl bases
his remarks, namely the 'Aryan Model' of ancient history. This (astonish-
ingly) only dates from the early decades of the nineteenth century and was
developed in England and Germany. Prior to this period, and indeed for
most of Western history, what Bernal calls the 'Ancient Model' of classical
civilization had been dominant. The latter model believed, amongst other
things, that the Egyptians invented philosophy, that philosophy was essentially imported into Greece from Egypt, and that Egypt – and remember
Plato visited there around 390 BCE – was the font of all philosophical
wisdom. In addition to the Egyptian influence on Greek civilization, it was
also widely assumed that Greece was subject to colonization and extensive
cultural influence from Phoenician traders and mariners, and that, therefore, Greek civilization and the philosophy expressed by that civilization
was largely a consequence of the influence of near-Eastern cultures on the

African and Asian continents. That is to say, Greek culture – like all culture – was a *hybrid ensemble*, a radically impure and mongrel assemblage, that was a result of a series of invasions, waves of immigration, cultural magpieism and ethnic and racial mixing and crossing.

Contesting this picture of the African and Asiatic roots of classical civilization given in the Ancient Model (a picture that Bernal wants to revise and defend), the Aryan Model claims that Greek civilization was purely Indo-European and a consequence of either the autochthonous genius of the pre-Hellenes – resulting in what is sometimes called 'The Greek Miracle', the transition from *mythos* to *logos* – or of alleged invasions from the North by shadowy Indo-European peoples. Bernal's polemical thesis is that the displacement of the Ancient Model by the Aryan Model was not so much driven by a concern for truth as by a desire for cultural and national purity which, for chauvinistic, imperialist and ultimately racist reasons, wanted to deny the influence of African or Semitic culture upon classical Greece, and by implication upon nineteenth-century northern Europe.

The influence of this Aryan Model in philosophy can be seen in the way the canon of the history of philosophy was transformed at the beginning of the nineteenth century.[8] Up until the end of the eighteenth century, the history of philosophy was habitually traced back to multiple so-called 'wisdom traditions' in Egyptian, Hebraic, Babylonian, Mesopotamian and Sumerian cultures. However, from the early 1800s, these traditions were generally excluded from the canonical definition of 'philosophy' either because of their allegedly mythical or pre-rational status or because they were largely anonymous; whereas the Greeks, like Thales, had names. The individual thinker rather than a body of thought becomes the criterion for philosophy. The consequence of this transformation of the canon is the belief that philosophy begins exclusively amongst the Greeks; which is also to say that philosophy is indigenous to the territory of Europe and is a result of Europe's unique spiritual geography – setting aside the unfortunate geographical location of certain pre-Socratics on the Ionian coast, which is usually explained away by calling them Greek colonies, an explanation that conceals a slightly anachronistic projection of the modern meaning of colonialism back into the ancient world.

The hegemony of the Aryan model can also be seen in the nineteenth-century development of the discipline of Classics in England based on the German model of *Altertumswissenschaft*. Both are premised upon a vision of the Greeks as quasi-divine, pure and authentic. What Bernal shows is the way in which this vision was complicit with certain northern European nationalisms and imperialisms (particularly in England and Germany), where contemplation of the Greeks was felt to be beneficial to the education of future administrators of the empire. It is on this point of a possible link between culture and imperialism that one can perhaps link Bernal's analysis to the wider problematic of the invention of tradition in the nineteenth century, as diagnosed by Eric Hobsbawm and others.[9] Hobsbawm shows that traditions were invented with extraordinary rapidity in this period by various nation states (notably Britain, France, Germany and the USA) in order to reinforce political authority and to ensure the smooth expansion of electoral democracy – for males at least.

More specifically, the traditions invented in this period – which in Britain were as grand as the fabrication of a modern monarchy complete with its jubilees and public processions, or as small as the invention of the postage stamp complete with image of the monarch as symbol of the nation; or, more widely, the proliferation of public statuary in France and Germany, with the ubiquitous image of Marianne in the former and Bismarck or Kaiser Wilhelm in the latter, or the spread of national anthems and national flags – culminate, claims Hobsbawm, in the emergence of *nationalism*. It was nationalism that became the quasi-Rousseauesque civic religion of the nineteenth century, and which, crucially, ensured social cohesion and patterns of national identification for the newly hegemonic middle classes, providing a model which could then be extended to the working classes, as and when they were allowed to enter the political process. The power of invented tradition consists in its ability to inculcate certain values and norms by sheer ritualization and imposed repetition, and to encourage the belief that those traditions are rooted in remotest antiquity, as in the case of English nationalism's sentimental myth of 'a thousand years of unbroken history'.

My concern, as someone who teaches philosophy, is the extent to which the version of tradition that is operative and goes largely unquestioned in much philosophical pedagogy and post-prandial parley (the belief in the exclusivity of the Greek beginning of philosophy and the centrality and linear continuity of the European philosophical tradition) remains tributary to an invented historical paradigm, barely two centuries old, in which we have come to believe by sheer force of inculcation and repetition. Is the vision of philosophy offered by those, like myself, working on the geographical and spiritual edges of the Continental tradition, tributary to the Aryan model of ancient history and thereby complicit with a Hellenomania that buttresses an implicit European chauvinism? Indeed – although this is not my direct concern here – might one not be suspicious of the nationalist motives that led to the retrieval, within an Anglo-American tradition suspicious of the high metaphysics of 'Continentalists', of a specifically 'British' empiricist tradition in the 1950s to justify either an Anglicized logical positivism or Oxford ordinary language philosophy? Might one not say the same about the self-conscious retrieval of pragmatism or transcendentalism as distinctively and independently *American* traditions in the work of thinkers as diverse as Stanley Cavell, Richard Rorty and Cornel West?[10]

All of which brings me to some critical questions: must the Greco-European story of the philosophical tradition – from ancient Greece to modern northern Europe, from Platonism to its inversion in Nietzsche – be accepted as a legitimating narrative by philosophers, even by those who call themselves philosophers only in remembrance? Must philosophy be haunted by a compulsion to repeat its Greek origin? And if so, what about the possibility of other traditions in philosophy, other beginnings, other spiritual adventures? Could philosophy, at least in its European moment, ever be in the position to repeat another origin, announce another beginning, invent another tradition, or tell another story?

More gravely, and with reference to Bernal and also to David Theo Goldberg's *Racist Culture*,[11] is there perhaps a racist logic intrinsic to European philosophy which is founded on a central *paradox*, hinted at above in the coincidence of the geographical and the spiritual or the particular and the universal in Husserl? That is, philosophy tells itself a story which affirms the link between individuality and universality by embodying that link either in the person of Socrates or by defining the (European) philosopher as 'the functionary of humanity',[12] but where at the same time universality is delimited or confined within one particular tradition, namely the Greco-European adventure? Philosophy demands universal validity, or is defined by this demand for universal validity, yet it can only begin here, in Europe. We are who we are, and our supra-national cultural identity as Europeans is founded in the universality of our claims and the particularity of our tradition; a tradition that, for Husserl, includes 'the English dominions', i.e. the USA, but does not extend to the gypsies, 'who constantly wander across Europe',[13] like some living memory trace of Egypt. No other culture could be like us, because we have exclusive rights to philosophy, to the scientific-theoretical attitude.

In the light of Edward Said's work, such philosophical sentiments do not seem far from the core belief of imperialism: namely, that it is the responsibility or *burden* of the metropolitan powers to bring our universal values to bear on native peoples; that is, to colonize and transform other cultures according to our own world-view and to conceal oppression under the cloak of a mission. As Said puts it,

why are most professional humanists unable or unwilling to make the connection between, on the one hand, the prolonged cruelty of practices such as
slavery, colonialism, imperial subjection and racial oppression, and, on the other
hand, the poetry, fiction and philosophy of the societies that engage in such
practices?[14]

However, if we provisionally admit that there is a racist or imperialist
logic in philosophy – and this is as much an accusation against myself as
against Husserl – then could it ever be otherwise? That is, would it be
conceivable for philosophy, or at least for 'we European philosophers', to
be in a position to repeat another origin? Wouldn't this be precisely the
fantasy of believing oneself to speak from the standpoint of the excluded
without being excluded, of wishing to speak from the margins whilst standing at the centre, that is to say, the fantasy of a romantic anti-Hellenism
or Rousseauesque anti-ethnocentrism? If so, where does this leave us? How
do we proceed? As a way of sharing my perplexity, rather than resolving it,
I shall try to illuminate these questions by taking a slightly different tack.

Sedimentation, Reactivation, Deconstruction

Tradition can be said to have two senses:
  1. as something inherited or handed down without questioning or
critical interrogation;
  2. as something made or produced through a critical engagement with
the first sense of tradition, as a de-traditionalization of tradition or an appeal
to tradition that is in no way traditional.

Of course, this distinction is artificial insofar as it could be claimed that
the consciousness of tradition *as such* only occurs in the process of its
destruction, that is to say, with the emergence of a *modernity* as that which
places in question the evidence of tradition.

However, it is this second sense of tradition, the philosophical sense, that
is shared – not without some substantial differences – by Husserl and
Heidegger. For the Husserl of *The Crisis of the European Sciences*, the two
senses of tradition correspond to the distinction between a *sedimented* and
a *reactivated* sense of tradition. Sedimentation, which in one passage of the
Crisis Husserl compares to 'traditionalization',[15] and which it is helpful to
think of in geological terms as a process of settling or consolidation, would
consist in the forgetfulness of the origin of a state of affairs. If we take
Husserl's celebrated example of geometry, a forgetfulness of the origin of

geometry leads to the forgetfulness of the historicity of such a discipline, of the genesis of the theoretical attitude expressed by geometry, and the way in which the theoretical attitude belongs to a determinate *Lebenswelt*. What is required to counter the sedimentation of tradition is the *reactivation* of the origin in what Husserl calls 'a teleological-historical reflection upon the origins of our critical scientific and philosophical situation'.[16] Thus, philosophy in the proper sense of the word, i.e. transcendental phenomenology, would be the product of critical-historical reflection upon the origin of tradition and the (re)active making of a new sense of tradition against the pernicious naïveties of objectivism and naturalism.

Matters are not so different with the early Heidegger's conception of *Destruktion*, the deconstruction of the history of ontology, which is precisely not a way of burying the past in nullity, but rather of seeking the positive tendencies of the tradition. *Destruktion* is the production of a tradition as something made and fashioned through a process of repetition or retrieval, what Heidegger calls *Wiederholung*. The latter is the assumption of the tradition as a genuine repetition, where the original meaning of a state of affairs (the temporal determination of the meaning of Being, to pick an example at random) is retrieved through a critical-historical reflection. In the period of *Being and Time*, Heidegger articulates the difference between a received and destroyed tradition in terms of the distinction between tradition (*Tradition*) and heritage (*Überlieferung*), where the possibilities of authentic existing are delivered over and disclosed.[17]

It is important to point out that the target of Husserl's and Heidegger's reflections on tradition – and this is equally true of Hegel's reflection on the history of Spirit and Nietzsche's conception of nihilism – is not the past as such, but the *present*, and precisely the *crisis* of the present. The true crisis of the European sciences (Husserl) or distress of the West (Heidegger) is felt in the absence of distress: 'crisis, what crisis?' At the present moment, when the Western techno-scientific-philosophical adventure is in the process of globalizing itself and reducing humanity to the status of happy consumers wearing Ronald McDonald Happy Hats, we are called upon to reactivate the origin of the tradition from which that adventure sprang, and to do this precisely in order to awaken a sense of crisis and distress. Thus, a reactivated sense of the tradition permits us a critical, perhaps even *tragic* consciousness of the present. As Gerald Bruns points out in an essay on tradition,

> On this line of thinking a good example of the encounter with tradition would be the story of Oedipus and his discovery of the truth of what has been said about him by seers, drunks, and oracles, not to mention what his own awakened

memory can tell him. I mean that from a hermeneutical standpoint the encounter with tradition is more likely to resemble satire than allegory, unmasking the present rather than translation of the past. Or, as I've tried to suggest, the hermeneutical experience of what comes down to us from the past is structurally *tragic* rather than comic. It is an event that exposes us to our own blindness or the limits of our historicality and extracts from us *an acknowledgement of our belongingness to something different*, reversing what we had thought. It's just the sort of event that might drive us to put out our eyes.[18]

The Husserlian-Heideggerian sense of reactivated tradition which destroys the past in order to enable us to confront the present achieves this by consigning us, as Derrida puts it,[19] to the security of the Greek element with a knowledge and confidence which are not comfortable, but which permit us to experience crisis, distress and tragedy.

But we must proceed carefully here: on the one hand, it seems that the Husserlian-Heideggerian demand for the reactivation of a sedimented tradition is a necessary and unavoidable move, it is the step into philosophy and critique – that is, into the realization of tradition as something made or fashioned (re)actively as a way of confronting the tragedy of the present. However, on the other hand, the problem here is that the tradition that is retrieved is uniquely and univocally Greek. It is only a Greek tragedy that will permit us to confront the distress of the present. The way in which globalized techno-scientific ideology is to be confronted is by learning to speak Greek. My problem with this conception of tradition, as pointed out above, is that it might be said to presuppose implicitly an imperialist, chauvinist or racist logic. One recalls the remark that Heidegger was reported to have made to Karl Löwith in 1936, when he asserted that his concept of historicity was at the basis of his political engagement with National Socialism.[20]

It is with this problem in mind that I want to make an excursion into Derrida's 1964 essay, 'Violence and Metaphysics', which deals with the thought of Emmanuel Levinas insofar as that work might be said to offer an ethical challenge to the Heideggerian and Husserlian conceptions of tradition. I think it is justified to claim that Derrida's thinking of tradition, at least in this early work, is dominated by the problem of closure, that play of belonging and non-belonging to the Greco-European tradition, which asserts both the necessity and impossibility of such a tradition. Broadly stated, the problem of closure describes the duplicitous or ambiguous historical moment – *now* – when our language, institutions, conceptuality and philosophy itself show themselves both to belong to a metaphysical (or logocentric) tradition that is theoretically exhausted, while at the same time searching for the breakthrough from that tradition. The problem of closure describes the liminal situation of late modernity out of which the deconstructive problematic arises, and which, I believe, Derrida inherits from Heidegger. Closure is the double refusal of both remaining within the limits of the tradition and of transgressing that limit. Closure is the hinge that articulates the double movement between the philosophical tradition and its other(s).

In 'Violence and Metaphysics', Derrida's general claim is that Levinas's project cannot succeed except by posing the question of closure, and that because this problem is not posed by Levinas in *Totality and Infinity*,[21] his dream of an ethical relation to the Other which is linguistic but which exceeds the totalizing language of the tradition, remains just that, a *dream*. Derrida calls it the dream of pure empiricism, that evaporates when language awakens. Levinas's discourse – and Derrida repeats this strategy with regard to all discourses that claim to exceed the tradition, those of Foucault, Artaud, Bataille or whoever – is caught, unbeknownst to itself, in an economy of betrayal, insofar as it tries to speak philosophically about that which cannot be spoken of philosophically.

Now, one conservative way of understanding the problem of closure is to argue that Derrida demonstrates the irresistibility of the claims of the Greco-German tradition and the impossibility of claiming any coherent position outside of this tradition – 'Hegel, Husserl and Heidegger are always right!' Although this interpretation is to some extent justified, it is by no means the whole story. The logic of closure works within a double bind; that is, if there is no outside to the philosophical tradition from which one can speak in order to criticize its inside, then, by the same token, there is no inside to the philosophical tradition from which one can speak without contamination by an outside. This is why closure describes the *liminal* situation of late modernity, and why it is a *double* refusal of both remaining within the limits of the tradition and of transgressing those limits. Thus, there is no pure Greek inside to the European tradition that can be claimed as an uncontaminated origin in confronting the crisis. This, I believe, explains Derrida's strategy when confronted with a unified conception of tradition, when he works to show how any such conception is premised upon certain exclusions which cannot be excluded. One thinks, for example, of his unpicking of Heidegger's reading of Nietzsche, or of Foucault's reading of Descartes, or again in *Glas* (as we saw in chapter 1), where the focus is on that which refuses the dialectico-historical logic of *Aufhebung*, and in *La carte postale*, where the Heideggerian unity of the Greek sending of Being (*envoi de l'être*) is undermined and multiplied into a plurality of sendings (*envois*).

Tradition as a Changing Same

Turning from the philosophical tradition to tradition as such, the deconstructive thinking of tradition leaves one in the situation of the double bind discussed by Derrida in relation to European cultural identity:

> It is necessary to make ourselves the guardians of an idea of Europe, of a difference of Europe, but of a Europe that consists precisely in not closing off in its own identity and in advancing itself in an exemplary way toward what it is not, toward the other heading or heading of the other, indeed – and this is perhaps something else altogether – toward the other of the heading, which would be the beyond of this modern tradition, another border structure, another shore.[22]

Although such statements are problematic, not least because Derrida tends to assume too much unity to the 'European culture' that is being deconstructed, it is clear that, for him, being European means obeying the irreducibility of a double duty (and why only a double duty? Why not a triple, quadruple or multiple duty?): to retrieve what Europe is or was, whilst at the same time opening Europe to the non-European, welcoming the foreigner in their alterity.

On a deconstructive account, then, any attempt to interpret tradition and culture in terms of a desire for unity, univocity and purity must be rigorously undermined in order to show how this desire is always already contaminated by that which it attempts to resist and exclude. If deconstruction has a sociology, then it is a sociology of impurity, of contamination. Culture and tradition are hybrid ensembles, they are the products of radically impure mixing and mongrelism. For example, being British today means recognizing the way in which the dominant English culture has been challenged and interpellated by previously dominated cultures, be they Scottish, Welsh, Irish, Afro-Caribbean or Asian. As Edward Said persuasively suggests, the consequence (and inverted triumph) of imperialism is the radical hybridity of culture, where histories and geographies are intertwined and overlapping, troubling any appeal to cultural and national exclusivity. Cultural identity (or perhaps one should say, cultural self-differentiation) is relationally negotiated from amongst competing claims that make conflicting and perhaps awkward demands upon the subject.

Of course, one response to this conflict is racism, or the essentialist identification of race, culture and nation that is shared by white supremacism, Thatcherite British nationalism and oppositional Black nationalism.

Needless to say, I do not think the last are the most felicitous responses to the hybridity of culture and tradition. But the cultural-political task facing the Left, as I see it, lies in *hegemonizing hybridity*. As Said intimates, this can only entail an internationalist politics, which would try to hegemonize those oppositional movements – Said speaks of the *intifada*, the women's movement, and various ecological and cultural movements – that resist the global political cynicism of 'hurrah capitalism'. The vocation of the intellectual (whatever that much-maligned word means at this point and whoever it includes and excludes) consists in trying to focus and exacerbate these internationalist energies by being the exilic consciousness of the present through the practice of what Said calls *contrapuntal criticism*. The latter would be a form of critical-historical, genealogical or deconstructive reflection that would bring us to the recognition of the hybridity of tradition, culture and identity. Contrapuntal criticism, the comparative analysis of the over-lapping geographies and intertwined histories of present cultural assemblages, would reveal hybrid ensembles *as* hybrid ensembles and not as unities or essences.

A stunning example of such a contrapuntal criticism, in my view, is Paul Gilroy's *The Black Atlantic*.[23] The basic polemical point of this book is to oppose any easy (and fatal) identification of race or culture with nation, where notions of racial purity function as legitimating discourses for nationalistic politics, for example, within Black nationalism. In opposition to the latter, the black Atlantic is a transnational and intercultural framework that exceeds the borders of existing or Utopian nation-states. It is a 'rhizomorphic, fractal structure' that opposes 'the ethnic absolutism that currently dominates black political culture'.[24] What is most impressive about Gilroy's book is the way in which the frequently reified and reifying discourse on race and roots is transposed onto a discourse of routes: a historical tableau of traversals and criss-crossings signifying upon a vast oceanic surface; a diaspora, that Gilroy courageously compares to Jewish experience, but where the potentially Mosaic discourse of the promised land is maintained as a mosaic of routes. Gilroy engages in what we might call a spatialization of history, where the potential essentialism of historical narrative is problematized through a recourse to geography.

But it is Gilroy's conception of tradition that, for me at least, forms the centre of the book and which speaks directly to the concerns of this chapter. Gilroy's basic historical thesis is that it is not possible to view slavery as an epiphenomenon within modernity, or as some residue of pre-modern barbarism carried over into modernity. Rather, using Zygmunt Bauman's terminology, slavery and black Atlantic experience as a whole constitute a distinct *counter-culture* within modernity that complicates and disrupts certain versions of modernity's emancipatory project. The question here is whether there is room for a memory of slavery within modernity; that is to say, for Gilroy, is there room for a personalized, sublime and perhaps pre-discursive moment of liberatory creativity within modern experience? This emphasis upon creativity and aesthetic experience takes us to Gilroy's main contention, which is that black expressive culture, particularly music, is the means for articulating this counter-culture and for activating this memory. For Gilroy, black music is 'a cipher for the ineffable, sublime, pre-discursive and anti-discursive elements in black expressive culture'.[25] Black music is, in Gilroy's words, a *changing same*. Taking the examples of dubbing, scratching, sampling, mixing, borrowing and alluding that one can find in Hip Hop, Rap, Reggae, and more recent musical hybrids like Jungle and Drum and Bass, Gilroy argues against the notion of an authentic racial art and the conception of black music as a fixed dialogue between a thinking racial self and a stable racial community. In this sense, black musical expression exemplifies the relation between identity and difference that is constitutive of cultural traditions and tradition as such. Thus, cultural traditions, like music, cannot be reduced to 'the transmission of a fixed essence through time', but are rather a series of 'breaks and interruptions'. In this sense tradition itself 'may be a distinct though covert response to the destabilizing flux of the post-contemporary world'.[26]

Tradition is a changing same – that is, by insisting on the place of the memory of slavery within modernity, Gilroy disputes the supposed opposition between tradition and modernity, where, for example, black nationalists might claim the purity and authenticity of an African tradition in order to oppose the oppression of European and American modernity. This can be seen vividly in George G. M. James's attempt to show how the Greco-European philosophical tradition that culminates in modernity and racism is, in fact, a stolen legacy from a prior Egyptian and African civilization.[27] In contradistinction to such attempts, Gilroy proposes a *black modernism*, that is to say, a self-consciously modernist relation to tradition, where the specificity of the modern lies precisely in the consciousness of the problematic relation between the past and the present, between tradition and the individual talent. For the modernist – and the resonances with Derrida's notion of closure here become apparent – tradition is that to which we simultaneously belong and do not belong, what Gilroy suggestively calls '*a non-traditional tradition*, an irreducibly modern, ex-centric, unstable and asymmetrical cultural ensemble that cannot be apprehended through the manichean logic of binary coding'.[28] Tradition is that duplicitous experience of continuity and rupture or of belonging and non-belonging that I have already tried to discuss in relation to Derrida. In response to this conception of tradition, what is required, according to Gilroy, is a Du Boisian experience of double consciousness, or simultaneous attraction and repulsion, where one recognizes the doubleness of one's identity as being shaped by modernity without feeling fully part of it.[29] *An experience of modernity as something which one is both unable to believe and unable to leave.* In Toni Morrison's words, tradition, like the supple and evasive rhythms of funk, 'slaps and it embraces, it slaps and it embraces'.[30] Tradition is the story of overlapping geographies and intertwined histories, perhaps an ultimately non-narratable narrative that thwarts the desire for cultural, racial or philosophical purity.

Contrapuntal Philosophy?

Drawing together the threads of this discussion into a conclusion, in addition to the two senses of tradition we introduced above, we are now in a position to add a third:

1. *Sedimented tradition*: where tradition is inherited as forgetfulness of origins, as pre-critical inheritance or pre-philosophical *doxa*, as the moral world-view that is inculcated into us by family, schooling, etc.

2. *Reactivated tradition*: the Socratic moment of a critical, philosophical engagement with the first sense and the retrieval of an 'authentic' Greco-European tradition (histories and genealogies of Spirit, of nihilism, of Being's oblivion, of the forgetfulness of origins). This is the *philosophical* articulation of sedimented tradition, which one might conceive as a defining characteristic of modernity.

3. *Deconstructed tradition*: where the unity, univocity and linearity of the reactivated traditions would be critically questioned, and where the founding presuppositions of such traditions would be shown to be premised upon certain exclusions that are non-excludable, leaving us in the double bind of closure, and encouraging us to face up to the doubleness (or more than doubleness) or hybridity of tradition, culture and identity. This would be the contrapuntal or double consciousness of tradition as a changing same.

So, deconstruction provides a third sense to the concept of tradition, where the reactivated philosophical-critical sense of tradition – an ever-incomplete modernity – is not rejected or set aside, but, rather, where its power for getting us to face the crisis of the present is both incorporated and – crucially – *contested*, where the philosophical tradition is forced to acknowledge the limits of its jurisdiction and the failure of its demand for exclusivity.

As I see it, the position I have argued for has three important consequences for those concerned with philosophy and its history:

1. the acceptance of the necessity of the Greco-European tradition as
the linguistic and conceptual resource with which what 'we Europeans'
(leaving the limits of this 'we' deliberately vague) call thinking takes place;

2. the necessary failure of any attempt to constitute an uncontaminated
Greco-European tradition, a pure inside that would presuppose the European exclusivity of philosophy and the privileging of the European over the
non-European. The identity of the European tradition is always impurely
traced and contaminated by the non-European other that it tries unsuccess-
fully to exclude;

3. the acceptance of the impossibility of a pure outside to the European
tradition for 'we Europeans', the irretrievability of another origin, the fantasy of a European anti-Eurocentrism, of anti-ethnocentrism, of romantic
anti-Hellenism, of all post-Rousseauesque versions of what Derrida calls
nost-Algérie.

Tradition, culture and identity are irreducibly hybrid ensembles. The
purpose of critical-historical, genealogical or deconstructive reflection –
contrapuntal criticism – is to bring us to a recognition of these ensembles *as*
ensembles. On analogy with the latter, I wonder – and this is the tentative
expression of a Utopian hope rather than the statement of a programme –
whether it would be possible to study and practise philosophy contrapunt-
ally. That is, to philosophize out of an experience of the utter contingency
of historical being (and Being as such insofar as the latter is constituted
historically) and with reference to the intertwining and overlapping of
those histories and geographies that make up something like a philosophical
canon or tradition. As I see it, this would mean studying the history of
philosophy not as a unified, universal, linear, narratable and geographic-
ally delimitable (i.e. European) procession stretching from the Athens of
Socrates to Western late modernity, but, rather, as a series of constructed,
contingent, invented and possible non-narratable contrapuntal ensembles
that would disrupt the authority of the hegemonic tradition.

Can one conceive of the philosophical tradition as a series of contrapuntal ensembles? I have two closing suggestions in this regard:

1. Might it be possible to conceive of the history of philosophy in terms
of what Derrida calls (with reference to Levinas) *sériature*, that is, an interrupted series, or series of interruptions that would constitute less a teleo-
logically destined succession of epochs or figures of Spirit and more a
multiplicity of sendings in the manner performed in *La carte postale*?[31]

2. Secondly, might the history of philosophy be approached *geographic-
ally* as a series of plateaux in the manner of Deleuze and Guattari, namely

as a multiplicity of dated, stratified assemblages? Might not such a contra-puntal consciousness of the philosophical tradition have the potential to transform philosophy into a practice of radical reflection rooted in the acceptance and affirmation of hybridity as the condition of possibility for philosophy's historical emergence and its future flourishing?[32]

Postscript (July 1995)

The intention behind the previous part of this chapter is the following: to see whether the concept of hybridity, so pervasive as an explanatory cat-egory in recent cultural theory, can be productively extended into a reflec-tion on philosophy and the philosophical tradition. This intention has a two-way motivation, as I see it:

1. to confront an under-interrogated philosophy of history – a Euro-centrism, an imperialism, a racism even – that is still hegemonic in much philosophical discussion and pedagogy;

2. to try and lend some philosophical gravity to debates in recent cultural theory which often seem to proceed with an unbearable lightness when it comes to the philosophical articulation and interrogation of their basic categories.

And yet, re-reading this chapter a year or so after writing it, a sceptical doubt troubles me. It concerns the alleged relation or equation between the category of hybridity and intellectual resistance. Throughout my paper, I follow Said's understanding of the intellectual as a nomadic or exilic figure; I implicitly assume that nomadism and exile can be interpreted as figures of cultural and political resistance to the contemporary world, to that bewil-dering network of what we all too readily and easily call 'late capitalism'. For Said, the critical intellectual has the obligation to speak the truth to power, to disrupt any and every consensus, to be the dissensual, oppositional Socratic gadfly in relation to whatever passes for common sense, to refuse academic specialization and professionalization by claiming the position of amateur and generalist, a position that Said assimilates to the nomadic experi-ence of exile, an exile at once actual or metaphorical, even metaphysical.[33]

But is such a view of the intellectual plausible? Is the intellectual (de-scribed with the figures of nomad, exile or agent of hybridity) really a source of resistance to late capitalism, or do not these figures rather suggest a troubling complicity with that which the intellectual intends to oppose? That is to say, might not hybridity, exile and nomadism better describe the deterritorializing force and the speculative flows of late capitalism and the theories of its management gurus and marketing consultants rather than constituting any resistance to it?[34] International capitalism, specifically the near-neurotic behaviour of the financial markets – testified to in the collapse of the Baring Bank in 1995 at the hands of the nomadic Nick Leeson – is, in the terminology of Deleuze and Guattari, a nomadic war machine, working largely and increasingly independently of the state apparatus, where the activity of business is the ever-transient reconfiguration of skills, knowledges and products in response to rapidly changing, hybridizing markets.

My question is: who is the nomad in these contemporary circumstances? Is it the entrepreneurial capitalist or the secular intellectual? Is it Edward Said or Nick Leeson? But if this is at least a question (and that is all I am claiming), then might this not lead one to be a little suspicious of notions of nomadism, exile and hybridity as categories in terms of which one can articulate intellectual resistance?

To follow this thought speculatively a little further, it can be asked: how is intellectual resistance possible? Is it even desirable? Is resistance itself the most felicitous response to late capitalism? Is it not too *reactive* in the Nietzschean sense? Should we not, rather than opposing late capitalism reactively, seek to think through some kind of *active affirmation* of its enormously creative and destructive energy? Should we not, as travelling theorists and jet-set professors, try to ride the surf of late capitalism in some sort of parasitic low-wage parody of the deterritorializing displacements of late capitalism, whose agents I sit next to on the aeroplane (he reads *Business Week*, I read Guy Debord), hoping that the enormously creative and destructive energy of late capitalism turns over into cyber-revolution?

Exciting as it sounds – and mania is, as Freud noted, one possible dysfunctional response to the trauma of mourning – I have my doubts about this apocalyptic version of Deleuze and Guattari (though there are, of course, less apocalyptic versions of their thought) and its concomitant economistic teleology and a-theodicy. But that still leaves open the question as to whether and how intellectual resistance is possible and what categories might be employed to articulate it.

What is so troubling about capitalism to many on the Left is precisely its extraordinary hybridizing energy, its ability to assume new forms, to hegemonize itself, to recuperate what was originally intended as opposition and sell it as a commodity (situationist graffiti crop up on CD packaging and T-shirts; as I write these words the new South African flag flashes across the television screen between the beer commercial of the programme sponsor and live action from the Rugby World Cup). But what is even more disturbing is capitalism's ability to renew and propagate itself, not out of any reactive gestures, but rather out of a cheerfully superficial affirmativeness – 'Don't worry, be happy'. The problem with the 'bad Nietzscheanism' of late capitalism is that it refuses to place in question the very social, economic and political premises of its own system and the gross iniquities, inequalities and wastefulness that it leaves in its wake. And it is here that we might finally be able to specify the difference between the nomadic entrepreneur and the nomadic intellectual, between Nick Leeson and Edward Said, because whereas the former does not place late capitalism in question, but accepts its language of forces and markets as a metaphysical reality, the latter precisely places that metaphysics in question, engaging in a genealogical ideology-critique that would trace the conditions of possibility for the emergence of late capitalism and expose its injustices and waste. In Adornian terms, which are interestingly echoed both by Said and Deleuze and Guattari,[35] what late capitalism lacks is a *critical* or *Utopian* moment, and the articulation of such a moment remains, to my mind, a *philosophical* task, at least according to the hopefully less impoverished version of philosophy argued for in this chapter. That is to say, it is therefore a question of hegemonizing the categories of hybridity, nomadism and exile in relation to the philosophical production of a critical and Utopian stance in a way that will serve as an effective basis for intellectual resistance.

Notes

1. First published in *Radical Philosophy*, no. 69, 1995, pp. 17–26. Reprinted with a new postscript in *Theoria*, no. 95, South Africa, 1995, pp. 79–98.

2. See Hegel, 'Tragedy and the Impiety of Socrates' in A. and H. Paolucci, eds, *Hegel on Tragedy*, New York: Harper and Row, 1975, pp. 345–66; and Nietzsche, *The Birth of Tragedy*, transl. W. Kaufmann, New York: Vintage, 1967; and 'The Problem of Socrates', in *Twilight of the Idols*, transl. R. J. Hollingdale, Harmondsworth: Penguin, 1968, pp. 29–34.

3. 'Tragedy and the Impiety of Socrates', p. 364.

4. 'Meditations on First Philosophy', in *The Philosophical Writings of Descartes* vol. 2, transl. J. Cottingham *et al.*, Cambridge: Cambridge University Press, 1984, p. 12.

5. 'Violence and Metaphysics', in *Writing and Difference*, transl. A. Bass, London and New York: Routledge, 1978, p. 81.

6. In *The Crisis of the European Sciences and Transcendental Phenomenology: An Introduction to Phenomenological Philosophy*, transl. D. Carr, Evanston: Northwestern University Press, 1970, pp. 269–99.

7. Martin Bernal, *Black Athena. The Afroasiatic Roots of Classical Civilization*, vol. 1, 'The Fabrication of Ancient Greece 1785–1985', London: Vintage, 1991.

8. I rely here on the work of Robert Bernasconi and in particular his paper, 'Heidegger and the Invention of the Western Philosophical Tradition', *Journal of the British Society for Phenomenology*, vol. 26, no. 3, 1995, pp. 240–54; and 'Philosophy's Paradoxical Parochialism: The Reinvention of Philosophy as Greek', in *Cultural Readings of Imperialism. Edward Said and the Gravity of History*, London: Lawrence and Wishart, 1998, pp. 212–26.

9. E. Hobsbawm and T. Ranger, eds, *The Invention of Tradition*, Cambridge: Cambridge University Press, 1983, see esp. pp. 1–14 and 263–307.

10. In this regard, see esp. Cornel West, *The American Evasion of Philosophy*, London: Macmillan, 1989.

11. David Theo Goldberg, *Racist Culture, Philosophy and the Politics of Meaning*, Oxford: Blackwell, 1993, p. 6. Also see in this regard Harry M. Bracken's 'Philosophy and Racism', *Philosophia*, vol. 8, 1978, pp. 241–60. In an innovative and provocative discussion of racism and empiricism, it is argued that Lockean (and to a lesser extent, Humean) empiricism facilitates 'the expression of racist ideology and that Locke was actively involved in formulating policies [compatible with those theories] and encouraging practices (e.g. the African slave trade and perpetual racial slavery) which were racist in character' (p. 255). In contrast to empiricism, and by way of a covert defence of the Cartesianism of Chomsky's linguistic theory, Bracken argues that Cartesianism contains 'a modest conceptual barrier to racism' (p. 254).

12. *The Crisis of the European Sciences*, p. 17.

13. Ibid., p. 273.

14. Edward Said, *Culture and Imperialism*, London: Chatto and Windus, 1993, p. xiv.

15. *The Crisis of the European Sciences*, p. 52.

16. Ibid., p. 3.

17. *Being and Time*, transl. J. Macquarrie and E. Robinson, Oxford: Blackwell, 1962; German pagination, p. 395; English pagination, p. 447.

18. Gerald L. Bruns, *Hermeneutics Ancient and Modern*, New Haven: Yale University Press, 1992, p. 204 (my emphasis).

19. 'Violence and Metaphysics', p. 82.

20. Karl Löwith, 'My Last Meeting with Heidegger in Rome, 1936', in R. Wolin, ed., *The Heidegger Controversy*, Cambridge Mass. and London: MIT Press, 1993, p. 142.

21. I argue that matters become much more complicated in Levinas's later work, *Otherwise than Being or Beyond Essence*. In this regard, see my 'Eine Vertiefung der ethischen Sprache und Methode', in *Deutsche Zeitschrift für Philosophie*, vol. 42, no. 4, 1994, pp. 643–51.

22. Derrida, *The Other Heading*, transl. P. A. Brault and M. Naas, Bloomington: Indiana University Press, 1992, p. 29.

23. Paul Gilroy, *The Black Atlantic. Modernity and Double Consciousness*, London: Verso, 1993.

24. Ibid., pp. 4–5.

25. Ibid., p. 120.

26. Ibid., p. 101.

27. George G. M. James, *Stolen Legacy. Greek Philosophy is Stolen Egyptian Philosophy*, Trenton NJ: Africa World Press, 1992, 1954.

28. *The Black Atlantic*, p. 198 (my emphasis).

29. Incidentally, this is also how Cornel West defines the situation of the prophetic critic in *Keeping Faith. Philosophy and Race in America,* London and New York: Routledge, 1993, p. xxi.

30. *The Black Atlantic*, p. 78.

31. For the notion of *sériature* in Derrida, see 'At this very moment in this work here I am', transl. R. Berezdivin, in R. Bernasconi and S. Critchley, eds, *Re-Reading Levinas*, Bloomington: Indiana University Press, 1991. See also *The Post Card*, transl. A. Bass, Chicago: University of Chicago Press, 1987.

32. Deleuze and Guattari, *A Thousand Plateaus. Capitalism and Schizophrenia*, transl. B. Massumi, London: Athlone, 1988. Although, with regard to Deleuze and Guattari, it should be noted that they also insist upon the exclusivity of the Greek beginning to philosophy: 'If we really want to say that philosophy originates with the Greeks, it is because the city, unlike the empire or state, invents the agon as the rule of society of "friends", of the community of free men as rivals (citizens)' (*What is Philosophy?* transl. G. Burchell and H. Tomlinson, London: Verso, 1994, p. 9; see also pp. 43–4 and especially chapter 3, 'Geophilosophy', pp. 85–113). Although Deleuze and Guattari insist upon the contingency of the historical origin of philosophy in Greece, and emphasize the crucial role that migrants and foreigners played in the formation and articulation of Greek culture, their representation of philosophy and the ancient world is pervaded by the power of invented tradition as presented in this chapter. For example, their representation of the space of the *polis* as the pre-philosophical plane of immanence and the condition of possibility for philosophical concept-creation would seem, in a manner that is absolutely traditional, to link the historical emergence of philosophy to the political form of democracy in opposition to the alleged hierarchy and transcendence of all forms of imperial or theological space. But this is precisely to forget that the space of the Greek *polis* was, at once, powerfully imperial, theological and exclusionary. My open question here is whether the possible radicality and innovativeness of Deleuze and Guattari's conception of Geophilosophy can be freed from this sedimented notion of history and tradition into a productive basis for philosophical praxis.

33. See Said's 1993 Reith Lectures, *Representations of the Intellectual*, London: Vintage, 1994; see esp. chapter 3, 'Intellectual Exile: Expatriates and Marginals', pp. 35–47.

34. I here follow closely an interesting line of argument developed by James Williams in 'Nomads and the Management of Liberation', unpublished typescript.

35. *Representations of the Intellectual*, pp. 40–4; *What is Philosophy?*, p. 99.

The Hypothesis, the Context, the Messianic, the Political, the Economic, the Technological: On Derrida's *Spectres of Marx*[1]

> I once said, perhaps rightly: The earlier culture will become a heap of rubble and finally a heap of ashes, but spirits will hover over the ashes.
>
> Wittgenstein, *Culture and Value*

To begin with, let me try to be quite clear about what Derrida is affirming in *Spectres of Marx* (SdM[2]). Although he claims from the beginning to the end of SdM that Marxism is *plus d'un* (both more than one and no longer one), and that deconstruction has neither been Marxist nor non-Marxist (SdM 126–7/75), and that, as Marx said before him, 'What is certain is that I am not a Marxist' (SdM 145/88), Derrida's affirmation in this text is the following:

> Deconstruction has never had any sense or interest, in my view at least, except as a radicalization, which is also to say *in the tradition* of a certain Marxism, in a certain *spirit of Marxism*. (SdM 151/92)

Although Derrida has understandable reservations about the felicity of the word 'radicalization', he elsewhere speaks, to use another word he has problematized, of the *position* (SdM 92/53) he is going to defend in terms of assuming the Marxist heritage, 'one must [*il faut* – with all the force that the *il faut* commands in a whole series of Derrida's texts] assume the heritage of Marxism' (SdM 93/54).

Deconstruction is Marxism, it would seem: a formula that we will have to put alongside Derrida's other hyperbolic formulations, that 'deconstruction is justice', or, more awkwardly, 'America is deconstruction'.[3] I don't know how shocking this identification of deconstruction with Marxism might appear. To readers of Derrida, it shouldn't exactly come as news, particularly regarding a number of elements in his career: his early interest in Tran Duc Thao's attempted reconciliation of phenomenology and dialectical materialism, his radicalization of the thought of economy from his earliest work, particularly in his essay on Bataille, and his revealing comments on Marxism during the 'Political Seminar' of *Les fins de l'homme*.[4] However, if deconstruction is a certain reception, continuation and continued radicalization of the Marxist heritage, then we are still no closer to understanding what this might mean. To do this I would like to begin by briefly discussing *the hypothesis* advanced in SdM and making a couple of remarks about *the context* for the book. I will then go on to discuss what I see as the central theme of SdM: *the messianic*. As a way of unpacking this theme, I will address a number of sub-themes in SdM: the injunction of *différance*, democracy to come (*la démocratie à venir*), justice, religion and the *es spukt* (it spooks). As a consequence of this discussion, I would like to turn to the theme of *the political* and address the sub-themes of hegemony, the decision and the New International. I conclude, more speculatively, with brief discussions of two more themes that arise out of the Marxist tradition: *the economic*, specifically the relation of deconstruction to capitalism, and *the technological*, where I focus on some of Derrida's hints on the relation of spectrality to technicity and try to approach Derrida as a thinker of originary technicity.

The Hypothesis

Derrida's hypothesis in SdM has a structure that will be familiar to readers of his work. He spells it out schematically in the concluding pages of the text:

> On the one hand [*D'une part*], Marx insists on respecting the originality and the proper efficacity, the autonomization and automatization of ideality as finite-infinite processes of *différance* (phantomatic, fantastic, fetishistic, or ideological) . . . But, on the other hand [*d'autre part*] . . . Marx continues to want to ground his critique of his exorcism of the spectral simulacrum in an ontology. It is a critical – but pre-deconstructive – ontology of presence as actual reality and as objectivity. This critical ontology means to deploy the possibility of dissipating the phantom, let us venture to say again of conjuring it away as the representative consciousness of the subject, and of bringing this representation back to the world of labour, production and exchange, so as to reduce it to its conditions.

Pre-deconstructive here does not mean false, unnecessary, or illusory. (SdM 269/170)

D'une part . . . d'autre part – this is the double gesture, the rhythm of double or what I call elsewhere *clôtural* reading that has *haunted* Derrida's work since the 1960s, of which the examples are legion, and which is the most distinctive motif of deconstruction as a way of reading.[5] As always, Derrida reads with two hands, following assiduously and indefatigably the unstable limit that divides what we might call the logic of a text – its fundamentally aporetic or undecidable basic concepts and distinctions – from the intentions that attempt to govern that text, the author-ity that tries dissolve or control those aporias. As is so often the case, Derrida focuses this double gesture in the ambivalent usage of a specific word by the author he is considering, in this case *Spectre, Gespenst*. Previous examples, of course, are *Geist* in Heidegger, *pharmakon* in Plato, *supplément* in Rousseau, and so on. So, at the formal level at least, SdM *'c'est du bon Derrida, n'est-ce pas?'* Always the same, yet always different in each particular instance of reading; a singular event and the eternal return of the same. But, after all, could we or should we expect Derrida not to be Derrida?

However, to operate strategically with a pre-deconstructive distinction, if the double gesture gives us the *form* of Derrida's reading of Marx, then what of the *content* to his hypothesis? To introduce some detail that will only become clear later on, the basic claim that Derrida makes is that, on the one hand, Marx respects the spectrality of *différance* at the basis of any conceptual order, political regime or mode of economic organization. For Derrida, this is exemplified in a number of specific ways, in Marx's treatment of technology and the media, his thinking of the spectrality of communism ('A spectre is haunting Europe – the spectre of communism'), and the spectrality of capital itself: the fetish character of the commodity form, the non-phenomenologizable mystery of exchange value, and the subtle evasiveness and tendency-to-invisibility of ideology. This leads Derrida to one side of his hypothesis, that the figure of the spectre or phantom is not just one figure amongst others in Marx's text, it is rather 'la figure cachée de toutes les figures' (SdM 194/120). The basic task of Derrida's reading in SdM is to survey this *phantomachia peri tes ousias* that runs through Marx's texts, which is traced in a partial reading of the *Communist Manifesto*, the second chapter of Volume 1 of *Capital* and, most impressively, a reading of Marx's critique of Stirner in *The German Ideology*.

This leads Derrida to the claim that there is, to use his neologism, a *hantologie* in Marx's text, a certain irreducible spectrality and *différance* at work, a logic of haunting that, for Derrida, is the condition of possibility and impossibility of any conceptual order.[6] One of the crucial distinctions in SdM turns, characteristically for Derrida, on a homonym, namely the difference between *ontologie* and *hantologie*, a difference that can only be marked grammatologically in writing, that by-passes phoneticization. I will specify ontology in a moment, but let it be noted that Derrida's claim early in the book is that this *hantologie* is not only more powerful and ample than any ontology or thinking of Being, i.e. Heidegger's, but contains within it, as a secondary effect, any eschatology or teleology linked to such onto-logy, whether that be an eschatology of Being, of class struggle, of divine revelation, or whatever (SdM 31/10). In a gesture that will be familiar to Derrida-watchers, *ontologie* is an apocalyptic discourse on or of the end, whereas *hantologie* is a discourse on the end of the end.[7]

Marx is therefore, according to Derrida, a *hantological* thinker. This is what his texts *say*. This is the logic that governs them, that makes them possible, *despite themselves*. However, following the other side of the double gesture – *d'autre part* – if Marx's texts respect a logic of spectrality that is (as Derrida implies in the above quote) deconstructive, then, as Derrida makes crystal-clear in his reading of the critique of Stirner in *The German Ideology*, Marx also wanted to be rid of phantoms and spectres. Of course, Marx shares this tendency with the Young Hegelians (Bauer, Feuerbach, Stirner) – and, I would claim, with Hegel himself – insofar as they wanted to free philosophy and consciousness of the illusions to which it had subjected itself in history, in particular the illusory spectrality of religion. However, as is well known, the young Marx's problem with the Young Hegelians was that they concerned themselves with 'German philosophy and not German reality', and restricted their critique of spectrality to the realm of conscious-ness and its objects. However, Marx's discourse was not only directed against the spectrality and *Vorstellungsdenken* of the Young Hegelians, but also against the spectre of ideology, namely 'the legal, political, religious, aes-thetic or philosophical'[8] forms through which the ideas of the hegemonic class become the ideas of the epoch, and also against the spectrality of bourgeois economy characterized by the fetish character of the commodity form and the phantom nature of exchange value.

Furthermore, Marx wanted to found his critique of spectrality on what Derrida refers to as an *ontology*, which is critical but pre-deconstructive. Why pre-deconstructive? Because, to echo Derrida's words, it is a critique of political economy that has as its horizon or foundation a conception of presence as effective reality or objectivity, what Derrida elsewhere refers to as the living present of life, praxis, production and labour. The unstable limit that Marx's text criss-crosses at various points is that between the deconstructive and the pre-deconstructive, between *hantologie* and *ontologie*. Thus, the general hypothesis here is that Marx's analysis and critique of the Young Hegelians, of the German Ideology, and of bourgeois political economy, is deconstructive and *hantological*, but it becomes pre-deconstructive when that critique is referred to or founded upon an ontology of presence, effectivity, praxis and objectivity. Derrida's characteristically quasi-transcendental claim is that *hantologie* is the condition of possibility for *ontologie*; that is, although Marx makes a decision to refer the critique of capital to an ontology of presence, this decision cannot repress what we might call the *spectral drive* or *différance* which would ruin any such ontology *avant la lettre*. Thus, although Derrida is reading with two hands, his reading is not even-handed, he is not offering an even choice between *hantologie* and *ontologie*; rather, he is showing how this ambivalence is structured or staged in Marx's text, but *hantologie* has theoretical priority, for the claim is that it is from this spectral drive that something like thought is born (SdM 261/165).

(I have a parenthetical worry here about what counts as Marx's ontology: Derrida refers to an ontology of presence in Marx but how are we to understand this? I take it that Marx's 'ontology' is located in what, at the beginning of *The German Ideology*, he refers to as the 'presuppositions' of his approach, namely that 'we begin with real individuals, together with their actions and the material conditions of life, those in which they find themselves, as well as those which they have created through their own efforts'.[9] That is, we begin with an insight into the fundamentality of the social production of life – 'As individuals express their life so they are' – in terms of a dialectic between individual forces of production and the arrangement of the relations of production into which those forces are born, and which constitutes the economic structure of society. I take it that Marx's ontology is located in his insight into the dialectic of forces and relations of production, which generates both the materialist conception of history and an agenda for political action – let's call it communism for old time's sake. Two thoughts on this:

1. Is this an ontology? To my knowledge, Marx doesn't use this word in this sense, and I imagine that many scholars of Marx would be suspicious of this terminology. For example, J. O'Malley in his helpful 1994 edition of Marx's *Early Political Writings* calls this 'ontology' a 'materialist guideline'.[10] Thus, the notion of ontology here would seem to presuppose the hermeneutic grid of a Heideggerian conception of metaphysics which is not, as Derrida has shown better than anyone, exempt from deconstruction.

2. Secondly, and more importantly, if the elements of Marx's 'ontology' are somehow 'pre-deconstructive', then what does this mean? Derrida is careful to point out in the above quote that pre-deconstructive does not mean 'false, unnecessary or illusory', but presumably neither does it mean 'true, necessary or real'. If the elements of Marx's 'ontology' are pre-deconstructive, then what remains that we might call (pre-deconstructively) *substantive* or at the level of *content* in a deconstructive Marxism? What force does Marxism retain if we set to one side its materialist account of life, production, economy, praxis and history? I completely agree with Derrida that there are certain ontologies that we can do without, for example the Marxist-Leninist economic determinism of dialectical materialism, and we must constantly resist the temptation to ossification and dogmatism into which Marx's discourse can fall, but does this qualification disqualify all ontologies? Can we do without ontology or, better, an ontological *moment* if we are Marxists, even deconstructive Marxists? And what remains of Marxism when we set to one side this ontological baggage? I will return to this question below in my discussion of the political.[11])

The Context

However, if Derrida's hypothesis in SdM claims a theoretical argument for the primacy of spectrality, then is this Derrida's only reason for writing SdM? Is there not, to use another pre-deconstructive palaeonym, a *norma-tive* claim running through SdM which allows us to establish something like the *context* for this text. Why read Marx now?

In the paragraph that follows the statement of the hypothesis that I have just been commenting on, Derrida makes the following remark:

> That the ontological and the critical are pre-deconstructive, has political conse-quences that are perhaps not negligible. And they are doubtless not negligible, to say it too quickly here, as concerns the concept of the political, as concerns the political itself. (SdM 270/170–1)

To express a thought telegraphically and in a way that I will try to make good below, the normative drive of SdM, and what I find so impressive about the text – so urgent and so clear – is its attempt at a politicization or, better, *re*-politicization (SdM 144/87) of deconstruction, an attempted reinvention of the political in terms of a Marxist *hantologie*. But what is Derrida arguing against? That is, what are the political consequences of a pre-deconstructive ontology and critique? They are twofold, or rather there are at least two elements to the context for SdM, one within Marxism, one outside of Marxism, the latter being much more important for Derrida. What they have in common is a refusal of spectrality.

1. Within Marxism, a strong point of Derrida's reading is the link he draws between what he rather euphemistically calls 'the totalitarian heritage of Marx's thought' (SdM 170/104) and the refusal of spectrality. Totalitarianism, or what Jean-Luc Nancy calls 'immanentism', in all its recent and less recent guises, is a political form of society governed by a logic of identification, where 'everything is political'. That is, it is a political form where all areas of social life are claimed to represent incarnate power: the proletariat is identified with the people, the party with the proletariat, the politburo with the party, the leader with the politburo, and so on. Totalitarianism is the phantasy of a completed and transparent social order, a unified people among whom difference or social division is denied. In terms of SdM, totalitarianism is premised upon a refusal of spectrality, it is, as Derrida puts it, a 'panic before the phantom in general'; that is, before something which escapes, transcends and returns to haunt the social order. Although totalitarianism is a grotesque distortion of Marx's thinking, particularly of what I would see as its fundamentally democratic ethos (which is, of course, powerfully and rightly critical of the formalism of bourgeois liberal democracy, of the latter's attempt to have political equality without economic equality), it is clear that totalitarianism inherits a certain conception of 'the end to politics' within Marx's text, what he called the abolition of the state and what Engels referred to as its 'withering away'. Against the troubling tendency to subordinate the political to the socio-economic within Marx's 'ontology', which was transformed into the economism of the Second International, Derrida's argument for a logic of spectrality within Marxism can be linked to the claim for the irreducibility of the political understood as that moment where the sedimented meanings of the socio-economic are contested. Following Ernesto Laclau's radicalization of Gramsci, one might link the logic of spectrality to the logic of hegemony; that is, if one renounces – as one must – the communist eschatological 'a-theodicy' of the economic contradictions of capitalism inevitably culminating in revolution, then politics and politico-cultural-ideological hegemonization is indispensable to the possibility of radical change. I will come back to this below.[12]

2. Outside of Marxism, and here we come to the real context for SdM, if there is a refusal of spectrality within totalitarianism, then there is an equal refusal of it in that anti-Marxist consensus that celebrates the 'collapse

of communism' in terms of the uncontestable triumph of liberal democracy. The context for SdM is the hegemony of the teleological discourse on
the death or end of Marxism, which, as I mentioned above, Derrida rightly
sees with a sense of *déjà vu*, as a rehearsal of the 1950s 'end of ideology'
thesis. Derrida detects a threefold thread to this hegemony in the recent
behaviour of the political class, the media and intellectuals (SdM 91–2/52–
3). As an example of this anti-Marxist hegemony, Derrida chooses Fukuyama's
The End of History and the Last Man, which is the focus of the engaging, but
perhaps over-lengthy, second chapter to SdM. Derrida quite rightly and
very persuasively places Fukuyama's end-of-history thesis in the tradition of
Americian Straussianism continued by Fukuyama's teacher, Allan Bloom,
and going back, via Leo Strauss, to Kojève's interpretation of Hegel. In a
way that recalls Derrida's discussion of an apocalyptic tone in philosophy,
he shows how Fukuyama's neo-liberal end-of-history euphoria is essentially
a Hegelian-Kojèvian theodicy where liberal democracy, allegedly rooted in
a recognition of the dignity of human beings and economic effectivity, is
the realization of the kingdom of God on earth. Thus, the end of history
would be the final eradication of the spectre of communism and the universal *incarnation* of liberal democracy. Thus, Fukuyama opposes the spectre
of Marxism to a certain Hegelian/Kojèvian Christian logic of incarnation
as the end of history.

Although seemingly diametrically opposed, both elements of the context for SdM (and these two elements by no means exhaust its context)
follow a logic that is premised upon a refusal of spectrality; they are both
discourses on and of the end – apocalyptic discourses. We could go further
and claim that both discourses are *Christian* in Hegel's sense of the word,
namely discourses of *incarnation* and *revelation*, ultimately the incarnation
of community, of absolute knowing as community, the system as socio-
political comedy (of course, there are other, and perhaps more persuasive,
certainly more tragic, readings of Hegel than this comic interpretation). This
thought can be linked to an opposition that runs throughout SdM, and
which is particularly important in the final chapter: between spectrality and
phenomenology. The spectre is precisely that which refuses phenomenologization, that retreats before the gaze that tries to see it, like the ghost of
Hamlet's father. The spectre is the apparition of the inapparent.[13] Phenomenology is here conceived in its Hegelian rather than Husserlian sense,[14] as that
active experience (*Erfahrung*) where objects in themselves become objects *for*
consciousness. In this sense, phenomenology is always a phenomenology of
spirit (subject becoming spirit and spirit becoming subject), or a becoming-
phenomenologizable of the spectre, in a logic which is both Christian, insofar

as Christ is the phenomenologization of the spectrality of the divine, and – as the Young Hegelians were perfectly aware – post-Christian insofar as Christianity is the self-alienation of consciousness or human essence. For Derrida, the irreducibility of the spectral is thematically linked to the irreducibility of the religious. But, in order to understand what this means we must turn to the central theme of SdM: *the messianic.*

The Messianic

First, a word on ghosts. In the characteristically elliptical opening to SdM, entitled 'Exordium' (which is possibly an allusion to Kierkegaard's *Fear and Trembling*), Derrida suggests that without speaking to and of ghosts we would not be able to be responsible either to the living or to the not-yet or no-longer living. Thus, the discourse on spectres is the condition for what, with Benjamin, we would call an anamnesic solidarity with the dead of history and for those as yet unborn.[15] Thus, the discourse with and on spectres proceeds in the name of justice, as this word is presented in the essay 'Force of Law', which is in many ways the *Ur*-text for SdM, although the former presents the barest bones of the latter.[16] Indeed, in SdM – as in 'Force of Law' – Derrida cites Levinas and employs the latter's conception of justice from *Totality and Infinity* to illustrate his own account (SdM 48–9/ 23). Justice here defines and is defined by the ethical relation to the other, '*la relation avec autrui – c'est à dire la justice*'. In Derridian terms, Justice is the undeconstructable condition of possibility for deconstruction, the 'for-the-sake-of-which' deconstruction takes place, 'but', Derrida notes, 'we can call it by other names'. The messianic will be one of those other names.

Thus, SdM proceeds in the name of justice, whether ethical or political, and speaks of spectres in order to try and do justice to the living, the dead and the unborn. Running through Derrida's opening remarks is a critique of any account of justice that would restrict responsibility only to the living, to the presently living, or to the living present. In a manner that is difficult to present cogently outside the dense allusiveness and performative compression of the opening pages of SdM, Derrida is weaving together his account of justice with his early deconstruction of the *lebendige Gegenwart* in Husserlian phenomenology, to suggest that justice is somehow constituted by *différance*.

Before unpacking this claim, one might note that there are two prime candidates for accounts of justice that would restrict responsibility to the living. Firstly in Marx himself, recall the famous words from *The German*

Ideology cited above – 'as individuals express their life, so they are' – where Marx's thinking would seem to be rooted in an ontology of life. Secondly, we can also note an oblique debate with Michel Henry's reading of Marx, for whom *life* – for Henry, the subjective praxis of living individuals – is the foundation upon which economic and meta-economic reality can be constructed. Marxism is not reducible to any economism or explicable through any notion of scientificity based on the fiction of *une coupure épistémologique*, but is, rather, a *philosophy of life*.[17]

Against Marx's and Henry's primacy of *la vie*, an approach that the latter would call phenomenological, Derrida posits a notion of *la sur-vie* (living-on, sur-vival), which one could trace back to his readings of Blanchot.[18] This notion, which only occurs, to my knowledge, on three occasions in the text (SdM 17/xx, 179/187 and 235–6/147), plays a quiet but organizing function. The nearest one gets to an explanation of *sur-vie* is when the debate with Henry surfaces in a long footnote (SdM 177–9/186–8). For Henry, Marx's metaphysical determination of reality in terms of praxis, production and, ultimately, life, gives rise to an entirely novel conception of subjectivity as 'une puissance immergée en soi et qui s'éprouve soi-même sans distance';[19] that is to say, as radically immanent subjectivity constituted through affectivity. Although Derrida might be said, in principle, to grant the *ontological* plausibility of Henry's reading of Marx, as 'the hyper-phenomenological principle of the flesh-and-blood presence of the living person' (SdM 230/191), Derrida opposes this reading with his own *haunto-logical* approach. After posing some persuasive critical questions to Henry, Derrida writes revealingly:

> We are attempting something else. To try to accede to the possibility of this very alternative (life and/or death), we are directing our attention to the effects or the petition of a living-on or survival [*une sur-vie*] or of a return of the dead (neither life nor death) on the sole basis of which one is able to speak of 'living subjectivity' (in opposition to its death). (SdM 179/187)

By following the path of the spectre and the logic of spectrality in Marx's text, Derrida is obviously seeking to deconstruct the limit between the living and the non-living and show that the seeming priority of life in fact presupposes a *sur-vie* that undermines this priority. We speak of ghosts in the name of justice.

However – and this is an extremely difficult thought to get to grips with, but it is a *capital* idea – to claim that justice is constituted by *différance* is not to imply that justice is deferred, delayed or indefinitely postponed: 'demain

on rase gratis', 'it's jam tomorrow'. *Différance* is falsely accused of procrastination or of evading the pressing needs of the present with the so-called
luxury of undecidability. On the contrary, Derrida's whole effort in SdM is
in thinking the *injunction*, be it the injunction of Marx (the title of the first
chapter) or the injunction of *différance*. As Derrida remarks in an interview
given at the time of the publication of SdM, 'There would be no *différance*
without urgency, emergency, imminence, precipitation, the ineluctable,
the unforeseen arrival of the other, to the other to whom reference and
deference are made'.[20] With an urgency that marks the whole tone of the
book, making its prose restless and light,[21] Derrida writes, and I quote at
length:

> In the incoercible *différance* the here-now [*l'ici-maintenant*] unfurls. Without late-
> ness, without delay, but without presence, it is the precipitation of an absolute
> singularity, singular because differing, precisely, and always other, binding itself
> necessarily to the form of the instant, in *imminence and in urgency*: even if it
> moves toward what remains to come, there is the *pledge* [*le* gage] (promise,
> engagement, injunction and response to the injunction, and so forth). The
> pledge is given here and now, even before, perhaps, a decision confirms it. It
> thus responds without delay to the demand of justice. The latter by definition is
> impatient, uncompromising, and unconditional. No *différance* without alterity,
> no alterity without singularity, no singularity without here-now. (SdM 60/31)

A full commentary on this compressed and rich passage would constitute
a separate chapter in itself. It would at the very least cause us to link the
urgency and injunction of Marx to the theme of *le gage* which is the key to
an understanding of Derrida's reading of Heidegger in *De l'esprit*.[22] However, the central thought here is that the injunction of SdM – of *différance*
and Marxism – is *l'ici maintenant sans présence*, that is, the absolute singularity
of justice happening now without presence. We should hear in the 'here and
now' both the classical and theological *hic et nunc* and the semantic richness
of the *maintenant*, understood both as the now, but also as the 'maintaining',
that is, the act of *maintenance* or maintaining/sustaining/bearing, where the
present participle connotes an *act* of presencing irreducible to the present
(*Gegenwart*). We might even hear the thought of the hand-holding (*manutenere*
– *manus, tenere*) of the now which appears in Derrida's reading of Heidegger.[23]

For Derrida, the ethico-political imperative of Marxism happens *now*,
it is maintained at this very moment and is not postponed to a Utopian
future.[24] It would seem to me that the entire plausibility of SdM rests upon
this difficult thought of the *here and maintaining-now without presence as an*

impossible experience of justice. If this thought proves absolutely unintelligible, then one can perhaps follow Derrida no further.

Derrida associates the injunction of *différance*, or the injunction of Marx, with his notion of *democracy to come* (*la démocratie à venir*), which has been an increasingly persistent theme in his recent work (SdM 110–11/64–5). Once again, Derrida is anxious to distinguish *la démocratie à venir* from any idea of a future democracy, where the future would be a modality of the *lebendige Gegenwart*, namely the not-yet-present. Derrida's discourse is full of negations at this point: democracy is *not* to be confused with the living present of liberal democracy, lauded as the end of history by Fukuyama, *neither* is it a regulative idea or an idea in the Kantian sense, *nor* even a Utopia, insofar as all these conceptions understand the future as a modality of presence (SdM 110/65). It is a question here of linking *la démocratie à venir* to *différance* understood in the above-mentioned sense as *l'ici maintenant sans présence*, as an experience of the impossible without which justice would be meaningless. In this sense, *la démocratie à venir* does not mean that tomorrow (and tomorrow and tomorrow) democracy will be realized, but rather that the experience of justice as the maintaining-now of the relation to an absolute singularity is the *à venir* of democracy, the temporality of democracy is *advent*, it is arrival happening now. As I have hypothesized elsewhere, democracy is the future of deconstruction, but this future is happening now, it is happening as the now blasting through the continuum of the present.[25] It would be a question here of developing at least three further points.

1. To show how the time of justice – the time of the injunction of *différance*, of Marxism and *la démocratie à venir* – can be understood as messianic time in the sense developed by Benjamin in the 'Theses on the Philosophy of History';[26] that is, as that *Jetztzeit*, which Derrida translates as 'l'à-présent' ('the at-present' SdM 96/181), that *now* which is not the empty and homogenous flow of objectivist history governed by the *Gegenwart*, and which Benjamin assimilates to a notion of historical materialism.

2. To show how the Benjaminian notion of messianic time can be thought in relation to Levinas's notion of ethical time or the temporality of what he calls, with great discretion in the Preface to *Totality and Infinity*, messianic eschatology.[27] Levinas opposes the time of justice to the ontological or economic notion of time and history that reduces and reifies individuals, determining them in terms of their works, relations of exchange and productivity. When Levinas claims that 'When man truly approaches the Other he is uprooted from history',[28] I think 'history' here refers to the objective history of the victors, or 'barbarism' in Benjamin's sense of the

word. At least on my reading, Levinas's work attempts to rub history against the grain, to find the 'ruptures in history',[29] to produce a history for those without works or texts, what I have elsewhere called *ethical* history.[30] The historical materialist, in Benjamin's sense, blasts open the continuum of objectivist history in the name of another history, in the name of justice, which would not be – for Benjamin, Levinas or Derrida – an end to history, but the continual working over of history as a work of infinite mourning, a politics of memory, the insomniac experience of being haunted by the spectres of the past. Levinas writes: 'Of peace there can only be an eschatology . . . That peace does not take place in the objective history disclosed by war, as the end of that war or as the end of history.'[31]

3. To show how the time of justice in Derrida, as the maintaining-now without presence, can be productively linked to the temporality of the ethical relation in Levinas. Levinas's later work proceeds from a distinction between two orders of time: synchrony and diachrony. Synchronic time is a linear, infinite series of punctual moments spread along the axes of past, present and future – what one might call, with Bergson, the spatial representation of time or, with Heidegger, the vulgar Aristotelian concept of time. Diachrony, on the other hand, is – literally – the coming apart of time, it is time as the punctual present falling out of phase with itself (*le déphasage de l'instant*) or the time of the lapse (*le laps*). In Bergson's sense, diachrony is the real time of subjectivity: the unique, unrepeatable and mobile temporality of *la durée*; in Heidegger's sense, it is the temporalization of time (*die Zeitigung der Zeit*), the authentic experience of time from which the inauthentic time of synchrony is derived. Levinas's basic and astonishing claim is that the concrete case in which time temporalizes itself as diachrony is in the everyday event of my responsibility for another.[32] Time is accomplished in a relation to the other. This relation is not an experience of presence for Levinas, but is, rather, a relation to the other that is underwritten by an experience of the trace, the trace of the infinite as that past which has never been present. For Levinas, the essence of time is *temporisation*: postponement, patience, the undergoing of time as senescence, the passivity of ageing. Time establishes a relation to the future that is not achieved through laying hold of the future, as Heidegger attempts in his analyses of *Verstehen* and *Entwurf*, but in a 'lack of any hold upon the future'.[33] For Levinas, the enigma of time – the time of justice – lies in an experience of time that differs from the present, both as an absolute past and an ungraspable future, precisely as trace and as *différance*. And yet, this experience of time happens *now*, blasting through the continuum of the present in a relation to the other, the experience of justice. Interestingly, this temporal and ethical

structure is what Levinas would call (and would Derrida call it?) *témoignage*: testimony or witness.[34]

However, we are still a little distant from the theme of the messianic, although it has been presupposed in everything that has been said in the last few pages. Something is rotten in the state of Denmark, the time is out of joint. The lesson that Hamlet learns from the political assassination of his father, according to Derrida, is that the order of law, of the state, is based on violence, vengeance and injustice. Given this identification of law and violence – which, Derrida rightly claims, is Shakespeare's question before it is Nietzsche's, Heidegger's or Benjamin's (and whose is it before Shakespeare's? Homer's?) – how is one to think of justice at this time of disjuncture? Derrida asks, and it is here that the messianic is introduced for the first time, qualified by a characteristically coy 'quasi':

> If right or law stems from vengeance, as Hamlet seems to complain . . . can one not yearn for a justice that one day, a day belonging no longer to history, a *quasi messianic* day, would finally be removed from the fatality of vengeance. (SdM 47/ 21, my emphasis)

In these fascinating pages, Derrida is weaving together a dense fabric of allusion and argument, where he associates: (1) the experience of *disjuncture* (a crucial word in these pages), of Hamlet's sense of the time being out of joint – the order of law as vengeance – with (2) the disjuncture of the ethical relation in Levinas, which is precisely that which cannot be assembled into a totality; and (3) Heidegger's meditation on time and justice in *Der Spruch der Anaximander*, where *dike* is translated as jointure or *Fug*, and which is thought together with *a-dikia* as *Unfug* or dis-juncture. Although I cannot go into the detail of Heidegger's text here,[35] what interests Derrida is Heidegger's attempt, firstly, to suspend all traditional conceptions of law as calculative, metaphysical and deconstructable, and to try and think justice in relation to the donation of time, namely the presencing of the present (*das Anwesende des Anwesen*), and to think something like Being non-metaphysically in relation to this presencing.

However, and in a way that will be familiar to readers of Derrida, he poses the following critical question to Heidegger:

> Once one has recognized the force and the necessity of thinking justice on the basis of the gift . . . is there not a risk of inscribing this whole movement of justice under the sign of presence, albeit the presence to meaning of the *Anwesen*, of the event as coming into presence, of Being as presence joined to itself, of the proper of the other as presence? (SdM 55/27)

Thus, if Heidegger thinks of justice in relation to the presencing of the present – that is, in terms of a jointure that gathers and harmonizes – Derrida's question is whether justice, understood with Levinas as a disjunctive relation to the other, 'supposes on the contrary the irreducible excess of a disjunction or an anachrony, some *Un-fuge*, some "out of joint" . . .' (SdM 55/27). Derrida engages in a reversal of Heidegger where he hypothesizes that justice as disjuncture – 'the de-totalizing condition of justice' (SdM 56/28) – is the condition for the presencing of the present. It is in this way (and Derrida recognizes the hastiness and provisionality of his formulations at this point) that the relation of deconstruction to the possibility of justice can be thought, where justice – 'that which must (without debt and without duty) render itself to the singularity of the other' (SdM 56/28) – is the undeconstructable condition of possibility for deconstruction.

Although the way in which Derrida links his argumentation to Heidegger and Shakespeare is novel, the above conclusion – deconstruction is justice – will hardly be surprising to readers of 'Force of Law'. However, what *is* novel are two subsidiary claims that Derrida tags on to the above argumentation: firstly, this account of justice is called a 'desert-like messianism' by Derrida: 'the messianic: the coming of the other, the absolute and unpredictable singularity of the *arrivant as justice*' (SdM 56/28). Secondly, this notion of the messianic is interpreted as 'an *ineffaceable* mark . . . of the heritage of Marx' (SdM 56/28). Thus, combining the two claims, the heritage of Marx that Derrida wants to endorse is that of a messianic appeal for justice.

The theme of the messianic, allied to the name of Marx, recurs at crucial points in SdM. After stating that he endorses the kind of critical analysis (of ideology and capital) that we have inherited from Marxism, Derrida links this to the '*schwache* messianische Kraft' of Benjamin's 'Theses on the Philosophy of History', what he calls, emphasizing the adjectival rather than substantive usage, a 'messianique sans messianisme' (SdM 96/181, and see 103/59, 112/65).

(A further parenthetical worry begins to take shape here: namely, if this messianic appeal for justice is the way in which the heritage of Marxism is to be assumed, then, Derrida goes on,

Failing which [*Faute de quoi*] one would reduce the event-ness [*l'événementalité*] of the event, the singularity and the alterity of the other. Failing which [*Faute de quoi*] justice risks being reduced once again to juridico–moral rules, norms of representations, within an inevitable totalizing moment . . . (SdM 56–57/28)

My question would be: is the passage from the messianic appeal for justice to laws, norms and rules always a fault (*une faute*), always in default? If so, why is it a fault and what sort of fault is it? Clearly for Derrida, to refer the messianic appeal for justice to moral and legal conditions is a transgression of the apparent priority, or indeed apriori antecedence of the messianic – what Derrida elsewhere calls 'the universal dimension of experience'[36] – but is this transgression not also a necessity? Is it not the most necessary of necessities, namely the moral-legal-social *instantiation* of justice, the aposteriori and particular event of the apriori status of the messianic? To employ the language of the above quote, is not totalization inevitable? Isn't the question not *whether* to totalize, but *how* to totalize, that is, *how* to link the apriori and the aposteriori, the universal and the particular, the transcendental and the empirical? As we will see below, the notion of the New International acknowledges the necessity for instantiation, totalization, the *aposteriori*, the particular and the empirical; but I have two further telegraphic thoughts in this regard:

1. Is not this faulty move from justice to law precisely that which is thought by Levinas in terms of the move from the other (*autrui*) to the third party (*le tiers*), from ethics to politics? It might also be noted that, in 'Idéologie et idéalisme', Levinas also interestingly defines Marxism as an ethical 'prophetic cry . . . the revolt of Marx and of Marxists beyond Marxist science'.[37] But, for Levinas, politics would be the *measure* brought to the ethical relation to the other, without which the latter would risk being 'angelic', 'the spirituality of angels' (if not spectres) that is the source of his critique of Buber's I–Thou relation. How is one to combine (is one to combine?) the thought of justice with the thought of measure, which, of course, also entails the question of judgement? (I shall return to this question in detail in chapter 12.)

2. In a debate with Axel Honneth, I have, with some significant and important reservations, attempted to support and amplify his attempt to show the possible compatibility or mutual supplementarity of Derrida's recent reflections on ethico-political issues with the Habermasian programme of discourse ethics, in order to show how the messianic appeal for justice conceived as a relation to the irreducible singularity of the other might be combined with a broadly Kantian and procedural theory of justice, capable of testing the validity of moral-political norms. The question here is: if it can be shown that the reciprocity and symmetry axiomatic to Habermasian discourse ethics stand in need of supplementation by a non-reciprocal, asymmetrical appeal to justice or the messianic, then is not the same true *vice versa*?[38])

However, on the question of Marxism and messianism, are we not evading a rather basic and crude question? Marx had many swingeing and unkind things to say about the Young Hegelians, but what he endorsed in their approach was the critique of religion, writing famously that 'Religion is the sigh of the oppressed creature, the feeling of a heartless world and the soul of soulless circumstances. It is the opium of the people.'[39] As the *Theses on Feuerbach* make clear, the problem with the Young Hegelians is that their concept of alienation is restricted to the critique of religion, a critique which is 'essentially complete'.[40] So, against Marx, Derrida would seem to want to maintain the irreducibility of the religious in its 'desert-like' form. Now, is this plausible? At least four features can be noted here:

1. For Derrida, the irreducibility of the spectral is linked to the irreducibility of the religious, where Marx's critique of religiosity would be part and parcel of his ontological approach. *Hantologie* would seem to be premised upon the irreducibility of forms of non-identity and alterity, where the religious is a privileged form of such alterity.

2. More specifically, in Derrida, the irreducibility of the religious is the desire to maintain the *sublimity* of the religious, which is expressed in Benjamin's messianism and elsewhere (in Levinas, in a certain version of negative theology). Derrida opposes – and this is a theme one can find dealt with at great length in *Glas* – any notion of religiosity rooted in what I called above a phenomenology of *incarnation* (which one might also call a phenomenology of the beautiful), the incarnation of the living presence of the divine in the form of the person of Christ and, ultimately, in the spiritual form of the community in Hegel and the material form of communism in Marx.

3. In opposing this logic of *incarnation* in religion, Derrida works to undermine (1) the historical teleology of religion in Hegel which leads irresistibly to Christianity, the *revealed* religion; (2) the *Aufhebung* of religion in philosophy found at the end of the *Phenomenology of Spirit* and *one* condition (only one, the other being the becoming-spirit of the subject) for the possibility of Absolute Knowing; and (3) the *Aufhebung* of the Young Hegelian critique of religion into the critique of political economy in Marx. All of these gestures would be ontological for Derrida.

4. Is one led to conclude from the above that the irreducibility of religious sublimity in Derrida's notion of the messianic allows one to identify his position with that accorded by Hegel to Judaism, as an abstract and formalistic religion of duty, where justice is placed above love? Is *hantological* Marxism a continuation of what we might call 'philosophical Judaism' by other means? And is this justifiable?

Derrida goes some way to addressing this question in his most revealing discussion of the messianic which comes close to the end of SdM (SdM

266–7/167–9). Derrida asks: what is the relation between Marxist messianism, as 'a universal structure' (SdM 266/167), and that other desert-like Abrahamic messianism of Judaism? Having set up the question nicely, Derrida doesn't really give a satisfying response, asking himself whether Abrahamic messianism would be a prefiguration or (to use Levinas's word, which is how he refers to the divine as the trace of illeity[41]) 'prénom' of Marxist messianism. Why not, perhaps? Nonetheless, and always in the interrogative mood, Derrida asks, 'Can one conceive an atheological heritage of the messianic?' (SdM 266/168) and suggests a few lines later that 'One may always take the *quasi-atheist* dryness of the messianic to be the condition of the religions of the Book' (SdM 267, my emphasis). Derrida goes on to qualify the messianic in terms which recall my discussion of *différance* and *la démocratie à venir* in terms of 'imminence' and 'urgency', and calls it 'a "messianism" that despairs' (SdM 268/169). A religion of despair, then? Perhaps.

However, taking as a cue Derrida's qualification of the messianic as 'quasi-atheist', another avenue can be briefly pursued. In his reading of *The German Ideology*, Derrida comes across Marx's citation of Stirner's words '*Ja*, es spukt in der ganzen Welt', poorly rendered into French as, '*Oui*, le monde entier est peuplé de fantômes' (SdM 216/136). What holds Derrida's attention is the phrase *es spukt, het spookt, it spooks*. Derrida comes back to this phrase right at the end of SdM (SdM 272/172); what interests him is the way in which the logic of spectrality is expressed *verbally* (*es spukt* from *spuken*), that is, as a movement, what Derrida calls the 'passive movement of an apprehension'. This passive movement is the very movement of haunting, of the ghost, of the ghosting of the ghost, *la revenance du revenant*. Derrida makes an interesting parallel between the spookiness of haunting and the experience of *Unheimlichkeit* in Freud and Heidegger (SdM 273–7/173–5). However, specifically in relation to the question of religion, I would like to associate the *es spukt* with the uncanniness of the *il y a* as this is figured in the work of Levinas and Blanchot.

Although I cannot go into detail here,[42] the *il y a* should not be confused with the Heideggerian *es gibt* (although might one not link the *es spukt* with the *es gibt: es spukt Sein, es spukt Zeit*?), for it is both Levinas's word for Being and his attempt to ruin the *Seinsfrage*. With the *il y a*, Levinas asks us to undertake a thought experiment: 'Let us imagine all beings, things and persons, reverting to nothingness?'. But what would remain after this annihilation of all *Seienden*? Nothing? Levinas claims that this very nothingness of all existents would itself be experienced as a kind of presence, not the presence of the *lebendige Gegenwart*, but what he calls elsewhere 'An atmospheric density, a plenitude of the void, or the murmur of silence'.[43]

To compress to the point of incomprehensibility, the experience of the *il y a* is what Blanchot would call *le neutre*, which is opened in the experience of writing and literature. I have claimed that the *il y a* is the secret of Blanchot's work, its primal scene, which is an experience of dis-aster, of the night without stars.[44]

What interests me here is the way in which the experience of the *es spukt*, that is, the impossible experience of spectrality (i.e. the ghost is there, but does not exist; it is neither present nor absent) shares certain features with the *il y a*. The latter is an experience of the night, the night of insomnia for Levinas or what Blanchot calls 'the other or essential night' towards which the desire of the writer tends. It is also, crucially, an experience of haunting; it is the night of ghosts, which Levinas illustrates with the example of Banquo's ghost which returns after its murder to haunt Macbeth.[45] In the night of the *il y a*, which is also the space of many of Blanchot's *récits*, the frontier between the living and the dead is criss-crossed: the living are unable either to live or die and the dead refuse to lie down. The *il y a* is an experience of the impossibility of death – horror of horrors – which Derrida has himself explored in his recent *Aporias*.[46] Death is the impossibility of my possibility, which outstrips my powers; it is that of which I am ultimately unable (*je ne peux plus pouvoir*). With this in mind, we might explore some of the spectres in Levinas's text, particularly his discussion of the return of *le revenant* of scepticism after its refutation, which, it has been claimed, is the spectre of Derrida in Levinas's *Autrement qu'être*.[47]

However, the thought that I would like to pursue here is the following: might not the 'quasi-atheist' messianism of SdM be linked with the *es spukt* and the *il y a*, not as a religious messianism, but precisely as an experience of atheist transcendence? Does the impossible experience of the *es spukt*, the spectrality of the messianic, look upwards to a divinity, divine justice, or even the starry heaven that frames the Moral Law; or, rather, does it not look into the radically atheist transcendence of the *il y a*, the absence, disaster and pure energy of the night that is beyond law?

The Political

I suggested above that what is perhaps most impressive and most urgent about SdM is its call for a re-politicization of deconstruction in terms of a Marxist *hantologie*. I also indicated two of the political consequences of a pre-deconstructive Marxist *ontologie*, and suggested that the logic of spectrality in Derrida could be linked to the neo-Gramscian logic of hegemony in the work of Ernesto Laclau. It is time to try and make good on these suggestions.

In what we might justifiably refer to as his deconstruction of Marxism – that is, a reading that identifies a double gesture within Marx's texts – Laclau radicalizes Gramsci's critique of the economistic stageism and historical determinism of traditional Marxism.[48] Roughly and readily, Laclau opposes the almost mechanistic vision of historical materialism advocated in the Second International and in certain Marxist texts (the example given is the Preface to the *Contribution to the Critique of Political Economy*), with an account of history based on the irreducibility of class struggle and antagonism, a tendency that one can also find within Marx's texts, for example at the beginning of the *Communist Manifesto*. Thus, although Laclau would endorse the traditional Marxist account of capitalism in terms of its often pernicious dislocatory effects, he does not think that these dislocations can simply be referred to the alleged economic and historical objectivity of contradictions between the forces and relations of production, the effects of the infrastructure on the superstructure; they are, rather, the consequence of continual 'hegemonic articulations' (for me, the key concept in Laclau's work), of incursions of the political and the ideological into the socio-economic-historical realm, where infrastructure and superstructure form what Gramsci would call a 'historical bloc'. Such hegemonic articulations temporarily fix or stabilize the meaning of social relations in a transient equilibrium. Such a 'hegemonic equilibrium' of the social is not to be transcended in a communist society free from power, contingency, antagonism and politics itself – the millenarian vision of communist society that sometimes gets the better of Marx and which, with the privilege of hindsight, it is all too easy to confuse with the totalitarian myth of social transparency.

In contradistinction to the traditional Marxist theodicy that would claim that the dislocations of capitalism lead inexorably to the simplification of the class structure, and the emergence of the proletariat as the revolutionary class and privileged agent of history, Laclau argues that the very dislocatory effects of late capitalism – what one might think of as the phenomenon of combined and uneven development – lead instead to a progressive fragmentation of the social and a proliferation of social actors (for example, the decline in the organizing power of the state and in the credibility of traditional political parties and the increasing prominence of ethnic, national, sexual or ecological protest movements). Perhaps Laclau's most challenging and controversial thesis is that these phenomena of dislocation and fragmentation lead not only to a proliferation of political possibilities, but are also the conditions under which something like freedom is possible; that freedom is a consequence of dislocation. The democratic transformation of society – what I still want to call socialism – is *one* of these political possibilities (and only one: there are others, particularly on the radical Right, which have been significantly more successful at hegemonizing in recent decades), but there is no economic or historical inevitability to such an outcome. Socialism will only be the consequence or, better, the permanent activity of intense hegemonic articulation and political effort. It is, to say the least, unclear whether the traditional notion of the political party, confined within the nation-state is adequate to such a task.

An expanded notion of hegemony becomes a way of arguing for the primacy of politics over socio-economic relations, although the former can in no way proceed without continual reference to the latter and the former is done for the sake of the latter. As such, the concept of hegemony points in two different temporal directions at once: first, with regard to history, hegemony is a way of explaining how certain social relations became fixed, and shows that such fixing is not the consequence of the 'objective' contradiction of forces and relations of production; it is, rather, the product of contingency, antagonism and power, that is to say, it is the consequence of a *decision* (i.e. the transformation of history into genealogy). Second, the concept of hegemony leaves the future radically open and indeterminate, which means that nothing is guaranteed, but neither is anything lost, at least not yet. On this view, rather than standing at the end of history, it might be said that we stand at some sort of beginning, at the point when we can recognize the radical contingency and limitedness of our finitude. Such a situation need not lead to the pessimism of an Adorno or the passivity or the resignation of a later Heidegger, but can also be the condition for a 'new militancy and new optimism'.[49]

If deconstruction is the attempt to show the constitutive undecidability, radical incompletion or untotalizability of textual, institutional, cultural, social and economic structures, then hegemony is a theory of decisions taken in the undecidable terrain opened up by deconstruction, and which, in my view, is precisely the way in which we might begin to think about the politics of deconstruction.[50] The burning question here is whether and how we can combine the logic of deconstruction with the logic of hegemony: does undecidability paralyse the possibility of the decision or does it, on the contrary, enable it?

With regard to SdM, the fate of the question of deconstruction and hegemony, to my mind, turns on how we interpret the following thought: in relation to the generalized dislocation of the contemporary world, Derrida claims, the messianic hesitates, it trembles: 'This messianic hesitation does not paralyze any decision, any affirmation, any responsibility. On the contrary, it grants them their elementary condition. It is their very experience' (SdM 269/169).

Is messianic hesitation the experience of the decision? That is the question, as Hamlet might soliloquize. If our response is positive, then we might be able to solder the logics of deconstruction and hegemony at this point.

In SdM, Derrida indeed speaks of hegemony, using the word – which is, to my knowledge, relatively new to his vocabulary[51] – on at least eight occasions (SdM 69 [× 2], 73 [× 2], 90, 91, 96–7, 149; in translation 37 [× 2], 40 [× 2], 51, 52, 55, 90), mostly during the discussion of Fukuyama and the so-called death of Marxism. The first time he uses the word, he even refers to Laclau's work, making the interesting and valid point that 'Haunting belongs to the structure of every hegemony' (SdM 69/37). However, rather than viewing hegemony as a theory of the decision and the positive possibility of politicization, Derrida (mis)understands hegemony negatively in its traditional sense as domination. He writes, for example, that 'a dogmatics is attempting to install its worldwide hegemony in paradoxical and suspect conditions. There is today in the world a *dominant* discourse . . .' (SdM 90/51). This is unfortunate. However, if the concept of hegemony is (mis)understood traditionally in SdM, there is nonetheless, I believe, a *logic* of hegemony at work in the text. This logic turns around a phrase that forms part of the book's subtitle, and which, in Georges Sorel's terminology, we might describe as the mobilizing 'myth' of SdM: *The New International*.[52] In many ways, this is the key to SdM, but my worry is whether the key fits the lock of the present political situation.

Derrida lists what he calls the ten afflictions of the 'New World Order' in a kind of *tableau noir* (SdM 134–9/81–4). After listing unemployment, homelessness and other woes, the final item on his list, which is privileged above the other terms ('*surtout, surtout*', he writes – SdM 138/83) is the present state of international law, which he rightly sees as being dominated by the interests of certain 'hegemonic' nation-states. In contradistinction to this, Derrida suggests that we require a New International that 'is being sought through these crises of international law, it already denounces the limits of a discourse on human rights that will remain inadequate, sometimes hypocritical, and in any case formalistic' (SdM 141/85). This reference to the formalism of human rights, echoing the Hegelian-Marxist critique of their abstraction and one-sidedness, is illuminating and is followed by some qualifications of the New International. He writes of the bond around which something like solidarity might form: 'It is a link of affinity, suffering and hope, a still discreet, almost secret link, like that around 1848, but more and more visible – we have more than a sign of it' (SdM 141/85). Thus, the New International would be focused around a common bond or link, that – at this point in history at least – is almost secret. Derrida goes on to claim that this bond would be 'without party, without country, without national community (International before, across, and beyond any national determination), without co-citizenship, without common belonging to a class' (SdM 142/85).

A strange bond, then: without reference to the figures of community, class, party, nation or the other traditional means of collective identification or hegemonization. Yet, Derrida insists, this bond of the New International is inspired by at least one of the spirits of Marxism. Which one? Clearly not the ontological Marxism of *the* proletariat, *the* party and *the* revolution characterized above as ontological. Derrida continues in a luminous passage, which I quote at length:

> Now if there is a spirit of Marxism which I will never be ready to renounce, it is not only the critical idea or the questioning stance [which Derrida qualifies on the previous page as the spirit of the Enlightenment] . . . It is rather a certain emancipatory and *messianic* affirmation, a certain experience of the promise that one can try to liberate from any dogmatics and even from any metaphysico-religious determination, from any *messianism*. And a promise must promise to be kept, that is, not to remain 'spiritual' or 'abstract', but to produce events, new forms of action, of practice, of organization, etc. To break with the 'party form' or with such and such a form of the State or the International does not mean to renounce every form of practical or effective organization. It is exactly the contrary that matters to us here. (SdM 146–7/89)

I couldn't agree more. The New International must be in the spirit of the Marxist idea of critique (critique of ideology and of capital) and the quasi-atheist notion of messianic affirmation or promise that we discussed above and which proceeds in the name of justice and emancipation. Furthermore, such critical and messianic promises must be made with the intention of being kept, and thus the promise of the New International must in its turn give rise to new forms of organization, activism and political aggregation. In relation to what I said above about the *injunctions* of *différance* and *la démocratie à venir*, the urgency of the New International cannot be deferred or postponed indefinitely; it must be approached in messianic terms as *l'ici maintenant sans présence*. The New International is happening now, at this very moment. Derrida writes: 'And there are signs. It is like a new International, but without a party, or organization, or membership. It is searching and suffering, it believes that something is wrong, it does not accept the "new world order".'[53]

To my mind, Derrida would here seem to be trying to sketch the pre-conditions for a new socialist hegemonic articulation, a political decision taken in the name of justice and in the face of the world's afflictions.

The only question I have here is the following: *how is the New International to be hegemonized?* What forms and means should it employ? Around what figures should it agitate? Should it agitate around figures? Who does it include? Who does it oppose? *Does* it oppose? *Does* it exclude?

I do not have convincing answers to these genuinely open questions, but let me hazard three critical thoughts:

1. I find Derrida's suggestions on the subject of the New International a little unspecific, suggesting that 'the new International belongs only to anonymity' (SdM 148/90). He goes on, in the same paragraph, to suggest that within the academic and intellectual world, the New International includes those who have resisted the anti-Marxist dogma of recent years and remained hyper-critical in the Enlightenment spirit, without renoun-cing the ideals of democracy and emancipation. Who does Derrida have in mind here? Jürgen Habermas?

2. Also, the limits of the New International begin to look a little vague when Derrida writes that 'Whether they wish it or know it or not, all men and women, all over the earth, are today to a certain extent the heirs of Marx and Marxism' (SdM 149/91). Perhaps this is right. But so what? Couldn't the same be said – perhaps with even greater justification – about Adam Smith or John Locke? Are we not all heirs to their marketing strat-egies? Thus, there is the risk of a rather empty universalism on Derrida's part at this point.

3. Finally, on the question of organization, although Derrida is rightly dubious of the idea of a communist party as the privileged and sole means for revolutionary transformation, he tends to link this to a rather question-able historical positivism which claims that 'What tends perhaps to disap-pear in the political world that is announcing itself, and perhaps in a new epoch of democracy, is the domination of this form of organization called the party' (SdM 167/102). Again, on the next page, he says of this hypoth-esis 'that this mutation has already begun; it is irreversible' (SdM 168/103). Derrida tags two claims onto this hypothesis: (1) that the correlate of the party, i.e. the state, is also exhausted; and (2) that the notion of the party cannot adapt to the exigencies of the contemporary public space with its domination by the media and tele-technology. In relation to this second

point, I have two words to offer: *Forza Italia*. If Derrida is right, how does one explain the brief but stunning electoral success of this alliance which would seem (entirely cynically, to my mind) to combine a fairly classical party structure with the exigencies of the televisual media forms? An analysis of the 1994 elections in South Africa (one recalls that SdM is dedicated to the memory of Chris Hani), although they had a more progressive outcome, might also consider this question of the relation between the party form (in this case, the ANC), the media and the democratic process. However, to return to the first point, my question is the following: if the political party is not an adequate vehicle for promoting something like a New International, which might be justified although I have my (doubtless nostalgic) doubts about this, then how does one hegemonize something like the New International outside of traditional party structures? What means of identification, figuration and hegemonization are available? Furthermore, how does one work outside traditional party structures without collapsing into a 'divide and rule' designer politics of individualism or confining oneself to the always modest socio-economic changes of single-issue politics, or, worst of all worlds, devoting oneself to an intra-academic politics of vacuous radicalism and reaction?

The Economic[54]

The concept of economy has played a continual, discreet, but perhaps organizing rôle in Derrida's work since the 1960s. One immediately thinks of the discussion of restricted and general economy in Bataille and of psychic economy in Freud in *Writing and Difference*.[55] Indeed, what Derrida calls 'the point of greatest obscurity' in his work, 'the very enigma of *différance*', can be redescribed in economic terms as a relation between two impossibilities. That is, thinking in particular of Derrida's reading of Bataille, two claims are made: (1) that the calculable expenditure, exchange and restitution that governs a restricted economy cannot but be interrupted by the force of a general economy, by an incalculable expenditure without reserve; (2) that there can be no pure giving or expenditure without reserve that does not fall back into the restricted economy it attempts to leave behind. Derrida's major insight might be thought of as the necessity of thinking together of two impossibilities, that of a purely restricted and a purely general economy. One might claim that *différance* is the name for this necessary and impossible thinking together, this relation between the economic and an-economic.[56]

Of course, as Gido Berns has shown, this distinction between the economic and the an-economic is classical and finds its philosophical origin in Aristotle's *Politics*.[57] As is well known, for the Greeks, economy was primarily concerned with establishing the rules or *nomoi* of the household or *oikos*. The *oikos*, what Derrida would call 'la clôture économique' (SdM 53/26) is the enclosed sphere of the home and the hearth, wherein Aristotle thought it possible to have a virtuous relation to economic goods insofar as one practises 'equalizing justice'; that is, insofar as economic exchange between *oikoi* takes place on the basis of service and mutual use, repaying good with good. Over against the sphere of economy – the sphere of the proper – stands what Aristotle calls *chrematistics*, money making. Berns has shown how, for Aristotle, the art of money making (*chrematistike techne* – and I note the association of chrematistics, capital accumulation and technics at this point, which is not peripheral to our concerns here) is essentially *improper* to ethical life and should not be part of the proper conduct of human nature. Chrematistics only arises when the use value of an object has been exceeded by exchange value, that is to say, when the de(con)structive infiniteness of accumulation and desire has been introduced into the finite circle of the *oikos*. In this sense, and I will return to this below, we might say, adapting one of Wallace Stevens's *Adages*, that '*money is a kind of deconstruction*'.[58] In this Aristotelian sense – counter-intuitively, insofar as we would associate chrematistics with modern capitalist economy – money is an-economic.

Aristotle's model of economy, tied as it is to ethical and political reflection, betrays, according to Berns, a nostalgia for small, quasi-agrarian communities. Such nostalgia has a long and powerful heritage, and modern analogues can be found firstly in the young Hegel's longing for *verlorene Sittlichkeit*, and perhaps even in the mature Hegel's concept of the State, where the latter's rational and ethical *telos* would attempt to contain or circumscribe the boundlessness of chrematistic desire. Also, it can be found in Marx's effective reproduction of the distinction of economy and chrematistics, where socialism would be identified with the former and capitalism with the latter. Economy is chrematistic under conditions of capitalist relations of production, but in a communist society, 'there will be no money-capital at all'.[59]

Of course, it should be noted that there is another, liberal and capitalist, tradition of economic reflection, beginning in Locke and definitively expressed by Adam Smith, which, whilst still articulating itself in relation to a moral vision (Adam Smith is the author of *The Theory of Moral Sentiments* as well as *The Wealth of Nations*), analyses the chrematistic nature of economy as an essentially autonomous, value-free domain. For Adam Smith, money is a consequence of the division of labour, a division rooted in that most advantageous feature of human nature, the propensity to truck and barter.

Before returning to SdM and trying to focus some critical questions, I would like to follow Berns one step further and look at a passage from Derrida's *Given Time*, where the distinction between economy and chrematistics is discussed in the context of Baudelaire's 'La fausse monnaie'.[60] Derrida summarizes Aristotle's distinction between economy and chrematistics, noting that 'for Aristotle, it is a matter of an ideal and desirable limit, a limit between the limit and the unlimited, between the true and finite good (the economic) and the illusory and indefinite good (the chrematistic)'.

Economy is the thought of a limit, it is the attempt to master that limit and control the thought of the unlimited, the *apeiron* that would overstep the *peras*. As such, the opposition between the economic and the chrematistic is that between 'the supposed finiteness of need and the presumed infinity of desire'.[61] Now, the infinity of desire will always transcend the finitude of need (and the fact that Derrida's language at this point recalls that of Levinas is perhaps not accidental, as Levinas is one of the rare thinkers who reserves a privileged place for money in his work[62]) once *money* has appeared on the scene. Derrida continues, in a gesture that will be familiar to readers of his work, 'As soon as there is monetary sign – and first of all sign – that is, *différance* and credit, the *oikos* is opened and cannot operate its limit'.[63] Thus, money is a kind of deconstruction, it opens the closure of the *oikos* to the unrestricted 'economy' of desire where money circulates and where wealth is accumulated or squandered – the nomadic and quasi-automatic flows of capital.

But – and this is what interests me – this ruination of the ethicality of economy, this transgression of its limits, which are the limits of the family, hearth and home, is also 'the chance for any kind of hospitality . . . the chance for the gift itself. The chance for the event.'[64] (Derrida is suggesting here, and we cannot go into the detail of his reading of Baudelaire at this point, that *money is the possibility of a form of an-economic giving*, for a donation without return, for an *event*. As a long footnote makes clear, the word 'event' is clearly to be understood in its Heideggerian sense as *Ereignis*, and where Derrida associates money (*to khrema*) with *der Brauch* or usage (*to khreon*), which, according to Heidegger, names Being as the presencing of the present in 'that oldest fragment of Western thinking'.[65] Thus, the possibility of money, that is to say, the possibility of '*différance* and credit', breaking the restricted economy of the proper, is also the possibility of the gift, of the 'ethicality' of the gift. We are, doubtless all too allusively, on the brink here of a new thought of the event, of *Ereignis* as the injunction, or what I called above the disjuncture of *différance* as the possibility of justice: *es gibt Sein, es gibt Geld.*

What is the bearing of this argumentation to SdM? How are we to link the injunction or disjuncture of *différance*, thought in relation to money making and capital, to the spirit of Marxism we spoke of above? For a book that deals with Marx and Marxism for 279 pages, Derrida is relatively reticent about economics. However, I have already discussed at length Derrida's suspicions of an ontological Marxism, which, at the level of economy, could be linked to the economistic stageism of traditional Marxism criticized by Gramsci and Laclau, and which leads to the assertion of the primacy of politics (i.e. *hantologie* and hegemony) over economics. In SdM itself, the economic is mentioned on a couple of occasions (SdM 48/23, 53/27), and is taken up in the discussion of the spectre of exchange value in chapter 5. Most interestingly, Derrida defines justice as the incalculability of the gift and 'l'ex-position an-économique à autrui' (SdM 48/23), where the relation to the other might be associated with a certain thought of ethical chrematistics.

However, the central economic question with regard to Derrida, in SdM and elsewhere, as I see it, is the following: *what is the relation between capital and deconstruction?* Doesn't the entire argument of SdM for the irreducibility of a logic of spectrality necessarily entail that capitalism cannot and should not be overcome, for it is only under the conditions of capitalist economy, with its unlimited chrematistic desire, that the radical donation of justice is possible? Is not capitalism the possibility of justice? Is this not the entire thrust of the discussion of the irreducible spectrality of exchange value and commodity fetishism in chapter 5 of SdM? If Derrida is trying to establish the spectral origin of capital and the spectres of Marx that must continue to haunt capitalism, as he would seem to be doing, then is he not also implying a certain dependence of the deconstructive logic of spectrality upon capitalism? Don't Derrida's suspicions of the ontology underpinning Marx's work at least imply the exorcizing of some *Spectres de Marx*, namely the spectre of the revolution and the transcendence of the bourgeois order in a communist society? Furthermore, if, as I have suggested, money is a kind of deconstruction, then is the reverse not also true, namely that deconstruction is a kind of money, perhaps even an art of money-making? For what is money if not a spectre or a sign, as Derrida himself suggests (SdM 80/45), the spectrality of *différance* that haunts the 'real' value of the notes and coins in our pockets? Might not deconstruction be redescribed as a *chrema-tologie*, a logic of money making?

These questions appear critical, but they needn't be at all. I mentioned above how Laclau claims that the possibility of radical democracy is directly linked to the structural dislocations of late capitalism, and that the increasing disorganization of these dislocations enables the possibility of new hegemonic articulations, some of which might lead to the democratic transformation of society. Should we not simply conclude that the only way to assume the heritage of Marxism at the present time is by presupposing capitalism as the unstable but staggeringly resilient economic form of the contemporary world? Capitalism, as Marx himself perspicuously foresaw, has become a global economic system that has pushed beyond the state boundaries of national economies and which exists in a near-neurotic state of permanent revolution, 'tearing down all obstacles that impeded the development of productive forces, the expansion of needs, the diversity of production and the exploitation and exchange of natural and intellectual forces'.[66]

Contemporary capitalism, particularly the activity of the financial markets, would indeed seem to be a total chrematistics that is increasingly free from the regulatory control of any particular economy, whether national or quasi-federal like the European Community. At once extraordinarily creative and wasteful, contemporary capitalism is a near-chaotic order (or a near-orderly chaos) whose endless mobility and movement – its sheer velocity, and strange love of chance – is its best protection against subversion.

How, then, does one respond to contemporary capitalism? In Derrida's words, it is necessary 'To calculate with the incalculable'.[67] That is to say – picking up on the definition of *différance* given above as the necessary and impossible thinking together of the economic and the an-economic – particular economies, such as states or federations of states, must attempt to negotiate with the radical chrematistics of late capitalism, for example by trying to control the value of a given currency against the vast speculative flows of the financial markets. As numerous recent examples show, this is an infinite, precarious and possibly futile task. But is this not the only possibility available for ensuring the integrity of the state or super-state territory and guaranteeing effective economic management, responsible government and adequate social provision for citizens of a given territory?

Maybe. The problem with such a response is that, in terms of the argument I have tried to develop here, it is simply the reactive defence or shoring up of economy against chrematistics – in many ways, it is the friendly old spectre of European social democracy. Although I have much sympathy with this position, does it not beg the question: *why* calculate with the incalculable? Why not rather *incalculate* with the incalculable?

As I argued in the Postscript to chapter 6, what is so troubling about contemporary capitalism to many on the Left is its extraordinary hybridizing
energy, its ability to assume new forms, to hegemonize itself, to recuperate
what was originally intended as opposition and to sell it as a commodity,
to renew and propagate itself not out of any reactive gestures but rather out
of a cheerfully superficial affirmativeness. I argued above that what contemporary capitalism lacked was a *critical*, *Utopian*, or, in Derrida's terms,
messianic moment that would place in question the very social, economic
and political premises of its own system and the iniquities, inequalities and
wastefulness that it creates. But if this argument is granted, the question that
is raised for me is the following: why oppose this extraordinary chrematistic
energy with a defensive, reactive strategy? Perhaps what is required is some
kind of exacerbation of the enormous creative energy of contemporary
capitalism, where those energies are comprehended, criticized and transformed, where rather than opposing capitalism with a reterritorialization
on the level of the economy, the state and law, one would try to accelerate
its deterritorializing effects. Such might well be the task of *philosophy*. As
Deleuze and Guattari write, 'Philosophy takes to the absolute the relative
deterritorialization of capital'.[68] Absolute deterritorialization, then. Is this
not a spectre of Marx?

The Technological

As is well known, Marx had some remarkably prescient things to say about
technology, showing how the capitalist drive for efficiency and the mastery
of time results in the increasing mechanization of the production process, the
creation of a reserve army of the unemployed and an opposition between,
on the one hand, technologized capital and, on the other hand, living
labour. However, Marx's views could not be said to be anti-technological –
unlike, say, the agrarian Utopia of Fourier – and a communist society
would resolve the contradiction between technology and labour by allowing the former to become the property of the latter, of free-associated
labour.

Derrida recognizes Marx as a thinker of technics (SdM 92/53), and the
question of technics, whilst not a dominant theme in SdM, is powerfully
linked to the logic of spectrality. In relation to the modern media or tele-
technologies, Derrida insists that the media still require a Marxist analysis.
Of course, Derrida is thinking of Marxism here in the sense of *hantologie*,
and the claim would seem to be that only such an approach is capable of

grasping the truly spectral nature of the media, of the ways in which the contemporary public space is constituted through tele-technology, a technology that is neither living nor dead, neither present nor absent, but which haunts our most intimate private spaces with its imagery of power.

In a footnote, Derrida reminds the reader that the portion of the heritage of Marx that he wants to preserve concerns the irreducibility of the spectral, which he then links to the *virtual* and the increasing virtualization of politics and the public space (SdM 225–6/190). It would here be a question of an affirmative thinking together of tele-technology or the media with what Derrida says of the public space of democracy. The link between the increasing virtualization and media-tization of the public space and the process of democratization becomes clearer in a second passage, which directly precedes the statement of the hypothesis with which we began this chapter:

> But also at stake, indissociably, is the différantiel of *techne,* of techno-science or tele-technology. It obliges us more than ever to think the virtualization of space and time, the possibility of virtual events whose movement and speed prohibit us more than ever . . . from opposing presence to its representation, 'real time' to 'deferred time', effectivity to its simulacrum, the living to the non-living, in short, the living to the living–dead of its ghosts. It obliges us to think, from there, another space for democracy. For *la démocratie à venir* and thus for justice. (SdM 268/169)

However, it should first be asked: what is technology, or better, technics? As Bernard Stiegler recalls at the beginning of *La technique et le temps*, a text footnoted in the above passage, Western philosophy arguably begins with the distinction of *techne* and *episteme*, where Socrates distinguishes himself from the Sophists by showing how the pursuit of knowledge in critical dialogue is superior to and independent of sophistic rhetoric and mnemotechnics.[69] As the *Phaedrus* shows, philosophy has no need of writing and rhetoric, technologies of the self which lead not to genuine knowledge but only to the loss of memory, or what Husserl called the forgetfulness of origins. In its ancient and modern forms, and in its major tradition, philosophy has sought to constitute the realm proper to it, the realm of the proper – whether this is the transformed space of the *polis*, the intersubjective space of dialogue and uncoerced communication, or the solitary realm of contemplation, reflection and the soul's dialogue with itself – by making any form of technicity secondary. In its drive for authenticity, philosophy has, as Stiegler puts it, repressed the question of technics, a repression that sees technics and technicization as a perversion, a corruption and a constant threat of contamination.[70]

Stiegler shows how this tradition of repression is continued in more recent philosophy, for example in Heidegger, where, despite his subtle remarks about the Janus face of *Gestell* and *Ereignis*, that is, where a meditation on the essence of technics would be a prelude to the appropriative event of time and Being, Heidegger's entire analysis proceeds upon the metaphysical distinction of actual technics, thought as pure calculation or reckoning, and the essence of technics. But equally in Habermas, technics is thought under the categories of Weberian rationalization or as an instance of *Zweckrationalität* leading to technocracy; that is, as a pathological perversion of the space of communicative action and a contamination of the *Lebenswelt*.

In contradistinction to this tradition where philosophy would coincide with the repression of the question of technics – a tradition which risks being rendered quite irrelevant by the sheer speed of the contemporary world, a speed which is that of technical acceleration – Stiegler hypothesizes a thought of *originary technicity*.[71] Technics would here be thought not as an inauthentic perversion secondary to properly philosophical activity, but, rather, as the very condition of possibility for the constitution of something like human life. Technics is that process of exteriorization, the use of means, of media and mediation whereby the human takes shape. Hominization is technicization. As Stiegler puts it, technics is the 'poursuite de la vie par d'autres moyens que la vie'.[72]

What of Derrida, then?[73] Although, to say the very least, this is not how he has been read, might not Derrida best be approached as a thinker of originary technicity? In this respect, it is worth reconsidering a number of examples of 'classical' deconstruction: if one thinks of Derrida's insistence on the role of writing given by Husserl in the constitution of ideality in 'The Origin of Geometry', or the irreducibility of the indicative sign in *La voix et le phénomène*, or the place of writing in the constitution of *logos* and *phone* in 'Plato's Pharmacy', or the logic of iterability in 'Signature, Event, Context', then each of these discrete arguments might plausibly be viewed as claims for the irreducibility of technics, where the grammatological would be equiprimordial with the technological.[74] That is, there is a *necessity* for a detour through technics in the constitution of the philosophical *episteme*, whether this is a realm of dialogue, of the soul conversing with itself, auto-affection, or the pure ideality of speech and meaning. Yet the necessity of the detour through technics is also the ruination or rendering impossible of the very project that it was intended to make possible. One way of following Derrida's work would be to see it as a claim for the irreducibility of technics in the constitution of the philosophical *episteme* and, more generally, in any attempt to constitute what is proper, authentic or appropriate to the human. Authenticity or appropriation are always impurely traced and contaminated by the inauthentic and the inappropriate. Indeed, the former are inconceivable without the latter. We might say that the human, or the *event* of the human, only comes to itself by virtue of technical mediation, by virtue of what Derrida calls the 'différantiel of *techne*' (SdM 268/169). There is no event of the human without technical *différance*, without the technological differentiation of the human from itself in relation to the non-human.

In this connection, some more examples might be illuminating. Think of the whole chain of technical figures that haunt Derrida's texts: the mystic writing pad in 'Freud and the Scene of Writing'; the machines that haunt his readings of Hegel, notably the *machine à draguer* in *Glas*; the persistent ringing of the telephone in *La carte postale*; the gramophone in the essay on Joyce; the photograph in the essay on Barthes; the ubiquitous Mackintosh in *Circonfession* (this list could be continued).[75] It should not therefore be surprising that Derrida should choose the question of technics, and specifically the *metaphysical* character of the distinction of the essence of technics from actual technics, as one his four *fils conducteurs* in his reading of Heidegger in *De l'esprit*.[76] For me, a privileged example of technicity in Derrida to be explored is the brief discussion of Leibniz's plan for a 'General Characteristic' (a kind of seventeenth-century mechanical artificial intelligence program) in *De la grammatologie*, where it might be possible to conceive of grammatology as a general grammar of technics and technicity as a condition of (im)possibility for logocentrism.[77] Thus, it would be a question here of wresting grammatology from its literary and philosophical receptions and even from the direction taken by some of Derrida's later work and reclaiming it as a general theory of technics.

The thesis of originary technicity, as the claim that the human only comes to itself as such through a movement of technical *différance*, opens the possibility of thinking the relation of the human to the non-human, of the *justice* of a relation to the non-human other, whether animal, vegetable, mineral or machine. This perhaps illuminates Derrida's persistent attempts to interrogate and deconstruct the limit that divides the human from the animal and to widen the notion of *le vivant* outside the realm of carnal sacrifice, and also, as we have seen in SdM, to employ the figure of the spectre or ghost to deconstruct the limit between the living and the non-living.[78] As Stiegler reminds us, *différance* is defined by Derrida as a process of *life* of which the human would only be a particular instance, and it would here be a question of linking technicity to biologization, of thinking through the implications of the new biological technologies and perhaps reactivating all the biological metaphors of Derrida's work: the pro-gramme, dehiscence, khora, invagination, etc.[79]

In this sense, I do not think that it would be at all implausible to recast the entire argument for a logic of spectrality in *Spectres of Marx* in terms of a claim for the irreducibility of technicity in the constitution of the human, social and political space of the contemporary world. Technicity is not a perversion but a fatality, a fatality that we should not approach reactively, but *amorously*, that is, affirmatively; perhaps even erotically.

The task barely broached here consists in trying to think together productively the following three elements: (1) originary technicity as both a media-ted and a biological process, (2) capitalization conceived in a relation of originary supplementarity with technics, and (3) the movement of democratization and the possibility of justice. But this task overflows not only the bounds of this chapter, but also the limits of your patience and my competence.

Notes

1. An abridged version of this text first appeared in *Philosophy and Social Criticism*, vol. 21, no. 3, May 1995, pp. 1–30; and in *Filozofski Vestnik*, Slovenian Academy of Sciences, vol. 16, no. 2, 1995, pp. 81–108. The present version first appeared in *Brief. Issues in Cultural Analysis*, ASCA Yearbook, Kampen: Kok Pharos, 1996, pp. 128–62.

2. References to SdM will be given to the pagination of the French text (Paris: Galilée, 1993), followed by a reference to the extremely accurate English translation by P. Kamuf (London and New York: Routledge, 1994).

3. Derrida momentarily ventures this hypothesis in *Mémoires for Paul de Man* (New York: Columbia University Press, 1986, p. 18) before quickly dismissing it. As Stanley Cavell points out, America is '*the* anti-Marxist country' (*Must We Mean What We Say*, Cambridge: Cambridge University Press, 1969, pp. 345–6). But if America were comparable to deconstruction, then what spirit of Marxism would haunt it? I am referring to other work of mine on Cavell, and in particular to the latter's extraordinary discussion of the Marx Brothers in 'Nothing Goes Without Saying' (*London Review of Books*, 6 January, 1994, pp. 3–5; see also *Very Little . . . Almost Nothing*, London and New York: Routledge, 1997, pp. 118–38), where, in the final paragraph, and in a clear allusion to Derrida, Cavell suggests that, better even than Emerson or Thoreau, access to 'that tangle of American culture' might best be had by 'a few days immersion in half a dozen Marx Brothers' films'. What is the spectre of Marx for America? Is it Karl-o or Harpo or Groucho? I return to this theme in a discussion of comedy in chapter 10.

4. On the influence of Tran Duc Thao's *Phénoménologie et matérialisme dialectique*, Paris: Éditions Minh-Tan, 1951, see Derrida's remarks in an interview with *Le Monde* in 1982 (*Entretiens avec 'Le Monde'*, Paris: Éditions la découverte, 1984, p. 79); and remarks in the 'Avertissement' to *Le problème de la genèse dans la philosophie de Husserl*, Paris: Presses Universitaires de France, 1990, p. vii. On economy, see 'From Restricted to General Economy: A Hegelianism Without Reserve', in *Writing and Difference*, transl. A. Bass, London and New York: Routledge, 1978, pp. 251–77. On politics, see *Les fins de l'homme. A partir du travail de Jacques Derrida*, Paris: Galilée, 1981, pp. 526–7.

5. See *The Ethics of Deconstruction: Derrida and Levinas*, Oxford: Blackwell, 1992, pp. 20–31 and 88–97.

6. On *hantologie*, see SdM 31/10, 89/51 and 255/161.

7. See 'Of an Apocalyptic Tone Recently Adopted in Philosophy', transl. J. P. Leavey, *Oxford Literary Review*, vol. 6, no. 2, 1984, pp. 3–37.

8. See 'Preface to a Contribution to the Critique of Political Economy', *Marx/Engels Selected Works*, London: Lawrence and Wishart, 1968, p. 182.

9. *The German Ideology*, London: Lawrence and Wishart, 1970, p. 42.

10. Cambridge: Cambridge University Press, 1994, p. xv.

11. A permanent risk of SdM, I feel, is its tendency to attempt to reinvent the wheel with respect to Marxism by ignoring the attempts, within the Marxist philosophical tradition itself, to refine and revise Marx's work and to save it from its theoretical and practical distortions, whether we think here of Lukàcs, Gramsci, or Adorno and Horkheimer. Might we not ascribe this tendency in Derrida to what one might call an Althusserian 'tic' in SdM (Althusser is clearly a spectre thoughout this text – SdM 147/89), that one can bracket out the previous history of Marxist philosophy insofar as it has somehow been contaminated by 'la grande dérive soviétique' and return to Marx's text, and, literally, *lire le Capital*. The only real exception to this rule is Benjamin, who is a decisive spectre in SdM. But why is Benjamin accorded this unique state of exception? For the most part, Derrida's scholarly sources on Marx (excluding references to external classical sources, like Freud and Heidegger) are exclusively French – Etienne Balibar is treated very well, Michel Henry less so, and Blanchot's short piece 'Les trois paroles de Marx' is the intellectual framework for chapter 1. Indeed, SdM could be seen as a contemporary rewriting of Blanchot's essay, particularly if we take seriously Derrida's extremely astute remarks on the analogies between the 1950s 'end of ideology' thesis and the 1989 'end of history' thesis.

12. Laclau has responded to the reading of *Spectres of Marx* attempted here in his review essay 'The Time is Out of Joint', in *Diacritics*, vol. 25, no. 2, 1995, pp. 86–97, which offers some important critical clarification of Derrida's arguments, particularly on the question of the necessity for discourses of incarnation and the irreducible teleology of the classical discourse of emancipation that Derrida supposedly wants to endorse. However, Laclau is unconvinced of the necessity for the move from a notion of messianic promise to an ethico-political injunction in the way I develop it in the present essay and in my other work. For Laclau, no ethical injunction of a Levinasian kind flows from undecidability, and democratic politics does not need to be anchored in such an injunction. He concludes by focusing what he sees as an ambiguity in Derrida's work, between undecidability as the

terrain of radicalization of the decision and undecidability as the source of an ethical injunction. If this is indeed an ambiguity in Derrida (and I am not wholly convinced of this), then Laclau and I stand at opposing poles of this ambiguity. However, my ambition in the discussion of the political given below is to show how these two poles can enter into some form of productive tension. The debate with Laclau is also discussed above in chapter 5 and continued in chapter 12.

13. Which still leaves open the question of whether there can be a phenomenology *of* spectrality, a phenomenology of the inapparent, to take up Heidegger's phrase from the Zähringen seminar in 1973. As the title of the final chapter of SdM ('L'apparition de l'inapparent: l'escomatage phénoménologique') suggests, Derrida is here alluding to debates about the status of French phenomenology and its alleged theological turn. On this debate, see Dominique Janicaud, *Le tournant théologique de la phénoménologie française*, Combas: L'éclat, 1991 and Jean-Luc Marion, *Réduction et donation. Recherches sur Husserl, Heidegger et la phénoménologie*, Paris: Presses Universitaires de France, 1989.

14. On Husserl, see the intriguing and slightly hurried note (SdM 215–16/189), where Derrida, pondering the question of the spectre in Husserlian phenomenology, focuses on the notion of the *noema* as that 'intentional but *non-real* component of phenomenological lived experience', which would be 'the condition of any experience'.

15. A view perversely paralleled in the Mormon doctrines of baptism for the dead and spirits for the unborn as described by Harold Bloom in *The American Religion*, New York: Simon and Schuster, 1992, pp. 112–28.

16. 'Force of Law: The Mystical Foundation of Authority', in D. Cornell *et al.*, eds, *Deconstruction and the Possibility of Justice*, London and New York: Routledge, 1992. For a discussion of this text, see above, chapter 4.

17. See *Marx*, 2 vols: 1. *Une philosophie de la réalité*. 2. *Une philosophie de l'économie*, Paris: Gallimard, 1976. For an abridged introduction to Henry's reading of Marx, see his essay 'Marx', in S. Critchley and W. Schroeder, eds, *A Companion to Continental Philosophy*, Oxford: Blackwell, 1998, pp. 118–27.

18. See, in particular, 'Sur-vivre', in *Parages*, Paris: Galilée, 1986, pp. 117–218. I take up this theme below in chapter 12.

19. In Henry, 'Marx', p. 126.

20. Derrida, 'The Deconstruction of Actuality', *Radical Philosophy*, no. 68, Autumn 1994, p. 32.

21. Mention of the restlessness and lightness of Derrida's prose in SdM can be related to a common complaint one often hears in circles otherwise highly sympathetic to Derrida's work. It is claimed that Derrida's early work, in particular *La voix et le phénomène*, is philosophically decisive in the deployment of deconstruction and that it possesses a rigour sadly lacking in his later work, which too often seems to have been written in undue haste. Perhaps there is some truth to such a claim. However, what such a complaint consistently overlooks is precisely the question of the *urgency*, or the *injunction* that drives Derrida's later work, and its relation to what one might call the *performativity* or *event-character* of deconstruction. *Spectres of Marx* is clearly not *La voix et le phénomène*. It is a text that was written with enormous urgency to address a specific context at a specific historical moment, to make an intervention at once theoretical, cultural and political. As such, I think that *Spectres*

of Marx should be viewed as a certain *enactment* of the injunction that the book seeks to describe or prescribe. Might we not view *Spectres of Marx* in terms of what it says about the event (SdM 125–6/74–5), namely the event of the injunction of *différance* happening here and now without presence? *Spectres of Marx* is an event, a performance, a staging which, as Samuel Weber has shown (I refer to an unpublished paper, 'Piece-Work', given at the University of Essex in October 1994), is utterly pervaded by its own *theatricality*, most obviously in Derrida's deployment of *Hamlet* as a frame for his reading. A serious question arises for me at this point, however: if we take on board Derrida's remarks on the need for a non-negative, non-reactive thinking of tele-technology and the media, might one not have doubts about whether the book – however staged, however theatrical, however performatively conceived – is the most felicitous medium for the enactment of such a singular event? How about the use of other media: theatre, television, CD-Rom, internet?

22. See 'The Question of the Question: An Ethico–Political Response to a Note in *Of Spirit*', in *The Ethics of Deconstruction*, pp. 190–200.

23. On the hand in Heidegger, see 'Geschlecht II: Heidegger's Hand', in J. Sallis, ed., *Deconstruction and Philosophy*, Chicago: Chicago University Press, 1987, pp. 161–96.

24. As already indicated in the opening note to chapter 5, Derrida distinguishes the thought of the messianic, as the here and now of justice, from the conventional meaning of Utopia (which does not exclude the possibility of other meanings for Utopia). See C. Mouffe, ed., *Deconstruction and Pragmatism*, London and New York: Routledge, 1996, pp. 82–3:

> The messianic experience of which I spoke takes place here and now; that is, the fact of promising and speaking is an event that takes place here and now and is not Utopian. This happens in the singular event of engagement, and when I speak of *la démocratie à venir* this does not mean that tomorrow democracy will be realized, and it does not refer to a future democracy, rather it means that there is an engagement with regard to democracy which consists in recognizing the irreducibility of the promise when, in the messianic moment, it can come [*ça peut venir*]. There is the future [*il y a de l'avenir*]. There is something to come [*il y a à venir*]. That can happen . . . that can happen, and I promise in opening the future or in leaving the future open. This is not utopian, it is what takes place here and now, in a here and now that I regularly try to dissociate from the present.

25. See *The Ethics of Deconstruction*, p. 241.

26. In *Illuminations*, transl. H. Zohn, London: Fontana/Collins, 1973, pp. 255–66.

27. *Totality and Infinity*, transl. A. Lingis, Pittsburgh: Duquesne University Press, 1969, pp. 22–4.

28. *Totality and Infinity*, p. 52.

29. Ibid., p. 52.

30. *The Ethics of Deconstruction*, p. 30.

31. *Totality and Infinity*, p. 24. Incidentally, if this view of Levinas's conception of history is at all plausible, then it makes little sense to claim that Levinas is an anti-historical thinker, as Derrida appears to do in 'Violence and Metaphysics' (in *Writing and Difference*, p. 94).

32. *Otherwise than Being or Beyond Essence*, transl. A. Lingis, Dordrecht: Kluwer, 1981, p. 10.

33. *Time and the Other*, transl. R. Cohen, Pittsburgh: Duquesne University Press, 1987, p. 80.

34. In this regard, see Levinas's 'Vérité du dévoilement et verité du témoignage', *Archivio di Filosofia*, 1972, pp. 101–10; transl. I. MacDonald, *Emmanuel Levinas: Basic Philosophical Writings*, A. Peperzak, S. Critchley and R. Bernasconi, eds, Bloomington: Indiana University Press, 1996, pp. 97–107.

35. 'The Anaximander Fragment', in *Early Greek Thinking*, transl. D. Krell and F. Capuzzi, New York: Harper and Row, 1975, pp. 13–58.

36. See 'The Deconstruction of Actuality', p. 36. On the apriori, see ibid., p. 32.

37. In *De dieu qui vient à l'idée*, Paris: Vrin, 1986, p. 19.

38. See 'Habermas und Derrida werden verheiratet: Antwort auf Axel Honneth', *Deutsche Zeitschrift für Philosophie*, vol. 42, no. 6, 1994, pp. 981–92.

39. See David McLellan, *The Thought of Karl Marx*, London: Macmillan, 1971, p. 23.

40. Ibid., p. 22.

41. *Otherwise than Being or Beyond Essence*, p. 185.

42. For a much fuller discussion of the *il y a*, see the text of the same name in my *Very Little . . . Almost Nothing*, London and New York: Routledge, 1997.

43. See *Existence and Existents*, transl. A. Lingis, Dordrecht: Kluwer, 1978, pp. 57–64.

44. *Very Little . . . Almost Nothing*, Lecture 1.

45. *Existence and Existents*, p. 62. It might be recalled that it is Levinas who writes in *Time and the Other*, p. 72, that 'it sometimes seems to me that the whole of philosophy is only a meditation on Shakespeare'.

46. Transl. D. Dutoit, Stanford: Stanford University Press, 1993.

47. See Robert Bernasconi, 'Skepticism in the Face of Philosophy', in *Re-reading Levinas*, Bloomington: Indiana University Press, 1991, pp. 149–61.

48. My brief presentation of Laclau's work is based on the eponymous opening essay from *New Reflections on the Revolution of our Time*, London: Verso, 1990, pp. 3–85, rather than Laclau and Mouffe's *Hegemony and Socialist Strategy*, London: Verso, 1985, which presents the same deconstruction of Marxism from within a genealogy of the concept of hegemony.

49. *New Reflections on the Revolution of our Time*, p. 82.

50. In this regard, see Laclau's helpful short article, 'Discourse', in R. Goodin and P. Pettit, eds, *The Blackwell Companion to Contemporary Political Philosophy*, Oxford: Blackwell, 1994, pp. 431–7.

51. Although Derrida speaks of 'l'hégémonie centralisatrice' and 'l'hégémonie nationale' in *L'autre cap*, Paris: Minuit, 1991, pp. 45 and 48.

52. This notion is first introduced in chapter 1 (SdM 58/29), but receives a fuller discussion as the centrepiece of chapter 3.

53. 'The Deconstruction of Actuality', p. 39.

54. These remarks on the question of the economic in Derrida are entirely indebted to the work of Gido Berns, and particular to a course given at Essex University in June 1994 on 'Economy and Difference'. For a brief outline of his

approach to Derrida's work, see his 'Politique et justice dans un style déconstructif', in *Filosfski Vestnik*, Slovenian Academy of Sciences, vol. 16, no. 2, 1995, pp. 15–21.

55. 'From Restricted to General Economy: A Hegelianism without Reserve', and 'Freud and the Scene of Writing', in *Writing and Difference*, London and New York: Routledge, 1978.

56. 'Différance', in *Margins of Philosophy*, transl. A. Bass, Chicago: University of Chicago Press, 1982, p. 19.

57. See Aristotle, *Politics*, I, 3, 1256a–1258b.

58. Stevens's adage reads: 'Money is a kind of poetry', in *Opus Posthumous*, London: Faber, 1957, p. 165.

59. Marx, *Capital*, vol. 2, Moscow, 1954, p. 318.

60. *Given Time*, Chicago: University of Chicago Press, 1992, pp. 158–9. It might be noted that these pages also offer a reading of Heidegger's 'Der Spruch der Anaximander', which we could connect to the discussion given above.

61. Ibid., p. 158.

62. Although there are many references to money scattered throughout Levinas's major works, see in particular 'Socialité et argent', *Emmanuel Levinas. Cahier de l'Herne*, Paris: Éditions de l'Herne, 1991, pp. 134–8.

63. *Given Time*, p. 158.

64. Ibid., p. 158.

65. Ibid., p. 159n; and 'The Anaximander Fragment', p. 52 et passim.

66. *Karl Marx. Selected Writings*, D. McLellan, ed., Oxford: Oxford University Press, 1977, p. 364.

67. 'Force of Law: The "Mystical Foundation of Authority"', p. 16.

68. *What is Philosophy?* transl. G. Burchell and H. Tomlinson, London: Verso, 1994, p. 99.

69. *La technique et le temps*, vol. 1, *La faute d'Epiméthée*, Paris: Galilée, 1994. Derrida and Stiegler have extensively collaborated in *Echographies de la télévision*, Paris: Galilée, 1996.

70. Ibid., p. 11.

71. Ibid., p. 30.

72. Ibid., p. 31.

73. The following remarks are deeply indebted to conversations with Richard Beardsworth. In this regard, see the important 'Conclusion' to his *Derrida and the Political*, London: Routledge, 1996, pp. 145–57, see esp. p. 149.

74. *Edmund Husserl's 'Origin of Geometry': An Introduction*, transl. J. P. Leavey, Lincoln: University of Nebraska Press, 1989; *Speech and Phenomena*, transl. D. Allison, Evanston: Northwestern University Press, 1973; 'Plato's Pharmacy' in *Dissemination*, transl. B. Johnson, Chicago: University of Chicago Press, 1981; 'Signature, Event, Context', in *Margins of Philosophy*, Chicago: University of Chicago Press, 1982.

75. See, respectively, *Writing and Difference*, pp. 196–231; *Glas*, transl. J. P. Leavey and R. Rand, Lincoln and London: University of Nebraska Press, 1986; *The Post Card: From Socrates to Freud and Beyond*, transl. A. Bass, Chicago: University of Chicago Press, 1987; 'Ulysses Gramophone: Hear Say Yes in Joyce', in D. Attridge, ed., *Acts of Literature*, London and New York: Routledge, 1991, pp. 253–309; 'Les morts de Roland Barthes', transl. P. A. Brault and M. Naas, in H. J. Silverman, ed.,

Continental Philosophy 1: Philosophy and Non-Philosophy since Merleau-Ponty, London and New York: Routledge, 1988, pp. 259–97; *Jacques Derrida*, transl. G. Bennington, Chicago: University of Chicago Press, 1993.

76. *Of Spirit*, transl. G. Bennington and R. Bowlby, Chicago: University of Chicago Press, 1989.

77. *Of Grammatology*, transl. G. C. Spivak, Baltimore and London: Johns Hopkins University Press, 1976, pp. 75–81.

78. ' "Eating Well", or the Calculation of the Subject: An Interview with Jacques Derrida', in E. Cadava, ed., *Who Comes After the Subject*, New York and London: Routledge, 1991, pp. 96–119.

79. See *La technique et le temps*, p. 147.

The Original Traumatism:
Levinas and Psychoanalysis[1]

Es gibt gar keine andern als moralische Erlebnisse,
selbst nicht im Bereich der Sinneswarnehmung.

Nietzsche, *Die Fröhliche Wissenschaft*

Two Hypotheses: Subjectivity and Ethical Language

Let me begin with a first working hypothesis: the condition of possibility
for the ethical relation to the other – that is, the condition of possibility for
ethical transcendence, communication and beyond that justice, politics and
the whole field of the third party with the specific meanings that Levinas
gives to these terms – is a conception of the subject.[2] Thus, it is only
because there is a *certain affective disposition towards alterity within the subject, as
the structure or pattern of subjectivity*, that there can be an ethical relation.
Levinas writes in the 1968 version of 'Substitution', that we will have more
than one occasion to come back to,

> It is from subjectivity understood as a self, from the excidence and dispossession
> of contraction, whereby the Ego does not appear but immolates itself, that the
> relationship with the other is possible as communication and transcendence.[3]

Or again,

> It is through the condition of being a hostage that there can be pity, compassion,
> pardon, and proximity in the world – even the little there is, even the simple
> 'after you sir'. (p. 91)

So, to make my claim crystal clear, Levinas's account of ethics understood as the relation to the other irreducible to comprehension and therefore to ontology finds its condition of possibility in a certain conception of the subject. In Kantian terms the ethical relation to the other presupposes a rather odd transcendental deduction of the subject. In other terms, it is only because there is a disposition towards alterity within the subject – whatever the origin of this disposition might be, which, as we will see, is the question of trauma – that the subject can be claimed by the other.

Levinas tries to capture this disposition towards alterity within the subject with a series of what he calls 'termes éthiques' or even 'un langage éthique': accusation, persecution, obsession, substitution and hostage. Of course, and this is already a huge issue, this is not what one normally thinks of as an ethical language. A related second working hypothesis announces itself here: the condition of possibility for the ethical relation lies in the deployment or articulation of a certain ethical language. This is already highly curious and would merit separate attention: namely, that Levinas deploys an ethical language that attempts to express what he calls 'the paradox in which phenomenology suddenly finds itself [le paradoxe où se trouve brusquement jetée la phénoménologie]' (p. 92). The paradox here is that what this ethical language seeks to thematize is by definition unthematizable, it is a conception of the subject constituted in a relation to alterity irreducible to ontology, that is to say, irreducible to thematization or conceptuality. Levinas's work is a phenomenology of the unphenomenologizable, or what he calls the order of the enigma as distinct from that of the phenomenon.

Of course, the claim that Levinas is offering a phenomenology of the unphenomenologizable does not make his work unique, and one thinks both of the late Heidegger's description of his thinking in his final Zähringen seminar in 1973 as the attempt at a 'phenomenology of the inapparent' (das Erscheinen des Unscheinbaren) and the important recent debates that this has given rise to in France about the alleged theological turn within French phenomenology (Janicaud, Marion, Henry), discussed in chapter 7. As Wittgenstein might have said, the ethicality of thought is revealed in its persistent attempt to run up or bump up against the limits of language. The ethical might well be nonsense within the bounds of sense demarcated by the Tractatus, but it is important or serious nonsense, and it is arguably the animating intention of both Wittgenstein's earlier and later work.

Thus, and here I bring together the two hypotheses, the disposition towards alterity within the subject that is the condition of possibility for the ethical relation to the other is expressed linguistically or articulated philosophically by recourse to an ethical language that has a paradoxical relation to that which it is attempting to thematize. As so often in the later Levinas, it is a question of trying to say that which cannot be said, or proposing that which cannot be propositionally stated, of enunciating that which cannot be enunciated, and what has to be said, stated or enunciated is subjectivity itself.

In this chapter, I want to discuss just one term in this ethical language, namely *trauma* or 'traumatisme'. Levinas tries to thematize the subject that is, according to me, the condition of possibility for the ethical relation with the notion of trauma. He thinks the subject as trauma – ethics is a trauma-tology.[4] I would like to interpret this word 'trauma', and its associated ethical language and conception of the subject, in *economic* rather than strictly philosophical terms; that is to say, in relation to the metapsychology of the second Freudian topography first elaborated in *Beyond the Pleasure Principle*. For Freud, it is the evidence of traumatic neurosis, clinically evidenced in war neurosis, that necessitates the introduction of the repetition compulsion. Now, it is the drive-like or pulsional character of repetition that overrides the pleasure principle and suggests a deeper instinctual function than the earlier distinction of the ego and sexual drives. Thus, for Freud, there is a direct link between the analysis of trauma and the introduction of the speculative hypothesis of the death drive, and it is this link that I would like to exploit as I read Levinas.

What is the justification for this economic understanding of Levinas? Well, there is absolutely none really, and certainly nothing in Levinas's *intentions* to justify this link. However, as is so often the case with Levinas, his *text* is in a most illuminating conflict with his intentions. It is only by reading *against* Levinas's denials and resistances that we might get some insight into what is going on in his text: its latencies, its possibilities, its radicalities. Although Levinas includes such terms as obsession, persecution and trauma in his ethical language – not to mention his invocation in one place of 'psychosis' (p. 102) and of the ethical subject as 'une conscience devenue folle' – he does this by specifically refusing and even ridiculing the categories of psychoanalysis. For example – and there are other examples – Levinas begins a paper given at a conference with the title 'La psychana-lyse est-elle une histoire juive?' with the confession, 'My embarrassment comes from the fact that I am absolutely outside the area of psychoanalytic research.'[5] For Levinas, psychoanalysis is simply part and parcel of the anti-humanism of the human sciences, which, in criticizing the sovereignty of 'Man' risks losing sight of the holiness of the human (*la sainteté de l'humain*).[6]

From Ego to Self: Levinas's Refusal of Psychoanalysis and the Paradox of the Unconscious

Before giving a more careful reading of Levinas and trying to make good on my initial hypotheses on the subject and ethical language, I would like to illustrate the tension between Levinas's intention and his text in relation to psychoanalysis with an example.

In the original version of 'Substitution', Levinas asks: 'Does consciousness exhaust the notion of subjectivity?' (p. 82). That is to say, is the ethical subject a conscious subject? The answer is a resounding 'no'. The whole Levinasian analysis of the subject proceeds from a rigorous distinction between subject and consciousness or between the *le Soi* (the self) and *le Moi* (the ego). Levinas's work, and this is something far too little recognized in much of the rather too edifying or fetishizing secondary literature on Levinas, proceeds from the rigorous distinction between consciousness and subjectivity, where 'c'est une question de ramener le moi à soi', of leading back the ego of ontology to its meta-ontological subjectivity. For Levinas, it is the reduction of subjectivity to consciousness and the order of representation that defines and dominates modern philosophy. It is necessary to reduce this reduction – such is the sense of Husserlian intentional analysis for Levinas, where what counts is the overflowing of objectivistic, naïve thought by a forgotten experience from which it lives; that is to say, the pre-conscious experience of the subject interlocuted by the other.[7] Levinas breaks the thread that ties the subject to the order of consciousness, knowledge, representation and presence. Levinas gives the name 'psychism' to this subject that constitutes itself and maintains itself in a relation to that which escapes representation and presence: the subject of the trace, of a past that has never been present, the immemorial, the anarchic, etc. In brief, consciousness is the belated, *nachträglich* effect of the subject as trace, the dissimulating effect of a subjective affect. *Consciousness is the effect of an affect*, and this affect is trauma.

Of course, the Freudian resonances in what I have already said will already be apparent, but any possible rapprochement between the Levinasian analysis of the subject and Freudian psychoanalysis is specifically and violently refused by Levinas in the text we are commenting upon. He writes, once again in the 1968 version of 'Substitution':

> But to speak of the hither side of consciousness is not to turn toward the unconscious. The unconscious in its clandestinity, rehearses the game played out in consciousness, namely the search for meaning and truth as the search for

the self. While this opening onto the self is certainly occluded and repressed, psychoanalysis still manages to break through and restore self-consciousness. It follows that our study will not be following the way of the unconscious . . . (p. 83)

It should hopefully go without saying that this is a pretty lamentable understanding of Freud. But, provisionally, one can note two things:

1. That if Levinas appears to believe that psychoanalysis seeks to restore self-consciousness, then it is interesting to note that he says exactly the opposite – and rightly – in an important text from 1954, 'Le moi et la totalité', where it is claimed that psychoanalysis, 'throws a fundamental suspicion on the most unimpeachable evidence of self-consciousness'.[8]

2. Although Freud arguably always harboured the therapeutic ambition of restoring self-consciousness, an ambition expressed in the famous formula, 'Wo Es war soll Ich werden', one should note that there are other ways of returning to the meaning of Freud, and other ways of reading that formula, notably that of Lacan, where he interprets the Freudian *Es* as the subject of the unconscious and where the imperative driving psychoanalysis is to arrive at the place of the subject beyond the imaginary *méconnaissance* of the conscious ego.[9]

However, the tension that interests me has not yet been established. Returning to the above quote on Levinas's refusal of the psychoanalytic concept of the unconscious, what is fascinating here and typical of the relation between Levinas's intentions and his text, is that Levinas's statement that he will not be following the way of the unconscious is flatly contradicted in a later footnote in the 1968 'Substitution' text, just after a couple of key references to trauma:

Persecution leads back the ego to the self, to the absolute accusative where the Ego is accused of a fault which it neither willed nor committed, and which disturbs its freedom. Persecution is a traumatism – violence par excellence, without warning, without apriori, without the possibility of apology, without logos. Persecution leads back to a resignation without consent and as a result traverses a night of the unconscious. *This is the meaning of the unconscious, the night where the ego comes back to the self under the traumatism of persecution* [nuit ou se fait le retournement de moi à soi sous le traumatisme de la persécution] – a passivity more passive than all passivity, on the hither side of identity, becoming the responsibility of substitution. (p. 183, my emphasis)[10]

Here is the paradox (or is it a simple contradiction?): in one breath, Levinas writes that he will not follow the psychoanalytic way of the unconscious because it seeks to restore self-consciousness. But, in the next breath, Levinas gives us the meaning of the unconscious conceived as the night where the ego comes back to the self under the traumatism of persecution. So, the concept of the unconscious, the *pierre angulaire* of psychoanalysis, is strategically denied and then reintroduced with a *méconnaissance* that is perhaps too easily understood within a Freudian logic of *Verneinung*.

My question to Levinas has already been announced but can now be more sharply formulated: *what does it mean to think the meaning of the unconscious in terms of the traumatism of persecution? What does it mean to think the subject – the subject of the unconscious – as trauma?*

The Levinasian Subject

In order to approach this question, I would like to return to my first hypothesis and try to show the central place of the subject in Levinas through a brief overview of the main argument of *Otherwise than Being or Beyond Essence.*[11] As I discussed in detail in chapter 3, Levinas begins his exposition by describing the movement from Husserlian intentional consciousness to a level of pre-conscious, pre-reflective sensing or sentience, a movement enacted in the title of the second chapter of the book, 'De l'intentionalité au sentir'. In a gesture that remains methodologically faithful to Heidegger's undermining of the theoretical comportment to the world (*Vorhandenheit*) and the subject–object distinction that supports epistemology and (on Levinas's early reading in his doctoral thesis) Husserlian phenomenology, the movement from intentionality to sensing, or in the language of *Totality and Infinity*, from representation to enjoyment, shows how intentional consciousness is conditioned by *life* (p. 56) But, against Heideggerian *Sorge*, life for Levinas is not a *blosses Leben*, it is sentience, enjoyment and nourishment. It is *jouissance* and *joie de vivre*. Life is love of life and love of what life lives from: the sensible, material world. Levinas's work is a reduction of the conscious intentional ego to the pre-conscious sentient subject of *jouissance*. Now, it is precisely this sentient subject of *jouissance* that is capable of being called into question by the other. The ethical relation, and this is important, takes place at the level of pre-reflective sensibility and not at the level of reflective consciousness. The ethical subject is a sentient subject not a conscious ego.

So, for Levinas, *the subject is subject*, and the form that this subjection assumes is that of sensibility or sentience. Sensibility is what Levinas often refers to as 'the way' of my subjection, vulnerability and passivity towards the other. The entire argumentative thrust of the exposition in *Otherwise than Being* is show how subjectivity is founded in *sensibility* (chapter 2) and to describe sensibility as a *proximity* to the other (chapter 3), a proximity whose basis is found in *substitution* (chapter 4), which is the core concept of *Otherwise than Being*. So, if the centre of Levinas's thinking is his conception of the subject, then the central discussion of the subject takes place in the 'Substitution' chapter of *Otherwise than Being*, that Levinas describes as 'la pièce centrale' (p. ix) or 'le germe du present ouvrage' (p. 125). However – a final philological qualification – the 'Substitution' chapter was originally presented as the second of two lectures given in Brussels in November 1967; the first was an early draft of 'Language and Proximity', which was published separately in the second edition of *En découvrant l'existence avec Husserl et Heidegger*, elements of which were redrafted in the third chapter of *Otherwise than Being*. The original published version of 'Substitution' appeared in the *Revue Philosophique de Louvain* in October 1968. Although much is missing from the first version of this text, particularly Levinas's qualified endorsement of Kant's ethics, I would say that it is philosophically more concentrated and easier to follow than the 1974 version. So, if the concept of the subject is the key to Levinas's thinking, then the original version of the 'Substitution' chapter might well provide a key to this key.

Subject as Trauma

I would now like to try and analyse this traumatic logic of substitution – a self-lacerating, even masochistic logic – where I am responsible for the persecution that I undergo, and where I am even responsible for my persecutor. No one can substitute themselves for me, but I am ready to substitute myself for the other, and even die in their place.

In the original version of 'Substitution', the first mention of trauma comes after a citation from *Lamentations*, '*Tendre la joue à celui qui frappe et être rassasié de honte*' ('To offer the cheek to the one who strikes him and to be filled with shame' p. 90). Thus, the subject is the one who suffers at the hands of the other and who is responsible for the suffering that he did not will. I am responsible for the persecution I undergo, for the outrage done to me. It is this situation of the subject being 'absolutely responsible for the persecution I undergo' (p. 90) that Levinas describes with the phrase 'le traumatisme originel'. Thus, the subject is constituted as a subject of persecution, outrage, suffering or whatever, through an original traumatism towards which I am utterly passive. This passage, and the pages from which the quote is taken, is dramatically expanded in the 1974 version of 'Substitution', and Levinas adds:

> A passivity of which the active source is not thematizable. Passivity of traumatism, but of the traumatism that prevents its own representation, the deafening trauma, breaking the thread of consciousness which should have welcomed it in its present: the passivity of persecution. But a passivity that only merits the epithet of complete or absolute if the persecuted is liable to respond to the persecutor. (p. 111)

This 'traumatisme assourdissant', this deafening traumatism (which incidentally recalls the opening lines of Baudelaire's 'A une passante', 'La rue assourdissante', where it refers to the traumatic noisiness of nineteenth-century Paris) is that towards which I relate in a passivity that exceeds representation, i.e. that exceeds the intentional act of consciousness, that cannot be experienced as an object, the noematic correlate of a *noesis*. Trauma is a 'non-intentional affectivity', it tears into my subjectivity like an explosion, like a bomb that detonates without warning, like a bullet that hits me in the dark, fired from an unseen gun and by an unknown assailant.[12]

Now, it is this absolute passivity towards that which exceeds representation, a non-relating relation of inadequate responsibility towards alterity experienced as persecuting hatred, that is then described in the 1974 version – very suggestively for my concerns – as *transference*, '*Ce transfert . . . est la subjectivité même*' ('This transference . . . is subjectivity itself', p. 111). Thus, *subjectivity would seem to be constituted for Levinas in a transferential relation to an original trauma*. In other terms, the subject is constituted – without its knowledge, prior to cognition and recognition – in a relation that exceeds representation, intentionality, symmetry, correspondence, coincidence, equality and reciprocity, that is to say, to any form of ontology, whether phenomenological or dialectical. The ethical relation might be described as the attempt to imagine a non-dialectical concept of transference, where the other is opaque, reflecting nothing of itself back to the subject. In Lacanian terms, that I will take up in detail in the following chapter, it would seem that the subject is articulated through a relation to the real, through the non-intentional affect of *jouissance*, where the original traumatism of the other is the Thing, *das Ding*. It is only by virtue of such a mechanism of trauma that one might speak of ethics.[13]

The second major reference to trauma in the 1968 version is a few pages further on and has already been partially cited and discussed. Reinforcing his claim about the subject as substitution, Levinas writes, rather awkwardly:

The condition – or non-condition – of the Self [*Soi*] is not originally an auto-affection presupposing the Ego [*Moi*] – but precisely an affection by the Other – an anarchic traumatism this side of auto-affection and auto-identification. But a traumatism of responsibility and not causality. (pp. 93–4)

Thus, the subject is constituted in a hetero–affection that divides the self and refuses all identification at the level of the ego. Such is the work of trauma, *die Trauma-Arbeit*, the event of an inassumable past, a lost time that can never be, *contra* Proust, *retrouvé*, a non-intentional affectivity that takes place as a subjection to the other, a subject subjected to the point of persecution.

It is at this point, and in order to elaborate critically this concept of the subject as trauma, that I would like to make a short detour into Freud.

Trauma in Freud

What is trauma? Trauma is etymologically defined in Larousse as *blessure*, as wounding, as 'violence produite par un agent extérieur agissant mécaniquement'. As such, trauma has both a physiological as well as psychical meaning, denoting a violence effected by an external agency, which can be a blow to the head, or a broken arm, as much as the emotional shock of bereavement. For Freud, trauma is an economic concept and refers to a massive cathexis of external stimulus that breaches the protective shield of the perceptual-consciousness system or ego. Trauma is shock and complete surprise. In terms of the Freudian model of the psychical apparatus governed by Fechner's constancy principle, trauma is an excess of excitation that disrupts psychical equilibrium and is consequently experienced as unpleasurable. In Lacanian terms, trauma is the subjective affect of contact with the real. It is the opening up of the ego to an exteriority that shatters its economic unity. Recalling Levinas's allusion to a 'deafening traumatism', trauma is like a bomb going off, producing a sudden and violent pain. With the breach in the ego caused by such a trauma, the pleasure principle is momentarily put out of action. However, the ego responds to the cathexis of stimulus caused by the trauma with an equivalent anti-cathexis, by a defensive strategy that seeks to transform the free or mobile energy of the trauma into bound, quiescent energy. If the defensive strategy succeeds, then the economy of the ego is restored and the pleasure principle resumes its reign.

Whence arises the riddle of traumatic neurosis. Traumatic neurosis is the disorder that arises after the experience of a trauma: sexual abuse, a car accident, torture, shell shock, terrorist bombing, Holocaust survival. In clinical terms, the neurosis can manifest itself in a number of ways: from chronic memory loss, depression and aggressive or self-destructive behaviour to paroxysms, severe anxiety attacks, states of profound agitation (compulsive twitching) or sheer mental confusion (shell shock).[14] What characterizes the symptoms of traumatic neurosis, like the other neuroses, is both their compulsive character – and compulsion is one of the main traits of the unconscious (*com-pulsare* = the constraint of a *pulsion*, a drive) – and their repetitiveness. In traumatic neurosis the original scene of the trauma, its deafening shock, is compulsively and unconsciously repeated in nightmares, insomnia or obsessive (another Levinasian term in 'Substitution') reflection. The subject endlessly attempts to relive that contact with the real that was the origin of the trauma, to repeat that painful *jouissance*. That is to say, the traumatized subject *wants* to suffer, to relive the *jouissance* of the real, to pick repeatedly at the scab that irritates it.

Freud writes in *Beyond the Pleasure Principle*:

> Das Studium des Traumes dürfen wir als den zuverlässigsten Weg zur Erforschung der seelischen Tiefenvorgänge betrachten. Nun zeigt das Traumleben der traumatischen Neurose den Charakter, das es den Kranken immer wieder in die Situation seines Unfalles zurückführt, aus der er mit neuem Schrecken erwacht. Darüber verwundert man sich viel zuwenig.

> [The study of dreams may be considered the most trustworthy method of investigating deep mental processes. Now dreams occurring in traumatic neurosis have the characteristic of repeatedly bringing the patient back into the situation of his accident, a situation from which he wakes up in another fright. This astonishes people far too little.][15]

Thus, the dream of the traumatic neurotic repeats the origin of the trauma. Freud's huge theoretical problem here is the following: if this is true – that is, if there is a repetition complusion at work in traumatic neurosis that repeats the origin of trauma – then how can this fact be consistent with the central thesis of his magnum opus, the *Traumdeutung*, where it is claimed that all dreams are wish-fulfilments and are governed by the pleasure principle? *It cannot*, and it is with the evidence of the repetition compulsion exhibited in traumatic neurosis and fate neurosis that the whole sublime architecture of the *Traumdeutung* and the first Freudian topography begins to fall apart. The move from the first to the second topography is that from *Traumdeutung* to *Trauma-Deutung*.

The dreams of traumatic neurotics are not, then, in obedience to the pleasure principle, but to the repetition compulsion. And not only is this true of traumatic neurosis, it is also true of dreams that bring back the traumas of childhood, hence the importance of the Fort/Da game in Freud, where the infant attempts to sublimate the absence of the mother with a game that repeats the trauma of her departure. Thus, the original function of dreams is not the dreamwork (*die Traumarbeit*) that permits the sleeper to sleep on, it is rather the interruption of sleep, *die Trauma-Arbeit*, that is beyond the pleasure principle. Insomnia is the truth of sleep. Freud writes:

Aber die obenerwähnten Träume der Unfallsneurotiker lassen sich nicht mehr unter den Gesichtspunkt der Wunscherfüllung bringen, und ebensowenig die in den Psychoanalysen vorfallended Träume, die uns die Erinnerung der psychischen Traumen der Kindheit wiederbringen. Sie gehorchen vielmehr dem Wieder-holungszwang, der in der Analyse allerdings durch den von der 'Suggestion' geförderten Wunsch, das Vergessene und Verdrängte heraufzubeschwören, unter-stützt wird.

[But it is impossible to classify as wish-fulfilments the dreams we have been discussing which occur in traumatic neuroses, or the dreams during psycho-analyses which bring to memory the psychical traumas of childhood. They arise, rather, in obedience to the compulsion to repeat, though it is true that in analysis that compulsion is supported by the wish (which is encouraged by 'suggestion') to conjure up what has been forgotten and repressed.][16]

In chapter 5 of *Beyond the Pleasure Principle*, Freud tries to establish the instinctual or 'drive-like' (*Triebhaft*) character of the repetition compulsion and, vice versa, to establish the repetitive character of the drives. Freud's claim is that the representatives or manifestations of the repetition compul-sion exhibit a highly *Triebhaft* character, being out of the control of the ego and giving the appearance of a 'daemonic' force at work – such is fate neurosis. Once Freud has established the *Triebhaft* character of the repetition compulsion, he is then in a position to introduce his central speculative hypothesis, namely that a drive is an inner urge or pressure in organic life to restore an earlier condition. That is the say, a drive is the expression of a *Trägheit*, an inertia, sluggishness, or laziness in organic life. It is this specu-lation about the fundamentally conservative nature of drives – wrapped up in a pseudo-biological phylogenetic myth of origin – that entails the extreme (and extremely Schopenhauerian) conclusion of *Beyond the Pleasure*

Principle: namely that 'Das Ziel alles Lebens ist der Tod' ('the aim of all life is death').[17] Thus, death would be the object that would satisfy the aim of the drives.

Levinas after Freud: The Structure of Ethical Experience

After this little detour, and by way of conclusion, I want to use the above Freudian insights to throw some light on what seems to be happening in Levinas. As I hope to have established, the subject is the key concept in Levinas's work. The subject's affective disposition towards alterity is the condition of possibility for the ethical relation to the other. Ethics does not take place at the level of consciousness or reflection, rather, it takes place at the level of sensibility or pre-conscious sentience. The Levinasian ethical subject is a sentient self (*un soi sentant*) before being a thinking ego (*un moi pensant*). The bond with the other is affective.

We have already seen the tension in Levinas's work where – on the one hand – he writes that his analysis of the subject is not going to follow the way of the unconscious because psychoanalysis seeks to restore self-consciousness, but – on the other hand – Levinas gives us the meaning of the unconscious as 'the night where the ego comes back to itself in the traumatism of persecution'. That is to say, Levinas seeks to think the subject at the level of the unconscious in relation to an original traumatism. The subject is constituted through a non-dialectical transference towards an originary traumatism. This is a seemingly strange claim to make, yet my wager is that if it does not go through then the entire Levinasian project is dead in the water.

How does Levinasian ethical subjectivity look from the perspective of the second Freudian topography? In the following way, perhaps: under the effect of the traumatism of persecution, the deafening shock or the violence of trauma, the subject becomes an internally divided or split self, an interiority that is radically non-self-coincidental, a gaping wound that will not heal, a subject lacerated by contact with an original traumatism that produces a scarred interiority inaccessible to consciousness and reflection, a subject that *wants* to repeat compulsively the origin of the trauma, a subject that becomes what Levinas calls a recurrence of the self without identification, a recurrence of trauma that is open to death, or – better – open to the passive movement of dying itself (*le mourir même*), dying as the first opening towards alterity, the impossibility of possibility as the very possibility of the ethical subject.[18]

The Levinasian subject is a traumatized self, a subject that is constituted through a self-relation that is experienced as a lack, where the self is
experienced as the inassumable source of what is lacking from the ego – a
subject of melancholia, then. But, this is a *good thing*. It is only because the
subject is unconsciously constituted through the trauma of contact with the
real that we might have the audacity to speak of goodness, transcendence,
compassion, etc.; and moreover to speak of these terms in relation to the
topology of desire and not simply in terms of some pious, reactionary and
ultimately nihilistic wish-fulfilment. Without trauma, there would be no
ethics in Levinas's particular sense of the word.

In this connection, one might generalize this structure and go so far as to
say (although in a provisional manner) that without a relation to trauma, or
at least without a relation to that which claims, calls, commands, summons,
interrupts or troubles the subject (whether the good beyond being in Plato,
God in Paul and Augustine, the fact of reason or respect for the moral law
in Kant, *das Ding* in Freud, the call of conscience in Heidegger, 'the jews'
in Lyotard), there would be no ethics, neither an ethics of phenomenology,
nor an ethics of psychoanalysis. Without a relation to that which summons
and challenges the subject, a summons that is experienced as a relation to
a Good in a way that exceeds the pleasure principle and any promise of
happiness (any *eudaimonism*), there would be no ethics. And without such a
relation to ethical experience – an experience that is strictly inassumable
and impossible, but which yet heteronomously defines the autonomy of the
ethical subject – one could not imagine a politics that would refuse the
category of totality. The passage to justice in Levinas – to the third party,
the community and politics – passes through or across the theoretical and
historical experience of trauma. No democracy without the death drive.
Now, there's a thought.

Notes

1. First published as 'Le traumatisme originel – Levinas avec la psychanalyse', *Rue
Descartes, Actes du Colloque 'Hommage à Levinas'*, Paris: Presses Universitaires de France,
1997, pp. 167–74. An English version appears in Richard Kearney and Mark Dooley
(eds), *Questioning Ethics*, London and New York: Routledge, 1998, pp. 230–42.

2. For an exhaustive and exhausting account of the subject in Levinas, see
Gérard Bailhache, *Le sujet chez Emmanuel Levinas*, Paris: PUF, 1994.

3. 'Substitution', transl. P. Atterton, G. Noctor and S. Critchley in A. Peperzak,
S. Critchley and R. Bernasconi, eds, *Emmanuel Levinas. Basic Philosophical Writings*,
Bloomington: Indiana University Press, 1996, p. 92. Subsequent page references to
this book are given in the body of text.

4. In this regard, see Elisabeth Weber, *Verfolgung und Trauma*, Vienna: Passagen Verlag, 1990; and Michel Haar, 'L'obsession de l'autre. L'éthique comme traumatisme', *Emmanuel Levinas*, Paris: L'Herne, 1991, pp. 444–53.

5. 'Quelques reflexions talmudiques sur le rêve', *La psychanalyse est-elle une histoire juive?* Paris: Seuil, 1981, p. 114.

6. On the importance of the notion of *la sainteté* in Levinas, see above chapters 1 and 2; for Levinas's relation to the anti-humanist and post-structuralist critique of the subject, see chapter 3.

7. Levinas, *Totality and Infinity*, transl. A. Lingis, Pittsburgh: Duquesne University Press, 1969, p. 28.

8.

Ce n'est pas la parole seulement que démolissent ainsi la psychanalyse et l'histoire. Elles aboutissent en réalité à la destruction du *je* s'identifiant du dedans. La réflexion du *cogito* ne peut plus surgir pour assurer la certitude de ce que je suis et à peine pour assurer la certitude de mon existence même. Cette existence tributaire de la reconnaissance par autrui, sans laquelle, insignifiante, elle se saisit comme réalité sans réalité, devient purement phénoménale. La psychanalyse jette une suspicion foncière sur le témoignage le plus irrécusable de la conscience de soi . . . Le *cogito* perd ainsi sa valeur de fondement. On ne peut plus reconstruire la réalité à partir d'éléments qui, indépendents de tout point de vue et indéformables par la conscience, permettent une connaissance philosophique.

'Le moi et la totalité', in *Entre nous. Essais sur le penser-à-l'autre*, Paris: Grasset, 1991, pp. 36–7; see also pp. 44–5.

[It is not only speech that psychoanalysis and history demolish in this way. In reality they lead to the destruction of the *I*, which identifies itself from within. The reflection of the *cogito* can no longer arise to ensure certainty about what I am, and can barely do so to ensure the certainty of my very existence. This existence, which is tributary of recognition by another, and insignificant without it, apprehends itself as a reality without reality; it becomes purely phenomenal. Psychoanalysis casts a basic suspicion on the most unimpeachable evidence of self-consciousness . . . The *cogito* then loses its value as a foundation. One can no longer reconstruct reality on the basis of elements which are taken to be independent of any point of view and undeformable by consciousness, and would thus make philosophical knowledge possible.]

'The Ego and Totality', in *Collected Philosophical Papers*, transl. A. Lingis, Dordrecht: Nijhoff, 1987, p. 34; see also p. 40.

9. Lacan, 'La chose freudienne', in *Écrits*, Paris: Seuil, 1966, pp. 416–18.

10. A similar line of thought is expressed in 'La ruine de la représentation', in *En découvrant l'existence avec Husserl et Heidegger*, Paris: Vrin, 1967, p. 130. Levinas writes:

Cette découverte de l'implicite qui n'est pas une simple 'deficience' ou 'chute' de l'explicite, apparaît comme monstruosité ou comme merveille dans une histoire des idées où le concept d'actualité coïncidait avec l'état de veille absolue, avec la lucidité de l'intellect. Que cette pensée se trouve tributaire d'une vie anonyme et obscure, de paysages oubliés qu'il faut restituer à l'objet même que la conscience croît pleinement tenir, voilà qui rejoint incontestablement les conceptions modernes de l'inconscient et des profondeurs. Mais, il en resulte non pas une nouvelle psychologie seulement. Une nouvelle ontologie commence: l'être se pose non pas seulement comme corrélatif d'une pensée, mais comme fondant déjà la pensée même qui, cependant, le constitue.

[This discovery of the implicit which is not a simple 'deficency' or 'fall' of the explicit, appears as a monstrosity or as a marvel in the history of ideas where the concept of actuality coincided with a state of absolute wakefulness, with the lucidity of the intellect. That this thinking finds itself to be tributary to an anonymous and obscure life, or forgotten landscapes that it is necessary to restitute to the very object that consciousness fully believes it hold to, this is exactly what brings us back to the modern conception of the unconscious and its depths. But it is not only a new psychology that results from this. A new ontology begins: being poses itself not only as the correlate of thinking, but as already founding the thinking which, however, constitutes it.]

11. Levinas, *Otherwise than Being or Beyond Essence*, transl. A. Lingis, The Hague: Nijhoff, 1981. Further page references are given in the body of the text.

12. See Andrew Tallon, 'Nonintentional Affectivity, Affective Intentionality, and the Ethical in Levinas's Philosophy', in Adriaan Peperzak, ed., *Ethics as First Philosophy*, London and New York: Routledge, 1995, pp. 107–21.

13. I have in mind Lacan's formula in his commentary on Sade, 'la jouissance est un mal. Freud là-dessus nous guide par le main – elle est un mal parce qu'elle comporte le mal du prochain [*Jouissance* is suffering. Freud guides us by the hand on this point – it is suffering because it involves or bears itself towards the suffering of the neighbour].' *L'éthique de la psychanalyse*, Paris: Seuil, 1986, p. 217. Also, think of Kant's remark in the *Critique of Practical Reason* that the relation of the subjective will to the moral law 'must produce a feeling which can be called pain' (transl. L. W. Beck, Indianapolis: Bobbs Merrill, 1956, p. 75). Hence, the Marquis de Sade is a true Kantian.

14. For an extremely rich account of trauma from a clinical point of view, see Dori Laub and Nanette C. Auerhahn, 'Knowing and Not Knowing Massive Psychic Trauma: Forms of Traumatic Memory', *International Journal of Psychoanalysis*, vol. 74, 1993, pp. 287–302.

15. *Psychologie des Unbewussten, Freud-Studienausgabe, Band 3*, Frankfurt am Main: Fischer, 1975, p. 223. *On Metapsychology*, vol. 11, Penguin Freud Library, Harmondsworth: Penguin, 1984, p. 282.

16. Ibid., p. 242; transl. p. 304.

17. Ibid., p. 248; transl. p. 311.

18. For a discussion of the distinction between *la mort*, death, and *le mourir*, dying, which I borrow from Blanchot, see my *Very Little . . . Almost Nothing*, London and New York: Routledge, 1997.

9

Das Ding: Lacan and Levinas[1]

The Ethics of the Real

In Seminar VII, *The Ethics of Psychoanalysis* (1959–60), Lacan's thesis is that the ethical as such is articulated in relation to the order of the real, which is variously and obscurely glossed as 'that which resists, the impossible, that which always come back to the same place, the limit of all symbolization' [etc., etc.] Indeed, this thesis is finessed in the following, crucial way: namely, that the ethical, which affirms itself in opposition to pleasure (hence Lacan's linking of the reality principle and the death drive, of Freud's very early and very late work, insofar as both are articulating what is opposed to or beyond the pleasure principle), is articulated in relation to the real insofar as the latter can be the guarantor of what Lacan calls, following a certain idiosyncratic and radical reading of Freud, *das Ding*, *la Chose*, the Thing.[2]

The whole thematic of *das Ding* – which, it would seem, only appears in Seminar VII (although what is named by *das Ding* might be said to be replaced later in Lacan's work in the guise of the '*objet petit a*' – the cause of desire in the subject) – is somewhat tortuous, overdetermined as it is with suggestive but unspecific Heideggerian and Kantian allusions. Although Lacan places *das Ding* at the very centre of Freud's work, insofar as that work is, for him, governed by a founding ethical intuition, the central Freudian text that motivates Lacan's discussion of *das Ding* appears very briefly towards the end of the 1895 *Entwurf einer Psychologie*, only published in 1950. As has often been remarked, the *Entwurf* is an uncannily prophetic piece of writing that anticipates the metapsychology of the First Topography elaborated in chapter VII of the *Traumdeutung* and much of the Second Topography, particularly the economic analysis of the death drive in chapters IV and V of *Beyond the Pleasure Principle*.[3] I shall examine the relevant passage from the *Entwurf* below, but the remark that is picked up and developed by Lacan is that the figure of the *Nebenmensch*, the fellow human being, the neighbour, what I shall call below *le petit bonhomme*, appears to the subject 'als *Ding*'.[4] Such is what Freud suggestively calls '*der Komplex des Nebenmenschen*', the complex of the fellow human being.

Of course, and here I come back to my theme in the previous chapter, it is because the ethical moment in Lacan articulates itself in relation to the real that it is *traumatic*. Contact with the real leaves the subject with the affect of trauma, and we might say with Kristeva that, '*Le traumatisme met à jour le rapport du sujet à la chose* [Traumatism illuminates the relation of the subject to the thing].'[5] Furthermore, what is particularly suggestive from a Levinasian point of view is that the cause of trauma in the subject is the figure of the neighbour, the fellow human being, namely that being with whom I am in an ethical relation.

Das Ding and the Face of the Other

Let me try and clarify my initial claim anecdotally: I remember a friend saying to me several years ago, 'What prevents the face of the other in Levinas from being *das Ding*?'. I didn't know quite what he meant at the time, but the question was clearly meant critically. I would like to answer the question directly now by saying that *nothing* prevents the face of the other being *das Ding* and, furthermore, that there is a *common formal structure to ethical experience in Levinas and Lacan*. To use Dieter Henrich's expression, what Levinas and Lacan share is a common concept of moral insight, a shared pathology of the moral, although the tone, form, method, sources and normative consequences of this pathology are starkly different.[6]

In the previous chapter, my aim was to borrow elements from Freudian psychoanalysis in order to delineate, criticize and complicate the structure of the subject that is at the basis of ethical experience in Levinas. What I would like to propose here is an extension of that argument that brings together the Levinasian conception of the subject with Lacan's account of ethical experience and attempts some kind of *rapprochement*. On the one hand, I am using psychoanalytical categories to challenge, clarify and (I hope) deepen what is going on in Levinas's work. However, on the other hand, it should be noted that this proposal also runs in the opposite direction: namely, that the analysis of the subject as trauma in Levinas does not lead into some supposed psychoanalytic an-ethicality, but, rather, opens up the possibility of emphasizing *the ethical dimension to psychoanalytic experience*, what Lacan sees as the revolutionary ethical intuition at the basis of Freud's work, namely that Freud's Copernican revolution, like that of Kant, although in a rather different way, also subscribes to the primacy of practical reason.

However, such statements and such an attempted *rapprochement*, although tempting, might be said to obscure the substantive differences between Levinas and Lacan. For example, their estimations of the validity of psychoanalysis obviously stand in stark contrast, as do their evaluations of Heidegger. However, their main philosophical difference might be said to concern the relation to Hegel – a certain Kojèvian Hegel, specifically the dialectic of intersubjectivity at the core of the Lacanian understanding of the subject, the symbolic order, and the concept of the transference. As has been argued by Peter Dews, the Lacanian claim that the truth of the subject takes place in 'the locus of the Big Other' is arguably the psychoanalytic restatement of Hegel's thesis that subjectivity is constituted through an intersubjective dialectic, a dialectic graphically represented in Schema L.[7] There can be no doubt that it is precisely this dialectical model of intersubjectivity that is refused from the beginning to the end of *Totality and Infinity*, where Levinas defies Hegel and the principle of non-contradiction by describing an absolute relation or *un rapport sans rapport*, that is to say, *a non-dialectical model of intersubjectivity*; what I proposed in the previous chapter as a non-dialectical concept of transference.

However, to construct this simple opposition between Levinas and Lacan on the basis of their relative debt to Hegel, and to understand the symbolic order as the intersubjective field of community, has to be complicated with reference to Seminar VII, where the order of the Real is introduced as the limit of symbolization, and where the ethical moment in psychoanalysis is articulated in the 'relationless relation' to *das Ding*. As Lacan says, 'I am concerned with the ethics of psychoanalysis, and I cannot at the same time discuss Hegelian ethics. But I do want to point out that they are not the same' (p. 126/105). To this one might add that, in Seminar VII, Lacan explicitly seeks to distance his dialectic of desire from any Hegelianism (p. 160/134), and furthermore – and the importance of this remark will become increasingly apparent – 'Hegel nowhere appears to me to be weaker than he is in the sphere of poetics, and this is especially true of what he has to say about *Antigone*' (p. 292/249).

Ethics and Aesthetics: The Problem of Sublimation, the Need for Tragedy

Of course, such an attempted rapprochement with Levinas raises interesting but unanswerable questions about the coherence and development of Lacan's teaching, and about the place of Seminar VII within that teaching. In its extensive use of Melanie Klein's work in relation to the body of the mother 'als *Ding*', Seminar VII can be seen to be articulating and anticipating Lacan's later developments on feminine sexuality in *Encore* (Seminar XX, 1972–73).[8] Also, along with the discussion of Joyce in the as yet unpublished *Le Sinthôme* seminar (Seminar XXIII, 1975–76), Seminar VII contains Lacan's most sustained discussion of aesthetics in his extended analysis of the *Antigone*, the literature of courtly love and the phenomenon of anamorphosis in art. But why is it that when Lacan discusses ethics, he also gives one of his most sustained discussions of aesthetics?

Obviously, the question of the relation of ethics to aesthetics raises the problem of sublimation, which is an absolutely essential topic of Seminar VII. Let me try and briefly broach this topic by summarizing what Lacan says at the beginning of the final séance of the seminar. What is *demanded* in analysis is happiness, nothing less. However, in the time since Aristotle – what Lacan variously and gnomically calls 'the crisis of ethics', implying a rather encoded but detectable *genealogy of ethics* (i.e. in Hegelian terms, the crisis of ethics is the disappearance of the world of *Sittlichkeit*, a crisis in the position of the master revealed *inter alia* in Hegel's master–slave dialectic) – the question of happiness is not amenable to an Aristotelian solution, it has become what Lacan calls a political matter, a matter for everyone, 'there is no satisfaction apart from the satisfaction of all'. That is to say, happiness is no longer referable to the position of the master or subsumable under the ideal of contemplation, as it was for Aristotle, but is, rather, referred to an abstract quantitative generality. Happiness becomes that of the greatest number. Of course, what Lacan is describing here is the Benthamite world of utilitarianism, which is surprisingly generously treated in Seminar VII, mainly through a reading of Bentham's *Theory of Fictions*, where Lacan picks up on the idea that fiction is not deception but is the structure of a truth, where he claims that Bentham approaches the question of ethics 'at the level of the signifier' (p. 269/228).[9]

However, despite this concesssion to Bentham, it is clear that within utilitarianism happiness becomes the object of a moral calculus, a question of the happiness of the greatest number. In this utilitarian context – and this is a highly significant context for Freud, as is clear from his early translations of John Stuart Mill – *the only possibility of happiness offered by psychoanalysis is through sublimation*, formulaically defined by Freud as satisfaction without repression. Sublimation is the satisfaction of a drive insofar as the drive is, through the work of sublimation, deflected from its aim (*Ziel*). For example, the sexual drive can be deflected from its aim through religious sublimation, as is evidenced in the ecstasies of female mystics discussed by Lacan in the

Encore seminar. In Lacanian terms, sublimation is the realization of one's desire, where one realizes that one's desire will not be realized, where one realizes the lack of being that one is. So, in the absence of the possibility of happiness – that is, in the awareness of the *tragic* dimension of human experience (a tragedy confronted on the couch in the form of symptoms) – only sublimation can save us.

Thus, Lacan dismisses the conventional idea of the moral goal of psychoanalysis, namely that it might be able to achieve some kind of psychological normalization, that the subject might be able to readjust to reality by achieving a new harmonization of drive and object. Such an idea of the ethics of psychoanalysis is nothing less than 'a kind of fraud [*une sorte d'escroquerie*]', 'To make oneself the guarantor that the subject might in any way be able to find its good itself [*son bien même*] in analysis is a kind of fraud' (p. 350/303). Within the conventional moralization of psychoanalysis, the success of analysis is reduced to providing individual comfort, or what Lacan refers to as 'the service of goods'. With a delightfully restrained sarcasm, he quips: 'There is absolutely no reason why we should make ourselves the guarantors of the bourgeois dream. A little more rigour and firmness is demanded in our confrontation with the human condition' (p. 350/303).

Thus, the moral goal of psychoanalysis does not consist in putting the subject in relation to the Sovereign Good, not only because s/he does not possess this Good, but also because s/he knows 'that there isn't any [*mais il sait qu'il n'y en a pas*]' (p. 347/300). Lacan adds in relation to the moot point of the end of analysis, 'To have carried through an analysis to its end is nothing other than to have encountered that limit where the entire problematic of desire is posed' (p. 347/300).

Rather, the moral goal of psychoanalysis consists in putting the subject in a relation to its desire, of confronting the lack of being that one is, which is always bound up with the relation to *death*. Such is what Lacan calls, with surprising forthrightness, 'the reality of the human condition [*la réalité de la condition humaine*]' (p. 351/303). In relation to the death-bound reality of desire, all the analyst can offer is not comfort but 'an experienced desire' (p. 348/301). This is the reason why, at the end of Seminar VII, Lacan writes that from a psychoanalytical point of view, 'the only thing of which one can be guilty is giving way on one's desire' (p. 370/321). Such is the categorical imperative of Freud's Copernican revolution – do not give way on your desire.

Thus, the problem of sublimation is pursued in relation to death, to the death drive as the fundamental aim or tendency of human life. The question is: *how can the human being have access to the death drive?* How can one grasp the meaning of human finitude or 'the reality of the human condition'? In Lacanian terms, it is only by virtue of the signifier, that is to say, through aesthetic form and the production of beauty. Thus, the function of the beautiful, of sublimation as the formation of the beautiful, is to reveal the human being's relation to death. But 'reveal' is perhaps too strong a verb here, for it is not that the aesthetic, in the form of beautiful sublimation, reveals, manifests or places the subject in a relation of adequation with the truth of finitude. It is, rather, that *the aesthetic intimates the excess of the ethical over the aesthetic.* In other terms, the real (as the realm of the ethical) exceeds the symbolic (the realm of the aesthetic) but the latter provides the only access to the former. Thus, access to the real or the ethical is only achieved through a form of symbolic sublimation that traces the excess within symbolization. There is no direct access to the real, only an oblique passage.

Hence, the importance of the figure of Antigone and the experience of the tragic in Seminar VII. Antigone, as the figure par excellence for the beautiful, embodies this excess of the ethical over the aesthetic. The effect of her beauty, or what Lacan refers to as her 'splendour', is to trace the sublime movement of the ethical within the aesthetic. The key term in Lacan's extraordinary reading of *Antigone* is *ate*, which he renders as 'transgression'. Thus, the function of art is transgression, the transgression *of* the aesthetic *through* the aesthetic. Namely, that Antigone transgresses the laws of Creon, refuses to feel any guilt for her transgression and, in so doing, does not give way on her desire, which is to say, she does not give way on 'the laws of heaven'. As Lacan remarks in the penultimate paragraph of Seminar VII, in allusive defiance of Hegel's interpretation of the *Antigone*, 'The laws of heaven in question are the laws of desire' (p. 375/325).

The law of desire is death, and Antigone goes all the way unto death because she will not give way on her desire. Thus, the work of the beautiful – of Antigone *as* the beautiful – takes the human being to the limit of a desire which cannot itself be represented; the work of sublimation traces the outline of something truly sublime, the aesthetic object describes the contour of *das Ding* at the heart of ethical experience, the shadow of *das Ding* falls across the aesthetic object. This is why, earlier in Seminar VII, Lacan says: 'Thus, the most general formula that I can give you of sublimation is the following: it raises the object . . . to the dignity of the Thing [*Elle élève un objet . . . à la dignité de la Chose*]' (p. 133/112).

On the basis of this summary reconstruction of parts of the argument of Seminar VII, the following schema can now be sketched (see figure 1). What I want to emphasize with this figure is the way in which sublimation produces a kind of aesthetic screen – a redemptive *Schein* or protective

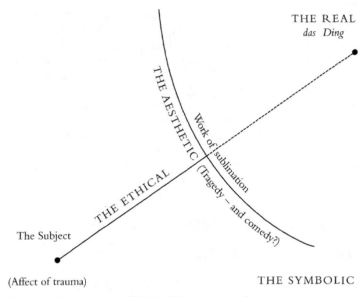

Figure 1   The Structure of Ethical Experience in Lacan

Schleier – which allows the profile of *das Ding* to be projected whilst not being adequate to its representation. The aesthetic – in this case the work of tragedy – is the ever-inadequate symbolization of that Thing that resists symbolization. This inadequate symbolization both allows the subject contact with the real (which leaves the affect of trauma in the psyche) and protects the subject from the direct glare of *das Ding*. We need art, in Nietzsche's words, lest we might perish from the truth. The aesthetic is a veil which permits an unveiling, *une voile* which allows *un dévoilement*, recalling the double structure of truth as *aletheia* in Heidegger, as the bivalence of concealment and unconcealment. The question that I shall pursue in the following chapter is whether comedy, rather than tragedy, is a form of sublimation that better describes the relation of the subject to *das Ding*.[10]

Sublimation in Levinas?

An interesting and open question that is raised here in passing by the problem of sublimation is the following: namely, given Levinas's refusal of the categories of psychoanalysis discussed in the previous chapter, what might be *imagined* as the place of sublimation in his work? Furthermore, and more importantly, is there not a need for sublimation in Levinasian ethics? What I mean is that, as some critics have pointed out, there is an undoubted ethical extremism in Levinas which, in my presentation of his work, centres around the theme of the subject as trauma. That is, Levinas seems to be describing ethical responsibility as the maintenance of a permanent state of trauma. Now, I think this raises a twofold question: firstly, what is our access to this state of trauma in Levinas? And secondly, is (or should) this state of trauma be sustainable?

Obviously, our access to this state of trauma, as Levinas describes it, occurs through Levinas's *writing*, through his ethical language that 'describes the paradox in which phenomenology suddenly finds itself'. Levinas's writing is an excessive and interrupted phenomenology, an aesthetic presentation that breaches the aesthetic and breaks with the order of presentation and presence.[11] The entire effort of Levinas's strangely hyperbolic rhetoric is to intimate or testify to a dimension of the unthematizable Saying within the thematics of the Said that, for him, characterizes philosophical discourse. That is, Levinas attempts to use the Said of philosophy against itself by letting the Saying resound within it. Levinas's books – and this is something that becomes increasingly explicit in his later writings – might be seen as an attempt at sublimation that keeps open the traumatic dimension of the sublime, allowing the Saying to circulate within the Said that both betrays and conveys it. There is no pure Saying, there is nothing prior to the mediation of the Said. Levinas's writing might be seen as an anti-aesthetic aesthetic.[12]

A further thought in relation to sublimation in Levinas would focus on the whole question of *philosophy* understood as 'the wisdom of love'. Recalling the analysis of chapter 3, I showed how the first four chapters of *Otherwise than Being* follow the itinerary of a phenomenological reduction from intentionality, through sensibility and proximity, to the subject of substitution conceived in terms of trauma. But what was omitted from this discussion was the move made in chapter 5 of *Otherwise than Being*, where Levinas shows the necessity for the passage from the Saying to the Said, not the pure Said of war and injustice that precedes the reduction, but what might be called *the justified Said*, the Said that is justified through being derived from a prior Saying. It is in this context that Levinas discusses the third party, justice, ontology, politics and consciousness, and where he inverts the usual definition of philosophy from 'the love of wisdom' to 'the wisdom of love'. 'Love' is here employed as a synonym for the ethical, and 'wisdom' is the discursive-theoretical articulation of the ethical in a discourse that aspires to justice. Philosophy is the wisdom of love 'at the service of love'.[13] Twisting the intention of Levinas's words, might one not say that philosophy itself – as the work of love in the name of justice – is the Levinasian discourse of sublimation? In a Kleinian register, might one not wonder whether the radical *separation* of trauma that defines the ethical subject, requires *reparation* in a work of love? With this in mind, might one not imagine the rhythm of Levinas's discourse as a movement between separation and reparation, between the tear and repair, between the traumatic wound and the healing sublimation, between the subject and consciousness, between ethics and ontology?[14] In this sense, Levinasian ethics would not simply be a one-way street from the Same to the Other, but would also, in a second move, consist in a return to the Same, but a Same that had been altered in itself.

Ethical Subjectivity in Lacan and Levinas

But let me now turn more directly to the glare of *das Ding* and try and make good some of the claims made above. Just after the initial discussion of *das Ding* in Seminar VII, Lacan imagines the following curious scenario. I quote at length:

> What if we brought a simple soul into this lecture hall, set him down in the front row and asked him what Lacan means.
>
> The simple soul will get up, go to the board and will give the following explanation: 'Since the beginning of the academic year Lacan has been talking to us about *das Ding* in the following terms. He situates it at the heart of a subjective world which is the one whose economy he has been describing to us from a Freudian perspective for years. This subjective world is defined by the fact that the signifier in man is already installed at the level of the unconscious, and that it combines its points of reference with the means of orientation that his functioning as a natural organism of a living being also gives him.'
>
> Simply by writing it on the board and putting *das Ding* at the centre, with the subjective world of the unconscious organized around in a series of signifying relations around it, you can see the difficulty of topographical representation. The reason is that *das Ding* is at the centre only in the sense that it is excluded. That is to say, in reality *das Ding* has to be posited as exterior, as the pre-historic Other that it is impossible to forget – the Other whose primacy of position Freud affirms in the sense of something *entfremdet*, something strange to me, although it is at the heart of me, something that on the level of the unconscious only a representation can represent. (p. 87/71)

My organizing claim here is that the structure of the Lacanian ethical subject organized around *das Ding* – as the pre-historic other that it is impossible to forget, as something strange or *entfremdet* that is at the heart of me
(*étranger à moi tout en étant au cœur de ce moi*) – has the same structure as the
Levinasian ethical subject that I sought to elucidate with the concept of
trauma and which Levinas tries to capture with various formulae, such as
'the other in the same', and which I described above as 'the inside of the
inside that is outside'. On this construal of their work, I think one can establish a formal or structural homology between ethical subjectivity in Levinas
and Lacan. As stated above, they share a common grammar of moral insight.

Of course, the consequences of such a homology between Lacan and
Levinas at the level of the concrete determination of the Good or in providing precriptions or procedures for action are far from being identical
and such is not my claim. To pursue this homology that far would raise
related and vexed questions that cut in two directions at once. For example,
in relation to Lacan: what is the *scope* of his teaching; i.e. is this only an
ethics *of* psychoanalysis, *for* psychoanalysts, or is this the basis for a more
general ethics? And in relation to Levinas: how exactly does the establish-
ment of ethics as first philosophy in Levinas relate to specific and – as he
calls them – pre-philosophical determinations of action at the level of social
life?[15] And perhaps what most clearly differentiates Lacan and Levinas is
what they initially seem to have in common, namely the attempt to think
ethics in relation to desire. It is at the very least questionable whether one
can identify Levinas's rather Platonic conception of metaphysical desire with
a Freudian ethics based on the unconscious sexual desire of the libidinal
body. It seems to me that one must not confuse physical and metaphysical
eros, or seek to reduce one to the other.

However, to return to my main argument for a structural or formal
homology between Lacanian and Levinasian ethics, which I will presently
attempt to pursue through an analysis of the figure of the *Nebenmensch* in
Freud, it is fortunate (or unfortunate, depending on how one looks at it)
to note that my argument has already been anticipated in an interesting
essay by Monique Schneider, 'La proximité chez Levinas et le *Nebenmensch*
freudien'.[16] The whole article is written without any reference to Lacan,
which is slightly bizarre, but what is useful to me about this essay is that the
link between Lacan and Levinas can be made stronger by showing how
Schneider establishes an independent link from Freud to Levinas.

The basic thesis of this essay (and Schneider tends to repeat this basic
point a little too insistently) concerns an interpretation of Freud; namely
that in Freud's *Entwurf*, specifically in the brief discussion of the *Nebemensch*

there is both a recognition of the essential intrication, '*l'enchevêtrement inextricable*' (p. 434), of the Same and the Other, and the evaluation of this intrication by Freud as a threat, as something to be excluded, 'in order to come back to a subject seen as a separated being'. Thus, Schneider's claim is that after the small breakthrough of the *Entwurf* in 1895, the entire subsequent Freudian enterprise is concerned with trying to erect a barrier between the same and the other and establishing a strict subject–object dualism. Although such a claim is doubtless justified insofar as Freud's work is often informed by rather traditional epistemolgical assumptions, one would, against Schneider, have to acknowledge that the question of subject–object dualism in Freud becomes much more richly entangled after the introduction of the concept of narcissism in 1914, with the splitting of the ego and the introduction of the agency of conscience or the super-ego in the second Freudian topography.

From the Levinasian perspective that Schneider adopts, Freud falls from an original ethicality into a traditional ontology. Thus, the whole analysis of the subject as substitution, where self and other are essentially intricated, is employed as a key for understanding the fate of ethics in Freudian theory: 'Levinas's text can thus be received as untangling what is strangled in the Freudian itinerary, a strangling that puts an end to the first attempt at an opening' (p. 436). And again, 'Levinas is thus placed as the *Nebenmensch* of the Freudian text.'

'If it screams': The *Nebenmensch* Complex in Freud

But what or who is this figure of the *Nebenmensch*? The key passage in Freud, which is at the centre of Lacan's *Ethics* seminar and again at the centre of Schneider's and Kristeva's contestations of a Lacanian approach (see note 19), is the following. I quote at length:

Nehmen wir an, das Objekt, welches (die) W(ahrnehmung) liefert, sei dem Subjekt, ähnlich, ein *Nebenmensch*. Das theoretische Interesse erklärt sich dann auch dadurch, dass ein *solches* Objekt gleichzeitig das erste Befiedigungsobjekt, im ferneren das erste feindliche Objekt ist, wie die einzige helfende Macht. Am Nebenmenschen lernt darum der Mensch erkennen. Dann werden die Wahrnehmungskomplexe, die von diesem Nebenmenschen ausgehen, zum Teil neu und unvergleichbar sein, sein *Züge*, etwa auf visuellem Gebiet, andere visuelle W(ahrnehmungen), z.B. die seine Handbewegungen, aber werden im Subjekt über die Er(innerung) eigener, ganz ähnlicher visueller Eindrücke vom eigenen Körper fallen, mit denen die Er(innerungen) von selbst erlebten Bewegungen

in Assoziation stehen. Noch andere Wahrnehmungen des Objekts, z.B. wenn
es schreit, wenn die Erinnerung, an eigenes Schreien und damit an eigene
Schmerzerlebnisse wecken. Und so sondert sich der Komplex der Nebenmenschen
in zwei Bestandteile, von denen der eine durch konstantes Gefüge imponiert, als
Ding beisammenbleibt, während der andere durch Erinnerungsarbeit *verstanden*,
d.h. auf eine Nachricht vom eigenen Körper zurückgeführt werden kann. Diese
Zerlegung eines Wahrnehmung-komplexes heisst ihn *erkennen*, enthält ein Urteil
und findet mit dem letzes erreichten Ziel ein Ende.[17]

Thus, the fellow human being is the object of both love and hate: s/he is
both the first satisfying object *and* the first hostile object, both the 'helpful
power' of the friend, and the enemy (*feindliche Objekt*). Note the logic of
Freud's text here, where the *Nebenmensch* is simultaneously (*gleichzeitig*) predicated with opposing attributes: s/he is both incomparable (*unvergleichbar*),
which is another word Levinas uses to describe the relation to the other, and
comparable. S/he is both capable of being understood by the subject, and
escapes understanding. And in this way, the *Nebenmensch* complex falls apart
into two components: *on the one hand*, the other stands over against me as
a thing – *als Ding* – or imposes itself through what Freud mysteriously calls
'konstantes Gefüge', which Lacan translates as 'un appareil constant', an
unchanging apparatus, which threatens to turn the other *als Ding* into some
sort of machine. *On the other hand*, the other can be understood or comprehended on the basis of its being similar to me; Freud's twice-repeated word
is *ähnlich*. The other is both my *semblable* and a stranger to me, what Lacan
called above 'something strange to me, although it is at the heart of me',
what Levinas would describe as 'the other within the same'. It can thus be
seen how the relation to *das Ding* corresponds to the logic of substitution.

Freud concludes the passage by claiming that the *Nebenmensch* complex is
resolved or attains its aim or end when cognition (*erkennen*) reduces the other
to the same through the activity of judgement. For Freud, the work of
judgement, like the structure of the unconscious *Wunsch* in the *Traumdeutung*,
reduces alterity by attempting to bring about a state of identity between drive
and object. It is tempting to give a rather Kantian interpretation of this last
sentence in the above quote, where the unconscious traumatic affect of the
relation to *das Ding* is resolved through the move to judgement as the subject's
conscious act of synthesis, where the subject lays hold of or takes possession
of the alterity of the manifold of intuition by placing it under concepts.
Although it must be noted that for Kant, like Lacan and Levinas, what is left
over as the inassimilable remainder of *das Ding* continually escapes the cognitive
power of the subject, whether the *Ding an sich* of the transcendent object X
in the First Critique, the relationless relation to the incomprehensibility of

the moral law in the Second Critique or the relation of the subject to the sublime in the Third Critique. However, the function of judgement in the above passsage from Freud has the function of resolving the *Nebenmensch* complex and restoring the subject–object dualism at the basis of the traditional predicament of philosophy.

But we have overlooked a crucial moment in Freud's text, a moment at the centre of Schneider's essay, namely that the relation to the *Nebenmensch* announces itself '*wenn es schreit*', if it screams, shouts, cries, or screeches. The fellow human being is perceived *als Ding* when it screams; that is, the other presents itself in a pre-linguistic scream that traumatically recalls the subject's own screaming and its own memory of experience of pain (*an eigenes Schreien und damit an eigenes Schmerzerlebnisse*). The other, which resists my attempts at comprehension, is presented to me in a scream that recalls me to the memory of my own screaming, my own trauma, my own 'pre-historic' experience of pain, an archaic memory laid down in relation to my first satisfying/hostile object. The *Nebenmensch als Ding* initiates a traumatic relation to the other that recalls me to my traumatic self-relation, to my wounded subjectivity. In relation to the two moments of the *Nebenmensch* complex, the scream both presents me with the other *als Ding* in a pre-linguistic affect, and allows me to understand the other insofar as their screaming recalls me to my own memory of my own painful affect. The important point here is that ethical subjectivity is constituted in the traumatic memory of wounding. This might become clearer in chapter 10 when I discuss Peter Chelsom's 1994 film *Funny Bones*, where the scream functions as mode of identification with the comic Thing.

This structure of the scream gives us the pattern of substitution in Levinas, where the scream would be the dimension of Saying that would elucidate the pre-history of the subject in its essential intrication with alterity. As with Rousseau's discussion of *la pitié* in the Second Discourse, the pre-linguistic '*aidez-moi!*', the scream or cry of the other gives the subject both its first opening towards alterity and places it radically in question.[18] The affective, pre-linguistic call of the other is in Levinasian terms the 'an-archic origin' of goodness, a 'natural' goodness that disappears within Rousseau's genealogy of morals in the Second Discourse.

Thing Becomes Word: Lacan on *das Ding*

With the above discussion in mind, let me now turn to Lacan's commentary on the figure of the *Nebenmensch* and its relation to *das Ding*, which is scattered here and there in the first section of Seminar VII. In a response to a presentation by Pontalis on Freud's *Entwurf*, Lacan makes the extraordinary claim: 'it is through the intermediary of the *Nebenmensch* as speaking subject that everything that has to do with the thought processes is able to take shape in the subjectivity of the subject' (p. 50/39).

I will come back to the question of whether the *Nebenmensch* is a speaking subject below, but the central discussion of *das Ding* comes slightly later, and one might note the Levinasian resonances in Lacan's description of the relation to others as 'beside yet alike, separation and identity':

> On that basis there enters into play what we will see function as the first apprehension of reality by the subject. And it is at this point that reality intervenes, which has the most intimate relationship to the subject – the *Nebenmensch*. A formula that is altogether striking in as much as it expresses powerfully the idea of beside yet alike, separation and identity [*l'à-côté et la similitude, la séparation et l'identité*].
>
> I ought to read you the whole passage but I will limit myself to the climactic sentence, 'Thus the complex of the *Nebenmensch* is separated into two parts, one of which affirms itself through an unchanging apparatus [*un appareil constant*], which remains together as a thing, *als Ding*.' (p. 64/51)

Thus, the subject's first apprehension of reality, of the order of the real, occurs in the relation to the *Nebenmensch als Ding*, that is, as alien, absolutely other and '*Fremde*' (p. 65/52). As Lacan goes on to remark, also playing with the etymology of *Ur-teil*, there is an 'original division' in the experience of the other, where the subject 'finds itself in the beginning led toward a first outside'. But Lacan makes the claim even stronger, arguing that '*tout le cheminement du sujet* [the whole march, advance or progress of the subject]' articulates itself around *das Ding*. In other terms, the *Nebenmensch als Ding* is 'the absolute Other of the subject' that is simultaneously at the heart of the subject, the other within the self that defines what is most central to the subject, a centrality that is not abstract but is completely bound up, for Lacan, with 'the world of desires'.

However, the really provocative passages on *das Ding* occur a couple of pages further on, for it is here that Lacan will conjure up the spectre of Harpo Marx. I quote at length:

> *Das Ding* is that which I will call the outside-of-the-signified [*le hors-signifié*]. It is as a function of the outside-of-the-signified, and from an emotional relation [*rapport pathétique*] with it that the subject keeps its distance and constitutes itself in a kind of relation, primary affect, anterior to all repression. The entire first articulation of the *Entwurf* takes place around it . . .

Well, here it is in relation to this original *das Ding* that the first orientation, the first choice, the first seat of subjective orientation takes place that we will sometimes call *Neuronenwahl*, the choice of the neurosis. This first grinding [*mouture première*] will henceforth regulate the entire function of the pleasure principle . . .

Today I only want to insist on this, that the Thing only presents itself to the extent that it becomes word [*qu'elle fait mot*], *hits the bull's eye* [fait mouche] as one says. In Freud's text, the way in which the stranger, the hostile one, appears in the first experience of reality for the human subject is the cry [*le cri*, which is Lacan's translation of *das Schreien*]. I would say that we do not have any need of this cry. Here I would like to make reference to something which is more inscribed in the French rather than the German language – each language has its advantages. In German, *das Wort* is at once word [*mot*] and speech [*parole*]. In French, the word *mot* has a particular weight and sense. *Mot* is essentially 'no response' [*pas de réponse*]. *Mot*, La Fontaine says somewhere, is what is silent [*se tait*], it is precisely that to which no *mot* is spoken. The things in question here – and some people could object to me as being placed at a higher level than the world of signifiers which I have said to you are the true resource of the functioning in man of that process designated as primary – are things insofar as they are mute. And mute things are not exactly the same thing as things that have no relation to words [*paroles*].

It is enough to evoke a figure which will be living to everyone of you, that of the terrible mute of the four Marx Brothers – Harpo. Is there anything which can pose a more present [*présente*], more pressing [*pressante*], more captivating [*prenante*], more disruptive, more nauseating, more calculated to throw into the abyss and nothingness everything that takes place before us, than the figure of Harpo Marx, marked with that smile of which one does not know whether it is that of the most extreme perversity or foolishness. This mute on his own is sufficient to sustain the atmosphere of placing in question and radical annihilation that is the stuff of the formidable farce of the Marx Brothers, of the uninterrupted play of *jokes* [in English in original] that makes their activity so valuable. (pp. 67–9/54–5)

The first couple of paragraphs amplify the thesis presented above, namely that the relation to *das Ding* is that 'outside-of-the-signified' of the relation to the real, a relation to an 'absolute Other' that is *un rapport pathétique*, a 'primary affect' that is constitutive of the subject. This relation or 'first grinding' of the subject governs the entire function of the pleasure principle for Lacan; that is, it overrides the pleasure principle in the name of its beyond.

But – and here is a rather moot point challenged by Kristeva in her discussion of precisely this passage from Seminar VII[19] – *das Ding* only presents itself for Lacan insofar as it becomes word. In Lacanian word play, the Thing *fait mouche* insofar as it *fait mot*, it hits the spot only when it becomes a word. Lacan then refers back to the passage from Freud's *Entwurf*, where he recalls the point that was discussed above, namely that the *Nebenmensch* presents itself *'wenn es schreit'*. He then adds significantly that we do not have any need of this scream or cry, a claim which is justified by one of Lacan's rather opportunistic Franco-German etymologies, where *das Wort* is translated as both *le mot* and *la parole*. That is, *das Ding fait mouche* insofar as it *fait mot*, and *mot* is understood in distinction from what is spoken (*la parole*) as *pas de réponse*, where the word is *ce qui se tait*, that which keeps silent. Thus, in a further play, *les mots* are *les choses muettes*, words are essentially mute. Hence the claim that *le mot* is present where no word is spoken (*parlé*). The word is unspoken, it is dumb.

It is in connection with this claim about the muteness of the word, a point that could also obviously be made in connection with silent movie comedians like Chaplin and Keaton, and in order to illustrate the relation of the subject to *das Ding*, that Lacan introduces the spectre of Harpo Marx. But I want to put Harpo on hold for a moment because what Lacan is at the point of saying here, which is the topic of the next chapter, is that *das Ding*, as the subject's ethical relation with an alterity that resists comprehension and which is constitutive for subjectivity and ethicality, opens in the experience of *jokes*, in the comic.

It is therefore, of course, a question of sublimation, and of what form or forms of symbolization are best able to evoke the in-adequate relation of the subject to *das Ding*. How is one to approach *das Ding*? Lacan privileges tragedy, and, as we will see, this privileging is hardly historically neutral or novel. *Contra* Lacan, I will raise the possibility of comedy because my worry is that tragedy is a form of sublimation that risks reducing the trauma of the relation to *das Ding* and disfiguring the problem of finitude. There is a risk of losing sight of the ethical dimension to psychoanalysis through its submission to what I shall call a tragic–heroic paradigm.

Notes

1. First published in *Research in Phenomenology*, vol. 28, 1998, pp. 72–90.
2. *L'éthique de la psychanalyse*, Livre VII, J.-A. Miller, ed., Paris: Seuil, 1986. *The Ethics of Psychoanalysis*, Book VII, 1959–60, transl. Dennis Porter, London and New York: Routledge, 1992, p. 76. Subsequent page references to the original and translation are given in the text. Cited passages from the *Ethics* seminar have been retranslated. The only full commentary I know on Seminar VII is Paul Moyaert's

excellent *Ethik en sublimatie*, Nijmegen: Sun, 1994. But see also Moyaert's more critical engagement with Seminar VII in 'Lacan on Neighbourly Love: The Relation to the Thing in the Other who is my Neighbour', *Epoche*, vol. 4, no. 1, 1996, pp. 1–31. See also John Rajchman's helpful introductory discussion of Lacan in *Truth and Eros. Foucault, Lacan and the Question of Ethics*, London and New York: Routledge, 1991, pp. 29–85; and Alenka Zupancic, *Die Ethik des Realen*, Vienna: Turia and Kant, 1995. A number of essays on the topic on the ethics of psychoanalysis are collected in *Fragmente. Schriftenreihe zur Psychoanalyse*, nos. 39–40, 1992; see esp. Hans-Dieter Gondek, 'Cogito und *séparation*', pp. 43–76. A collection of essays on Seminar VII, which focus on the relation of Lacan to Kant, are in H. D. Gondek and P. Widmer, eds, *Ethik und Psychoanalyse. Vom kategorischen Imperativ zum Gesetz des Begehrens: Kant und Lacan*, Frankfurt am Main: Fischer, 1994. On the relation of Levinas to Lacan, see Pierre-Laurent Assoun, 'Le sujet et l'autre chez Levinas et Lacan', *Rue Descartes*, no. 7, 1993, pp. 123–45.

3. On the importance of the *Entwurf*, see, for example, Richard Wollheim's discussion in his *Freud*, London: Fontana, 1971, pp. 42–64; and John Forrester's *La langage aux origines de la psychanalyse*, Paris: Gallimard, 1984.

4. *Entwurf einer Psychologie* was first published in Marie Bonaparte, Anna Freud and Ernst Kris, eds, *Aus den Anfängen der Psychoanalyse*, London: Imago, 1950, pp. 371–466. Reprinted in Angela Richards, ed., *Gesammelte Werke, Nachtragsband*, Texte aus den Jahren 1885–1938, Frankfurt am Main: Fischer, 1987, pp. 387–487.

5. 'L'impossibilité de perdre', in *Les Cahiers de l'Institut de Psycho-Pathologie Clinique*, no. 8, November 1988, special issue on 'Trauma réel, trauma psychique', p. 40.

6. See Henrich's classic 1960 essay, 'The Concept of Moral Insight and Kant's Doctrine of the Fact of Reason', in *The Unity of Reason: Essays on Kant's Philosophy*, Cambridge Mass.: Harvard University Press, 1994, pp. 55–87, see esp. pp. 61–7. I owe this reference to Henrich to an ongoing debate with Jay Bernstein. See his critique of my position in 'After Auschwitz – Grammar, Ethics, Trauma', unpublished typescript, 1997.

7. For Lacan's discussion of 'Schema L', see 'La chose freudienne', in *Écrits*, Paris: Seuil, 1966, pp. 429–30. In this regard, see Dews, 'The Truth of the Subject. Language, Validity and Transcendence in Lacan and Habermas', in S. Critchley and P. Dews, eds, *Deconstructive Subjectivities*, Albany: SUNY Press, 1996, pp. 149–68.

8. Obviously, the whole problematic of sublimation in Seminar VII is provoked by the work of Klein and the Kleinians, where, in Lacanian terms, sublimation is the symbolic repair of the lesions in the imaginary caused by the real of the mother's body (see esp. 'The Object and the Thing', pp. 121–37/101–14). Sublimation is reparation, the work of love. It would also be a question here of linking together the analysis of the subject as trauma as the affect of the real with an analysis of the relation to the female body, specifically the body of the mother that stands in for *das Ding*. Lacan writes:

> The whole development of psychoanalysis confirms it in an increasingly weighty manner, while at the same time it emphasizes it less and less. I mean that the whole development at the level of the mother/child interpsychology . . . is nothing more than an immense development of the essential character of the maternal thing, of the mother, insofar as she occupies the place of that thing, of *das Ding*. (p. 82/67)

And again, with explicit reference to Klein,

> Let me suggest to you that you reconsider the whole of Lacanian theory with the following key, namely, Kleinian theory depends on its having situated the mythic body of the mother at the central place of *das Ding*. (p. 127/106)

9. In this regard, see the extremely interesting French/English parallel edition of Bentham, published with a Lacanian editor: *Theorie des Fictions*, Paris: Éditions de l'association freudienne internationale, 1996. And see in particular the annex to this edition by J. Parin, 'Réel et symbolique chez Jeremy Bentham', ibid., pp. 3–10.

10. In passing, one might note that the Lacanian thesis on sublimation, in particular its use of tragedy as exemplary in articulating the ethics of psychoanalysis, shows certain similarities with Nietzsche's early – and extremely Schopenhauerian – theory of tragedy in *The Birth of Tragedy*. Nietzsche is only mentioned twice in Seminar VII, and not in connection to his theory of tragedy (pp. 38/46, 198/233–4). For the latter, ancient tragedy was the aesthetic presentation of the fundamental coupling and conflict between the two divine orders of the Apollinian and the Dionysian, which are analogous to *Vorstellung* and *Wille* in Schopenhauer. For Nietzsche, we require the redemptive *Schein* of the Apollinian in order both to reveal the excess of the Dionysian within it, the abyssal 'reality of the human condition', and to save us from contact with that reality.

11. I have tried to analyse Levinas's method in terms of what he calls 'the reduction', in *The Ethics of Deconstruction*, Oxford: Blackwell, 1992, pp. 8, 163–6.

12. On the vexed question of the aesthetic in Levinas, see Gary Peters's excellent article, 'The Rhythm of Alterity: Levinas and Aesthetics', *Radical Philosophy*, no. 82, 1997, pp. 9–16.

13. *Otherwise than Being or Beyond Essence*, The Hague: Nijhoff, 1974, p. 161.

14. I owe these insights to conversations with Axel Honneth.

15. On pre-philosophical experiences in Levinas, see Robert Bernasconi's '"Only the Persecuted . . .": Language of the Oppressor, Language of the Oppressed', in A. Peperzak, ed., *Ethics as First Philosophy*, London and New York: Routledge, 1995, pp. 77–86.

16. *Cahier de l'Herne*, Paris: Herne, 1991, pp. 431–43. Further page references are given in the text.

17. Freud, 'Entwurf einer Psychologie', *Gesammelte Werke*, pp. 426–7.

18. Rousseau, *Discours sur l'origine de l'inégalité parmi les hommes*, Paris: Garnier, 1962, p. 37.

19. In 1988, a short while after the publication of *Soleil noir* (Paris: Gallimard, 1987; *Black Sun*, transl. L. Roudiez, New York: Columbia University Press, 1989), Kristeva presented a paper to a Parisian psychoanalytic group on the question of trauma ('L'impossibilité de perdre'). Kristeva studies trauma in relation to depression and tries to focus on the object relation maintained by the depressive person, specifically the narcissistically depressed person. The latter is depressed by feeling afflicted by a fundamental fault or lack; their sadness is the expression of an unsymbolizable, unnamable narcissistic wound. That is, the depressed person is depressed not in relation to an object but to *das Ding*. Depression is the dumb articulation of that unknown loss that defines the structure of melancholia in Freud.

For Kristeva, *das Ding* is 'the real in rebellion against signification', the pole of attraction and repulsion, the dwelling place of sexuality from which the object of desire will detach itself. *Das Ding* is the *soleil noir*, the black sun of melancholia, what Kristeva calls '*une insistance sans présence*', a light without representation, the unknown object that throws its shadow across the ego. When faced with this seemingly archaic or 'pre-historic' attachment to *das Ding*, the depressive person has the impression of being disinherited from an unnamable supreme good.

Now, Kristeva's difference with Lacan is precisely on the interpretation of *das Ding* and refers to the specific passage from Freud's *Entwurf* discussed in Seminar VII, 'In commenting on the notion of *das Ding* in Freud's *Entwurf*, Lacan claims that however withdrawn the Freudian Thing may be from judging consciousness, it is always already given in the presence of language.' Kristeva's claim is that Lacan, by making the Thing a word, prioritizes language in the ethical relation to *das Ding*. So – and here Kristeva is making the same point as Schneider – although for Freud *das Ding* presents itself as the scream, Lacan translates this as *mot*, even if it is a word that remains silent. Thus, Lacan reduces the primary affect of *das Ding* to language. Now, the importance of this is that Lacan, in Kristeva's terms, reduces the *semiotic* to the *symbolic*, that is, he reduces the pre-verbal affective energy of the drives to linguistic categories. And I think that Kristeva has a point here, and there is something quite wilful and wayward about Lacan's attempt to understand the relation to *das Ding* in terms of the word, however widely the latter is understood. In depression, it seems to me, we are transfixed by our Thing, standing mute before its affect, like Harpo. This affect cannot simply be understood linguistically, but subtends the activity of language. The relation to *das Ding* is not the word, but the subjective affect of trauma.

Comedy and Finitude:
Displacing the Tragic-Heroic Paradigm
in Philosophy and Psychoanalysis

I never saw anything funny that wasn't terrible, that didn't cause pain.

Freddy 'Parrot Face' Davies[1]

Why do you particularly suppose I pointed out to you the mixture of pain and pleasure in comedy?

Socrates, *Philebus*

The Privilege of the Tragic in Post-Kantian Philosophy

One version of the post-Kantian settlement in philosophy is that the critical dismantling of the claims of dogmatic metaphysics in the *Critique of Pure Reason* has the consequence that questions concerning the ultimate meaning and value of human life pass from the category of the religious to that of the aesthetic. Kant bequeathes a problem to his idealist, romantic and even Marxist inheritors in the European tradition, a problem that he grapples with himself in the *Critique of Judgement*, where he attempts to throw a bridge between the faculties of the Understanding (epistemology) and Reason (ethics) through a critique of the faculty of Judgement, where the latter would be the mediator between the domains of nature and freedom and would harmonize the elements of the critical project.

This problem might be restated in the following way: the Kantian critique of metaphysics, if justified, achieves the remarkable feat of both showing the *cognitive* meaninglessness of the traditional claims of speculative, dogmatic metaphysics, whilst establishing the regulative *moral* necessity for the primacy of practical reason, that is, the concept of freedom. Yet, the question that this raises is the following: how is freedom to be instantiated or to take effect in the world of nature, if the latter is governed by causality and mechanistically determined by scientifically established natural laws? How is the causality of the natural world reconcilable with what Kant calls the causality of freedom?[2] How, to allude to Emerson alluding to the language of Kant's Third Critique, is genius to be transformed into practical power?[3] Doesn't Kant leave human beings in what Hegel might have called the *amphibious* position of being both freely subject to the moral law and determined by an objective world of nature that has been stripped of any value and which stands over against human beings as a world of alienation?

Thus, the task of a critique of aesthetic and teleological judgement is to build a bridge between the realms of pure and practical reason, nature and freedom, epistemology and ethics, that Kant had laid asunder. Laying to one side the important matter of teleological judgement, one can see the consequences of this enormous privileging of the category of the aesthetic in post-Kantian philosophy, in, say, Schiller's *Letters on the Aesthetic Education of Man* (1795). More particularly, for the concerns of this chapter, the privileging of the aesthetic can be seen in Schelling's 'Identity Philosophy', the young Hegel and, of course, Hölderlin. For each of these thinkers, in decisively different ways, in relation to their related but often opposed estimations of the possibilities of art in modernity, the highest exemplar of the aesthetic is dramatic art. And the model for dramatic art, even when it is, as in Hegel's *Aesthetics*, subordinated to comedy, is ancient tragedy, in particular Sophoclean tragedy. Schelling discusses *Oedipus Rex* briefly in the last of his *Letters on Dogmatism and Criticism*, written in 1795, and again in more detail in the 1802–03 lectures on *The Philosophy of Art*. Hegel famously interprets the *Antigone* in the *Phenomenology of Spirit* (1807), although tragedy is also central to the 1803 essay on 'Scientific Ways of Treating Natural Law'. Also in 1803, Hölderlin wrote his remarks on both *Oedipus Rex* and *Antigone*, although the tragic is the central theme of the earlier *Grund zum Empedocles* and *Über das Werden im Vergehen* (both 1798–1800), and the ever-incomplete tragedy *Death of Empedocles*.

To summarize rather violently, if the aesthetic is, in Schelling's formulation in the 1800 *System of Transcendental Idealism*, 'the keystone in [the] entire arch'[4] that will span the regions of pure and practical reason that Kant had divorced, then ancient tragedy is the determining exemplar of the aesthetic, even when, as Hegel insists, art is judged to be a thing of the past. The privileging of tragedy as the aesthetic form that would reconcile the freedom of the subject and the necessity of nature, can be most clearly seen in the version given by Schelling in *The Philosophy of Art*:

> The essence of *tragedy* is thus an actual and objective conflict between freedom in the subject on the one hand, and necessity on the other, a conflict that does not end such that one or the other succumbs, but rather such that both are manifested in perfect indifference as simultaneously victorious and vanquished.[5]

What begins with Schelling is not so much a poetics of tragedy as what Peter Szondi calls a *philosophy of the tragic*, which has an almost uncanny persistence in the German intellectual tradition.[6] In Hegel, tragedy is employed to illustrate what he calls *die Tragödie im Sittlichen*, the tragic condition of modern ethical life. Against the alleged formalism of Kant and Fichte, the model of tragedy allows Hegel to diagnose what I called above the amphibious character of modernity, the diremption or, better, the self-diremption of the individual subject from the substantiality of Spirit.[7] This tragic paradigm is most obviously evident in Nietzsche's early 1871 account of the birth of tragedy, with its desire for a rebirth of tragedy through the music of Wagner, a desire self-criticized as an 'artist's metaphysics' by the later Nietzsche, although he maintains to the end the idea of art as a tragic affirmation.[8]

However, this massive privileging of the tragic can also be found elsewhere in the nineteenth century, in the work of Solger, Schopenhauer, Hebbel, and in a more complex way in Kierkegaard, where the latter shows how the tragic must be overcome through humour, irony and, finally, the leap of faith.[9] Moving into the twentieth century, one can obviously see this tragic paradigm at work in Freud's use of the Oedipus myth as the structuring narrative of infant development, in Georg Simmel's 1912 essay 'Der Begriff und die Tragödie der Kultur', in Max Scheler's 1915 essay 'Zum Phänomen des Tragischen', and in Heidegger's two readings of the second stasimon of the *Antigone* in *Einführung in die Metaphysik* (1935) and the lecture course on *Der Ister* (1942). I will turn to Heidegger in a moment, whose interpretation of the *Antigone*, for reasons that are perhaps more ideological than philosophical, is not even mentioned by Szondi, who completes his account of the philosophy of the tragic with Scheler. To complete this thumbnail sketch of the philosophy of the tragic in the German tradition, the tragic paradigm is both continued and contested in Benjamin's *Ursprung des deutschen Trauerspiels* (1924–25, published 1928) through the opposition between tragedy and *Trauerspiel*, that is to say, between the mythicality and heroic sacrifice of the latter and the historicality and flawed mundanity of the latter.

Two Paradigms and the Question of Finitude (Heidegger)

Moving from the German to the French context, all that I would like to establish in this chapter is how this tragic paradigm in continued in Lacanian psychoanalysis, at least in Seminar VII, *The Ethics of Psychoanalysis* (1959–60).[10] I think it is justified to say that, for Lacan, Antigone becomes the tragic heroine of psychoanalysis: she who does not give way on her desire, she who follows the law of desire, which is what Hegel would call 'the law of heaven', and follows that law all the way to her death.[11] We might say that Lacan is the psychoanalytic extension of the German philosophy of the tragic, and that he extends the tragic paradigm through his choice of Antigone as the heroine of psychoanalysis, as she who embodies the ethical imperative of psychoanalysis: *ne pas ceder sur votre désir*.

If I am right in my suggestion that there is a tragic paradigm in Lacanian psychoanalysis, and I will try and make good on this claim below, then the critical question that follows for me is very simple: *what about the comic?* Is there not an Oedipus complex in post-Kantian philosophy, or an Antigone complex, at the least a Sophocles complex, that has the consequence of subordinating the comic to the tragic and hence marginalizing the phenomena of jokes, humour and laughter?

But what is at stake in this question? The following, I think: returning to my opening sentence, if the post-Kantian settlement in philosophy has the consequence that questions concerning the ultimate meaning and value of human life pass from the category of the religious to that of the aesthetic – which initiates the philosophy of the tragic – then what is presupposed in this passage is the recognition of the essential *finitude* of the human being. That is, the question of the meaning and value of human life becomes a matter of what *sense* can be *made* from the fact of finitude. Given the collapse of the possibility – at least for 'we moderns' – of traditional religious belief, it is a question of what forms of aesthetic production and creation might begin to fill the void left by the historical self-consciousness of the death of God.

The critical hypothesis that I would like to explore is that the above-sketched tragic paradigm in post-Kantian philosophy indeed provides a way for thinking through the question of finitude, but that it is a thinking-through which *disfigures* finitude by making the human being *heroic*. This is a large claim and I cannot hope to begin to substantiate it within the limitations of this chapter. Furthermore, I would not want to advance this claim against all the authors mentioned above: Benjamin and Kierkegaard stand as obvious exceptions, not to mention the complexity of the treatment of the tragic in Hölderlin and its critical or, better, *Zeitdiagnostisch* employment in Hegel and in the tradition inspired by him, for example in Simmel. My modest ambition in this chapter is to begin to develop this critical hypothesis by using the example of Lacan's *Ethics* seminar.[12]

Simply as a heuristic device, I would like to propose two paradigms for thinking through the question of finitude: *the tragic-heroic paradigm* and *the comic anti-heroic paradigm*. As I have intimated, this tragic-heroic paradigm can be traced back through Heidegger and Nietzsche to elements within German idealism and romanticism. Let me try and explain this paradigm in Heideggerian terms.

In relation to Heidegger, the question of the tragic-heroic paradigm turns on whether death can be conceived as a *possibility* of the human being, of *Dasein*. In the Second Division of *Being and Time*, the condition of possibility for getting the totality of *Dasein*'s existence in our grasp, which is, in turn, the condition of possibility for authenticity, is that *Dasein* should be able to comprehend its end; that is, its death – *Sein-zum-Ende* – is *Sein-zum-Tode*.[13] As Heidegger writes in the introduction to Division Two, '*Das "Ende" des In-der-Welt-seins ist der Tod* [The "end" of Being-in-the-world is death]' (p. 234/276–7). To be able to comprehend my death means that *Dasein* conceives of death as its ownmost possibility, what Heidegger calls 'the possibility of the absolute impossibility of Dasein' (p. 250/294). When *Dasein* relates to the possibility of its death in the mode of anticipation (*das Vorlaufen*), then it is *free* insofar as *Dasein* has been released from the illusions of the Platonic cave of *das Man*. Freedom is 'Freiheit zum Tode' (p. 266/311). As Heidegger makes clear in the crucial later paragraph 74 on 'The Basic Constitution of Historicity', 'Only being-free *for* death [*Freisein für den Tod*] . . . brings Dasein into the simplicity of its fate [*seines Schicksals*]' (p. 384/435). In terms that curiously recall the above quote from Schelling's *Philosophy of Art*, through an anticipatory relation to its death, *Dasein* can freely assume its fate, its historicity, and achieve the individual union of freedom and necessity. Such is, as Schelling writes, the essence of tragedy and the core experience of the tragic hero, whether Oedipus or Lear. Furthermore, this fateful freedom, this 'shattering itself against death' (p. 385/437) as the basis for an understanding of historicity, is also the condition of possibility for a co-historicizing (*Mitgeschehen*) and for the determination of the community of the people (*das Volk*) as a destiny (*als Geschick* – p. 384/436). Of course, it is only a small step from paragraph 74 of *Sein und Zeit* to Heidegger's Promethean (mis)understanding of the relation between philosophy and politics some years later.

As such, authentically historical *Dasein* can 'choose its hero'; that is, either choose itself as a tragic hero, a freely fateful being holding itself out into the nothingness of death, or choose *das Man* and hence fall back into inauthenticity (pp. 371/422 and 385/437). These tragic-heroic thematics of authenticity are powerfully at work in Heidegger's above-mentioned and even more Promethean interpretation of the *Antigone*, an interpretation which seems to have influenced Lacan, as we shall see presently.[14] For Heidegger, the second stasimon from the *Antigone* provides not only the 'authentic Greek definition of the human being' but also the basic trait of human essence, namely to be the uncanniest one (*'das Unheimlichste zu sein, ist der Grunzug der Menschenwesens'* – p. 116/151). Greek tragedy understands human essence as *to deinotaton*, as that which throws itself out into the uncanny, leaving behind the ground of history in the *polis* and becoming *upsipolis* or *apolis*. The tragic hero – and this is a word which, as we have seen in the previous chapter, is at the centre of Lacan's reading of the *Antigone*, where it is used to describe her transgressive splendour – is possessed by *ate*, the violent drive for truth that leads to what Heidegger calls 'ruin, disaster' (*'der Verderb, das Unheil'* p. 116/152). But the violent transgression of the tragic hero is also, for Heidegger, a *necessity* or *need* (*Notwendigkeit, die Not* – p. 124/162–3) insofar as it is only by opposing the inauthentic historical ground of the *polis* that *Dasein* can become authentically historical. Through the ruin of the tragic hero, history is literally *made* as the confirmation or verification of Being ('Als Geschichte *bestätigt sich werkhaft das Überwältigende, das Sein*' p. 125/164). But, to return to the question of finitude, such tragic violence confronts one thing:

> All this vio-lence [*Gewalt-tätigkeit*] shatters against one thing. That is death. Death up-ends all consummation, it out-limits all limits [*Er über-endet alle Vollendung, er über-grenzt alle Grenzen*] . . . Insofar as the human being *is*, it stands in the issuelessness [*Ausweglosigkeit*] of death. (p. 121/158)

So much for the tragic-heroic paradigm. Having set up the latter, I would like to oppose it with a *comic anti-heroic* paradigm. As I will try and show in the course of this chapter, this second paradigm is based in the recognition not of the possibility of death, but of its impossibility. Against Heidegger and with Blanchot and Levinas, death is conceived as the impossibility of possibility: Death is that in the face of which the subject is not *able to be able* – this *Dasein* cannot choose its hero. On such a view, finitude is not something that can be heroically assumed in a free fatefulness but is, rather, something radically ungraspable, a weaker and ever-weakening conception of finitude.[15] My intuition is that laughter, a certain sort of laughter, opens up this ungraspable and ever-weakening relation to finitude. As Jean Paul remarks in *Vorschule der Ästhetik*, '*komisches Heldengedicht ist ein Widerspruch* [a comic heroic poem is a contradiction in terms]'.[16]

Of course, I have no pretension to novelty with this suggestion of a comic anti-heroic paradigm. It is rather that with the kind of minimal aspect change I am proposing, one might begin to *imagine*, alongside the history of the philosophy of the tragic, a history (or histories) of the philosophy (or non-philosophy) of the comic. The philosophical roots of this comic tradition obviously extend back to Aristotle's much-mooted but non-extant second half of the *Poetics*, at the centre of the drama in Umberto Eco's *The Name of the Rose*. But this comic tradition might be said to be given its decisive modern expression in Shaftesbury's *Sensus Communis: An Essay on the Freedom of Wit and Humour* (1709), which exerted such a powerful influence in Germany on Lessing and Moses Mendolsohn, and the traces of which can be found in Friedrich Schlegel's theory of wit and irony. But the true roots of such an imagined history would, I think, be found in literature rather than philosophy: from Aristophanes' comedies to Petronius' *Satyricon*, through to Chaucer, Rabelais, Erasmus, Nashe, Swift and Sterne, a carnivalesque or Juvenalian tradition of what Bakhtin euphemistically calls 'the material lower bodily stratum'.[17]

Freud's Sense of Humour and Two Senses of Laughter

Playing off Freud against Lacan, the importance of the phenomena of jokes, laughter and the comic is obviously something central to Freudian psychoanalysis, most obviously in his 1905 *Jokes and their Relation to the Unconscious*. Sarah Kofman rightly and wittily views the Jokebook as Freud's most philosophical work, with its tripartite systematic division of the argument into analytic, synthetic and theoretic parts.[18] And this work significantly influenced Lacan because of its extended attention to language. But if there is an Antigone complex in post-Kantian philosophy and Lacanian psychoanalysis, then as a *Gegengift* we might recall Freud's little aside in the Jokebook:

> Once when the *Antigone* was produced in Berlin, the critics complained that the production was lacking in the proper character of antiquity. Berlin wit made the criticism its own in the following words: *Antik? Oh, nee.*
>
> An analogous dividing-up joke is at home in medical circles. If one inquires from a youthful patient whether he has ever had anything to do with masturbation, the answer is sure to be: *O na nie.*[19]

The *Antigone* becomes 'Antik? Oh, nee', and then in the next paragraph 'O na, nie', onanism. Freud resolves the tragic-heroic paradigm into a wanking joke.

But more seriously, the importance of the comic is something that Freud recognizes even more acutely in his brilliant but brief late essay called 'Der Humor' (1927), where he analyses humour not from the economical point of view that prevailed in the 1905 Jokebook, but also from the perspective of what one might call a phenomenology of *Gefühl*, of feeling.[20] In the space of a few pages, and with the telegraphic conciseness of his late style, Freud shows how the phenomenon of humour is the contribution made to the comic by the super-ego. That is to say, in humour, the super-ego observes the ego from an inflated position, which makes the ego itself look tiny and trivial. As well as unwittingly recalling Jean Paul's idea of the comic as that which opposes the sublimity of the tragic with 'das unendliche Kleine',[21] what should be stressed is that Freud's remarks on humour constitute an unexpectedly positive development of the internal logic of narcissism which finally finds a positive place for the super-ego. Freud's comic example in 'Der Humor' is of a criminal who is being led out to the gallows to be hanged, and who remarks, 'Na, die Woche fängt gut an' (p. 253/161) In Freudian terms, the humour here is generated by the super-ego observing the ego, which produces a black humour that is not depressing but rather liberating and elevating. Freud concludes, 'Look! Here is the world, which seems so dangerous! It is nothing but a game for children – just worth making a jest about' (p. 258/166). Hence, the narcissistic splitting of the ego, which shapes the whole landscape of the Second Topography, does not only produce the alternating pathologies of melancholia and mania, what Freud calls the endless 'Abwechslung von Melancolie und Manie' (p. 257/165), but instead produces humour – dark, sardonic, wicked humour. In this sense, I would argue, humour recalls us to the modesty and limitedness of the human condition, a limitedness that calls not for tragic affirmation but comic *acknowledgement*, not heroic authenticity but a laughable inauthenticity.

So, my question is the following: what might comedy tell us about the question of finitude? That is, might not our relation to finitude be transformed if we learn to laugh, and – crucially – not to laugh the golden Nietzschean laughter of tragic affirmation that so influenced Bataille, but a weaker Freudian laughter, a laughter that recognizes that finitude is not something to be affirmed, but acknowledged. For there is laughter and *laughter*. What I mean is that, on the one hand, there is the laughter of eternal return, laughter *as* eternal return, which laughs in the face of a firing squad – a laughter that I always suspect of emanating from the mountain tops, from Sils-Maria. This is a *manic* laughter: solitary, hysterical, verging on sobbing. This is the ego bloated and triumphant in empty solitude. As Beckett quips in his *Proust*, '"Live dangerously," that victorious hiccough in vacuo, as the national anthem of the true ego exiled in habit'.[22] On the other hand, there is the laughter of someone like Lawrence Sterne or Samuel Beckett, but equally the comic genius of a Frankie Howerd or a Tommy Cooper, which is more sardonic and which arises out of a palpable sense of inability, inauthenticity, impotence and impossibility. Tommy Cooper was the magician that couldn't perform a trick, Frankie Howerd was the comedian who couldn't tell a joke. But – for me at least, but there is no accounting for taste – it is this second laughter that is more joyful (not to mention being a lot funnier), and also more tragic. As Beckett's Malone remarks, paralysed in his death-bed, 'If I had the use of my body I would throw it out of the window. But perhaps it is the knowledge of my impotence that emboldens me to that thought.' Or as Stephen Daedalus remarks with what Joyce calls 'saturnine spleen', 'Death is the highest form of life. Ba!' Provisionally – and doubtless rashly – one might say that the problem with the tragic-heroic paradigm is that it is not tragic enough and that only comedy is truly tragic.[23]

Contra Lacan, to anticipate my conclusion, to live between two deaths is not to live tragically, but is perhaps the life of comedy, where finitude is not something to be affirmed by the tragic hero, but comically acknowledged. Antigone? *O na nie!*

Acting in Conformity with Your Desire: Tragedy in Lacan

Let me now try and specify this all-too-huge a topic by turning to Lacan's *The Ethics of Psychoanalysis* and, in particular, to the final séance of Seminar VII, 'The Paradoxes of Ethics, or Have you Acted in Conformity with your Desire?'

Lacan defines an ethics as a judgement on an action (i.e. is an action good or bad?). Now, if there is an ethics of psychoanalysis, then it is only to the extent that it provides a *measure* (an Aristotelian *metron*) for our action, a measure that would be able to guide judgement, some sort of criterion. It is clear that, for Lacan, this measure is desire, unconscious sexual desire in the Freudian sense. The imperative implied by this ethical measure – although I am simplifying the logic of Lacan's text at this point – is *ne pas ceder sur votre désir*. I think this explains Lacan's closing Hegelian allusion in

Seminar VII, that 'The laws of heaven in question are the laws of desire' (p. 325/375), namely that the laws of heaven for psychoanalysis, that provide a measure for ethical judgement, are the laws of desire.

Looking back over the course of the seminar, Lacan says that he asked his auditors to enter into a thought experiment by adopting the standpoint of the Last Judgement, namely to ask oneself the question, 'Have you acted in conformity with the desire that is in you?' (p. 362/314). That is to say, the question of ethics is raised as a matter of the relation of action to unconscious desire. It is therefore a question of what form or forms of action would be appropriate to desire? Which forms of action would be ethical? Of course, the rather circular answer to this question has already been given insofar as the only form of action that is ethical is the following: *not to act in such a way that you give way on your desire*. Now it would be something of an understatement to say that the precise normative consequences of this imperative are not exactly clear, although Alain Badiou has made some significant advances in this direction, as I discuss elsewhere.[24]

In order to explain the relation between action and desire, Lacan has recourse to tragedy; namely, that tragic action might be an index for ethical action that would conform to one's desire. The ethics of psychoanalysis entails a relation to 'the reality of the human condition' (p. 351/303) that I emphasized in the last chapter. This 'reality' can be expressed with what Lacan calls 'the tragic sense of life'. Such a tragic sense of life has, for Lacan, nothing to do with what he calls 'speculation about prescriptions for, or the regulation of, what I have called the service of goods' (p. 362/314). The notion of 'service of goods' is the position that Lacan also describes as that of 'traditional ethics' (p. 362/314), and is represented – dubiously, I think – by the person of Creon. (As something of a provocation, might one not ask: is not Creon the true tragic hero rather than Antigone? For is it not Creon who, through the mediation of Teiresias, recognizes his error and turns himself around to confront freely his fate, thereby fulfilling both the Aristotelian and the Schellingian criteria for the tragic hero? Why, with the notable exception of Hegel, is the tragic role of Creon so systematically ignored in the Antigone complex of post-Kantian philosophy? This is a question that cannot be divorced from a certain androcentric philosophical idealization of the feminine as the divine victim.[25])

With these precisions in mind, I can now turn to the passage I want to discuss. I quote at length:

> It is in the tragic dimension that actions are inscribed and we are called to take our bearing with regard to values. Moreover, this is also the case with the comic

dimension and when I began to speak to you about the formations of the unconscious, it was, as you know, the comic that I had in mind.

Let us say as a first approximation that the relation of action to the desire which inhabits it in the tragic dimension functions in the sense of a triumph of death. I taught you to rectify the latter as triumph of being-towards-death [*triomphe de l'être-pour-la-mort*], that is formulated in Oedipus's *me phunai*, where this *me* figures, the negation that is identical to the entrance of the subject supported by the signifier. This is the fundamental character of all tragic action.

In the comic dimension, as a first approximation, it is less a question of triumph as of a futile and derisory play of vision. *However little I have up to now tried to approach the comic with you* [my emphasis], you have been able to see there too the relation of action to desire, and of the fundamental failure of the former to catch up with the latter.

The comic dimension is created by the presence at its centre of a hidden signifier, but which, in the Old Comedy, is there in person – the phallus. Who cares if it is subsequently whisked away? One must simply remember that what satisfies us in comedy, what makes us laugh, that makes us appreciate it in its full human dimension, not excluding the unconscious, is not so much the triumph of life as its flight, the fact that life slides away, steals away, flees, escapes all those barriers that oppose it, and precisely those that are most essential, those that are constituted by the agency of the signifier.

The phallus is nothing other than a signifier, the signifier of this flight. Life goes by, triumphs all the same, whatever happens. When the comic hero trips up and falls in the soup, the little fellow still survives.

The pathetic side of this dimension is, you see, exactly the opposite, the counterpart of tragedy. They are not incompatible, since the tragi-comic exists. That is where the experience of human action resides, and it is because we know better than those who have gone before how to recognize the nature of desire that is at the heart of this experience, that an ethical revision is possible, that an ethical judgement is possible, that represents this question with its value of the Last Judgement – have you acted in conformity with the desire that is in you? (pp. 361–2/313–14)

This is an extremely suggestive passage that would merit much commentary, but let me just attempt a provisional double reading of this text, both with and against the grain of Lacan's argumentation. To understand the relation between action and desire, Lacan has recourse to tragedy. Now, Lacan goes on to make the extremely Heideggerian claim that the relation between action and desire in the space of tragedy functions in the direction of being a triumph of being-towards-death, *une triomphe de l'être-pour-la-mort*, which is simply the French rendering of *Sein-zum-Tode*. This reading of tragedy finds confirmation in an earlier series of allusions to Oedipus, where the words *me phunai* are interpreted in terms that recall Nietzsche's use of the wisdom of Silenus in *The Birth of Tragedy*, namely 'plutôt, ne pas être' (p. 306/353) – the best thing is not to be born, the second best is to die soon. Thus, Lacan's thesis here would seem to be that tragedy provides an exemplary model of ethical action in conformity with one's desire, insofar as desire is bound up in a relation to death. Thus, the appropriate ethical comportment in the face of death is being-towards-death, where we act in such a way that we do not give way on our desire. Thus, one way of understanding the ethics of psychoanalysis is in terms of the aspiration to a Schellingian-Heideggerian correspondence between free ethical action and fateful deathly desire, that the subject *should*, through the work of analysis, aspire to the *Freiheit-zum-Tode* that is the core of tragic experience and the tragic-heroic paradigm for thinking finitude.

This line of thought is also connected to what Lacan says at the beginning of the penultimate séance about helplessness (*Hilflosigkeit*, p. 351/303–4), where helplessness describes our fundamental relation to finitude. But helplessness is not described, as it was for Freud in the *Entwurf*, as the signal of anxiety. Interestingly, Lacan says that such a relation to finitude is 'not so much *Abwarten* as *Erwartung*'; that is, not so much the helplessness of waiting but, rather, the passive openness of expectation or anticipation, something perhaps much closer to Heideggerian *Gelassenheit*. Thus, tragic experience is one of 'absolute disarray' (p. 361/304), where the tragic hero – Lear as much as Oedipus – finds himself 'alone and betrayed' (p. 353/305), cast out from the *polis* to become *upsipolis*, the uncanniest one who, in breaking with all familiarity, *makes* history. For Lacan, in this tragic ruination of the hero, a certain catharsis of desire is achieved. Tragic action achieves a purification of desire in relation to its object, namely death.

Lacan's Catharism

It is with this use of the concept of catharsis that one can attempt an excursus on the use of Catharism in Seminar VII, the celebrated heresy that preached a radical metaphysical dualism of Good and Evil, and which appeared in many places across Europe between the twelfth and fourteenth centuries, most famously in Languedoc.[26] This theme appears intermittently, but significantly, in Seminar VII, initially as a historical antecedent to the rituals of Courtly Love. Lacan employs the Aristotelian concept of catharsis to explain what takes place in tragic action, but he also extends its usage, so that one can speak of psychoanalysis itself, insofar as it returns to the otherwise hidden meaning of an action, as a form of catharsis: a cleansing, a purgation, a decantation, a purification through sacrifice. It is on the basis of this link, and the possible (but possibly questionable) etymological link between *katharos* and *katharsis*, that Lacan makes a series of allusions to the Cathars: 'The Cathars, who are they? They are the pure. *Katharos*, is a pure one [*un pur*]. And the term, in its original resonance, does not mean illumination or discharge, but purification' (p. 287/245).[27]

My worry here is that Lacan's account of the ethics of psychoanalysis, insofar as it employs the model of tragic action and stands under the imperative 'do not give way on your desire', is too Catharistic, too pure, too decanted, too clean, too heroic. The Cathar, like Antigone, does not give way on his/her desire, and the price of this desire, this desire for a pure desire, is death. The Cathar is like a whole series of Saint Catharines (of Alexandria, of Bologna, of Genoa, of Ricci, of Sweden, of Siena, of Tekakwitha, and the nineteenth-century Cathérine Labouré), the eternally pure, the *aei katharos*, whose usually gruesome death is an act of martyrdom because they were not willing to give way on their desire, they refused to subordinate a Christian conception of the Good to the pragmatic demands of the *polis*.

According to this rather static, non-dialectical, logic, death is dealt to the *katharos* by the various representatives of 'traditional ethics': Creon in the case of Antigone, Simon de Montfort (leader of the so-called Albigensian Crusade) in the case of the Cathars, Emperor Maxentius in the case of St Catharine of Alexandria. In Lacan's sense, one might see the final holocaust of the Cathars in Montségur in 1326, where *les Parfaits* allegedly jumped happily into the flames to meet their death, as authentic tragic action in relation to desire.

The really intriguing question that the link to Catharism throws back to Lacan's understanding of tragic action is the question of materiality, of the evil in matter that was the basic tenet of Cathar metaphysical dualism. That is, if the principle of evil is within matter itself, insofar as the visible creation was created by the Evil One, then Goodness and God are not of this world – I recall the Cathar maxim, 'nous ne sommes pas de ce monde et ce monde n'est pas de nous'. The question would therefore be whether Lacan elevates the tragic figure of Antigone by purifying her of all materiality. If matter is evil (and one also thinks of Sade here), then it follows that death is nothing to fear, for it is only a liberation from evil, throwing off the filthy husk of the body. Comedy in this sense would be the return of materiality.

Spectres of (Harpo) Marx: Lacan's Sense of Humour

Now, returning to the passage quoted above, I have chosen to analyse it because it is one of the few places in Seminar VII where Lacan acknowledges and analyses the comic. In contradistinction to tragedy, comedy is not the triumph of life, but 'life's flight', 'a futile and derisory play of vision'. If the lesson of tragedy for psychoanalysis is that one should act in conformity with one's desire, aspiring to the fateful freedom of an anticipatory relation to death, then comedy *shows the failure of action to keep up with desire.* Comedy is the permanent suspension, postponement or parody of catharsis, where all attempts at lofty, solitary heroism collapse into anti-heroic mirth – think of *Hamlet* performed by the National Theatre of Brent, or Peter Sellars's rendition of the Beatles's 'A Hard Day's Night' in the guise of Lawrence Olivier playing a very hammy Richard III. Comedy is the eruption of materiality into the spiritual purity of tragic action and desire. In comedy, Antigone would break wind on the way to her death; feeling the flames about to consume him, the Cathar would suddenly see the validity of St Augustine's refutation of Manicheism; Freud's condemned man would get a fearful erection on the gallows. As Milan Kundera says, 'Someone's hat drops on the coffin in a freshly dug grave, the funeral loses its meaning and laughter is born.'[28] The body, in all its dreadful fallibility, is the site of the comic. However, the revealing remark in the above passage is when Lacan admits: 'However little I have up to now tried to approach the comic with you'. Why so little time? Although one must obviously acknowledge the extraordinary difficulty of writing anything interesting, let alone funny, about comedy, might one not wonder why this is the case?

Contra Lacan, is it not rather that comedy opens a different relation to finitude, where, to use Lacan's own words, what makes us laugh is not the triumph of life, whatever that might be, but its flight, that life slips away, runs off, dissipates? The very phallus worn by the satyr in the old comedy is not some sort of patriarchal affirmation of male domination, but the signifier of flight, a sign of weakness, of the dis-possession of the phallus. The very comic exaggeration of the body that one can find in the whole tradition of clowning, is what recalls the very weakness and vulnerability of the body. Rather than being overawed with the Promethean, monstrous magnitude of the tragic hero, in comedy we are presented with 'the infinitely small', the *petit bonhomme* – Harpo, Chaplin, Keaton, Monsieur Hulot, Mr Bean – who keeps tripping up and falling in the soup.

And it is here that I would finally like to come back to the spectre of Harpo Marx that was conjured up in the last chapter and left rather hanging in the air. Let me recall the words with which Lacan concludes his central discussion of *das Ding*:

> It is enough to evoke a figure which will be living to everyone of you, that of the terrible mute of the four Marx Brothers – Harpo. Is there anything which can pose a more present [*présente*], more pressing [*pressante*], more captivating [*prenante*], more disruptive, more nauseating, more calculated to throw into the abyss and nothingness everything that takes place before us, than the figure of Harpo Marx, marked with that smile of which one does not know whether it is that of the most extreme perversity or foolishness. This mute on his own is sufficient to sustain the atmosphere of placing in question and radical annihilation that is the stuff of the formidable farce of the Marx Brothers, of the uninterrupted play of *jokes* [in English in original] that makes their activity so valuable. (pp. 67–9/54–5)

As I said above, what Lacan is at the point of admitting here is that the relation to *das Ding*, as that relation with an inassimilable alterity that resists comprehension and which is constitutive for subjectivity and ethicality, opens in the experience of *jokes*, in the comic. Thus, if there is, as I believe there is, a tragic-heroic paradigm at work in Lacan's *Ethics* seminar, then there are also some resources for thinking against this paradigm within his own text.

Let's go back to Harpo? What or who is he? He is a fool. And what is a fool? A fool is a thing – an uncanny mixture of perversity and simplicity, of wisdom and stupidity, of familiarity and strangeness – who speaks the truth, often by remaining mute, *un mot muet qui fait mouche*, to recall Lacan's words. The fool is that thing that speaks the truth to power, that speaks in refusing speech, that subverts protocols of everyday, polite language: 'Do you believe in the life to come?', 'Mine was always that'; 'Have you lived in Blackpool all your life?', 'Not yet'; 'Do you want to use a pen?', 'I can't write', 'That's OK, there wasn't any ink in it anyway'; 'I could dance with you until the cows come home', 'Yes?', 'On second thoughts I'd rather dance with the cows until you come home'; 'Why I've never been so insulted in my life', 'Well it's early yet'. And so on. The fool is that thing who does not speak to please the king, but who says, like Hamlet in his folly, 'The King is a thing'. In speaking thus, the fool says the truth. Of course, as Lacan realized, such is the topsy-turvy logic of Erasmus's *Praise of Folly*,[29] and the traditions of both the folly of the cross and the divine fool that one can also find in Anselm's so-called 'ontological proof' of the existence of God.

Staying with Shakespeare, think also of Lear, an example all too briefly discussed by Lacan (pp. 352–3/305), who approaches truth through his folly in his nonsensically raving dialogue with his fool in the famous storm scene. And note the figure of Cordelia in *King Lear*, an obvious, if more ambiguous, analogue to Antigone, who says 'Nothing my lord', who refuses to speak, who says nothing *as* the truth, for to say more would be to lie. Of course, there is a venerable tradition within Shakespearean scholarship that identifies Cordelia with the Fool. The justification for such an identification is that the two characters never appear on stage at the same time, and therefore could be played by the same actor. But the tie that binds Cordelia to the Fool is perhaps even stronger and more macabre, inasmuch as when Lear says, 'And my poor fool is hung', the instrument of death is *la corde*, the rope.

In relation to psychoanalytic practice, we might also think about the relative dumbness of the analyst, of the analyst as a fool: 'Why do you like being an analyst?', 'Because I can spend so much time looking out of the window'. Or again, think of the comic silence of the analyst as anonymously related in the following anecdote about Lacan: a patient wanted to terminate their analysis with Lacan because it clearly wasn't working. But Lacan refused to have any of it, insisting that the patient kept seeing him. Eventually, the patient decided, after several attempts to confront Lacan, to tell him he was leaving and simply get up and go. The patient left, descended the short staircase and walked out through the courtyard. Quickly glancing up to the window of Lacan's room, the patient saw him with a vase of flowers in his hand, which Lacan then threw at the patient, narrowly missing him and shattering on the ground. In Jean Allouch's book, *132 bon mots avec Jacques Lacan*, the anecdote has an appropriate English title: *say it with flowers*.[30]

So Harpo is dumb, and yet in his muteness, in his *point de réponse*, a word is articulated that hits the bull's eye – *il fait mouche en faisant mot*. And Lacan has a strong point here, namely that Harpo's wide-eyed dumb grin is extremely ambiguous, particularly with regard to its sexual intent. He is that impish, foolish mixture of perversity and simplicity, particularly if one thinks of his scenes with women in the various Marx Brothers movies, where his childlike innocence seems to be the veneer for a ravenous guile, a rapacious and probably perverse sexual desire. Thus, it is Harpo's ambiguity, his mixture of perversity and simplicity, hostility and familiarity, or vulnerability and menace that corresponds to the structure of the *Nebenmensch* complex in Freudian terms. Harpo's face is a mute *mot*, a void that the subject cannot avoid, an abyss into which all attempts at comprehension or judgement are annihilated. Harpo stands over against the subject *als Ding*, his muteness blocks the subject's attempts at judgement and comprehension.

In the endlessly surrealistic play of the Marx Brothers, in the sheer calling into question of the subject who still laughs in a recognition that destroys recognition, an identification that annihilates identity, a relation to *das Ding* is opened. At the heart of the laughter's complicity is hidden an ethical relation of *Fremdheit* that radically calls the subject into question.

Funny Bones

This is something wonderfully illustrated by Peter Chelsom's 1994 film *Funny Bones*, and in particular through the character of Jack Parker. This film, shot in the fading splendour of Blackpool, deals with the theme of comedy and finitude with an affective depth and sheer visual power that defies commentary. As one of the legendary Parker Brothers says in his first words in twelve years, 'Nobody's pain is greater than ours, but the moon's dark side draws the tides.' Of course, Freud had a holiday in Blackpool in 1908, and this very Freudian film is focused around the question of the family secret, of the Oedipal struggle between father and son, and the identification of the son with the mother and of the latter with depression. Jack Parker is the often dumb, illiterate, illegitimate 'laugh child', who stands under the threat of death at the hands of a corrupt police officer. Jack stole some of the powder of immortality, which miraculously rejuvenates the ageing Parker Brothers for their comeback performance towards the end of the film. But whereas Jack is dead funny, his newly arrived and newly discovered American half-brother, Tommy Foulkes, has neither 'funny bones', nor can he 'talk funny'. He is told this by his father, the hugely successful (and hugely self-regarding and corrupt) funny man, George Foulkes, played by a corpulent Jerry Lewis. George, it turns out, is also Jack's father and had to leave Blackpool suddenly when it was discovered that Jack's mother was pregnant. Tommy Foulkes also stands under the threat of death, repeatedly claiming that 'he only has only two weeks to live', which was the supposed length of his disastrous residency in Las Vegas. In response to the kind elderly solicitor's inquiry about his father, 'Didn't he die in Las Vegas?', Tommy replies, 'No, *I* died in Vegas'. Both characters scream out early in the film, 'I'M GONNA DIE!!!'

These themes of comic death, of dying on stage, or corpsing out, come to a climax in the closing scenes of *Funny Bones* where Jack Parker returns to the circus ring where years earlier he had murdered his mother's lover with a metal bar disguised in a rolled up newspaper, and was banned from ever appearing on stage again. Disguised as his stepfather, and exuding a genuine Thing-like menace, Jack performs on the swing pole, the camera in close-up on his face, locked in a vast grimace, looking like a death's head. The film ends happily enough, with the legitimate son, Tommy Foulkes, redeemed by finally being made funny. Jack's closing words are 'Tommy, I think they're beginning to like you.' But the point of the film is clear: as Freddy 'Parrot Face' Davies says, 'I never saw anything funny that wasn't terrible, that didn't cause pain.' Whoever has funny bones is cursed with a deep morbidity (the name of Tony Hancock comes to mind), and possesses a Thing-like quality that troubles and threatens the audience as they laugh. When laughter lowers your resistance, it is then that the punchline hits hardest and hurts most. What we recall when we laugh is the sheer proximity and dumbness of our pain.

But the logic of humour here is complex. As Freud suggests in the 1905 Jokebook, it is the very difference between oneself and the comic anti-hero that permits one an identification that allows an economization of psychical expenditure and which is experienced as pleasurable. However, it is also the case that the comic anti-hero stands over against us *als Ding*, denying us any identification. We might even say that the comedian traumatizes the subject or that laughter can return us to the place of the guilty family secret. Putting these two aspects of comedy together – which are nothing else but the two components of the *Nebenmensch* complex described above – one might say that in comedy we identify with that which refuses identification. The very fact that the comic hero evokes not life's triumph, but its slipping away, also entails that we are not adequate to the Thing that comedy presents. Even as we laugh at and with the comic Thing, it laughs at us, making us look ridiculous. Comedy is a relief that permits no escape, but which rather returns us all the more forcefully to the fact of being riveted to oneself, the idea of *être rivé à soi* that is the basic intuition of Levinas's earliest philosophical work.[31]

Such is the Freudian logic of humour, where the very exaggeration of the super-ego over the ego both humiliates the latter, producing a comic effect – 'Well, the week's beginning nicely' – and introduces some humility into the subject. In comedy there is a radical abasement of the subject that requires a new form of acknowledgement, but whose effect is not depressive, but liberating, elevating ('*befreiend, erhebend*').[32] Woody Allen seems to get this just about right in the characterization of Mickey Sachs in *Hannah and her Sisters*. Mickey is suicidally depressed because the fact of the death of God has just hit him. In despair, he wanders into a cinema and by chance the Marx Brothers' *Duck Soup* is playing. Mickey recalls the effect the film has on him:

And I went upstairs to the balcony, and I sat down and you know, the movie was a-a-a film that I'd seen many times in my life since I was a kid, an-and I always u-uh, loved it. And, you know, I'm, I'm watching these people up on the screen, and I start getting hooked on the film, you know? And I start to feel how can you even think of killing yourself? I mean, isn't it so stupid? I mean, I look at the people up there on the screen. You know, they're really funny, and, and what if the worst is true? What if there's no god . . .?[33]

The Punchline

Let me conclude with some general reflections on laughter and comedy. Laughter is an acknowledgement of finitude, precisely not as a manic affirmation of finitude in the solitary, Nietzschean laughter of the mountain tops, but as an affirmation that finitude cannot be affirmed because it cannot be grasped. Laughter returns us to the limited condition of our finitude, the shabby and degenerating state of our upper and lower bodily strata, and it is here that the comic allows the windows to fly open onto our tragic condition. Tragedy is insufficently tragic because it is too heroic. Only comedy is truly tragic. Comedy is tragic by not being a tragedy.

Pushing this a little further – maybe too far – I would even go so far as to claim that the sardonic laughter that resounds within the ribs of the person moved by what they find funny can be a site of resistance to the alleged total administration of society, a node of non–identity in the idealizing rage of commodification that returns us not to a fully integrated and harmonious *Lebenswelt* but lights up the comic feebleness of our embodiment. Laughter might here be approached as a form of resistance, of critique, of the sudden feeling of solidarity that follows the eruption of laughter in a bus queue, watching a party political broadcast in a pub, or when someone farts in a lift. As a radical German street slogan, whose origin is Italian, expresses it, '*Es wird ein Lachen sein, das Euch beerdigt* [It will be a laugh that buries you]'. Laughter is a convulsive movement, it is like sobbing or like an orgasm, it is involuntary, it sometimes even hurts.[34] It is contagious and solidaristic, think of the intersubjective dimensions of giggling, particularly when it concerns something obscene.[35] In this way, perhaps, we might say that laughter in its solidaristic dimension has an ethical function insofar as the simple sharing of a joke recalls to us what is shared in our life-world practices, not in a heroic way, but more quietly and discreetly. One might begin to speak here of laughter as a minimal form of *sensus communis*. The extraordinary thing about comedy is that it returns us to the very ordinariness of the ordinary, it returns us to the familiar by making it fantastic. Comedy might be said to provide us with *an oblique phenomenology of the ordinary*. At its most powerful, say in those inanely punning dialogues between Groucho and Chico, comedy is a paradoxical form of speech and action that defeats our expectations, producing laughter with its unexpected verbal inversions, contortions and explosions, a refusal of everyday speech that lights up the everyday: estranged, indigent and distorted, 'as it will appear one day in the messianic light'.[36]

Let me return to my starting point in Kant. In one of those fascinating by-ways of the Third Critique, Kant writes, rightly, 'Voltaire said that heaven has given us two things to compensate for the many miseries of life, *hope* and *sleep*. He might have added *laughter* to the list.'[37] Indeed, Kant might have added orgasm to the list, but the point is well made. However, if laughter compensates for the miseries of life, then it is not simply because it allows us to escape them, to compensate or *economize* upon the expenditure of affect, as Freud claimed in his Jokebook. Laughter does not *just* economize upon expenditure of affect, it also indicates obliquely the source of that affect, as Freud was also well aware. If psychoanalysis shows us one Thing, it is that the It, the *Es*, the Id, speaks where there is pain. And maybe it only hurts when you laugh.

Notes

1. Cited from Peter Chelsom's *Funny Bones* (1994).

2. *The Critique of Judgement*, transl. James Creed Meredith, Oxford: Oxford University Press, 1952, p. 37.

3. Emerson, 'Experience', in L. Ziff, ed., *Selected Essays*, Harmondsworth: Penguin, 1982, p. 311.

4. *System of Transcendental Idealism*, transl. P. Heath, Charlottesville: University of Virginia Press, 1978, p. 12.

5. *Philosophy of Art*, transl. D. W. Stott, Minneapolis: University of Minnesota Press, 1989, p. 251.

6. For Szondi's definitive historical account of the philosophy of the tragic, which I follow here, see his *Versuch über das Tragische*, in *Schriften I*, Frankfurt am Main: Suhrkamp, 1978, pp. 149–260, see esp. pp. 151–210. See also Jacques Taminiaux's fascinating *Le théâtre des philosophes*, Grenoble: Millon, 1995, which begins thus: 'De Schelling à Heidegger les lectures germaniques de la Grèce ont attribué une importance extrême à la tragédie'. Taminiaux's thesis is to show how the German privileging of tragedy remains, with the sole exception of Hölderlin, determined by the Platonic subordinaton of *praxis* to *poeisis*.

7. In this regard, see Christoph Menke's *Tragödie im Sittlichen. Gerechtigkeit und Freiheit nach Hegel*, Frankfurt am Main: Suhrkamp, 1996.

8. For Nietzsche's reference to his earlier Schopenhauerian 'Artist's Metaphysics', see his 1886 Preface to *The Birth of Tragedy*, 'An Attempt at Self-Criticism', transl. W. Kaufmann, New York: Vintage, 1967, p. 18–27.

9. For discussions of these authors, see Szondi, pp. 174–93.

10. *L'éthique de la psychanalyse*, Livre VII, J.-A. Miller, ed., Paris: Seuil, 1986; *The Ethics of Psychoanalysis*, transl. Dennis Porter, Book VII, 1959–60, London and New York: Routledge, 1992, p. 76. Subsequent page references to the original and translation are given in the text. Cited passages from the *Ethics* seminar have been retranslated. My reading of Lacan is restricted to Seminar VII. Although this seminar held a special place in Lacan's work – as is clear from the opening remarks of the *Encore* seminar, 'It came to pass that I did not publish *The Ethics of Psychoanalysis*' (*Encore*, Livre XX, Paris: Seuil, 1975, p. 9) – my interpretation could at the very least be complicated with reference to other texts of Lacan, perhaps most obviously Seminar XI, *The Four Fundamental Concepts of Psychoanalysis*, where the question of ethics is also discussed but with a different inflection. This chapter is a first and limited attempt to understand these questions.

11. I borrow freely here from Philippe Van Haute's 'Antigone: Heroine of Psychoanalysis?', unpublished typescript, 1997. For discussions of Lacan's interpretation of the *Antigone*, see the contributions of Philippe Lacoue-Labarthe, Françoise Duroux, Nicole Loraux, Samuel Weber and Patrick Guyomard in *Lacan avec les philosophes*, Paris: Albin Michel, 1991. See also Guyomard's more extended critical treatment of Lacan's *Antigone* interpretation in *La jouissance du tragique*, Paris: Flammarion, 1998 [1992].

12. On the existential heroism of Lacan's interpretation of the *Antigone*, see Hans-Dieter Gondek, 'Lacan und die Ethik der Psychoanalyse', in H.-D. Gondek and P. Widmer, eds, *Ethik und Psychoanalyse*, Frankfurt am Main: Fischer, 1994, pp. 217 and 220.

13. Heidegger, *Sein und Zeit*, 15th edn, Tübingen: Niemeyer, 1984, p. 245; transl. J. Macquarrie and E. Robinson, Oxford: Blackwell, 1962, p. 289. All subsequent page references to the original and translation are given in the text.

14. *Einführung in die Metaphysik*, 2nd edn, Tübingen: Niemeyer, 1958, pp. 112–26; *An Introduction to Metaphysics*, transl. R. Manheim, New Haven: Yale University Press, 1959, pp. 146–65. Further page references are given in the text.

15. This claim is analysed in much more detail in my *Very Little . . . Almost Nothing*, London and New York: Routledge, 1997.

16. Jean Paul, *Vorschule der Ästhetik*, 1804 and 1813, Hamburg: Meiner, 1990, p. 105. Once again, for a more extended discussion of finitude in terms of the impossibility of death, with particular reference to Blanchot, see my *Very Little . . . Almost Nothing*.

17. Mikhail Bakhtin, *Rabelais and his World*, transl. Helen Iswolsky, Cambridge Mass.: MIT, 1965.

18. For Kofman's detailed reading of Freud's Jokebook, which is particularly interesting on the complexity of the Jewish dimension of Freud's examples of jokes, see *Pourquoi rit-on. Freud et le mot d'esprit*, Paris: Galilée, 1986.

19. *Der Witz und seine Beziehung zum Unbewussten*, Frankfurt am Main: Fischer, 1992 [1905], p. 47; *Jokes and their Relation to the Unconscious*, vol. 6, Penguin Freud Library, Harmondsworth: Penguin, 1960, p. 64.

20. 'Der Humor', in *Der Witz und seine Beziehung zum Unbewussten*, pp. 253–8; 'Humour', transl. J. Riviere, Standard Edition, vol. 21, pp. 161–6. Subsequent page references to the original and translation are given in the text.

21. Jean Paul, *Vorschule der Ästhetik*, p. 105.

22. Beckett, *Proust and Three Dialogues*, London: J. Calder, 1949, pp. 8–9.

23. This distinction between two forms of laughter is analogous to that suggested by Milan Kundera in *The Book of Laughter and Forgetting*, Harmondsworth: Penguin, 1983, pp. 56–62 and 232–3, between the laughter of angels and the laughter of the devil. The laughter of angels is the serious laughter that expresses one's sheer joy of being, the superabundance of meaning. The laughter of the devil is the dissolution of meaning in the sheer scepticism of deflationary laughter. What interests me is the latter: the contagious, sardonic laughter of the devil, what Kundera refers to as the 'original' laughter (p. 62).

24. See Badiou, *L'éthique. Essai sur la conscience du Mal*, Paris: Hatier, 1993. See my 'How Not to Give Way on Your Desire. Notes on Alain Badiou's *Ethics*', in *Parallax*, no. 6, 1998, pp. 97–100.

25. These questions were suggested by conversations with Philippe Van Haute. In this regard, see his 'Antigone: Heroine of Psychoanalysis?'.

26. Lacan's knowledge of Catharism appears to be derived from his reading of the admirable historical work of René Nelli. The book to which Lacan refers is *Spiritualité de l'hérésie, le catharisme*, Paris: PUF, 1953. A very helpful account of the basic theology of Catharism can also be found in Nelli's *La philosophie du catharisme. Le dualisme radical au XIIIe siècle*, Paris: Payot, 1975.

27. For Lacan's other references to the Cathars, see pp. 148–9/123–4, 183/153, 254–5/215.

28. From Kundera's conversation with Philip Roth that appears as an afterword to *The Book of Laughter and Forgetting*, pp. 232–3.

29. Lacan performs an *imitatio* of Erasmus in 'La chose freudienne', in *Écrits*, Paris: Seuil, 1966, pp. 408–11; 'The Freudian Thing', in *Écrits. A Selection*, London: Tavistock, 1977, pp. 121–3.

30. Jean Allouch, *132 bons mots avec Jacques Lacan*, Toulouse: Éditions Érès, 1985. See Lacan's short, but extremely illuminating, discussion of the figure of the fool in Chaucer and Shakespeare (pp. 214–15/182–3).

31. See Levinas, *De l'évasion*, Montpellier: Fata Morgana, 1982 [1935].

32. Freud, 'Der Humor', p. 258; transl. p. 166.

33. Cited in Karl French's Introduction to The Marx Brothers, *Monkey Business, Duck Soup, and A Day at the Races*, London: Faber, 1993, p. 1.

34. I borrow here from Helmuth Plessner's *Lachen und Weinen*, Bern: Francke, 1961.

35. Slavoj Zizek makes a similar claim, with a different intent, when he speaks of 'obscene laughter bearing witness to a deep solidarity', in *The Indivisible Remainder. An Essay on Schelling and Related Matters*, London: Verso, 1996, p. 3.

36. Adorno, *Minima Moralia*, transl. E. F. N. Jephcott, London: Verso, 1974, p. 247.

37. Kant, *The Critique of Judgement*, p. 20.

11

With Being-With?
Notes on Jean-Luc Nancy's
Rewriting of *Being and Time*[1]

As a consequence of the argument developed in chapters 8, 9 and 10, in particular with regard to what I said about the structure of ethical experience, I would simply like to offer some expository and finally critical remarks on Jean-Luc Nancy's recent book, *Être singulier pluriel*.[2] I would like to focus on the central theme of his book, namely the concept of 'being-with' (*être-avec*), which is obviously the French rendering of Heidegger's *Mitsein*. Let me begin by summarizing the admirable philosophical ambition of *Être singulier pluriel* in three reading hypotheses.

1. What Nancy is attempting is what he calls 'a co-existential analytic', an existential ontology of being-with which has the ambition of being a first philosophy, *une philosophie première* (p. 13). For Nancy 'It is thus a "first philosophy" that is necessary, in the canonical sense of the term, that is to say an ontology' (p. 45). Of course, first philosophy (*philosophia protè*) is how Aristotle defines the area of inquiry later called 'metaphysics'. Although – and here an initial question can be raised – Nancy's will ostensibly be a non-metaphysical metaphysics; that is, a metaphysics that respects the severe qualifications placed on the possibility of metaphysical thinking by the later Heidegger. Of course, one might ask: how exactly is first philosophy possible in the light of Heidegger's account of the history of being? That is, how is it possible to conceive of a non-metaphysical first philosophy? Isn't this simply a contradiction in terms? A subsidiary but related question can also be raised: what exactly is the difference between metaphysics and ontology given that the former is defined by Heidegger (in complete fidelity to Aristotle) as onto-theo-logy?

For Nancy – and rightly – the last great first philosophy in the European tradition was Heidegger's project of fundamental ontology. It is this project that needs to be remade for determinate and hopefully fairly evident historical and political reasons. Nancy writes: '*il faut refaire l'ontologie fondamentale . . . à partir de* l'être-avec [it is necessary to remake fundamental ontology . . . starting from *being-with*]' (p. 45). This brings me to my second hypothesis.

2. What Nancy is proposing is a rewriting of Heidegger's *Being and Time*, where the concept of *Mitsein* would be essential (or co-essential) and originary. Nancy writes in a footnote, with another *il faut*, '*Il faut réécrire* Sein und Zeit [*Sein und Zeit* must be rewritten]' (p. 118n). Obviously, what is compelling the need for this rewriting, as with so much of Nancy's work, is the question of *the political*. Namely, that *Being and Time* must be rewritten because of the political fate of the project of fundamental ontology and the *Dasein*-analytic. That is to say, *Being and Time* must be rewritten without the autarchic telos and tragic-heroic pathos of the thematics of authenticity, where, in Paragraph 74, *Mitsein* is determined in terms of 'the people' and its 'destiny'. Although this would have to be explained in much greater detail, such is what Lacoue-Labarthe has called Heidegger's 'archi-fascism'.[3] If the awful political pathos of the thematics of authenticity is to be avoided, then *Being and Time*, it would seem, must be rewritten from the perspective of the inauthenticity of the *Mitsein*-analytic. Nancy would appear to be claiming – and incidentally, I completely agree with him – that the genuine philosophical radicality of *Being and Time* lies in the existential analytic of inauthenticity. What has to be recovered from the wreckage of Heidegger's political commitment is his phenomenology of everyday life, the sheer banality of our contact (*cotoîment*) with the world and with others, what Nancy calls 'the extremely humble layer of our everyday experience' (p. 27)

3. Thus, what is entailed by the second hypothesis is that the question of co-existence becomes *the* ontological question. The question of Being is (or, as we will see below, 'must be' with another *il faut*) equiprimordial with the question of being-with. Therefore, one might say – and once again, I agree – that the *Seinsfrage* loses some of its relative autonomy. The *Seinsfrage* has to be posed and pursued through the *Mitseinsfrage*. To express this thought in terms that Nancy always places between scare quotes (doubtless because of Heideggerian or Arendtian worries about the decline of the *polis* into the *socius*), 'The question of what we still see as a "question of social being" should in fact constitute *the* ontological question' (p. 78). Thus, the question of the meaning of Being – and by implication Heidegger's later questions of the truth and history of Being and the entire thinking of *das Ereignis* – must take root in and be referred to the question of the *socius*. *Being and Time* must be rewritten as a 'social' ontology.

In the light of this third hypothesis, I would like to consider briefly the political context for *Être singulier pluriel*, a context that is dramatically apparent from the untitled but dated opening page of the book (Nancy writes in Summer 1995) with its extraordinary list of those in struggle or oppressed across the world, an oppression for which the name of Sarajevo is an emblem (pp. 11–12).

The Withdrawal of the Political: Situationism, Law, Critique

For Nancy, in the wake of the collapse of the various communisms and socialisms, what should be retained is the exigency that communism maintained within it: the exigency to say 'we', to say 'we' to ourselves when neither a God nor a leader can say it for us. That is, to say 'we' when we have witnessed the withdrawal of what Nancy calls 'the theologico–political', i.e. the possibility of a religious legitimation of community. For Nancy, to say 'we' is for existence to reclaim its due or to find its condition in co-existence.

Nancy's thesis here is that the collapse of communism only brings to light all the more clearly the *sense* (perhaps Nancy's master word[4]) that underpinned it. Or rather, the collapse of socialism reveals *the making of sense* that is implicit within the socialist project. Nancy writes: 'What Marx understood by alienation . . . was ultimately the alienation of sense' (p. 62). For Nancy, communism is a *praxis of sense*,[5] a making of sense by us, by the 'we' that we are, that is our being. What would seem to be implicit here is a fairly traditional secularization thesis (collapse or withdrawal of the theologico–political, the death of God), namely that in modernity sense has to be something made by us, by the 'we', because we cannot depend upon God or our political leaders to make sense for us. Thus, communism is the recognition within modernity of the fact that the question of sense has devolved upon the 'we', upon finite humanity, and that the question of being-with is *the* ontological question that requires a political settlement.

Thus, for Nancy, our fin-de-siècle disenchantment does not result in political cynicism or liberalism ('that cynicism called "liberalism"' p. 64), but instead points us all the more powerfully to the question of what constitutes 'us' today, who 'we' are today, namely the question of 'social being'. In other words, the question of co-existence, the ontological question of the political (*le politique*) arises at the moment of the evaporation of the possibility of a polity that would incarnate such a being-with. This hopefully familiar logic of what Lacoue-Labarthe and Nancy have since the early 1980s called *le retrait du politique* should be noted here: the question of the political (*le politique*) can be retraced or retreated because politics itself (*la politique*) has withdrawn. It is by virtue of – rather than despite – the collapse of communism that the question of being-with can be raised.

In Nancy's work, as I have tried to show elsewhere, the withdrawal of the political raises the question of *figure* and *figuration* (*Gestalt* and *Gestaltung*).[6] That is, the withdrawal of the theologico-political in modernity – *as* modernity – means nothing else but the withdrawal of every possible figure for community. This means that what is lacking is a means of *identification* (in the Freudian sense) for being-with, given that previous forms of identification for the political reconstitution of the social have become degraded: people, nation, race, party, leader, proletariat or whatever. In Claude Lefort's sense, the place of power has become 'un lieu vide'. The vast question here is whether being-with can do without some figure, without some form of identification, without some form of what Nancy would call 'civil religion'. Nancy responds to this question with his concept of *comparution*, which I shall analyse in detail below.

In Nancy's *Zeitdiagnose*, as a consequence of the collapse of the theologico-political, the withdrawal of the political occurs in two dominant forms: (1) into law, and (2) into a specular self-representation.

1. In relation to law, the theologico-political can retreat into the formal abstraction of law, into that cynicism that Nancy calls liberalism. But it can also retreat into an ethics premised upon the transcendental unrepresentability of law, that is to say, the radical alterity of law or the law as the law of the other. This would presumably be Nancy's critique of Levinasian ethics, but equally of Lyotard's reading of Kant, or Lacan's ethics of psychoanalysis, i.e. to what I have attempted to describe as the structure of ethical experience. One might note in passing Nancy's apparent opposition to Lacanian psychoanalysis, where he writes: 'In a remarkable way, it is here that one sometimes sees how psychoanalysis seeks to conform to a substantialist and authoritarian vision of society' (p. 68 and cf. p. 29). I will come back to these themes below, where I detect a certain communistic flattening or neutralizing of transcendence in Nancy's work. However, it should be noted that, for Nancy, it is not a question of opposing law, it is rather a question of

'doing justice' both to the singular plural of the origin . . . [and], as regards law, to what might be termed the 'originary anarchy' or the very origin of law in what is 'legitimately without law' [*de droit sans droit*]: existence unjustifiable as such. (p. 69)

It is thus a question of doing justice to an existence in itself unjustifiable, of deriving law from originary anarchy, a thought which strangely recalls Levinas's analyses in *Otherwise than Being or Beyond Essence*.

2. The second form of the withdrawal of the theologico-political is in specular self-representation, where society implodes into a specular mirror play, namely Guy Debord's society of the spectacle, where a completely commodified society collapses into the radical immanentism of an auto-simulation or auto-dissimulation, into the society criticized by situationism in the 1960s. For Nancy – and there are strongly autobiographical elements to his remarks here, as he was closely connected with the Situationist International in Paris and Strasbourg – situationism appears as '*la dernière ressource critique dans un monde sans critique* [the final critical resource in a world without critique]' (p. 70). However, the Situationist critique, although necessary, was available for complete recuperation because of its metaphysical assumptions. That is, situationism criticizes the society of the spectacle, a society based on entirely imaginary constructions, but it does two things as a consequence: first, it attempts to replace this capitalist imaginary with a concept of creative imagination that remains tributary to a romantic conception of genius. Second, it understands appearance as mere appearance, namely as that which is opposed to an authentic reality or presence. Thus, the situationist critique remains unwaveringly obedient to the Platonist tradition, opposing an order of essential truth ('desire', 'imagination') to the false order of the spectacle.

Bringing together the two strands of the above critique in Hegelian fashion, Nancy's claim is that the two forms of the withdrawal of the theologico-political collapse into an ontology of same and other: either (1) the uncritical submission to the unrepresentable alterity of law, or (2) the finally traditional sameness of the spectacle and its critique. We thus require, according to Nancy, a different ontology of being with one another, a co-ontology of being-with that will provide the basis for a form of critique.

A guiding and vital concern in the central pages of *Être singulier pluriel* concerns this question of the possibility of critique, and the extent to which all previous forms of critique, with situationism as the last great example, have remained 'paradoxically and unconsciously subject to a classical model of reality opposed to appearance' (p. 75). This means that the lesson has not been learnt from Nietzsche's critique of Platonism, namely that when the true world becomes a fable, then the world of appearance – which only made sense in opposition to reality – also disappears. And if this is so, then the meta-question that this opens is whether the critical attitude is possible at all, and if it is not, then what alternatives are available apart from uncritical resignation?

In the light of the above questions, the lesson of critique is that we are confronted with an appeal to provide the sense of being-in-common according to what is in-common or the 'with', but not in accordance with some metaphysical essence of the common. To put it crudely, what is required is a thinking of the in-common or the being of the social which enables critique whilst being cognizant of the Nietzschean and Heideggerian critiques of metaphysics; that is, the critiques of metaphysical critique. For Nancy, this thinking will be that of *comparution*. To translate this into Anglo-American terms, one might say that what Nancy is after is a post-foundationalist conception of intersubjectivity that will provide a non-essentialist 'basis' for a critical ethics and politics.

Comparution

La comparution is the title of an earlier, shorter and much more polemical book from 1991 that I discuss elsewhere.[7] In everyday French, the verb *comparaître* means to appear in a court of law, and it is this sense of the word that is employed, for example by Levinas when he writes in *Autrement qu'être*, 'La façon dont j'apparais est une comparution.'[8] However, for Nancy, *comparution* has the etymological sense of an appearing-with, although the notion of 'appearing' needs heavy qualification for good Nietzschean and Heideggerian reasons. That is, for Nancy, the primordinal requirement for ontology, as first philosophy, must henceforth be that the concept of being should not be presupposed in the manner of classical metaphysics (as in Aristotle or Aquinas, say). Rather, being is simply the being of that which exists, it is not the presupposition for that existence. Now, existence always exists in the plural, it is the being-in-common of many. Thus, the meaning of the phrase *être singulier pluriel* is that *being one can only be understood on the basis of plurality within being, the singularity of being is plural*. In other words, as I said in my third reading hypothesis above, the question of social being is *the* ontological question.

Nancy suggests, a little hopefully perhaps, that we are living through a new Copernican revolution (p. 78), which is neither the cosmological revolution of Copernicus, nor the critical revolution of Kant, nor the turn towards the unconscious in Freud, but a revolution at the level of social being. This revolution would be, and this is an interesting but question-begging formulation, 'la mise à nu de la réalité sociale – du réel même de l'être-social – dans, par et comme la symbolicité qui la constitue [the laying bare of social reality – of the *real* itself of social being – in, through and as the symbolicity that constitutes it]' (p. 79). Given the discussion of Lacan in the previous chapters, the stakes of this remark should be clear. Nancy would appear to be claiming that not only is the reality of the social revealed by symbolicity, or the symbolic order, but that the latter also constitutes the former. This would seem to imply that the real is the effect of the symbolic, and that the former has no meaning outside the latter. Nancy goes on to qualify his use of symbolic and imaginary (pp. 79–80), but the claim that social reality is laid bare 'in, through and as the symbolicity that constitutes it' entails that 'society' is understood (as distinct from within situationism) as being nothing other than the appearance of itself, and not as referring back to a background of being, essence or whatever. So, appearance does not in any way mean 'mere appearance', but is similar to the notion of 'phenomenon' in Heidegger as the showing of that which shows itself, where being would be understood in terms of phenomenality. *Symbolizing* here does not therefore mean something standing in for something else, in the way a flag symbolizes a nation or the eucharist symbolizes the body of Christ, but, rather, in the etymological sense of *sumbolon* as the joining together of what is broken. Nancy's claim is that *the manner in which social being faces itself, symbolizes itself, is as* comparution.

So, for Nancy, *comparution* means that the 'appearing' – the fact of the world, of coming into the world, the symbolic constitution of the real – is inseparable from the *cum*, from the with. It is here that we can begin to detect a (or the) fundamental ontological structure, described in absolutist terms with yet another *il faut*: '*Que l'être, absolument, est être-avec, voilà ce qu'il nous faut penser* [That being, absolutely, is being-with, this is what we must think]' (pp. 83–4). As Nancy rather candidly puts it in the penultimate paragraph of his book on Hegel, '*L'absolu est entre nous.*'[9]

However, what becomes clear a couple of pages further on is that this fundamental ontology of being-with, this originary symbolizing of social reality as *comparution*, is not only an ontology. It is also, it must be (*doit être*) an *ethos* and a *praxis*, 'cette ontologie doit être, identiquement, un *ethos* est une *praxis*' (p. 87). This claim, which is mentioned only in passing (and in parenthesis) is developed in a later paper on Heidegger's *Brief über den Humanismus*, itself footnoted in *Être singulier pluriel* (p. 87n).[10] Thus, *comparution* as a (or the) fundamental ontological structure is also the structure of an originary ethics, or what Lacoue-Labarthe has called (also with reference to Heidegger) an archi-ethics.[11] Thus, to express this in a speculative proposition: *fundamental ontology is ethical and ethics is fundamentally ontological.*

I shall have another reason to return to these last propositions below, but let me briefly return to the question of what one might think of as a possible psychoanalytic critique of Nancy's project. I am thinking of Lacan here, because the identification of the ethical with the ontological would also entail the collapsing of the order of the real into the symbolic. For Lacan, as I discussed in chapter 9, ethics articulates itself in relation to the real, and Freudian ethics testifies to a certain contact with the real as the guarantor of what Lacan calls *das Ding*. My question here is whether this identification of the ethical and the ontological in Nancy, which would also seem to run parallel to the claim for the symbolic constitution of the real, does not run the risk of turning so-called 'originary ethics' into a yearning for a symbolic order and for forms of symbolic identification inconceivable or only available in a degraded form in modernity?

For Nancy, there would seem to be no dimension of the real outside of the symbolicity of *comparution*. All conceptualizations of the real that would allow it to stand apart from and support the symbolic would be metaphysical and pre-Heideggerian. On such a reading, Lacan is therefore a metaphysician. But, despite these claims, where might one look for the dimension of the real in Nancy? What is there in his work that would stand in for the place of the *das Ding*? One response to this question would be to refer to his beautiful 1988 essay, 'Le cœur des choses'.[12] This essay and later work on the body (*corpus*) attempt precisely to identify that thing 'At the heart of thinking . . . that defies all appropriation', the immemorial source of thinking towards which thinking proves itself inadequate like a 'black hole' that absorbs all light without reflecting anything back. Indeed, in *Être singulier pluriel*, Nancy insists in the penultimate section – 'Corps, langage' – that 'the ontology of being-with is an ontology of bodies' (p. 107), where body would seem to denote the dimension of exteriority, of the outside to the incorporeal working of language. However, the above question remains in an altered form: namely, what might be said to be the relation between this thinking of the materiality or exteriority of *das Ding* and the *ethos* of Nancy's first philosophy? Obviously, for Lacan, there is a connection between the materiality of unconscious desire and ethical experience. What of such a connection from Nancy's perspective? Does not the claim that the real is symbolically constituted as *comparution* entail that ethical experience is restricted to the symbolic order, thereby making the relation to *das Ding* pre-ethical?

The Co-existential Sense of Self

Let me now return to my opening reading hypothesis on the question of Nancy's co-existential analytic. With admirable philosophical honesty but questionable hyperbole, he writes in the final pages of *Être singulier pluriel*,

The existential analytic of *Being and Time* is the enterprise from which *all ulterior thinking* [toute pensée ultérieure] remains tributary, whether it is a question of Heidegger himself or of our thoughts, such as they are and whatever relation of conflict or overcoming they want with regard to Heidegger himself. (p. 117, my emphasis)

Although I would need a little more convincing on this point as to whether *all ulterior thinking* remains tributary to Heidegger (doesn't Wittgenstein at least merit a passing reference?), Nancy goes on to claim that the above is not the faithful profession of a Heideggerianism, and neither does it mean that every word of the existential analytic is definitive. Rather, what took place in *Being and Time* is a paradigm shift in the history of philosophy analogous to that of Descartes or Kant. In Nancy's own language, *Being and Time* registered 'the seismic shift of a decisive rupture in the constitution or in the consideration of sense' (p. 117). Although I agree with Nancy that *Being and Time* does indeed represent a decisive paradigm shift in the history of philosophy – indeed, a thinker as suspicious of Heidegger as Habermas would assent to this – but I would rather express this thought in a more sceptical manner: namely, that if it is granted that there is no way that one can be consequentially pre-Heideggerian in philosophy (no more than one can be pre-Kantian), this is also accompanied by the profound need to leave the climate of Heidegger's thinking for reasons at once metaphysical, ethical, sociological and political.[13]

Indeed, Nancy goes some way towards conceding this point, as I pointed out in my second reading hypothesis above. That is, although *Being and Time* sketches (*esquisse*, a verb repeated in these pages of *Être singulier pluriel*) the co-existential analytic of being-with, where *Mitsein* is shown to be co-essential with *Dasein*, Nancy acknowledges that it also contains 'the principle of a closure of its own opening' (p. 117) insofar as Heidegger in Paragraph 74 seeks to determine *Mitsein* in terms of 'the people' and its 'destiny'. Although, for Nancy, it is not at all a question of completing *Being and Time*, or surgically transforming the torso of the published book into *un corps propre*, it is certainly a matter of strongly emphasizing that the co-essentiality of *Mitsein* entails the co-originality of meaning and thus that the question of the meaning of Being would not be what it is – the dimension of pre-comprehension as the constitution of existence – if it was not first given in *Mitsein*, as being-with. If one were to push this claim a little further, one might simply say that there is a straightforward incoherence in Heidegger's *Being and Time*, between the analysis of *Mitsein* in Division I and the determination of *Mitsein* as *das Volk* in Division II.

On this question of sense or meaning (*sens*), Nancy writes: 'Il n'y a de "sens" qu'en raison d'un "soi"' (p. 118). That is, there is no meaning or sense without a self. In his way, Nancy would appear to be committed to the *subjective ideality of meaning*, namely that meaning comes into being through the creative activity of what Hegel would call the Subject, a self that is for-itself in being for-the-other. However, if there is no sense without a self, then there is no self without being-with, and the self is fundamentally structured co-existentially. As Nancy somewhat hyperbolically points out, '*tel devrait être l'axiome d'une analytique désormais co-existentiale* [such must henceforth be the axiom of a co-existential analytic]' (p. 118). The subjective ideality of meaning is structured intersubjectively.

However, Nancy has another – and rather troubling – way of formulating the basic axiom of the co-existential analytic. Namely, to say that sense is dependent on the self and that the self is always already co-existentially mediated is to say that being-with as the axiom of a new first philosophy is a thought of pure *mediation*.[14] As Nancy puts it in a parenthesis, 'it is a question here of mediation without a mediator' (p. 118). Thus, Nancy places out of court the idea of the other (of any other: human, animal, vegetable, mineral) as a form of mediation that might be constitutive of intersubjectivity. There would seem to be no fundamentally ontological (or ethically pre-ontological) dimension to the encounter with the other: the dimension of surprise, challenge, placing in question, falling in love or into hatred, being overcome by desire, acknowledging, refusing, blaming, forgiving or even cruelly murdering the other, or simply being moved by another's suffering. Such phenomena would presumably only be *ontic* modifications of a fundamental ontological structure.

But Nancy's reasons for refusing the role of mediation are even more revealing and troubling, namely that the 'prototype' of the figure of 'the Mediator' is 'Christ' ('Autre est toujours le Médiateur: son prototype est le Christ' p. 118). Although thinkers from non-Christian traditions might conceivably object to the thought that the figure of Christ is *the* prototype for the mediation between the divine and human, let us grant Nancy his rather Hegelian premise. He then goes on to claim that the thought of being-with as mediation without a mediator is

> Not Christ, but only such a mi-lieu: and this would no longer be the cross, but only the crossing [*croisement*], the intersection and spacing [*écartement*], the lighting up with stars [*étoilement*] of the very di-mension of the world. It would be the very apogee and abyss of a deconstruction of Christianity. (p. 119)

As an earlier note indicates, this project of a deconstruction of Christianity is future research for Nancy (p. 34). However, one cannot avoid a slight feeling of *déjà vu* in the face of such remarks, for one might say that the desire for mediation without a mediator is precisely the motivation behind the Third Person of the Holy Trinity: *Spirit*, whether in its Augustinian formulation or in Hegel, where it is the element in which the thinking of community, of the 'we', of being-with, would take place. Absolute Knowing in Hegel can be thought of as the community for which Spirit has become Subject and Subject has become Spirit; that is, where the self recognizes itself in and through absolute otherness. As Hegel puts it, 'Spirit is the image of God, the divinity of the human.'[15] Might one not say Hegel too is attempting a deconstruction of Christianity (both apogee and abyss) insofar as Spirit would be achieved by the Subject when it had successfully overcome all forms of *Vorstellungsdenken* (Christ as representation or figuration) and attained the pure mediation of the *Begriff*, where religion passes over into philosophy. My worry here concerns the way in which the fundamental ontological drive for mediation without a mediator in Nancy seems to entail both a subordination of the concrete ontic other to ontological otherness *überhaupt*, and the extent to which this seemingly pure move within first philosophy is parasitic upon a more or less latent, more or less deconstructed Christianity.

Is Ontology Fundamental?

Returning to the main strand of Nancy's argument, his sense of the self is the element in which I, you and we take place. The self is the element that comes to itself in the there of the world, it is a self that finds itself (*sich befinden*) there in the world, in the event of the world. The self is that which exists ecstatically, the self is *auprès-de-soi*, alongside itself and affectively disposed into the there of the world. That is to say, self is *Dasein*. It is '*être-le-là*': a pre-cognitive affective disposition towards the world. Such is Nancy's creative reconstruction of the arguments of Division I of *Being and Time*.

Nancy illustrates these arguments in the closing pages of *Être singulier pluriel* with an image, '*Quelqu'un entre dans une pièce* [Someone enters a room]' (p. 121). That is, before being the possible subject of a representation, a *res cogitans* or an 'I think', the self disposes itself within and towards the room, the self comes to itself insofar as it is disposed (pre-reflectively, pre-cognitively, pre-representationally) towards the world. Of course, this recalls Heidegger's analysis of *Dasein*'s spatiality, but Nancy goes on to qualify the image: '*Mais le monde n'est pas une pièce dans laquelle on pourrait entrer* [The world is not a room we might enter]' (p. 121). We cannot begin philosophizing from the solitary, solipsistic subject who is apart from the world. Being a self, for Nancy, is through and through based in the 'with', the with-world and the with-others. Thus, 'Being-with cannot be added to being-there' (p. 122). To-be-there is to-be-with and to-be-with is to make sense, to understand that sense is something that 'we' make.

Nancy concludes in Kantian terms: if pure reason is by itself practical, and not practical only through reference or reverence for some transcendent norm, it is because it is a *sensus communis* from the beginning. That is, the praxis of the 'with' is the foundation of practical reason. Thus, '*Il n'y a pas de différence entre l'éthique et l'ontologique: "l'éthique" expose ce que "l'ontologie" dispose* [there is no difference between the ethical and the ontological: "ethics" exposes what "ontology" disposes]' (p. 123). The ontological dimension of the 'with' which is the co-existential foundation of any sense of self and any making of sense is always already an *ethos*, an originary ethics. Ontology is ethical, ethics is ontological.

But is ontology fundamental? From the nuanced and minimal Levinasian point of view argued for in this book, the identification of the ethical and the ontological – that is, the collapsing of the former into the latter – is the very gesture that governs and defines the philosophical tradition. This tradition is called 'ontology' by Levinas and reaches its final and critical articulation in Heidegger's *Being and Time*. From this perspective, Nancy's first philosophy of being-with and *comparution* rejoins the philosophical tradition of ontology, with its suppression of ontic plurality and multiplicity. Yet, how is this possible given that Nancy's book is devoted to the question of the singular plurality of being?

Levinas's work seeks to describe a relation to an alterity irreducible to comprehension, that is to say, irreducible to what he sees as the *ontological* relation to others where alterity is reduced to what he calls the Same. Even the Heideggerian and post-Heideggerian ontology of Nancy, an ontology that exceeds and precedes Husserlian intellectualism and theoreticism, is unable to describe this relation because the particular being is always already understood within the pre-comprehension of Being. Both singularity and plurality are always understood from within Being and not as being otherwise than Being, a dimension of otherness that is refractory to *Seins*- or *Mitseinsverständnis*. The Heideggerian prioritization of the ontological over the ontic, however subtly this ontological difference is nuanced, subordinates the relation to the other to the relation to Being. In other words, although Heidegger acknowledges that *Dasein* is *Mitsein*, this question is only a moment of an existential analytic whose ambition is the elaboration of the question of the meaning of Being.

Of course, this last claim is not true of Nancy's work, as I have tried to show, where the ambition is to rewite *Being and Time* as a 'social' ontology where *die Seinsfrage* must be subordinated to *die Mitseinsfrage*. However, despite this laudable advance on Heidegger, Nancy might still be said to fall foul of the same critique insofar as the relation to the other, as mediator, always already presupposes the ontological pre-comprehension of my *Mitseinsverstädis*: pure mediation, apogee and abyss of Christianity. And perhaps more apogee than abyss.

Thus, even given the radicality of Nancy's rewriting of *Being and Time*, his conception of being-with constitutes what one might call *a neutralizing of ethical transcendence* or a *flattening of the structure of ethical experience*. What I mean is that the other person is no longer 'the widow, the orphan, the stranger' who stands to me in an asymmetrical relation of height, but the other becomes my colleague, my comrade, my *semblable*, perhaps also my lover. Nancy's conception of being-with risks reducing intersubjectivity to a relation of reciprocity, equality and symmetry, where I rub shoulders or stand shoulder to shoulder with the other, but where I do not *face* him. That is, I do not see in the other person that dimension of surprise, separateness or secrecy that continually defies my attempts at comprehension and appropriation. In more Hegelian terms, it would seem that the self in Nancy is constituted through the desire for recognition, the dialectic of intersubjectivity that defines the Subject through its appropriation of absolute otherness. The other is my other or an other for me, a logic that must always think intersubjectivity on the model of *love*.[16] For Nancy, I speak of 'me' and 'you' as a 'we', and speak of our world as a 'with'-world. But perhaps ontology is not fundamental. That is, perhaps I am never fundamentally 'with' the other and the relation to the other is, as Sartre suggested, a hole in the world, a tear in the ontological fabric of *In-der-Welt-sein*. Perhaps I am also 'without' the other, and perhaps most of all in love, in a relation that demands my *acknowledgement* because it exceeds the bounds of my knowledge. Perhaps the co-existential structures of being-with overlay a prior level of 'being-without', a being-without the other that is without being.

Nancy's model of being-with might be said to produce the desired political virtue of solidarity. Yet, my view is that unless solidarity is underpinned by the separation, distance and radical non-solidarity of the ethical relation to the other, a relation that I have sought to understand in previous

chapters in terms of the psychoanalytic model of trauma, then it will ineluct-
ably lead back to an ontological tradition that has shown itself incapable of
acknowledging that which resists knowledge, i.e. the source of ethical experience – what Levinas identifies as the other, what Lacan calls *das Ding*, what
Genet calls 'saintliness', what Derrida calls justice, and what Lyotard more
provocatively (and not unproblematically) names 'the jews'. The face-to-
face risks effacing itself in the reciprocity of the 'with'; it is therefore a
matter – ontologically, ethically, politically – not of thinking without the
'with', but of thinking the 'without' within this 'with'.

Notes

1. First published in *Phänomenologische Forschungen*, vol. 2, October 1998, pp. 1–
14.
2. *Être singulier pluriel*, Paris: Galilée, 1996. All subsequent page references are
given in the text; the translations are mine.
3. Philippe Lacoue-Labarthe, *Le courage de la poésie*, Paris: Le Perroquet, 1993,
p. 9. Lacoue-Labarthe also uses this phrase in his 'The Spirit of National Socialism
and its Destiny', in Simon Sparks, ed., *Re-Tracing the Political*, London and New
York: Routledge, 1997, p. 149. However, for the definitive version of Lacoue-
Labarthe's understanding of the relation between philosophy and politics in Heidegger,
see 'Transcendence Ends in Politics', transl. P. Caws in *Typographies*, Cambridge
Mass.: Harvard University Press, 1989.
4. See Nancy, *Le sens du monde*, Paris: Galilée, 1993.
5. Nancy also uses precisely these words in describing Hegel's concept of
philosophy in *Hegel. L'inquiétude du négatif*, Paris: Hachette, 1997, pp. 15 and 80.
See also the discussion of the 'we' in relation to Hegel, ibid., pp. 113–17.
6. See 'Re-Tracing the Political: Politics and Community in the Work of
Philippe Lacoue-Labarthe and Jean-Luc Nancy', in *The Political Subject of Violence*,
Manchester and New York: Manchester University Press, 1993, pp. 73–93. See also
Simon Sparks's Introduction to *Retreating the Political*, pp. xx–xxv.
7. *La comparution*, with Jean-Christophe Bailly, Paris: Christian Bourgois, 1991.
I discuss this book in the final pages of 'Re-Tracing the Political', see above note 3.
8. *Autrement qu'être ou au-delà de l'essence*, The Hague: Martinus Nijhoff, 1974,
p. 77.
9. *Hegel. L'inquiétude du négatif*, p. 117.
10. 'L'éthique originaire de Heidegger'. I refer to an unpublished typescript.
For a very similar reading of Heidegger, which makes explicit reference to Nancy,
see Roberto Esposito, 'Die ursprüngliche Gemeinschaft', *Deutsche Zeitschrift für Philosophie*, vol. 45, no. 4, 1997, pp. 551–8.
11. *Le courage de la poésie*, p. 10.
12. Reprinted in *La pensée finie*, Paris: Galilée, 1990, pp. 197–223. In this
regard, see also *Corpus*, Paris: Anne-Marie Métailié, 1992.

13. I allude to Levinas's remarks in the Introduction to *Existence and Existents*, Dordrecht: Kluwer, 1978, p. 19.

14. On mediation, see *Hegel. L'inquiétude du négatif*, pp. 74–8.

15. This passage from the *Encyclopaedia of the Philosophical Sciences* (paragraph 441) is cited by Nancy in *Hegel. L'inquiétude du négatif*, p. 139.

16. For these Hegelian themes in Nancy, see *Hegel. L'inquiétude du négatif*, pp. 86–90. For my critique of the Hegelian model of intersubjectivity, see above, chapters 1 and 2.

12

The Other's Decision in Me
(What Are the Politics of Friendship?)[1]

> We will then ask *ourselves* what a decision is and *who* decides.
> And if a decision is – as we are told – active, free, conscious and
> voluntary, sovereign. What would happen if we kept this word
> and this concept, but changed these last determinations?
>
> Derrida, *Politiques de l'amitié*

What is friendship? And what is the relation between friendship and democracy? In more Derridian terms, what is the relation between a certain non-
traditional – that is, non-androcentric, non-fraternalistic, non-patriarchal
– concept of friendship, an *aimance* unthought within (or only thought on
the margins of) the historical determinations of friendship in the West, and
a thinking of the political, a thinking that Derrida places under the sign
of *a democracy to come* (une démocratie à venir)? Of course, this is the very
question with which Derrida frames the entire argumentation of *Politiques
de l'amitié* (PdA 12–4 and 339–40; PF viii–ix and 305–6): if the concept
of the political is, in the Western tradition, as Derrida claims, thought in
relation to a fraternalist, androcentric and familial schema, then, as Derrida
writes, 'Let us ask ourselves what would then be a politics of such a
"beyond the principle of fraternity"?' To which he adds the crucial caveat,
'Would this still deserve the name "politics"?' To which we might also add
the question: would such a politics also merit what Derrida calls 'le vieux
nom' of democracy? And what might this mean?

The Three Non-Ecstases of Temporality: Friendship in Blanchot

In this chapter, for reasons that will soon become clear, I would like to
approach this question of the nature of friendship and the relation of the

latter to democracy by way of a reading of Blanchot and through a consideration of Derrida's reading of Blanchot in *Politiques de l'amitié*. This will permit me to make a transition to Derrida's recent *Adieu à Emmanuel Levinas* and to focus on the question of the relation between ethics and politics, which is a central theme of both the latter book and my own. In this way, my hope is that I will be able to reformulate as persuasively as possible the politics of deconstruction.

Now, although there are numerous important, but passing, references to Blanchot in *Politiques de l'amitié*, Derrida's reading of Blanchot occupies the second half of the final chapter 'For the First Time in the History of Humanity' (PdA 322–40/PF 290–306). Despite the fact that Derrida's book cannot be said to reach a conclusion or point of final closure, but, rather, opens a series of potentially endless recoils within the canonical history of friendship, the reading of Blanchot still occupies a quite crucial place in its exposition and argumentation. Indeed, in the original English version of 'The Politics of Friendship', delivered at the American Philosophical Association in 1988, Blanchot occupies a similar place in Derrida's argumentation, where he is first mentioned in the final two paragraphs of the text, and then cited at length and approvingly in the long final footnote.[2]

Although I shall turn presently to Derrida's reading of Blanchot in *Politiques de l'amitié*, and I will have those pages constantly in mind in everything I say, I would like to approach the theme of friendship in Blanchot and Derrida through a reflection on a short text that appeared too late to be mentioned in *Politiques de l'amitié*. This is Blanchot's preface to *À la recherche d'un communisme de pensée*, which is a memoir and testament of his friendship for Dionys Mascolo, which was originally published in 1993 and then republished separately in late 1996 as *Pour l'amitié*.[3]

In *Pour l'amitié* – a title whose very simplicity ('for friendship' connoting both the sense of 'in favour of', and 'out of friendship for'), as always with Blanchot's titles, evokes a much deeper complexity that allows the entire *Sache* to be discreetly profiled – Blanchot draws a classical distinction between friendship and camaraderie, between *Freundschaft* and *Kamaradschaft* (PA 31). At least within the Germanic languages, there is an association between friendship and the semantic chain *Freiheit* and *Friede*, where friendship is the peaceful and reciprocal recognition of the other's freedom. But friendship also resides in the intimacy of trust, in the secrecy of what is only shared between friends. As Kant writes in his *Metaphysik der Sitten*, '*Moralische Freundschaft ist das völlige Vertrauen zweier Personen in Wechselseitiger Eröffnung ihrer geheimen Urteilen und Empfindungen* [Moral friendship is the complete trust of two persons in the mutual disclosure of their secret judgements and feelings]'.[4] In this sense, the real sin against friendship is a breach of trust. What also characterizes *Freundschaft* is its connection to *Verwandtschaft*, as both kinship and twinship, as consanguinity and affinity, where the other who is my friend is my brother, and fraternity is based on an actual or symbolic blood-brothership.

The intimacy and secrecy of *Freundschaft* can be contrasted to *Kamaradschaft,* which is essentially public and stems from military vocabulary. *Kamaradschaft* is *esprit de corps* and tends towards a transparent collectivity that is profoundly exclusivist, a term that in German is strongly associated with the *Nationalsozialistische Jugendbewegung,* and more recently with the *Jugendgruppe* in the former DDR.[5] Derrida himself discusses this opposition in the final chapter of *Politiques de l'amitié* in relation to Nietzsche's remark, 'Es gibt Kamaradschaft: möge es Freundschaft geben' (PdA 284/PF 316).[6]

Blanchot emphasizes that this distinction between friendship and camaraderie is expressed in the distinction the pronouns *tu* and *vous*, between the comrades with whom one *tutoyer* and the friends with whom one *vousvoyer.* At this late stage in Blanchot's short memoir, the context is 1968.[7] The distinction is between, on the one hand, the camaraderie of *Les Comités d'action,* which '*n'admettaient . . . différence d'âge* [did not admit . . . age differences]' – where, in a street slogan that Blanchot traces to a source in the Talmud, '*il est interdit de vieillir* [it is forbidden to grow old]' (PA 31) – and, on the other hand, the friendship which takes time, a fidelity that is perennial and which demands patience and perseverance – step by step, little by little. *Pour l'amitié* begins thus:

> la pensée de l'amitié: je crois qu'on sait quand l'amitié prend fin (même si elle dure encore), par un désaccord qu'un phénoménologue nommerait existential, un drame, un acte malheureux. Mais sait-on quand elle commence? Il n'y a pas de coup de foudre de l'amitié, plutôt un peu à peu, un lent travail de temps. On était amis et on ne le savait pas. (PA 9)

> [The thought of friendship: I think that one knows when friendship ends (even if it still endures), with a disagreement that a phenomenologist would call existential, a drama, an unfortunate act. But does one know when it begins? Friendship does not begin with a bolt from the blue, but rather little by little, the slow work of time. We were friends and we didn't know it.]

Friendship, unlike camaraderie, is bound up with an experience of time's passing, of time not as the explosion of the *Augenblick* or *Jetztpunkt,* or indeed the mystical *scintilla dei* so dear to the various fatal political romanticisms of this century – a Fourieresque romanticism articulated in '68 by the Situationist International – but, rather, time as the experience of passage, procrastination, temporization, delay, one might even say *différance*. If camaraderie is an experience of the present, of the present of the *coup de foudre*, the sublimity of the Now of revolution for the exclusive élite of comrades, then friendship opens an experience of the future, what we might call a non-ecstatic experience of the future. This is non-ecstatic because it is a conception of the future irreducible to the autarchy that still determines the ecstasies of *Dasein*. The time of friendship is strongly linked with the experience of ageing, of senescence, of old friends leaning together like bookends, of being an old friend even when one is relatively young. The temporality of the future in friendship is an experience of slow protraction, the future tense as distension, as stretching out.

So, friendship is rooted in the passage of time, of a certain counting of time which allows one to count on one's friends and to hold them to account, to be accountable. This picks up on an insistent and guiding theme in *Politiques de l'amitié*: the question of *number*, of the demography of friendship. That is, how many friends are there? How many will we be? – 'Combien sont-ils? Combien serons-nous?' (PdA 14/PF x).

But the time of friendship is also essentially linked to a non-ecstatic experience of the past. Friendship is the time of recollection, testimony, testament, narration and memoir. Thus, the experience of friendship is deeply bound up with the experience of memory, both of friends recalling the past together, but – more importantly perhaps – of one friend recalling alone, in solitude, what Derrida calls in connection with Blanchot, 'amitié du solitaire pour le solitaire' (PdA 328/PF 295). This is also why the experience of friendship – and this is something obvious in Blanchot, but also, as Derrida shows, in Cicero, Montaigne and others – is so intimately connected with the experience of loss, of mourning, where *die Stimme des Freundes* is the voice from beyond the grave. The voice of the friend comes from the beyond the grave, and the voice of the friend who lives on, who sur-vives, speaks to the memory of a person who is no more: 'O mes amis, il n'y a nul amy'. As Derrida writes, in an unintended response to Blanchot's perplexity, '*l'amitié commence par se survivre* [friendship begins by surviving]' (PdA 324/PF 291). Although the relation between friendship, memory and mortality will presently become more complex, we can at least now provisionally make sense of the Ciceronian epigraph to *Politiques de l'amitié*: 'Quocirca et absentes adsunt . . . et quod difficilius dictu est, mortui vivunt'. Although it is indeed 'difficult to say', it is because of friendship that the *dead live* (*mortui vivunt*), and the condition of possibility for friendship is memory. The dead live because they are recalled by friends, they survive after death because they are not forgotten. In this sense, *philia* is *necro-philia*.

However, this experience of friendship as loss, as a work of mourning, where, as Freud says in 'Mourning and Melancholia', 'by taking flight into the ego love escapes extinction',[8] is also essentially the here and now of writing, the *present* time of inscription, of iterability: the writing of *Pour l'amitié* for Dionys Mascolo, of 'L'amitié' for Georges Bataille, of *Michel Foucault tel que je l'imagine*, but equally of *Mémoires, pour Paul de Man*, and of *Adieu à Emmanuel Levinas*. One writes here and now out of friendship, for friendship, in favour of friendship, for the future of friendship. And one does this in saying *adieu*, in trying to evoke the past, in seeking to recollect one's loss. One is most for the other in taking one's leave, in parting's sweet sorrow.

Thus, to summarize these remarks into what we might call 'the unity of the three non-ecstasies of temporality', the (present) time of writing, the moment of iterability that writes for friendship, for the other (future) is provoked by an experience of loss (past). One writes here and now for the future of friendship by recalling the past. And yet, as Blanchot insists in the most radical moment on his reflection on friendship, and this is where Derrida will follow him one step further, perhaps the greatest suffering ('*profonde douleur*') of friendship is the awareness that this effort of memory might have to recognize a more fundamental forgetfulness, '*C'est là sa profonde douleur. Il faut qu'elle accompagne l'amitié dans l'oubli* [This is its profound suffering. It must accompany friendship into forgetfulness]' (A 330).[9] In his commentary on this passage, Derrida simply writes, '*Il faut l'oubli* [Forgetfulness is necessary]' and then more abruptly, imperatively, and untranslatably in the next paragraph, '*Faut l'oubli* [Forgetfulness must]' (PdA 328/PF 295).

Although I am simply anticipating themes that I will pick up in more detail below, it should be noted that this imperative 'Faut l'oubli' contradicts the classical insistence on the link between friendship and memory, found in Cicero and Montaigne, where *mortui vivunt* because the dead are recalled to the memory of the friend. In my view, Derrida's treatment of friendship is aiming at (if not pretending to attain) a rather different conception of memory and a transformed conception of finitude and death, what he calls *sur-vivance*. Namely, that if *philia* is *necrophilia* in the classical conception of friendship, then this presupposes that a clear distinction can be made between the living and the dead, and presupposes the appropriative activity of memory as that which allows the dead to live. By contrast, *survivance* is for Derrida something irreducible to the opposition between life and death; it is the dimension of the *spectral*, that which deconstructs the line that divides the living from the dead. As such, although I have not presented the argument for this yet, one might say that *sur-vivance is the first opening onto alterity insofar as alterity opens in the relation to mortality.* This is not so much *philia* as *necrophilia* but, rather, friendship for the other *as* mortal, where the precondition for friendship is the acknowledgement of mortality. In this sense, the task is one of thinking friendship in relation to a more originary finitude – spectral and sur-viving, the night of Banquo's ghost. But I will come back to this below.

Friendship and its Other

At the end of *Pour l'amitié*, in an almost pleading tone that evokes the very evanescence of the time of friendship, Blanchot writes: '*J'avais eu le projet naïf de discuter avec Aristote, avec Montaigne, de leur conception de l'amitié. Mais à quel bon?* [I had the naive intention of discussing with Aristotle and Montaigne their conception of friendship. But to what end?]' (PA 33–4). After a quotation from Villon, whose sentiment Blanchot distrusts, a quotation that also appears at the beginning of Derrida's discussion of Blanchot in *Politiques de l'amitié* (PdA 322/PF 290), '*Que sont mes amis devenus?* [What has become of my friends?]', Blanchot concludes with an acknowledgement of contradiction:

> Vers émouvants, mais menteurs. Ici, je contredis mon commencement. Fidelité, constance, endurance, peut-être perennité, tels sont les traits de l'amitié ou du moins les dons qu'elle m'accordés. (PA 34)

> [Moving but deceptive lines. Here, I contradict my starting point. Fidelity, constancy, endurance, and perhaps perennity, such are the traits of friendship or at least the gifts that it has accorded to me.]

But he has not yet quite concluded, as we will see presently, and the contradiction he mentions is more complex that it appears. The classical distinction between *amitié* and *camaraderie*, between *vous* and *tu*, also echoes the distinctions between the personal and the political, or the private and the public. And it should be noted that, for Blanchot, the political is more personal than the personal, and the public is more private than the private. That is to say, the public realm of camaraderie is a zone of *tutoiement, Mitsein* and intimacy which is actually physically closer than the personal relation of friendship expressed in the *vous* ('nous marchions, bra-dessus, bras-dessous, avec Marguerite [Duras] entre nous' PA 33). However, that said, this distinction between *amitié* and *camaraderie* is then nicely and brusquely subverted in a closing allusion to Levinas, which is given in a short afterword to *Pour l'amitié*. Blanchot finally concludes:

> la *philia* grecque est reciprocité, échange du Même avec le Même, mais jamais ouverture à *l'Autre*, découverte d'Autrui en tant que responsable de lui, reconnaissance de sa pré-excellence, éveil et dégrisement par cet Autrui, qui ne me laisse jamais tranquille, jouissance (sans concupiscence, comme dit Pascal) de sa Hauteur, de ce qui le rend toujours plus près du Bien que 'moi'.
>
> C'est là mon salut à Emmanuel Levinas, le seul ami – ah ami lointain – que je tutoie et qui me tutoie, cela est arrivé, non pas parce que nous étions jeunes, mais par une décision délibérée, un pacte auquel j'espère ne jamais manquer. (PA 35)

> [Greek *philia* is reciprocity, the exchange of the Same with the Same, but never an opening to the *Other*, discovery of the other [*autrui*] insofar as one is responsible for them, a recognition of their pre-eminence, an awakening and disillusionment by this Other [*Autrui*], who never leaves me in peace, enjoyment (without concupiscence, as Pascal would say) of their Height, of that which always makes the other closer to the Good than 'me'.
>
> This is my salute to Emmanuel Levinas, the only friend – ah distant friend – who says *tu* to me and to whom I say *tu*, and this happened not because we were young, but because of a deliberate decision, a pact that I hope I will never fail to observe.]

This is an extraordinarily rich and provocative passage, that merits long meditation, but let me provisionally make six comments.

1. The virtues of friendship – the above-cited virtues of fidelity, constancy, endurance and perennity – are assimilated, perhaps too quickly, perhaps too easily, into the Greek concept of *philia*. The latter is then defined as reciprocity, as the economic exchange that takes place within the *oikos* and the *agora*, what Levinas would refer to as 'the economy of the Same', where the same and the other form a totality. Thus, in Levinas's terminology, the intersubjective relation of *philia* is *ontological* and must be demarcated from the *ethical* relation to *Autrui*.

(Let us note here, following Derrida, that this determination of *philia* is in complete contradiction with Blanchot's remarks in *Michel Foucault tel que je l'imagine*, where he claims that

> la *philia*, qui, chez les Grecs et même chez les Romains, reste le modèle de ce qu'il y a d'excellent dans les relations humaines . . . peut être acceuillie comme un héritage toujours capable d'être enrichi. (PdA 332–3)

[*Philia* which, for the Greeks and even for the Romans, remains the model of what is excellent in human relations . . . can be received as a heritage that is always capable of being enriched.] (PF 299)

Although I would say that the text on Foucault is the exception rather than the rule in relation to Blanchot's meditations on friendship, it is necessary to acknowledge the force of what Derrida calls *la question grecque* in relation to Blanchot (PdA 332–5/PF 299–302). However – which is perhaps even more important and more disturbing – it is also necessary to acknowledge the force of *la question juive* in Blanchot, where he is led to say in a letter to Salomon Malka, analysed in the closing paragraphs of *Politiques de l'amitié*, that '*les juifs étaient nos frères* [the Jews were our brothers]' (PdA 337/PF 304). It would here be a question of linking the above distinction of *philia* from the relation to *Autrui*, of the Greek from the Jew, with the question of what we might provocatively call Blanchot's *philo-semitism* in a series of texts extending from 'Être juif' in 1962, through his reading of Robert Antelme's memoirs of Buchenwald, through to his somewhat questionable discussion of the Holocaust in *L'écriture du désastre*. Although, for reasons we will see below in connection with Levinas, it is extremely tempting to speak of a *hebraicization* of the concept of *philia* in Blanchot, of a certain Judaic fracturing of the Greek model of friendship, such a move is too easy because it presupposes a radically de-historicized and unnuanced conception of the Hebraic that derives from an extremely questionable nineteenth-century tradition of philology, found, for example, in Matthew Arnold's *Culture and Anarchy*, and which risks creating many more problems than it begins to solve.)

2. Returning to the above quote, the reciprocity of *philia* is demarcated from the opening to the other, to *Autre* understood as *Autrui*, which is then defined in terms of responsibility or recognition of the pre-eminence of the other, which is to say that it is a relation that exceeds any dialectical *Kampf um Anerkennung*, whether metaphysical (Hegel), 'post-metaphysical' (Habermas, Honneth) or even post-historical (Kojève). The relation to the other is also described – in a striking formulation that could occasion an interesting digression into Lacan – as the 'jouissance de sa Hauteur', an enjoyment that would certainly exceed the pleasure principle and any eudaimonism, and where moral feeling would be an experience of pain (*Schmerz*), as Kant suggests in the Second Critique, or trauma, as Levinas suggests in *Autrement qu'être*.[10] But what the various formulations in the above quote attempt to evoke is the experience of a relation to the other irreducible to comprehension and hence (for Levinas) to ontology, a relation

that can be described with the adjective 'ethical'. Although we should note that if Blanchot mentions 'le Bien', he is careful not to use the word 'ethics'. Moreover, the latter is consistent with his powerfully reconstructive reading of Levinas in *L'entretien infini*, as we will see presently. Of course, the adjective 'ethical' might be replaced with other equally contingent terms, such as 'religious' or 'holy' (*saint*). As Derrida reminds us in his funeral oration for Levinas, perhaps *la sainteté* is a more important word than 'ethics' in describing the ambition of Levinas's work.

3. Thus, the consequence of the above is that we appear to have a distinction between *philia* and the relation to the other, between reciprocity and responsibility, between mediation and immediacy, between pleasure and *jouissance*, between Greek and Jew, between the virtues of fidelity, constancy, endurance and perennity, and the experience of disillusionment, awakening, and the absence of tranquility.

4. But this consequence is then complicated in a parting *salut*, an *adieu* to Levinas, who is the only friend 'que je tutoie et qui me tutoie'. A small, but significant, contradiction can be glimpsed and teased out here: the distinction between *amitié* and *camaraderie* was drawn above in terms of the difference between the *tu* and the *vous*. Yet here, in Blanchot's recollection of his friendship for Levinas, we have an account of friendship which takes place in a *tutoiement* that was above reserved for the experience of camaraderie. Blanchot's friendship for Levinas is the distance of 'ah, ami lointain', expressed in the intimacy of a camaraderie, 'le seul ami . . . que je tutoie et qui me tutoie'. Such a friendship can be described oxymoronically as the utter intimacy of distance, the absolute proximity to the one who is far off. This is a logic that recalls the dedication in *Pour l'amitié*, 'À tous mes amis, connus et inconnus, proches et lointains* [To all my friends, known and unknown, close and distant]'.

5. Also note that Blanchot writes that this use of the *tu* form is a deliberate *decision* on his and Levinas's part, a decision which again is in stark contrast to the whole drift of the other testimonies of friendship in *Pour l'amitié*, 'Mais sait-on quand elle commence?'. The friendship between Levinas and Blanchot, or at least their use of the *tu* form, begins with a decision, a datable, definable pact, although we are not told what it is, and we are not told why. And yet, who decides to say *tu*? This introduces a major theme of *Politiques de l'amitié*, namely the question of the *decision* indicated in my epigraph and which I will come back to below when I discuss the relation between ethics to politics. To anticipate a little, it is a question of trying to think the decision outside of its traditionally voluntaristic and 'decisionistic' determinations, for example in Carl Schmitt, where the

possibility of the decision presupposes the existence of the *sovereign* subject defined in terms of consciousness, activity, freedom and will. Derrida's ambition in *Politiques de l'amitié*, as he makes clear in a footnote to *Adieu à Emmanuel Levinas* (AEL 52, n. 2), is to think a conception of 'la décision passive' or 'la décision inconsciente', the passive or unconscious decision. In this sense, the decision is not something taken by a subject, but rather the subject (insofar as one can still employ this word post-deconstructively)[11] is *taken by the decision* that is made without its volition. In this sense, the moment of the decision is the subject's relation to an alterity within itself, something which corresponds to the structure of the Levinasian subject passively constituted through trauma, as I showed in chapter 8. Derrida tries to capture this transformed concept of the decision in the following terms:

> La décision passive, condition de l'événement, c'est toujours en moi, structurellement, une autre décision, une décision déchirante comme décision de l'autre. De l'autre absolu en moi, de l'autre comme absolu qui décide de moi en moi. (AEL 87)

> [The passive decision, condition of the event, is always in me, structurally, an other decision, a rending decision as the decision of the other. Of the absolutely other in me, of the other as the absolute who decides of me in me.][12]

Returning to Blanchot's words, if it is a 'deliberate decision' on Levinas's and Blanchot's part to say *tu*, then in a sense we might say that the decision was deliberated by the other, the decision came from the other, calling me to respond.

6. Thus, in terms of the opening schema we established, Blanchot's friendship for Levinas, at least as it is expressed in *Pour l'amitié*, cuts across, undercuts or maybe even *deconstructs* the distinction between *amitié* and *camaraderie*, between the virtuous fidelity and perennial endurance of *philia* and the *éclatment du présent* or *coup de foudre* of the feeling of solidarity.

The Relation without Relation: Blanchot's Reconstruction of Levinas

But what does all this mean? Perhaps the following: that the relation to *Autrui* that is not acknowledged in the Greek conception of *philia*, a relation evoked *in* and *as* Blanchot's *salut* to his friendship for Levinas, is an experience of 'friendship' irreducible to the distinction between *amitié* and *camaraderie*. Blanchot's friendship for Levinas is a 'friendship' that takes us beyond friendship into an opening onto the other, *découverte d'Autrui*, that defines, for Levinas, that experience that is called 'ethical'. One might speculate as to why *Pour l'amitié*, this little memoir ostensibly written *for* Dionys Mascolo, should conclude with this closing memoir *for* Levinas, which is *for* a conception of friendship that undercuts the friendship *for* which Blanchot writes. If Blanchot is *pour l'amitié*, then – and this is the thought that I would now like to explore – he is *for* a conception of friendship perhaps as yet unthought within, or at least only thought in rela-tion to the ruptures of, the Western tradition. Recalling the 'Avant-Propos' of *Politiques de l'amitié*, this would be a conception of friendship that, recalling Derrida, disrupts fraternity, patriarchy, androcentrism and 'the familial schema'. This friendship beyond the traditional figures of friendship is what Derrida seems to mean by the term *aimance*, that I will come back to below, but which is a compound of *amour* and *amitié*, *'l'aimance au-delà de l'amour et de l'amitié selon leurs figures déterminées* [*aimance* beyond love and friendship following their determined figures]' (PdA 88/PF 69), and which collapses the ever unstable historical and conceptual limit that distinguishes friendship from love.

But let me try and make some of these claims a little more concrete by turning to Blanchot's fascinating reading of Levinas's *Totalité et infini* in *L'entretien infini*.[13] In the latter work, Blanchot gives his first extended *critical* attention to a theme central to his *récits*, namely the question of *Autrui* and the nature of the relation to *Autrui*. What fascinates Blanchot in his three *entretiens* with Levinas is the notion of an absolute relation – *le rapport sans rapport* – that monstrous contradiction (that refuses to recognize the prin-ciple of non-contradiction) that is the theoretical core of *Totality and Infin-ity*, where the terms of the relation simultaneously absolve themselves from the relation. For Blanchot, the absolute relation offers what might be called a *non-dialectical account of intersubjectivity*;[14] that is, a picture of the relation between humans which is not, as I said above, the struggle for recognition where the self is dependent upon the other for its constitution as a sub-ject. For Levinas, the interhuman relation is an event of radical asymmetry which resists the symmetry and reciprocity of Hegelian and post-Hegelian models of intersubjectivity through what Levinas calls, in a favourite for-mulation of Blanchot's, 'the curvature of intersubjective space'. For Levinas, the radical alterity of the ethical relation is only conceivable on the basis of the absolute separation between self and other.

For Blanchot, Levinas restores the strangeness and terror of the interhuman relation as the central concern of philosophy and shows how transcendence can be understood in terms of the interhuman relation. But, and here we move onto a discreet but powerful critique of Levinas, Blanchot carefully (and, to my mind – although that is a separate matter – rightly) holds back from two Levinasian affirmations. Firstly, that the relation to alterity can be understood *ethically* in some novel metaphysical sense and, secondly, that the relation has '*theological*' implications, namely that the ethical relation is directed *à-Dieu* in some substantial metaphysical sense. So, in embracing Levinas's account of the relation to *autrui*, Blanchot places quotation marks around the terms 'ethics' and 'God', and hence holds back from the metaphysical affirmation of the Good beyond Being. Blanchot holds to the ambiguity or tension in the relation to *autrui* that cannot be reduced either through the affirmation of the positivity of the Good or the negativity of Evil. The relation to the Other is neither positive nor negative in any absolute metaphysical sense; rather, it is what Blanchot calls *le rapport du troisième genre*, or *un rapport neutre*.[15] That is to say, the relationless relation no longer takes place at the level of 'me' or 'you', but rather at the level of the neutral *il*, an anonymous neutrality that recalls, as I have argued at length elsewhere, Levinas's conception of the *il y a*.[16]

Now, and this is my point, it is this relationless relation or *rapport du troisième genre* that seems to define, for Blanchot, the non-traditional conception of friendship. It is this conception of 'friendship' that cuts across, runs beneath or deconstructs the traditional conceptions of *philia* and camaraderie, informing both whilst being reducible to neither. That is to say, the relation to the other is the quasi-transcendental condition for both *amitié* and camaraderie, 'quasi' because it announces the conditions of both their possibility and impossibility. Such a conception of 'friendship' cuts across or deconstructs the distinctions between the private and the public, between the personal (the pre-political) and the political.

In passing, I would also claim that it is this conception of 'friendship', as the relationless relation to the other, that Derrida defines as *justice*, when, in 'Force of Law' and *Spectres of Marx*, he illustrates the undeconstructibility of justice with the following quotation from *Totalité et infini*, 'La relation avec autrui – c'est à dire la justice'.[17] 'But', as Derrida insists, we can call justice 'by other names' – and the *messianic* is one of those other names. In this way, one can begin to construct a linguistic chain – *aimance*, justice, the messianic, *démocratie à venir*, unconditional hospitality – within which the terms seem to have a similar, but not identical, conceptual function. These terms function as what Hent de Vries would call 'non-synonymous substitutions', and what I have elsewhere called 'palaeonymic displacements'.[18] That is to say, they are not chosen arbitrarily as mere nicknames. Rather, each of them is chosen seriously in relation to the weight of the traditions out of which they arise, and in this sense palaeonymy is the responsibility for what we might call a *heritage*, even – and perhaps most of all – when it is that heritage that is being deconstructed.

The Finitude of Friendship in Blanchot

Some of the above thoughts on Blanchot would seem to be confirmed if one turns to his 1971 collection, *L'amitié*, which Derrida calls 'one of the great canonical meditations on friendship'.[19] I shall turn to the key text presently, namely Blanchot's memoir for Bataille, simply called 'L'amitié', which is carefully discussed by Derrida (PdA 327–9/PF 294–6). But what is also intriguing about the 1971 collection for our reading of *Pour l'amitié* is that one can find an earlier discussion of Dionys Mascolo, originally published in 1953 as 'Sur une approche du communisme'. However, for the 1971 reprinting of this short text, and in a way that is utterly characteristic of Blanchot's work (a long, serious and scholarly book could be written on the way in which Blanchot edits his critical texts for republication in his collections of essays: what imperatives govern his additions, his omissions, and his extensive reorganization of material[20]), he added the following footnote:

> Mais, ici, la question se pose: peut-on distinguer, aussi facilement, entre rapports privés et rapports collectifs? Dans les deux cas, ne s'agit-il pas de relations de sujet à objet, ni même de sujet à sujet, mais telles que *le rapport de l'un à l'autre puisse s'y affirmer comme infini et discontinu?* [my emphasis] De là que l'exigence, l'urgence *d'un rapport par le désir* [my emphasis] et par la parole, rapport toujours en déplacement, où *l'autre* – l'impossible – serait accueilli, constituent, au sens le plus fort, *une mode essentiel de décision et d'affirmation politique* [my emphasis]. Je crois que Dionys Mascolo l'admettrait. Reste enfin que le concept de besoin n'est pas simple et que le besoin, lui aussi, peut être travesti, de même que, dans un certain état d'oppression, les hommes peuvent tomber au-dessous des besoins. (A 112)

> [But here the question can be posed: can one distinguish this easily between private and collective relations? Is it not a matter, in both cases, of subject–object relations, not even of relations of the subject to itself, in such a way that *the relation of the one to the other can there be affirmed as infinite and discontinuous?* [my emphasis] From whence arises the urgent demand for a *relation of desire* [my

emphasis] and of speech, a relation that is always being displaced, where *the other* – the impossible – would be welcomed, constituting *an essential mode of decision and political affirmation* [my emphasis] in the strongest sense of the word. I think that Dionys Mascolo would grant this. For finally the concept of need is not simple, and need can also be misrepresented, in the sense that in a certain state of oppression human beings can fall below the level of needs.]

A word of clarification on the context here. Mascolo, according to Blanchot, defends a conception of communism based on an analysis of commodities and need. That is, as Marx writes, 'the reign of freedom begins with the end of the reign of needs and exterior ends'. Thus, the communistic understanding of the public, political realm is dominated by the question of need, against which we can indeed have a private life, what Blanchot describes as a life of friendship, '*l'homme peut devenir l'impossible ami de l'homme* [a human being can become the impossible friend of a human being]' (A 112). So, if Mascolo wants to demarcate clearly the domains of friendship and camaraderie, the domains of the public and private, in much the same way – paradoxically enough, given the political context – as Richard Rorty, then Blanchot wants to claim that this demarcation is undercut by the movement of *desire*. What would seem to me meant here (which is not unproblematic) is desire in Levinas's sense, where it describes a relation between self and other that can be affirmed 'comme infini et discontinu': the relation without relation.

However, Blanchot goes on to write that the welcoming (a word I shall have occasion to come back to below) of the other, which Blanchot describes as 'impossible', would also constitute 'an essential mode of decision and political affirmation'. Thus, and this question will assume increasing prominence in this chapter, there would seem to be a path or passage – although not a deduction, an algorithmic inference or a determinate judgement – from a certain conception of the relationless relation to the other, the *aimance* of an as yet unheard-of conception of friendship, to the dimension of the political decision, where the concept of decision will also be rethought outside its traditional subjectivistic, voluntaristic determinations. This conception of friendship, like Blanchot's *salut* to his friendship with Levinas, cuts across the public–private distinction, or the division between friendship and camaraderie, whilst informing both dimensions.

Turning now to the text on Bataille, we can see how Blanchot's reconstructed account of Levinas's notion of the relationless relation defines his concept of friendship. I will not cite the whole text, but restrict myself to the essential details. Blanchot writes:

L'amitié, ce rapport sans dépendance, sans épisode et où entre cependant toute
la simplicité de la vie, passe par la reconnaissance de l'étrangeté commune qui
ne nous permet pas de parler de nos amis, mais seulement de leur parler [Derrida's
emphasis], non d'en faire un thème de conversations (ou d'articles), mais le
mouvement de l'entente où, nous parlant, ils réservent, même dans la plus
grande familiarité, la distance infinie, cette séparation fondamentale à partir de
laquelle ce qui sépare devient rapport. (A 328, PdA 327)

[Friendship, this relation without dependence, without episode, into which,
however, the utter simplicity of life enters, implies the common strangeness
which *does not allow us to speak of our friends, but only to speak to them*, not to make
of them a theme of conversations (or articles), but the movement of the understanding in which, speaking to us, they reserve, even in their greatest familiarity,
the infinite distance, this fundamental separation starting from which that which
separates becomes relation.] (PF 294)

Friendship, then, is this relation without dependence, a relation thought
on the basis of a radical separation, the pre-ethical separation described in
Section II of *Totalité et infini*, 'Interiority and Economy', that is constitutive
for ethical relatedness in Levinas. In this sense, friendship is what speaks
across an infinite distance, what Blanchot calls a few lines further on,
'*l'intervalle, le pur intervalle . . . de moi à cet autrui qu'est un ami* [the interval,
the pure interval . . . from myself to that other who is a friend]' (A 328).
The words of friendship are '*paroles d'une rive à l'autre rive* [words from
one shore to another]' (A 329), a metaphor that directly evokes Levinas's
repeated insistence on the other speaking from 'un autre rivage'. This is
why we cannot speak *of* our friends but only speak *to* them, namely that
any conception of friendship that totalized the relation to the other would
reduce it to the ontological reciprocity of *philia*.[21]

In Levinasian terms, the ontological relation that comprehends the other
must presuppose his or her ethical incomprehensibility. This is why Blanchot
describes friendship, in the same passage from 'L'amitié', as '*l'interruption
d'être* [the interruption of being]'. The ethical relation to the other is otherwise than being because the same and the other cannot be totalized. Such
is the logic of the 'en ce moment même' that Derrida has so carefully identified elsewhere in relation to Levinas's work.[22] Indeed, Blanchot's distinction
between speaking *of* and speaking *to* seems to recall a key moment in *Totalité
et infini*, namely that,

And if I set forth, as in a final and absolute vision, the separation and transcendence of which it is a question in this very work [*dans cet ouvrage même*], these

relations, which I claim form the fabric of being itself, are already knotted together within my present discourse addressed to my interlocutors: inevitably the other faces me – hostile, *friend* [my emphasis], my master, my student – across my idea of the Infinite.[23]

At this very moment, here I am within a relation to the other *of* which I cannot speak but *to* whom I am obliged to speak, *to* whom I am already responding.

But *to* whom do I speak? As I said above, *die Stimme des Freundes* is spectral and speaks from beyond the grave. It is *to* this memory and out of this loss that I speak – 'Thou art a Scholler; speake to it Horatio'. Thus, and this is a key point, the relationless relation of friendship opens in the relation to death, not the tragic heroism of death as possibility described in chapter 10, where *Dasein* must assume death as the condition of possibility for authentic selfhood, but, rather, where death is radically impossible, it is that which divests me of possibility and authenticity. This is what Blanchot calls in 'L'amitié', '*la démesure du mouvement de mourir* [the excessiveness of the movement of dying]' (A 329). This recognition of death as exemplifying the relationless relation to alterity is something broached powerfully in Levinas's early work, particularly in *Le temps et l'autre*, but arguably not satisfactorily pursued. For the early Levinas, the first experience of an alterity that cannot be reduced to the self occurs in the relation to death, to the ungraspable *facticity* of dying.[24] Thus, if death is not a self-relation, if it does not result in the autarchy of authentic selfhood, then this means that a certain plurality has insinuated itself at the heart of the self. It is the facticity of dying that structures the self as being-for-the-other, which also means that death is not revealed in the relation to my death, but rather to the very alterity of death, the death of the other.

And this is why Blanchot writes at the end of 'L'amitié', in its very last words which were partially cited above,

> But thinking knows that one does not remember: without memory, without thinking, it struggles already in the invisible where everything falls back into indifference. That is its profound suffering. It must accompany friendship into forgetfulness.

That is, if friendship is what speaks *to* the other, to the dead friend whom I mourn, then *il faut l'oubli* or *Faut l'oubli*. Forgetfulness must. Why? Paradoxically perhaps it is in order to remember that this speaking *to* is a response, a responsibility to that which I can never adequately respond, a speaking *to* that speaks *out of* the impossible experience of *le mourir*.

This brings me back to what I said above about the relation of friendship to originary finitude and the question of *sur-vivance*. Namely, that if *philia* is *necrophilia* in the traditional conception of friendship, then this presupposes a clear distinction between the living and the dead and assumes the appropriative work of memory as that which allows the dead to live: *mortui vivunt*. *Sur-vivance* is a spectrality irreducible to the opposition between life and death. It is the very experience of *das Unheimliche* in Freud. But with the above remarks in mind, I think we can better understand what I claimed above about *sur-vivance* as the first opening onto alterity insofar as alterity opens in the relation to mortality. It is a question of an *aimance* for the other *as* mortal, where the precondition for a non-traditional conception of friendship is an acknowledgement of both the ubiquity and ungraspability of finitude. One is only a friend of that which is going to die.

Interestingly, this line of thought finds an echo in the closing pages of *Adieu à Emmanuel Levinas*, where Derrida significantly picks up the theme of death, claiming that, '*toute la pensée de Levinas, du début à la fin, fut une méditation de la mort* [from the beginning to the end, the entirety of Levinas's thinking was a meditation on death]' (AEL 206). Not only do I think this claim is justified, it is also a good deal more critical than it first appears. One might claim that what Derrida is very discreetly trying to do in *Adieu* is to interpret Levinas's work in terms of an originary finitude. In this sense, the very word *adieu* becomes significant, because it is at the point of death that one says *adieu*. But this mention of God does not necessarily bring with it any theological baggage. It is rather that the one who says *adieu* to the living and the friend who says *adieu* to the one who has died are both employing this word as an acknowledgement of the other's mortality, of *aimance* as the acknowledgement of that mortality. That is why '*Faut l'oubli*'. Nothing more. As Blanchot says, 'Let's leave God out of it'.[25]

What is to be Done? Blanchot's Politics of Friendship

It should be noted that Derrida's reading of Blanchot in *Politiques de l'amitié*, although overwhelmingly appreciative of his work, is not without criticism. Derrida poses three critical questions to Blanchot's conception of friendship: the question of community, the Greek question and the question of fraternity (PdA 329–38/PF 296–305) I would like to consider the first of these questions, the question of how one is to think the being-in-common of human beings, of community and political responsibility, on the basis of Blanchot's conception of friendship. Given the radical dissociation or *déliaison* that characterizes friendship for Blanchot, how is one to think the *association of sociation* on this basis? As Derrida puts it early in *Politiques de l'amitié*, and I shall come back in detail to the question of foundation, '*Comment fonder une politique de la séparation?* [How is a politics of separation to be founded?]' (PdA 73/PF 55).

More deviously, I would like to use Derrida's critical question to Blanchot as a way of raising a question directly to Derrida, the question I posed at the beginning of this chapter, namely the relation or non-relation between a non-traditional, non-androcentric, non-fraternalistic conception of friendship and a thinking of the political, specifically the political thought in terms of *la démocratie à venir*. What, for Derrida, are the *politics* of friendship?

In this regard, Derrida's response to the passages of Blanchot's 'L'amitié' discussed above is rather interesting and surprisingly classical. Describing the experience of friendship in Blanchot variously as 'hyperbole', 'insoutenable', or 'un vertige' (PdA 329, 330/PF 295, 296),[26] Derrida asks, '*Sans partage et sans réciprocité, pourra-t-on parler encore d'égalité et de fraternité* [Without sharing and without reciprocity can one still speak of equality and fraternity?]' (PdA 328/PF 296). And in the next paragraph, speaking of the 'réponse' to 'la proximité du plus lointain' that describes the experience of friendship for Blanchot in *L'écriture du désastre*, he continues, 'How could such a "response" ever translate into ethical or political responsibility, the one which, in the philosophical and Christian West, has always been associated with friendship?' (PdA 329/PF 296).

Of course, given the overall argument of *Politiques de l'amitié* and its attempt to deconstruct the Western and Christian conception of friendship, one might wonder why Blanchot *should* be expected to answer these questions at all? Don't all such questions of equality, fraternity and ethical and political responsibility fall back within the traditional conception of the politics of friendship that Derrida is seeking to displace?

The problem with such questions is that they risk reducing the double bind of deconstruction to a matter of taking sides. But the point here is that Derrida's question as to how one might translate Blanchot's conception of friendship into ethical and political responsibility, becomes the question of how one is to think the being-in-common of human beings on such a vertiginous basis, particularly if *die Stimme des Freundes* comes from beyond the grave? How does one think the commonality of what we called in the last chapter, with Jean-Luc Nancy, *être-avec*, in relation to this infinite distance of friendship. Derrida writes: '*On se demandera ce que veut encore dire "commun", dès lors que l'amitié porte au-delà de toute communauté vivante?* [It will be asked what "common" can still mean as soon as friendship goes beyond all *living* community?]' (PdA 329/PF 296).

Staying with Derrida's text, this question then becomes more directly stated in a repeated Leninesque refrain of 'Que faire' – 'What is to be done?':

> The question is not only the one which brings on semantic vertigo, but the one which asks 'what is to be done?' What is to be done today, politically, with this vertigo and its necessity? What is to be done with the 'what is to be done?' [*Que faire du 'que faire?'*]. And what other politics – which would nevertheless still be a politics, supposing this word could still resist this very vertigo – can this other communality of the 'common' dictate to us? (PdA 330/PF 297)

Such are Derrida's questions to Blanchot. And they are, for me, compelling questions, because they are the very ones that I would like to pose to Derrida himself, and to that extent they seem indirectly self-referential. So let me put these questions back to Derrida and approach my framing question of the relation of friendship to democracy.

The Distance Between Derrida and Levinas

Which brings me back to my opening question: what is the relation between a non-traditional conception of friendship, like that of Blanchot, and what might be called a politics of friendship? Does a non-traditional conception of friendship, in the classical manner, *found* politics, does undecidability allow for a procedural *deduction* of the political decision?

Or are not matters precisely the other way around: namely, that there is no *passage assuré* between friendship and politics, no deduction from one to the other, no foundation? That is, might there not be a *hiatus* between friendship and politics, that far from inducing paralysis or resignation, perhaps opens onto an experience of the political decision? It is this possibility that I would now like to open in closing this book.

In raising these questions in this way, I am alluding to Derrida's recent *Adieu à Emmanuel Levinas*. Indeed, the latter text might well have also been entitled, in all its ambiguity, *Pour l'amitié de Levinas*, and it functions as some kind of supplement to *Politiques de l'amitié*. To my knowledge, Levinas is only mentioned in passing in *Politiques de l'amitié* (see PdA 295, 326/PF 264, 293). However, if we see *Adieu* as a supplement to *Politiques de l'amitié*, then this also allows us to view the important distance between Derrida's and Levinas's work. What I mean is that one way of reading *Adieu* is in terms of the increasingly close philosophical proximity of Derrida to Levinas, which builids upon Derrida's 1986 remark where he said, 'Faced with a thinking like that of Levinas, I never have an objection. I am ready to subscribe to everything that he says.'[27] This is an understandable reading and I have myself advanced arguments for such a proximity in this book and elsewhere. But despite this undoubted homology, and despite the relative absence of criticism in *Adieu*, perhaps the latter paradoxically permits us to see that Derrida is further away from Levinas than it might at first appear. If we view *Adieu* from the perspective of the themes raised in *Politiques de l'amitié*, then the following five problems in Levinas's work can be profiled:

1. The continual linking of the problematic of justice, commuity and *le tiers* to what Levinas calls 'fraternity', which shows the utterly classical conception of the politics of friendship in Levinas's work. Let me pick one example amongst many, 'The other is from the first the *brother* to all the other men.'[28]

2. The linking of fraternity to the question of God, and the idea that the political community is essentially *monotheistic*. That is, the universality of fraternity is ensured through the mediation of the divine, which recalls the classical Christian, esssentially Augustinian, conception of friendship. This is the meaning of Levinas's phrase, 'It is thanks to God that I am an other for the others [*C'est grâce à Dieu que je suis un autre pour les autres*]'.[29] Or again, this time from *Totality and Infinity*, 'Monotheism signifies this human kinship, this idea of a human race that refers back to the approach of the other [*autrui*] in the face, in a dimension of height, in the responsibility for oneself and for the other [*autrui*]'.[30]

3. Levinas's profoundly *androcentric* conception of friendship, fraternity and political community, where the feminine is the essential, but essentially pre-ethical, opening of the ethical basis of community. Friendship between women is only admitted on analogy with fraternity. To that extent, I even have difficulty with Derrida's thought experiment (for it is nothing more than that) in *Adieu*, where he suggests reading Levinas on the question of the dwelling and the feminine, as a kind of 'manifeste feministe' (AEL 83).

4. The way in which the androcentric logic of fraternity is continually linked to what Derrida would call 'the family schema'. That is, the logic of filiality in Levinas, where the child is always the son, or thought on analogy with the son, is linked to the logics of paternity and fraternity, as that which makes 'the strange conjuncture of the family possible'.[31] It should not be forgotten that *Totality and Infinity* concludes with an invocation of 'the marvel of the family'.[32]

5. Finally, and most significantly, it would be a question of linking each of these four themes to what we might call (and I choose my words carefully here, thinking of Heidegger) the *political fate* of Levinasian ethics, namely the vexed question of Israel. The risk here (which is admittedly only a risk, but a significant one) is that, as Richard Beardsworth puts it, 'the non-place of alterity has become the place of Israel's borders'.[33] I attempted to complicate this political fate in chapter 2 through my use of Levinas to illuminate Genet's relation to the Palestinians.

Each of these themes would be the occasion for a long discussion, which I will not go into here. Indeed, these themes are only suggested and not developed by Derrida in *Adieu*, and I raise them here simply as a way of signposting some problems in the excessive identification of Derrida's work with that of Levinas. Let me now return to the questions I raised above and try and make matters more perspicuous by analysing the main argument of *Adieu à Emmanuel Levinas*.

The Hiatus Between Ethics and Politics

In 'Le mot d'accueil', Derrida focuses on one seemingly contingent word in Levinas's vocabulary – welcome (*acceuil*) – which he then links to the theme of hospitality, which has been a central topic of Derrida's seminars in recent years. Through a careful, immanent and systematic textual analysis, Derrida shows how the hospitality of welcome defines the various meanings given to ethics in Levinas's work. Derrida rightly argues that Levinas's *Totality and Infinity* can be read as 'an immense treatise on hospitality', where ethics is defined as a welcome to the other, as an unconditional hospitality.

Yet the question that Derrida is seeking to explore in this text concerns the relation between an ethics of hospitality and a politics or law of hospitality in Levinas's work. And Derrida's procedure in this regard is utterly typical of his practice of reading: namely, that through a commentary on Levinas he establishes an aporia or hiatus on the question of the passage from ethics to politics, an aporia which is not paralysing but which permits him to leave the order of commentary and begin to pose the problem in his own terms. And what is always fascinating in Derrida's readings of Levinas is the way his questions to the latter are really questions to himself and his own project.[34]

So the question is whether an ethics of hospitality can, in the classical manner, *found* the spheres of politics and law? That is, does the formal

ethical imperative of Levinas's work ('tu ne tueras point') lead to a deter-
minable political or legal content? Can one deduce politics from ethics?
Derrida's claim, which in my view could be at the very least complicated –
perhaps even contested – is that although Levinas sees the necessity for such
a deduction, he leaves us perplexed as to how it might be achieved, and his
text is marked by a silence on this crucial point. As Derrida says,

> To state it in a classical philosophical discourse, a silence is kept on the rules and
> schemas . . . that would procure for us the 'best' or the least worst mediations:
> between, on the one hand, an ethics or saintliness [sainteté] of messianic hos-
> pitality and, on the other hand, the 'peace process', the process of political peace.
> (AEL 197)[35]

However, and this is the really interesting move in the argument, rather
than judging this hiatus negatively, Derrida claims that the absence of a
plausible deduction from ethics to politics should not induce paralysis or
resignation. The claim is therefore that if there is no deduction from ethics
to politics, then this can be both ethically and politically welcome. On the
one hand, ethics is left defined as the infinite responsibility of unconditional
hospitality. Whilst, on the other hand, the political can be defined as the
taking of a decision without any determinate transcendental guarantees.
Thus, the hiatus in Levinas allows Derrida both to affirm the primacy of
an ethics of hospitality, whilst leaving open the sphere of the political as a
realm of risk and danger. Such danger calls for decisions or what Derrida,
citing Levinas, calls 'political invention' (AEL 144), an invention taken in
the name of the other without this being reducible to some sort of moral
calculus. Derrida writes, 'As always, the decision remains heterogenous to
the calculation, knowledge and science that nonetheless condition it' (AEL
199–200).

In this regard, perhaps, Derrida's questions to Blanchot in *Politiques de
l'amitié* are slightly too classical, appearing, as they do, to demand some sort
of deduction from the infinite distance of friendship to the questions of
equality, fraternity, community and political responsibility. Thinking now of
Derrida's question to Levinas, might we not already have a response to his
'*Que faire?*' question to Blanchot, namely that a responsible decision must
be taken – here and now, again and again – without any transcendental
guarantees, without any ontological foundation, and furthermore that only
such a decision might have the honour of being called *just*.

And this response to the question 'what is to be done?' does not, I think,
collapse into a vapid formalism or empty universalism. Derrida emphasizes

how the very indeterminacy of the passage from ethics to politics entails that the taking of a political decision must be a response to the utter singularity of a particular and inexhaustible context.[36] The infinite ethical demand of deconstruction arises as a response to a singular context and calls forth the invention of a political decision. Politics itself can here be thought of as *the art of response to the singular demand of the other*, a demand that arises in a particular context – although the infinite demand cannot simply be reduced to its context – and calls for political invention, for creation.

Politics and Foundationalism

With this in mind, we can, I think, reformulate the problem of the relation of politics to foundationalism in six steps:

1. For Derrida, politics cannot be founded because such a foundation would limit the freedom of the decision. In politics there are no guarantees. Politics must be open to the dimension of the 'perhaps' or the 'maybe', which is the constant refrain of the early and central chapters of *Politiques de l'amitié*. For Derrida, nothing would be more irresponsible and totalitarian (AEL 201) than the attempt apriori to exclude the monstrous or the terrible, 'Without the possibility of radical evil, of perjury, and of absolute crime, there is no responsibility, no freedom, no decision' (PdA 247/PF 219).

2. So the relation of ethics to politics is that there is a gap or hiatus between these two domains. And here we confront a crucial qualification of the problem of ethics and politics: namely that if politics is not founded in the classical manner, *then it is also not arbitrary*, for this would take us back to some *libertas arbitrarium* and its concomitant voluntaristic and sovereign conception of the will. That is, it would lead us back to an undeconstructed Schmittianism. So, if politics is non-foundational (because that would limit freedom) and non-arbitrary (because that would derive from a conception of freedom), then what follows from this? How does one think a non-foundational and yet non-arbitrary relation between ethics and politics, or between friendship and democracy?

3. Derrida's claim would seem to be that there is indeed a link between a non-traditional conception of friendship and his conception of democracy to come, between ethics and politics. In *Adieu*, Derrida puts the point more strongly, claiming that '*This relation is necessary* [il faut ce rapport], it must exist, it is necessary to deduce a politics and a law from ethics' (AEL 198). In this sense, as I have argued in this chapter, the non-traditional

conception of friendship described in the reading of Blanchot in *Politiques de l'amitié* is the redescription of the Levinasian ethical relation to the other thought out of an originary finitude. This, according to me and despite their differences, is the irreducibly Levinasian moment in Derrida, a moment that can be found shot through Derrida's remarks on justice and the messianic, a moment of formal universality. What has to be acknowledged is the irreducibly heteronomous opening of autonomy (which does not at all mean that autonomy is abandoned), the unconditional priority of the other (which does not at all mean that the economy of the same can be done without). It is this sense of a non-foundational and non-arbitrary relation between ethics and politics that Derrida tries to capture with the notion of *the other's decision is made in me*, a decision made but with regard to which I am passive.

4. Politics, then, or the articulation of democracy to come, is the task of political invention in relation to the other's decision in me. Non-foundationally, but non-arbitrarily. But how does one do this exactly? Perhaps in the following way: each decision is necessarily different, each time I decide I have to *invent* a new rule, a new norm, which must be absolutely singular in relation to the other's infinite demand made on me and the finite context within which this demand arises. This is what Derrida means by his qualified Kierkegaardian emphasis on the madness of the decision, namely that each decision is a leap of faith made in relation to the singularity of a context.

5. So, the political decision is made *ex nihilo*, and is not deduced or read off procedurally from a pre-given conception of justice or the moral law, as in Habermas, say, and yet it is not arbitrary. *It is the demand provoked by the other's decision in me that calls forth political invention, that provokes me into inventing a norm and taking a decision.* The *singularity* of the context in which the demand arises provokes an act of invention whose criterion is *universal*.

6. So, to summarize, what we seem to have here is a relation between friendship and democracy, or ethics and politics, which is both non-foundational and non-arbitrary, which leaves the decision open for invention whilst acknowledging that the decision comes from the other. The other's decision in me is not so much a Kantian *Faktum der Vernunft* as a *Faktum des Anderen*, the heteronomous ethical source for autonomous political action.[37] That is, there is a universal criterion for action, but I am passive in relation to this criterion, I have a non-subsumptive relation to this *Faktum*, and the specific form of political action must be singular and context-dependent.

Ethical Form and Political Content: The New International

This understanding of the hiatus between ethics and politics, permits Derrida to make an absolutely crucial move in his reading of Levinas: on the one hand, it enables him to accept the *formal* notion of the ethical relation to the other in Levinas – what Derrida calls here and elsewhere a 'structural' or 'apriori' notion of the messianic (AEL 204) – whilst refusing the specific political *content* that Levinasian ethics seems to entail, namely the vexed question of Levinas's Zionism (not to mention his Eurocentrism: 'Man is Europe and the Bible, everything else can be translated'[38]) and his persist-ent if nuanced defence of *une certaine idée d'Israel*: 'A State where prophetic morality and the idea of peace should be incarnated'.[39] Derrida writes that

> the *formal* injunction of the deduction remains irrefusable . . . ethics entails pol-itics and law . . . But, on the other hand, the political or juridical *content* thus assigned remains indeterminate, to be determined beyond knowledge and any possible presentation, concept or intuition, singularly in the speeech and respons-ibility *taken* by everyone in each situation. (AEL 199)

Having established this hiatus or discontinuity between the form and con-tent of Levinas's work, Derrida goes on, a few pages later,

> Moreover this discontinuity allows one to subscribe to everything that Levinas says to us about peace or messianic hospitality, of the beyond of the political within the political, without necessarily sharing all the 'opinions' which, within his discourse, arise from an intra-political analysis of real situations or of an effectivity happening today, of the terrestrial Jerusalem . . . (AEL 202)

Thus, Derrida makes this seemingly formalistic move in order to avoid what I called above the possible political fate of Levinas's work, namely the latter's 'opinions' on the 'terrestrial Jerusalem', which, whilst not simply 'un nationalisme de plus' (AEL 202), continually run the risk of being conflated with the latter. What has to be continually deconstructed is the guarantee of a full *incarnation* of the universal in the particular, or the privileging of a specific particularity because it *embodies* the universal. However, it is hugely important to point out that Derrida's avoidance of the possible political fate of Levinasian ethics is not done in order to *avoid* concrete political ques-tions, questions of the specific content of political decisions, but on the contrary to *defend* what he has elsewhere called in relation to Marx, 'The New International'. The latter is, for me, a key notion in Derrida's recent work, and which I see as *a reactivation or rearticulation of the emancipatory promise of modernity*.[40] In response to the question, 'Que faire?', we might say that what is required is, as Derrida writes, is 'another international law, another politics of frontiers, another humanitarian politics, even a humanitarian engagement that would hold itself *effectively* outside the interest of nation states' (AEL 176).

As there is no conception of the political without an enemy, it might be asked: who would be the enemy of such a New International? The logic of Derrida's argument would seem to entail that the enemy would be any form of nationalism, whether French, Israeli, British or whatever. That is, the enemy of the New International is the attempted identification of justice with the destiny of 'the people' or 'the nation', a nationalism that believes that justice can be incarnated within the frontiers of the state or the words of the tribe. (An open question for me would be as to the sufficiency of this notion of 'the enemy'. Namely, that nationalists are fairly easy enemies to have, and matters get more complicated when one faces other 'internationals' with different and perhaps opposing political objectives. I am thinking here not only of the various international humanitarian organizations, but also of the many multinational corporations and financial institutions, such as the World Bank.)

Democracy to Come and Democratization: Derrida's Re-Politicization of Marxism

Having (I hope) begun to clarify the relation between a non-traditional conception of friendship, derived from Derrida's reading of Blanchot, and the question of the political, let me close by trying to make clear the link to democracy, specifically what Derrida calls *la démocratie à venir*. Derrida concludes *Politiques de l'amitié* with the following question, which comes directly after his discussion of Blanchot, and which picks up the discussion of the problem of foundationalism:

> If one wishes to retranslate this pledge into a hypothesis or a question, it would, then, perhaps, – by way of a temporary conclusion – take the following form: is it possible to think and to implement democracy, that which would keep the old name 'democracy', while uprooting from it all these figures of friendship (philosophical and religious) which prescribe fraternity: the family and the androcentric ethnic group? Is it possible, in assuming a certain faithful memory of democratic reason and reason *tout court* – I would even say, the Enlightenment of a certain

Aufklärung (thus leaving open the abyss which is again opening today under these words) – not to found, where it is no longer a matter of *founding*, but to open out to the future, or rather, to the 'come', of a certain democracy [*non pas de fonder, là où il ne s'agit sans doute plus de* fonder, *mais d'ouvrir à l'avenir, ou plutôt au 'viens' d'une certaine démocratie*]. (PdA 339/PF 306)

Of course, these are rhetorical questions in the classical French style, and the answer is 'yes'. As Derrida admits, this is '*Juste une question, mais qui suppose une affirmation* [Just a question, but one that presupposes an affirmation]' (PdA 339/PF 306). The affirmation here is that of *la démocratie à venir*, but the question is: *how* might such a notion of democracy be conceived?

La démocratie à venir is much easier to describe in negative rather than positive terms. To turn back to *Spectres of Marx* and to pick up the analysis of *la démocratie à venir* given above in chapter 7, Derrida is particularly anxious to distinguish the idea of democracy to come from any idea of a *future* democracy, where the future would be a modality of the *lebendige Gegenwart*, namely the not-yet-present. Democracy to come is *not* to be confused with the living present of liberal democracy, lauded as the end of history by Fukuyama, but *neither* is it a regulative idea or an idea in the Kantian sense; *nor* is it even a Utopia, insofar as all these conceptions understand the future as a modality of presence. As we saw above, it is a question of linking *la démocratie à venir* to *différance* understood as it is in *Spectres of Marx* as *l'ici maintenant sans présence*, as a messianic experience of the *now* without which justice would be meaningless. The experience of justice as the maintaining-now (*le maintenant*) of the relation to an absolute singularity *is* the *à venir* of democracy. The temporality of democracy is *advent*, but it is arrival happening *now*, it happens as the now blasting through the continuum of the present.

La démocratie à venir is an extremely difficult notion to get hold of because it has an essentially contradictory structure: that is, it has both the structure of a promise, of something futural 'to come', and it is something that takes place, that happens right *now*. In other words, *la démocratie à venir* has the character of what Derrida tends to call 'the incalculable', an irreducible *Faktum* or remainder that cannot simply become the source of a deduction, or the object of a determinate judgement. However it is understood, it is clear that *la démocratie à venir* belongs to what we referred to above as the linguistic chain of 'non-synonymous substitutions' or 'palae-onymic displacements' which seem to have a similar, but not identical, conceptual function in Derrida's work: justice, the messianic, *aimance*, un-conditional hospitality. As such, *la démocratie à venir* has the character of an ethical demand or injunction, an incalculable *Faktum* that takes place now, but which permits the profile of a promisory task to be glimpsed.

Now, it is the *political* character of this incalculable promise and the tasks that it sets for us that I would like to discuss in closing. In 'Force of Law', Derrida insists that it is necessary 'to calculate with the incalculable',[41] and it seems to me to be absolutely essential to think the incalculability of *La démocratie à venir* together the calculability of politicization, namely perfectibility as a political task in relation to what we might call 'actually existing democracy'. Returning to what I said above, this is what I see as the force of Derrida's notion of the New International.

I claimed that Derrida's endorsement of a formal notion of the ethical in Levinas was not done in order to avoid concrete political questions, but rather in order to defend a new internationalism in relation to those questions, what I called a new articulation of the emancipatory promise of modernity, and what Derrida called 'another humanitarian politics . . . that would hold itself *effectively* outside the interest of nation states'. It is therefore a matter of thinking the ethical imperative of *la démocratie à venir* together with a form or forms of democratic action that move outside, beyond and against the state, as the *national* form of democratic government or indeed against any restriction of democracy to territory. In this sense, democracy should not be understood as a fixed political form of society, but rather as a *process* or, better, *processes* of what I would like to call, adapting William Connolly's formulation, *deterritorialized democratization*.[42] Such processes of democratization, evidenced in numerous examples (new social movements, Greenpeace, Amnesty International, etc.), would work across, above, beneath and within the territory of the democratic state, not in the vain hope of achieving some sort of 'society without the state', but rather as providing constant pressure upon the state, a pressure of emancipatory intent aiming at its infinite amelioration, the perfectibility of politics, the endless betterment of actually existing democracy.

It is then finally, for me at least, a question of understanding this notion of deterritorialized democratization as a spectre of Marx; that is, of insisting upon a Marxist haunting of the political present. What I am thinking of here can be nicely illustrated with the example of Miguel Abensour's recent book, *La démocratie contre l'État. Marx et le moment machiavélien*.[43] This book is essentially a reading of Marx's 1843 Critique of Hegel's *Rechtsphilosophie*, and what interests Abensour in this text is Marx's talk of 'true democracy', which can be understood as the opposition of any reduction of democracy to state form. Thus, the young Marx *thinks democracy against the state*, and this enables Abensour to disengage and defend a notion of radical democracy or what I have called 'democratization' in the young Marx. The other feature of this early text by Marx that interests Abensour is the theme of the political, understood as the moment of the political decision which cannot simply be subordinated to socio-economic calculations as in classical Marxism. This moment of the political decision, what Claude Lefort would call the democratic institution of the social, is the 'Machiavellian moment' in Marx, a Marxism rooted in the recognition of conflict, struggle and the necessarily aleatory character of democratic action. Abensour writes:

> In order to get access to this strangeness of democracy, it is not only necessary to reject the ideologies of consensus, notably the consensus between democracy and the State, but also to debanalize the idea of conflict, to keep oneself from inclining towards compromise in order to maximize the charge of conflict, that is to say, the always possible emergence of the struggle of human beings . . . Democracy, as paradoxically as that might appear, is that political society that institutes a human bond across the struggle of human beings [*un lien humain à travers la lutte des hommes*].[44]

But what is perhaps most suggestive to me in Abensour's reading of Marx, and which connects with the themes of this chapter and the book as a whole, is the linking together of supra- and infra-state forms of democratization conceived in terms of a Marxist conception of the political, with a certain affirmation of a Levinasian ethical anarchism. *La démocratie contre l'État* concludes by citing a footnote from *Otherwise than Being*, where Levinas defines the ethical meaning of anarchy, which is precisely pre-political, as that which 'can only disturb the State' and which means that 'The State cannot set itself up as a Whole'.[45] That is, the infinite and incalculable ethical demand of deconstruction or *la démocratie à venir* is the pre-political opening of the political, and in this sense it is the *anarchic* source of the political *arche*, the disorderly ethical root of the political order. It is this demand, this infinite demand for justice, that rages against the injustice of the political order and which initiates forms of human struggle and conflict in the name of *le lien humain*, and which acknowledges those points where the human is challenged by what surpasses the human.

Democratization or politicization is the hegemonization of such struggle into forms of dissensual emancipatory praxis that work against the consensual horizon of the state, not in order to do away with either the state or consensus, but rather in order to bring about its endless betterment. Democratization is a task that always demands '*encore un effort*'. Returning to Derrida and keeping Abensour in mind, we might say that what Derrida is thinking with his notion of democracy to come is an ethical injunction, a pre-political source for the political, that generates a movement of politicization or democratization that is not linked to the teleology of the state or the horizon of social consensus. To put it as boldly as possible, we might say that what Derrida is attempting in his recent work is nothing less than a *repoliticization of Marxism*; that is, the reactivation of the political in terms of its ethical source, a repoliticization waged against both the subordination of the political to the socio-economic in classical Marxism, but most of all against the gnawing cynicism of neo-liberalism and its disempowering ideology of 'globalization'.

However, this is where a final question is opened for me. For, as Mick Jagger perspicuously remarked long ago, 'you can't always get what you want'. What I mean is that it is perhaps at this point that we might need to turn to other attempts to repoliticize Marxism, notably the Gramscian tradition that still inspires Ernesto Laclau and Chantal Mouffe, even though, in my view, they both lack the very dimension of ethicality that radical democracy must presuppose in order to be effective.[46] What the infinite ethical demand of deconstruction requires is a theory of *hegemonization*, that is, an account of the political conceived in terms of strategy and tactics, power and force, as well as an account of institutionalization, and – most importantly – the fraught question of the figure(s) around which a radical democratic politics can articulate itself and become effective – the question of identification, of social movements, and the credibility of the party form. The logics of deconstruction and hegemony need to be soldered at this point, I think, in a reciprocal relation of supplementarity. For if what deconstruction lacks in its thinking of the political is a thematization of democratization as hegemony, then what the theory of hegemony lacks is the kind of messianic, ethical injunction to infinite responsibility that prevents it collapsing into a voluntaristic decisionism. If ethics without politics is empty, then politics without ethics is blind.

Notes

1. Parts of the concluding pages of this text appeared in 'Taking an Ethical Turn', *Times Literary Supplement*, no. 4933, October 1997, pp. 14–15. A shortened version appeared in *The European Journal of Social Theory*, vol. 1, no. 2, 1998, pp. 263–83. I would like to thank Gido Berns for giving me the occasion to write this text for a conference on Derrida's *Politiques de l'amitié* held at Tilburg University in June 1997, and I would to thank Jacques Derrida for his extremely helpful

responses both at Tilburg and at a conference on the same theme held at the Institute for Contemporary Arts, London, in November 1997. Discussions with Paola Marratti, Rudi Visker, Hent de Vries, Ernesto Laclau, Chantal Mouffe, Geoffrey Bennington and others were valuable.

2. See 'The Politics of Friendship', *The Journal of Philosophy*, vol. 85, 1988, pp. 633–44. These passages are an abbreviated version of some of the closing pages of chapter 10 of *Politiques de l'amitié*, cf. pp. 322–9/290–6.

3. Dionys Mascolo, *À la recherche d'un communisme de pensée*, Paris: Éditions Fourbis, 1993. The translations of PA are my own.

4. *Metaphysik der Sitten*, Part II, pp. 46–7. Kant's concept of friendship is discussed, with particular reference to secrecy, on p. 288/257 et passim.

5. Johannes Hoffmeister, *Wörterbuch der philosophischen Begriffe*, Hamburg: Felix Meiner, 1955, p. 238. See also in this regard a helpful article by Erich Heintel, 'Vom Sinn der Freundschaft', *Von der Notwendigkeit der Philosophie in der Gegenwart*, H. Kohlenberger and W. Lütterfelds, eds, Vienna: Oldenbourg, 1976, pp. 190–221; see esp. pp. 192–3 and 199–200.

6. Nietzsche's words are also cited towards the end of the original English version of 'The Politics of Friendship', p. 643. Derrida also discusses the distinction between friendship and camaraderie with reference to Aristotle in PdA 229/PF 202.

7. It would be necessary to read Blanchot's remarks on 1968 together with *La communauté inavouable*, Paris: Minuit, 1983, a text itself mentioned by Derrida in a series of footnotes to PdA 56–7, 89/PF 46–7, 70; and see especially PdA 337 fn. 1/PF 304 n. 32.

8. 'Mourning and Melancholia', *On Metapsychology: The Theory of Psychoanalysis*, vol. 11, Penguin Freud Library, Harmondsworth: Penguin, 1984, p. 267.

9. The translations of A are my own.

10. On this question, see above, chapters 8 and 9.

11. See above, chapter 3.

12. The translations of AEL are my own.

13. *L'entretien infini*, Paris: Gallimard, 1969, pp. 70–105.

14. Ibid., pp. 100–1.

15. Ibid., pp. 94 and 104.

16. For this argument, see 'Il y a', in *Very Little . . . Almost Nothing*, London and New York: Routledge, 1997, pp. 31–83. See also on this question Gerald Bruns's excellent book, *Maurice Blanchot. The Refusal of Philosophy*, Baltimore: Johns Hopkins University Press, 1997, see esp. pp. 119–21.

17. See *Totalité et infini*, The Hague: Nijhoff, 1961, p. 62; *Totality and Infinity*, transl. Alphonso Lingis, Pittsburgh: Duquesne University Press, 1969, p. 89. Cited in *Spectres de Marx*, Paris: Galilee, 1993, p. 48, and cf. 'The Force of Law: The "Mystical Foundation of Authority" ', in D. Cornell, M. Rosenfeld and D. G. Carlson, eds, *Deconstruction and the Possibility of Justice*, London and New York: Routledge, 1992, p. 22.

18. I refer to Hent De Vries's paper given at the above-mentioned Tilburg conference on *Politiques de l'amitié*. For a discussion of palaeonymic displacements in relation to Levinas, see above, chapter 3.

19. For the Derrida quote, see 'The Politics of Friendship', p. 643. Derrida uses the same formulation to describe Blanchot in PdA 322/PF 290.

20. This important work has been begun by Michael Holland in his editor's introduction and commentaries to *The Blanchot Reader*, Oxford: Blackwell, 1995.

21. Derrida takes up this distinction between 'speaking to' and 'speaking of' at length in chapters 7 and 8 of PdA in order to differentiate what he terms the 'canonical' and 'recoil' readings of the phrase, 'O my friends, there is no friend'.

22. 'En ce moment même dans cet ouvrage me voici', in *Textes pour Emmanuel Levinas*, Paris: Éditions Jean-Michel Place, 1980, pp. 21–60; 'At this very moment in this work here I am', transl. R. Berezdivin, in R. Bernasconi and S. Critchley, eds, *Re-Reading Levinas*, Bloomington: Indiana University Press, 1991, pp. 11–48.

23. *Totalité et infini*, p. 53/transl. p. 81.

24. *Le temps et l'autre*, Montpellier: Fata Morgana, 1979, pp. 51–69.

25. 'Laissons Dieu de côté', *L'entretien infini*, p. 71.

26. I note that the latter word also appears in AEL, where Derrida writes, '*Le tiers protégerait contre le vertige de la violence éthique même* [The third party would protect against the vertigo of ethical violence itself]' (AEL 66).

27. See *Altérités*, Paris: Osiris, 1986, p. 74. I discuss this remark in more detail in *The Ethics of Deconstruction*, pp. 9–13.

28. *Otherwise than Being or Beyond Essence*, transl. A. Lingis, The Hague: Nijhoff, 1981, p. 158.

29. Ibid., p. 158.

30. *Totality and Infinity*, p. 214. See also in this regard, 'Pour une politique monothéiste', in 'L'état de César et l'état de David', in *L'au-delà du verset*, Paris: Minuit, 1982, pp. 219–20. This text is discussed by Derrida in AEL 135–42.

31. *Totality and Infinity*, p. 279; for the elision between the child and the son in Levinas, see p. 277. I analyse this question in depth in *The Ethics of Deconstruction*, pp. 130–7.

32. *Totality and Infinity*, p. 306.

33. Richard Beardsworth, *Derrida and the Political*, London and New York: Routledge, 1996, p. 144.

34. Derrida finally pulls away from the order of commentary when he writes on p. 198, twelve pages before the end of the text, that 'I *interpret* this silence between ethics and politics, between ethics and law' (my emphasis).

35. For a much more nuanced account of the relation between ethics and politics in Levinas, see Robert Bernasconi's 'The Third Party. Levinas on the Intersection of the Ethical and the Political', *Journal of the British Society for Phenomenology*, forthcoming. Bernasconi concludes his paper in the following terms:

> There is no ethics without politics, no desire without need and no saying without a said. To ignore institutions and politics would be like remaining on the spiritual level of desire, thereby approaching the Other with empty hands. It would be to seek the condition of empirical situations, while ignoring the concretization which specifies their meaning. The ethical interrupts the political, not to direct it in the sense of determining what must be done, but to challenge its sense that it embodies the ultimate wisdom of 'the bottom line'. Levinas's thought cannot be assimilated to what conventionally passes as political philosophy, but it was never intended to do so and that is its strength.

36. On this point, see AEL 199.

37. Derrida uses the word *Faktum* to describe the hiatus between ethics and politics in *Adieu* (p. 201).

38. 'Je dis parfois: l'homme, c'est l'Europe et la Bible, et tout le reste peut s'y traduire.' From Levinas's conversations with François Poirié, *Emmanuel Levinas, 'Qui êtes-vous?'*, Paris: La Manufacture, 1987, p. 136.

39. See 'Politique après!', *L'au-delà du verset*, p. 228. Derrida gives a careful reading of this text in AEL 93, 120–2, 143–52, et passim.

40. The notion of The New International is critically discussed above in chapter 7.

41. 'The Force of Law: The "Mystical Foundation of Authority"', p. 16.

42. To be precise, Connolly speaks of *nonterritorial democratization*: 'The contemporary need, perhaps, is to supplement and challenge structures of territorial democracy with a politics of nonterritorial democratization of global issues', *Identity/Difference*, Ithaca: Cornell University Press, 1992, p. 218, and see pp. 198–222. See also chapter 2 of his *Ethos of Pluralization*, Minneapolis: University of Minnesota Press, 1995, pp. 135–61.

43. Paris: Presses Universitaires de France, 1997.

44. Ibid., pp. 113–14.

45. *Otherwise than Being or Beyond Essence*, p. 194.

46. I take up this issue with respect to Ernesto Laclau's work in my Response to Rorty in chapter 5, but also see the attempted rapprochement between deconstruction and hegemony attempted in chapter 7.

Abbreviations

A – Maurice Blanchot, *L'amitié*, Paris: Gallimard, 1971.

AEL – Jacques Derrida, *Adieu à Emmanuel Levinas*, Paris: Galilée, 1997.

PA – Maurice Blanchot, *Pour l'amitié*, Paris: Éditions Fourbis, 1996.

PdA – Jacques Derrida, *Politiques de l'amitié*, Paris: Galilée, 1994.

PF – Jacques Derrida, *Politics of Friendship*, transl. George Collins, London and New York: Verso, 1997.

Index

Printed in the United States
By Bookmasters